The Leader's Change Handbook

The Leader's Change Handbook

An Essential Guide to Setting Direction and Taking Action

Jay A. Conger

Gretchen M. Spreitzer

Edward E. Lawler III

Editors

Jossey-Bass Publishers • San Francisco

Jossey-Bass books and products are available through most bookstores. To contact Jossey-Bass directly, call (888) 378–2537, fax to (800) 605–2665, or visit our website at www.josseybass.com.

Substantial discounts on bulk quantities of Jossey-Bass books are available to corporations, professional associations, and other organizations. For details and discount information, contact the special sales department at Jossey-Bass.

For sales outside the United States, please contact your local Simon & Schuster International Office.

TCF Manufactured in the United States of America on Lyons Falls Turin Book. This paper is acid-free and 100 percent totally chlorine-free.

Library of Congress Cataloging-in-Publication Data

The leader's change handbook : an essential guide to setting direction and taking
    action / Jay A. Conger, Gretchen M. Spreitzer, Edward E. Lawler III, editors.
        p. cm. — (The Jossey-Bass business & management series)
    Includes bibliographical references and index.
    ISBN 0-7879-4351-7 (alk. paper)
    1. Leadership.   2. Organizational change.   I. Conger, Jay Alden.   II. Spreitzer,
Gretchen M.   III. Lawler, Edward E.   IV. Series.
HD57.7 .L423   1999
658.4'092—ddc21   98-40101

first edition
HB Printing   10 9 8 7 6 5 4 3 2 1

The Jossey-Bass
Business & Management Series

Contents

Foreword

Toward the end of 1997, the Leadership Institute and the Center for Organization Effectiveness of the University of Southern California convened a two-day seminar on the current status of leadership theory and practice. The "usual suspects" were all there: eminent and highly visible scholars and consultants. Looked at one way, they were rather a diverse group, representing a wide range of disciplines from psychiatry to social psychology and economics. In a far more important way, they had a lot in common: many years of pondering and writing about leadership and, for the most part, attempting to understand the complexity of leading change in what's often referred to as the New Economy—this spastic, turbulent, confusing, vertiginous, messy, and awesomely complex world that all of our human institutions are creating, participating in, and overwhelmed by. As one of my CEO friends put it, if you're not confused, you don't know what's going on.

The chapters in this book resulted from that conference and, one way or another, address the role of leadership in contemporary organizations. I think the book is a prize for all who are interested in leadership. Open it just about anywhere and it gleams with insight, experience, professional knowledge, and useful generalizations. The editors, with phenomenal grasp of leadership research and with an instinct for relevance, have done what could be done in one volume to bring some coherence to this complex topic. The result is a treasury.

I want to draw a few generalizations from the papers and conversation the papers elicited. First of all, it became clear that the last word on leadership will never be said, not in the papers that follow or the books the participants have written. In fact, reading over these papers reminded me of that famous Indian legend about the Blind Men and the Elephant, written in the middle of the nineteenth century. One of the blind men accidentally falls into the side of the elephant and thinks it's a wall, another happens to take the squirming trunk in his hand and thinks it's a snake. Another grabs on to the tusk and thinks it's a spear, and so on and so on. The poem ends: Though each was partly in the right, it was six men of Indostan and all were in the wrong! And of course, all were in the right!

So there are two kinds of subjects that we academics tackle. Some, like dry-fly fishing or English seventeenth-century poetry, can be plumbed to their depths. Others, like leadership, are so vast and complex that they can only be explored. The latter subjects are inevitably the more important ones. Just don't expect consensus or a unified theory or easy answers, as Heifetz reminds us.

Which segues into another generalization about the papers and dialogue the papers evoked. What is most refreshing about the book, stated on just about every page, is how achingly complex the topic of leadership is. Refreshing because the number of books on leadership mounting in our local book chains and on amazon.com— it's practically a heavy industry these days—tends to reduce the gnarly paradoxes into misleading recipes or Dilbertian cliches, trapping uneasy managers in false dreams. You know, take these Three Rules and you, too, can become Jack Welch; put yourself in a microwave and out pops a McLeader. Not! I prefer the atonal cacophony of voices these papers express, frustratingly contradictory and discordant as they are. Don't we all prefer nice, tidy answers to vexing problems? Well, you're not going to get them here. Yes, seek simplicity as Whitehead implores, but, as he goes on to say, distrust it!

My final generalization: Dilbert's Revenge. We all know that Scott Adams, Dilbert's alter ego, has become a multimillionaire based on the fallout of downsizing and the fact that about 25 percent of the U.S. workforce has been dumped since 1985. The resulting cynicism and distrust has seriously frayed, if not substantially broken, the implicit social contract between the workforce and The Corporation. But now, with unemployment plummeting to unprecedented levels—note that only 1.9 percent of college graduates are unemployed—workers are now stiffing The Corporation. Witness a recent cover story in *Fortune*. "Yo, Corporate America," it goes, picturing a twenty–something techie with a parakeet on his shoulder, "I want a fat salary, a signing bonus, and a cappuccino machine—oh, and I'm bringing my bird to work. I'm the New Organization Man. You need me." And he got it, birdcage and all. Although some of the authors in this volume disagree whether heroic leadership is viable or even relevant, they are all heroic in attempting to illuminate the darkness around a profoundly important issue: leading change in an achingly changing, helter-skelter world.

University of Southern California   WARREN BENNIS
September 1998

Preface

This book has its origins in a conference sponsored by the Center for Effective Organizations (CEO) and the Leadership Institute of the Marshall School of Business at the University of Southern California. The conference, entitled Leading Change, was held in Los Angeles. Its intent was to bring together a group of leading thinkers—both academics and practitioners—who had been conducting cutting-edge research on the issue of leadership and organizational change. The conference was all we had hoped for and more. Given the many vantage points represented by the participants, the dialogue generated pushed the envelope of our knowledge on leading change. The group attended to many unresolved issues, asked difficult questions, and helped us each learn about what it means to lead significant organizational change as we approach the new millennium. The chapters in this volume are the product of this remarkable group.

Audience

This volume brings together a highly respected group of scholars and thinkers to shed light on cutting-edge issues related to leadership and organizational change. Drawing together the most recent theories and research about leading change, it shows how this work can be applied to solving the leadership issues that many contemporary organizations face today. It is also a wonderfully balanced discussion of research, practice, and theory. Executives and managers wrestling with how to effectively orchestrate change should find this book a particularly rich resource. In addition to general guidelines and detailed case studies, it offers them specific advice and interventions. The book also holds important insights and ideas for consultants, human resources professionals, and organizational development practitioners who wish to enhance the success of their own interventions. Academics and researchers who study the issues of change management and leadership will find it an invaluable resource as well. It presents the most recent and important research on the topic.

Overview of the Contents

This book begins with an introduction that focuses on the key challenges facing leaders as they attempt to radically transform contemporary organizations. It describes the twin challenges of creating leaner, more responsive organizations while empowering their workforces. It stresses environmental conditions such as intense global competition and rapid technological change that create increasing demands for organizational change, transformation, and leadership.

Part One (Chapters One and Two) is concerned with leaders in action. It provides two in-depth case discussions of leaders in the process of transforming their organizations. Chapter One, by David Nadler, is a case study of the transformation of Lucent Technologies as it emerged as a spinoff from AT&T. It demonstrates how an insider-outsider leadership team collaborated to lead Lucent through a major change, including the setting of direction, creation of a new corporate identity, and formation of participative processes that involved employees at all levels of the organizational hierarchy.

Chapter Two, by Christopher Bartlett and Sumantra Ghoshal, provides a model for how to create corporate transformation that moves beyond incremental process reengineering to more radical people rejuvenation. The authors illustrate with the case of Jack Welch at General Electric the processes for moving beyond discipline and support to build stretch and trust in the revitalization process.

Part Two (Chapters Three, Four, and Five) focuses on articulating guiding principles for leading change. These chapters move beyond case studies to elicit the key elements of the effective leadership of change.

Chapter Three, by Ronald Heifetz and Donald Laurie, observes that leaders cannot solve strategic or operating problems without doing adaptive work—work for which no satisfactory response has been developed. Under such conditions, no single individual in authority possesses the solution and no established procedures will suffice. Instead, to succeed in adaptive work, deeply held beliefs and old skills must be relinquished for new ones. They argue that adaptive work can only be achieved by mobilizing people to make painful adjustments in their attitudes, work habits, and lives and to exhibit leadership at all levels.

Chapter Four, by John Kotter, examines why transformation efforts fail. He offers eight time-proven steps for the effective change of leadership. He suggests that leadership must begin by establishing a sense of urgency and then creating and communicating a focused vision. With a vision in place, then the leader can turn to implementation by empowering others to act and by creating short-term wins. The last steps in leading change include consolidating improvements and institutionalizing new approaches.

Chapter Five, by Donald Hambrick and Kristen Stucker, draws from an extensive, multistage research project on corporate spinoffs with the objective of providing guidance to managers on the effective leadership of spinoff companies. The authors recognize the major implications of these situations for leaders—instant autonomy, the history of the parent company, the need to interact and demonstrate legitimacy with key stakeholders.

Part Three (Chapters Six, Seven, Eight, and Nine) looks more specifically at designing leadership interventions that help the leader learn about leading change. These chapters examine detailed intervention strategies that were employed to assist senior leaders in implementing change successfully.

In Chapter Six, Michael Beer starts by rejecting the notion of the all-knowing, heroic leader who is in a position to miraculously save an organization. He points out the unintended and undesirable by-products of such notions when it comes to implementing change. He suggests instead that the leadership of change must begin in a structured dialogue between the leadership team and the lower levels of the organization that are connected to implementing the strategic tasks of the organization. He illustrates this action learning intervention through a process called Organizational Fitness Profiling.

Chapter Seven, by Robert Quinn and Nancy Snyder, introduces Advanced Change Theory, arguing that the leader must change him- or herself first to ensure that his or her deed and actions are consistent with the vision of the future before expecting others to change. They explore the applicability of Advance Change Theory in an account of a cultural change effort at Whirlpool under the leadership of its CEO David Whitwam.

Chapter Eight, by Richard Pascale, affords a new angle on the subject of leadership in focusing on complex adaptive systems. This complexity view of leadership extends situational models by asserting that social systems contain latent properties. The primary task of the leader, then, is to create a context that calls forth and taps this emergent potential.

Chapter Nine, by Robert Miles, provides a general framework for orchestrating large-scale corporate transformation. It addresses the key levers that executive leaders have at their disposal to launch and guide such an undertaking. The framework provides a robust, field-tested approach that can be adapted to meet a variety of corporate transformation challenges, executive styles, and organization skill sets.

Part Four (Chapters Ten, Eleven, Twelve, and Thirteen) gets down to a fundamental issue by asking whether leadership really matters in change efforts. Do leaders actually have discretion in making change or are the environment and other organizational forces so powerful that a leader's actions are largely irrelevant?

In Chapter Ten, Susan Mohrman takes the perspective of lower-level employees on the leadership of change, a perspective largely ignored in the other chapters. In an extensive research study of more than twenty companies experiencing significant change, she found that leaders must create shared understanding through new social, market, and technological architectures. She also highlights the need for contemporary leaders to shape the new employment relationship away from the traditional focus on lifetime employment.

Chapter Eleven, by Thomas Cummings, presents a balanced view of the role of top leaders in transformational change. He recognizes the constraints on leader discretion and identifies the characteristics of change situations where leaders are likely to have their greatest effects and those where they are expected to have little effect. He closes by speculating on what may be powerful substitutes for leadership in the change process.

In Chapter Twelve, we look toward the future. Raymond Miles and Grant Miles suggest that a central leadership challenge as we approach the new millennium will be the legitimization of collaboration. Collaboration is a necessity for the creation of new knowledge both inside and outside the firm in order to promote efficient innovation. A key emphasis of their chapter is the development of the philosophical underpinnings of collaboration as it relates to leadership and adaptation.

In the closing chapter, the editors look across the chapters to summarize key lessons about the leadership of change. We also highlight the unresolved issues that have been raised with an emphasis on those that must be addressed in future work. We close the book by identifying relevant issues for the future of the leadership of change.

Acknowledgments

We have many people to thank for their help in the development of this book and its embedded ideas. Both the Center for Effective Organizations and the Leadership Institute are part of the Marshall School of Business at the University of Southern California. We are grateful for the enthusiastic support we received from the administration and departments of the Marshall school. We would like to acknowledge Warren Bennis, founding chairman of the Leadership Institute at the Marshall School of Business. His work has guided many of the ideas presented in this volume. Moreover, his participation in and support of the conference have been invaluable. We have also received support from many faculty members in the Marshall School of Business. Many of the faculty participated in the conference as discussants for the papers or participants in the discussions. They include Arvind Bhambri, Robert Coffey, David Finegold, Larry Greiner, Sam Hariharan, Gerry Ledford, Julia Liebeskind, Morgan McCall, Ian Mitroff, Nandini Rajagopalan, and Kathleen Reardon. We would also like to thank Deletha Gafford and Annette Yakushi for their help in organizing the conference and in the production of this book.

Los Angeles, California
September 1998

Jay A. Conger
Gretchen M. Spreitzer
Edward E. Lawler III

The Authors

Jay A. Conger is professor of management and organization, Marshall School of Business, University of Southern California. He also chairs the Marshall School's Leadership Institute. He received his B.A. degree in anthropology from Dartmouth College, his M.B.A. degree from the University of Virginia, and his D.B.A. degree in organizational behavior from the Harvard Business School. The author of more than sixty articles and book chapters, he researches executive leadership, the management of organizational change, executive boardrooms, and the training and development of leaders and managers. His books include *Winning 'Em Over* (1998), *Charismatic Leadership in Organizations* (1998), *Spirit at Work,* (1994), *Learning to Lead* (1992), *The Charismatic Leader* (1989), and *Charismatic Leadership* (1988). He has consulted with a wide variety of companies on issues of organizational change and leadership. An outstanding teacher, Conger was selected by *Business Week* as the nation's top professor to teach leadership to executives.

Gretchen M. Spreitzer is on the faculty of management and organization at the University of Southern California Graduate School of Business Administration, where she is also a faculty affiliate of the Center for Effective Organizations and the Leadership Institute. She earned her B.S. degree in systems analysis from Miami University of Ohio and completed her doctoral work at the University of Michigan School of Business in organizational behavior and human resource management. Prior to completing her Ph.D., Spreitzer worked with the management consulting group at Price Waterhouse's government services office and with a not-for-profit urban planning firm in Washington, D.C. Spreitzer's main research activities have focused on employee empowerment, leadership development, and strategic and organizational change (including recent work on downsizing). Her work has been published in leading management journals. She consults with companies in several industries on the managerial applications of her research. She is a member of several editorial boards and has also served on the executive board of the Western Academy of Management and the Organization Development and Change Division of the Academy of Management.

Edward E. Lawler III is professor of management and organization in the Marshall School of Business at the University of Southern California. He joined USC in 1978 and in 1979 founded and became director of the university's Center for Effective Organizations. He has consulted with over one hundred organizations on employee involvement, organizational change, and compensation and has been honored as a top contributor to the fields of organizational development, organizational behavior, and compensation. The author of more than two hundred articles and twenty-eight books, his works have been translated into seven languages. His most recent books include *Strategies for High-Performance Organizations* (Jossey-Bass, 1998), *Tomorrow's Organization* (Jossey-Bass, 1998), *From the Ground Up: Six Principles for Creating the New Logic Corporation* (Jossey-Bass, 1996), *Creating High Performance Organizations* (Jossey-Bass, 1995), *Organizing for the Future* (Jossey-Bass, 1993), *Employee Involvement and Total Quality Management* (Jossey-Bass, 1992), *The Ultimate Advantage* (Jossey-Bass, 1992), and *Strategic Pay* (Jossey-Bass, 1990).

Christopher A. Bartlett holds the MBA Class of 1966 Chair of Business Administration at Harvard Graduate School of Business Administration. Prior to joining the faculty, he received an economics degree from the University of Queensland, Australia (1964), and both masters and doctorate degrees in business administration from Harvard University (1971 and 1979). He has also worked as a marketing manager with Alcoa, a management consultant at McKinsey and Company's London office, and general manager of Baxter Laboratories' subsidiary company in France. Since joining the faculty of Harvard Business School in 1979, his interests have focused on the general management challenges faced particularly in multinational corporations. He has taught courses in business policy, international management, management ethics, general management, and organizational leadership. He has served as Chair of the school's International Senior Management Program and as Chair of the General Management Unit at HBS. He currently teaches in Harvard's Program for Global Leadership. Bartlett is the author or coauthor of six books, including (with Sumantra Ghoshal) *Managing Across Borders: The Transnational Solution* (HBS Press, 1989), which has been translated into nine languages and adapted into a video program. His articles have appeared in journals such as *Harvard Business Review, Sloan Management Review, California Management Review, McKinsey Quarterly, Strategic Management Journal, Academy of Management Review,* and *Journal of International Business Studies.* He has just completed a major research program focusing on the way a new corporate model is redefining management roles and responsibilities of managers, and the implications of these changes for the skills and qualifications required of today's managers. Some of the findings of this project appeared in a three-part series of *Harvard Business Review* articles called "Changing the Role of the Top Management," and the book reporting on the project, *The Individualized Corporation* (coauthored with Sumantra Ghoshal), was published by Harper in October 1997. In addition to his academic responsibilities, Bartlett maintains ongoing consulting and advisory relationships with several major corporations, particularly in areas relating to his current research.

Michael Beer is Chaners-Rabb Professor of Business Administration at Harvard Business School, where he teaches in the school's Advanced Management Program, a residential executive development program for senior executives from around the globe. His research and expertise are in the areas of organizational effectiveness, organizational change, and human resource management. Prior to joining the faculty at Harvard, Beer was director of organization research and development at Corning, Inc. He has authored or coauthored seven books as well as numerous book chapters and articles, and consults with a number of Fortune 500 companies. *The Critical Path to Corporate Renewal* (Harvard Business School Press, 1990) won the Johnson, Smith, and Knisely New Perspectives on Executive Leadership award and was a finalist for the Academy of Management book of the year award in 1990.

Thomas G. Cummings is professor and Chair of the Department of Management and Organization at the Marshall School of Business. He received his B.A. and M.B.A. degrees from Cornell University and his Ph.D. in socio-technical systems from the University of California at Los Angeles. He was previously on the faculty at Case Western Reserve University. He has authored thirteen books, written more than forty scholarly articles, and given numerous invited papers at national and international conferences. He is associate editor of the *Journal of Organizational Behavior,* former editor in chief of the *Journal of Management Inquiry,* chairman of the Organizational Development and Change Division of the Academy of Management, and president of the Western Academy of Management. His major research and consulting interests include designing high-performing organizations and strategic change management. He has conducted several large-scale organization design and change projects and has consulted with a variety of private- and public-sector organizations in the United States, Europe, Mexico, and Scandinavia.

Sumantra Ghoshal holds the Robert P. Bauman Chair in Strategic Leadership at London Business School, where he also directs the Strategic Leadership Research Programme. Previously he was a Professor of Business Policy at INSEAD in Fontainebleau, France. Sumantra's research, writing, and consulting focuses on the management of large worldwide firms. He has published a number of articles, award-winning case studies, and books, including *Managing Across Borders: The Transnational Solution* (coauthored with Christopher A. Bartlett and published in nine languages), *Organization Theory and the Multinational Corporation* (with Eleanor Westney), *The Strategy Process: European Perspective* (with Henry Mintzberg and J. B. Quinn), and *The Differentiated Network* (with Nitin Nohria). He consults with a number of major European and American corporations.

Donald C. Hambrick is the Samuel Bronfman Professor of Democratic Business Enterprise at the Graduate School of Business, Columbia University. He is coeditor (with David Nadler and Michael Tushman) of the recent book *Navigating Change: How CEOs, Boards, and Top Teams Steer Transformation* and coauthor (with Sydney

Finkelstein) of *Strategic Leadership: Top Executives and Their Effects on Organization.* In addition, Hambrick's work has appeared in numerous professional and scholarly journals, including *Administrative Science Quarterly, Academy of Management Journal, Academy of Management Review,* and *Strategic Management Journal.* He is an active consultant and speaker to companies in the United States and abroad.

Ronald A. Heifetz directs the Leadership Education Project at Harvard University's John F. Kennedy School of Government. For the last fourteen years, he has been responsible for developing a theory of leadership and a method for leadership development. His research aims to provide strategy and tactics for mobilizing adaptive work in politics, businesses, and nonprofits. His courses on leadership and authority are among the most popular in the university. His widely acclaimed book, *Leadership Without Easy Answers,* was published by Belknap Press in September 1994. Formerly director of Cor Associates, a research and development group, and clinical instructor in psychiatry at Harvard Medical School, Heifetz works extensively with leaders in government and industry. His consultations and seminars with individuals, executive committees, and leadership teams focus on the work of leaders in generating and sustaining adaptive change across political boundaries, operating units, product divisions, and functions in politics, government agencies, and international businesses. Heifetz is a graduate of Columbia University, Harvard Medical School, and the John F. Kennedy School of Government. He is also a cellist and former student of Gregor Piatigorsky.

John P. Kotter is Konosuke Matsushita Professor of Leadership at the Harvard Business School. He is a graduate of MIT and Harvard and has been on the Harvard Business School faculty since 1972. In 1980, at the age of 33, he was given tenure and a full professorship at the school, making him one of the youngest people in the history of the university to be so honored. Kotter is author of *The General Managers* (1982), *Power and Influence: Beyond Formal Authority* (1985), *The Leadership Factor* (1987), *A Force for Change: How Leadership Differs from Management* (1990), *Corporate Culture and Performance* (1992, with Jim Heskett), *The New Rules: How to Succeed in*

Today's Post-Corporate World (1995), and *Leading Change* (1996), all best-sellers among business books in the United States. He has also created two highly acclaimed executive videos, *Leadership* (1991) and *Corporate Culture* (1993). His articles in the Harvard Business Review over the past twenty years have sold more reprints than any of the hundreds of distinguished authors who have written for that publication during the same period. In 1997, HBS Press released an educational CD-ROM based on the *Leading Change* book, and Simon & Schuster's Free Press published *Matsushita Leadership: Lessons from the 20th Century's Most Remarkable Entrepreneur.* The many honors won by Kotter include an Exxon Award for Innovation in Graduate Business School Curriculum (Design), a Johnson, Smith, and Knisely Award for New Perspectives in Business Leadership, and a McKinsey Award for best *Harvard Business Review* article. Kotter is widely regarded as the best speaker in the world on the topics of leadership and change. He lives in Cambridge, Massachusetts and on Squam Lake in New Hampshire with his wife, Nancy, daughter, Caroline, and son, Jonathan.

Donald L. Laurie is founder and managing director of the management consulting firm Laurie International Limited. His work focuses on strategic management issues relevant to chairmen and chief executives. His corporate assignments have been with clients concerned with crafting strategic architecture, inventing new businesses, managing change, and improving the quality of leadership. Laurie has worked with leaders and their organizations in British Airways, Xerox, IBM, Philips, Unilever, Shell, Chase Manhattan Bank, KPMG, British Telecom, British Petroleum, and others. He is coauthor with Ronald A. Heifetz of "The Work of Leadership" in the January-February 1997 issue of *Harvard Business Review.* His book on leadership will be published in 1998.

Grant Miles is assistant professor of management in the College of Business Administration at the University of North Texas. His research interests include the study of industry variety and evolution, strategic alliances, and new organizational forms. His research has been published in *Strategic Management Journal, Academy of Management Executive,* and *Journal of Business Ethics.* His current work is focused on the implications of knowledge and learning on organizational structures and processes.

Raymond E. Miles is Trefethen Professor Emeritus and former dean of the Haas School of Business at the University of California, Berkeley. He has written widely on organization and management, and he serves on the board of directors of two large companies. He is coauthor (with Charles Snow) of *Fit, Failure, and the Hall of Fame: How Companies Succeed or Fail* (Free Press, 1994). He currently is conducting a study of twenty-first–century organizational forms, funded by the Carnegie Bosch Institute for Applied Studies in International Management.

Robert H. Miles, founder and principal of Atlanta-based Corporate Transformation Resources, is a leading thought and practice leader in the areas of corporate transformation and executive leadership. Over the past two decades, he has been intensively involved in shaping some of the world's most important business transformations. He is the author of several books on the subject, including, most recently, *Leading Corporate Transformation* (Jossey-Bass, 1997). Before concentrating full-time on corporate transformations, Miles was a charter faculty member at the Yale School of Management, faculty chairman of the innovative Managing Organizational Effectiveness program for business leaders and their teams at Harvard Business School, Hopkins Professor and dean of the faculty at the Goizueta Business School at Emory University, and a frequent guest lecturer at the Stanford Executive Institute.

Susan Albers Mohrman is a senior research scientist at the Center for Effective Organizations, Marshall School of Business, University of Southern California. She received her A.B. degree in psychology from Stanford University, her M.Ed. degree from the University of Cincinnati, and her Ph.D. degree in organizational behavior from Northwestern University. Mohrman's research and publications focus on innovations in organizational design processes, team-based and other forms of lateral organization, high-involvement management, organizational learning and change, and human resource management. She has consulted with a variety of organizations, helping to introduce innovative management approaches and redesign structures and systems. Her books include *Self-Designing Organizations: Learning How to Create High Performance* (with T. G. Cummings), *Large-Scale Organizational Change* (with A. M. Mohrman Jr., G. E. Ledford Jr., T. G. Cummings, E. E. Lawler III, and

Associates), *Creating High Performance Organizations: Practices and Results of Employee Involvement* and *Total Quality Management in Fortune 1000 Companies* (with E. E. Lawler III and G. E. Ledford Jr.), *Designing Team-Based Organizations: New Forms for Knowledge Work* (with S. G. Cohen and A. M. Mohrman Jr.), and *Tomorrow's Organization: Crafting Winning Capabilities in a Dynamic World* (with J. Galbraith and E. E. Lawler III). She serves on the board of governors of the Academy of Management and on the review and editorial boards of several journals.

David A. Nadler, founder and chairman of Delta Consulting Group, Inc., is an internationally recognized leader in the field of strategic organizational change. Cited by Business Week (1992) as one of "management's new gurus," he and his firm employ a highly customized approach to executive-level consulting that combines a thorough grounding in the behavioral sciences with years of practical experience in change management at more than a hundred public and private organizations, including more than seventy Fortune 500 companies. Nadler advises CEOs and other senior corporate leaders on a range of issues related to the design and management of organizational change, including strategy, organizational architecture, operating environment, and leadership. Since its founding in 1980, Delta has grown to a firm of more than seventy-five employees with annual revenues close to $30 million. From its headquarters in New York and a major office in San Francisco, Delta serves a list of distinguished clients that currently include Xerox, Chase Manhattan, Lucent, Bristol-Myers Squibb, the New York Times, Corning, and The Limited. Before launching the firm, Nadler served for six years on the faculty of the Graduate School of Business, Columbia University. Prior to that, he was on the staff of the Survey Research Center, Institute for Social Research, University of Michigan. He holds a B.A. in international affairs from George Washington University, an M.B.A. from Harvard Business School, and an M.A. and Ph.D. in psychology from the University of Michigan. He is a member of the Academy of Management and was elected a Fellow of the American Psychological Association. Nadler has published extensively in the field of organizational behavior and change management and has authored or edited more than a dozen books. The most recent of these include

Competing by Design: The Power of Organizational Architecture (with Michael L. Tushman) and *Executive Teams* and *Champions of Change,* both published by Jossey-Bass.

Richard T. Pascale is an Associate Fellow of Oxford University and a Visiting Scholar of the Santa Fe Institute. He was a member of the faculty at Stanford's Graduate School of Business for twenty years. He is a leading business consultant worldwide, a best-selling author, and a respected scholar. Pascale is coauthor of *The Art of Japanese Management,* a New York Times best-seller, and author of *Managing on the Edge.* His seminal *Harvard Business Review* article, "Zen and the Art of Management," won a McKinsey Award. His most recent works include "Changing the Way We Change" (*Harvard Business Review,* November-December 1997; co-authored with Mark Millermann and Linda Gioja), "The Re-Invention Roller Coaster" (with Tracy Goss and Anthony Athos, *Harvard Business Review,* November-December 1993), and a BBC television series on transformation. He is currently completing a book with Mark Millermann and Linda Gioja to be published in Fall 1998 that encompasses recent work on complex adaptive systems and ties these findings to practical steps in the journey of organizational transformation. Pascale has worked closely with two dozen of the CEOs and top management teams of Fortune 500 firms engaged in organizational transformation, including General Electric, British Petroleum, Intel, Morgan Guaranty Bank, and Royal Dutch Shell.

Robert E. Quinn is the M. E. Tracy Distinguished Professor of Organizational Behavior and Human Resource Management at the University of Michigan Business School. He is particularly interested in issues of personal and organizational change and has published numerous journal articles on change-related topics. Four of his recent books are *Beyond Rational Management, Becoming a Master Manager, Deep Change: Discovering the Leader Within,* and *Diagnosing and Changing Organizational Culture* (forthcoming). He can be contacted at requinn@umich.edu.

Nancy T. Snyder is currently chief learning officer for Whirlpool Corporation. In this capacity she is responsible for creating and implementing corporate strategies that facilitate globalization and leverage learning around the world. She is currently assisting the chairman and CEO in developing a shared corporate culture worldwide. She heads the Brandywine Creek Performance Center, Whirlpool's corporate university. She can be contacted at Nancy_T_Snyder@email.whirlpool.com.

Kristin Stucker is a Ph.D. candidate in strategic management at Columbia University. Her research interests include the management of spinoff firms, internal versus external pressures for conformity in organizations, and multinational management.

Introduction:
The Challenges of
Effective Change Leadership

Jay Conger
Gretchen Spreitzer
Edward E. Lawler III

Today's fast-changing business environment requires corporations to adapt or risk death. Cutting-edge technology, the triumph of capitalism over communism, a burgeoning global economy, a billion new entrants to the global workforce, and a surplus of products all feed into an environment that is highly competitive and fast-changing. To survive, incremental performance improvements are not enough; dramatic, sometimes revolutionary, change is often necessary. No organization can sit on its laurels. The days of secure business niches insulated by government protection, geographic location, proprietary technology, or weak competition are all but gone. Today, corporations must adapt as never before in order to survive.

Compounding the challenges posed by today's competitive business environment is the growing complexity of organizations themselves. Fewer and fewer corporations are designed around neatly defined functions. Instead, cross-functional matrices and a web of joint-venture and alliance operations characterize many organization charts. Many of these new forms have a global character. Not only do companies like Ford, General Electric, and Sony span the globe, but increasing numbers of middle and small-sized organizations have operations in distant corners of the world as well.

Moreover, waves of mergers and acquisitions are adding to the complexity and dynamism of today's corporate world. In 1996 alone, more than ten thousand mergers were consummated, totaling some $660 billion. In many mergers, the big got bigger and more complex. The recent merger of Boeing and McDonnell Douglas, for example, combined the world's largest commercial aircraft manufacturer with the world's largest military aircraft manufacturer. At the same time, divestitures via spinoffs are up; Pepsico recently spun off Taco Bell, KFC, and Pizza Hut as a separate restaurant entity so that it could concentrate on its core beverage business. Increasingly, autonomous subunits of corporate giants are being spun off from parent companies.

All these changes, from the harsh competitive realities of the marketplace to the complexity of new organizational forms, pose demands on corporations to transform themselves frequently, rapidly, and effectively. These trends have made obsolete many of the traditional sources of competitive advantage, leaving organizational design and management as one of the few available sources of significant, sustained competitive advantage. Competitive advantage in today's world increasingly is in the hands of companies that are better at organizing and managing their operations.[1,2] General Electric, Hewlett-Packard, and Wal-Mart are just a few of the most visible companies that have thrived due at least in part to their ability to organize and manage their people and operations. To fit in to today's environment, organizations must develop new and unique approaches to management and change.

The difficulty of leading organizational change is ratcheted even higher given the seemingly paradoxical trend of companies trying to become leaner even as they empower their workforce.[3] Employee downsizing has become favored by many companies attempting to cope with fundamental structural changes in the increasingly global economy. Those employees who survive repeated downsizing are often less loyal and committed to the organization. Downsizing may also condition employees to be risk averse, worried that their own jobs will be the next to go. Corporations must find ways to more fully involve their employees in the effective management of the organization. Top managers today do not have the knowledge to make all decisions themselves. They must depend on lower-level employees who directly interface with customers and competitors and who understand the changing needs and requirements of the marketplace. Thus, a key challenge becomes how to lead radical change while simultaneously garnering employee initiative and involvement.

It is becoming increasingly clear that a new psychological or employment contract must be created that is not built around the notion of loyalty through lifetime employment.[4] Although we have little understanding of what the new psychological contract might look like, early clues indicate that it must offer employees the opportunity for a stake in the company through rewards such as profit sharing and stock options. In addition, it must focus on developing employee skills to increase their employability should downsizing become reality. Thus, today's leaders must help shape the changing employment relationship in order to keep employees committed and energized.

The Demand for Leadership

It is one thing to argue that organizations need to reinvent themselves and develop new, more effective approaches to organizing, and quite another to accomplish it. Large-scale organizational transformation is, at best, a developing art that has yet to produce any clear formulas for success, but more and more attention is being turned to executives as the principle agents of change and adaptation. It is increasingly common to assume that leadership plays the crucial role in an organization's successful adaptation to a changing world. Companies are paying record compensation to attract the best and brightest executive talent to lead them safely through today's turbulent business environment. Many boards and executive recruiters assume that there exists an elite corps of individuals who possess leadership skills that have almost universal application. Take, for example, Louis Gerstner, who moved from RJR Nabisco, a packaged food and tobacco company, to the high-technology giant IBM. Similarly, Randall Tobias leaped from telecommunications leader AT&T to pharmaceutical company Eli Lilly. Both have succeeded in organizations and industries radically different from those of their prior positions. They saved their organizations from the brink of financial distress.

Yet this type of heroic leadership appears rare. There seem to be as many if not more stories of leadership failures. Witness the hiring of Gilbert Amelio, the former head of National Semiconductor, to run the ailing Apple Computer. After a year and a half of not being able to turn the company around, he was fired very publicly by the Apple board. Or take the case of John Walter, who moved from printing giant R. R. Donnelly to succeed Robert Allen at AT&T. Less than a year later, he found himself fired by the AT&T board. Likewise CEO Robert Palmer, who after several years of management shakeups and turnaround schemes failed to successfully reposition Digital Equipment Corporation, which soon was acquired by Compaq Computer. The myth of the superleader seems to persist in spite of well-publicized leadership failures. Such a mixed record implies that leading organizational change is not a matter of following the simple set of formulas or steps often recounted in popular accounts of successful leaders. Leadership ability in general, much less the heroic form, appears to be scarce; in a survey conducted by John Kotter of Harvard Business School, executives in successful U.S. corporations concluded that their organizations had far too few people with leadership ability and too many who were simply strong at managing.[5]

Given these concerns, more attention in recent years has been directed toward understanding the fundamentals of effective leadership. For example, in previous decades the terms management and leadership were treated as synonymous. With the realization that organizations once considered paragons of management effectiveness were faltering in the face of dramatic competitive challenges, many began to suspect that the two roles involved different skill sets. It was conceivable that a company could be well managed but poorly led. In good times, a well-managed company might enjoy great success. But in difficult times, as the tide recedes, such a company's efficient managerial character would fail to compensate for its lack of foresight and vision. In these cases, management is not enough—these companies require effective leadership.

As a result, a small group of academics (including Bass,[5] Bennis and Nanus,[6] Conger and Kanungo,[7] Kotter,[8] Kouzes and Posner,[9] Peters and Waterman,[10] and Tichy and Devanna[11]) has drawn a strong distinction between management and leadership. Their models suggest different but complementary skill sets and time frames for the two roles. For example, management attends to shorter-term demands—to day-to-day operating challenges. Leadership focuses on the longer-term issues—to where the organization must be in the future. Management gains commitment to performance through contractual arrangements, leadership through empowerment. As the corporate world has become better aware of these essential distinctions, more and more resources have gone into training and educating about leadership competencies. Popular interest has also created an enormous demand for books and articles on leadership. Today they number in the thousands, with titles suggesting a remarkable range of viewpoints—from *The Leadership Secrets of Attila the Hun* to *The Tao of Leadership*.

Clearly, there has been a renaissance in the study of, development of, and general focus on the role of leaders in complex organizations. Despite this flowering of interest in and research on leadership's role in organizational change and effectiveness, our knowledge of the topic, particularly the leadership of change, remains limited. We are in the Bronze Age in terms of our insight. This becomes most apparent when one realizes that after two decades of research on leadership and organizational change there exists no universal set of prescriptions or step-by-step formulas that leaders can use in all situations to guide change.

Out of this murky state of affairs, however, there is widespread agreement on one fact: the change process is extremely messy and chaotic, wherever it occurs. This is in sharp contrast to popular notions that orchestrating change can be accomplished by following a neat set of sequential and universal steps, much like assembling a complicated electronics kit at home: patiently follow the right steps and success will be right around the corner. Clearly, the leadership of organizational change is complex and difficult, with no easy answers. The purpose of this volume is to draw together some of the outstanding thinkers on the topic of leadership and change to push the envelope of our knowledge of it.

New Directions in Leading Change

The many issues related to change leadership can be structured around multiple themes. They include leader behaviors for effective change, sources of change, different change strategies, whether leadership really matters, and the development of change leaders.

Leader Actions and Behaviors

From prior research on leadership, we have a limited understanding of the key leader actions and behaviors required for effective change. In this book we gain a greater understanding of some key behaviors involved in leading change that specifically focus on vision, alignment, and empowerment.

Creating a Vision

Most leadership scholars emphasize the importance of developing a vision or direction as the first step in leading change. This direction is critical in making sure that everyone is moving in the same direction. It is, however, an open question whether a vision is really necessary for leading change. IBM's CEO Louis Gerstner is famous for his assertion that "the last thing IBM needs right now is a vision" during the time IBM was desperately trying to recreate itself. If a vision is just another flavor-of-the-month activity, it will likely have little bearing on the functioning of the organization.

But if a vision is necessary, how does the leader go about creating one? In some organizations this is a top-down process announced by the leader; in others it involves lower-level employees. One chapter in this book relays the story of how a new leader was unable to create a vision until he had learned from employees at all levels of the organization what the key issues facing the organization were. In today's complex environment, it is probably not realistic to expect that one person can create an effective vision for the entire organization; more probably it will involve employees in different roles at many levels. Nor is it very realistic to think of vision as something relatively set or static; it may make more sense to think of a vision as something dynamic that evolves and develops over time.[12]

Aligning Constituencies to the Vision

Once a vision has been created, how does the leader communicate it to key stakeholders? Some leaders put their visions on plastic cards that employees can carry with them. Others make pronouncements by closed-circuit TV or videos. Still others create town-hall meetings where they lead discussions of the vision. Which alignment strategies build buy-in versus passive acceptance of a vision? Does real buy-in require the involvement of employees in the development of the vision itself? It is quite conceivable that change is not a sequence that starts with a vision and proceeds in a series of linear steps. Instead it may best be thought of as a dynamic, evolving process.

Empowering Employees to Implement the Vision

Once the leader has buy-in, what is involved in implementing the vision? A key issue, particularly in the literature on charismatic leadership, is how to create a sense of empowerment and ownership for employees. One argument is that this requires giving employees the autonomy to determine appropriate means for implementing the vision.[13] Prior research has shown that employees are most motivated when they have the freedom to determine what works best given their talents and skills.[14] However, we also know that in order for such autonomy to work employees must have access to the resources necessary for implementation and to information about the competition and the financial situation of their organization; without these they are likely to feel helpless in bringing about change. Also, rewards may be particularly helpful in building a sense of ownership.[15]

Symbolic Actions

Often leaders must engage in actions or behaviors that symbolize the commitment and energy the leader has toward change. These may speak strongly and take on almost legendary status. For example, when Lee Iacocca was brought in to help Chrysler back to life in the 1980s, he chose to forgo a salary for several difficult years. Although this was not a huge sacrifice given the substantial stock options he was poised to receive if the company rebounded, it was nevertheless important in symbolizing to employees Chrysler's dire straits and Iacocca's commitment to turning things around. Similarly, Herb Kelleher, CEO of Southwest Airlines, often joins employees and serves customers on flights around the country. This helps employees see that he is interested in them and values the work they do and also demonstrates to them the importance he places on customer service. Such symbolic acts, in tandem with the more substantive acts already described, seem to facilitate the effective leadership of change, but how important are they?

The Sources of Change

Few would disagree that change needs to be led, but less clear is the origin and type of leadership required for effective change. Chapters in this volume identify several different sources of change.

The Heroic Leader

One source of change is consistent with American tradition: leadership from the top, especially by the CEO and top management. The business literature of the 1980s and 1990s has been enamored with and focused on the impact of heroic leaders such as Andy Grove of Intel, Jack Welch of General Electric, and Larry Bossidy of AlliedSignal. They are often credited with providing their companies with the strong direction required for effective change. But is their type of heroic leadership the best way to run major corporations, and should we attribute the success of their companies to their leadership ability? Several chapters in this volume provide a clearer understanding of the heroic leader.

It certainly is an open question whether heroic leaders produce lasting change. For example, what happens when the heroic leader moves on or retires? What type of successor is required for hero-led change to be maintained? Many organizations have found it quite difficult to transfer the reins of power from a heroic leader to a successor and to sustain gains attained.

Leadership by a Team

As organizations and the business environment become increasingly complex, it becomes more difficult for any single executive to lead. Today, as a result, more emphasis is being placed on the top management team—a group of senior executives who work together to lead the company. Often it includes the top executives from finance, marketing, operations, and human resources, as well as the CEO and president. Such a team brings a great range of skills to the leadership challenge, and this diversity often provides unique insights not available to any one executive. The Lucent spinoff from AT&T was, until very recently, effectively led in tandem by its CEO and president, who made decisions together on all aspects of the business. Many agree that this helped Lucent through its infancy with little turmoil. But it remains an open question how and when a leadership team can be effective.

Bottom-Up Approaches to Change

Heroic leadership does not prevent or necessarily argue against the importance of others in an organization stepping forward and providing leadership supportive of CEO-led change. Several authors argue that change needs to be led by individuals throughout the organization. In essence, they argue for shared leadership and a bottom-up orientation to change. Although this does not totally conflict with CEO-led change, it certainly puts it in a different context. In essence, it argues that CEOs need to enroll others in the change process and that an organization without emerging leaders is likely to be poor at the initial change process. Further, they are particularly unlikely to demonstrate sustained organizational effectiveness.

Historically, writings advocating employee involvement have suggested that change can even begin as a bottom-up process. They cite the success of "greenfield" plants built on a highly participative model thanks to the leadership of local plant and division managers. Although there is no question that many such plants are successful, the degree to which bottom-up changes lead to or stimulate organization-wide change is in doubt. Some literature suggests that leaders of this kind of change can end up virtual outcasts because their efforts are encapsulated and they are ostracized by the rest of the organization.

Environmental Stimuli for Change

Regardless of whether change is led from the top or the bottom, one frequently made point about leader-generated change is that leaders must create a felt need for it. But though the organizational change literature has consistently emphasized the importance of felt need, it has not always emphasized the importance of leaders in creating that need. Indeed, the literature has often stressed the environment as a key factor in producing change; the leader, for his or her part, is typically pictured as crystallizing the need for change by calling attention to the environmental forces driving it.

But sometimes a leader can create a felt need for change in the absence of any readily foreseen crisis posed by the environment.

Jack Welch of General Electric, for example, is often cited as a leader who accomplished change without an immediate crisis posed externally; GE was doing well when Welch took over but, as described later in this book by Bartlett and Ghoshal, he was able to produce change by creating his own crisis—one based on his demands for superior performance and the need to change before a crisis was imminent.

The Role of Outsiders and Consultants

Over the last several decades, two interesting trends have gained popularity and prominence. The first is the replacement of sitting CEOs with outsiders specifically to create and direct major organizational change. In many cases these come not just from outside the company but outside the industry as well. Bucking a tradition of promoting from within, IBM brought in Louis Gerstner, a senior executive from RJR Nabisco, to help spearhead its turnaround. Michael Armstrong, former CEO of Hughes Aircraft, got the top job at AT&T over a well-respected insider. There are several reasons why companies are turning to outsiders. Clearly, outsiders bring fresh perspectives and are unencumbered by a history of investment and personal commitments; as a result, they may be more willing than insiders to make tough decisions. They may also have talent and leadership ability unavailable inside the organization.

Still, there are questions about how quickly a leader from outside can grasp a complex business and make the right strategic decisions. On the one hand, if the taking-hold process drags on awhile there is the danger of missing a key opportunity for change; on the other, making quick strategic decisions may take the organization in the wrong direction. In any case, it is not obvious that either the insider or outsider has a strategic advantage in leading change in a large corporation.

An alternative to the outsider CEO is to bring in a consultant to help insider CEOs manage the change process. In many respects this makes sense, because most CEOs don't have much experience leading large-scale change efforts. A few move from company to company doing their thing at each, but most grow up in a single organization and get only one shot at leading a major change effort. Unless they sit on the board of another major corporation that underwent change, they are unlikely to have even seen a large-scale change effort unfold. Most companies do not have a staff support group capable of helping a CEO manage the change process. At best, an internal organization development group may exist that is capable of managing small-scale changes in different parts of the organization, but typically it too has no experience with large-scale change. Thus it is not surprising that, increasingly, strategy- and change-consulting firms offer to assist CEOs with large-scale change. Nevertheless, and despite the claims of many firms and consultants, it remains open what the best role is for them in supporting organizational change—and, indeed, how much value they add to large-scale change efforts.

Change Strategies

The literature on organizational change consistently argues that in order for large-scale change to be successful, the major components of an organization need to be changed. These are often identified as the business strategy, the formal organization structure, the reward system, the people, and, finally, the information and decision processes.[16] The literature on organization design argues that all these elements need to be in alignment in order for an organization to be effective.[17] Thus, the assumption is that if one element is changed the others have to be changed—otherwise, the organization is destabilized and potentially less effective than before the change process began.

It is one thing to say that all systems in an organization have to be changed, but quite another to orchestrate an effort that actually realigns them into a good fit. In essence, there are two ways to do so. One might be called the big bang theory, the second the incrementalist approach. In the big bang theory, one of several different approaches can be used to produce an almost simultaneous changeover. The most popular and successful approach, mentioned earlier, is the "greenfield," in which new divisions or locations are simply started with a new alignment of key organizational elements. This has proved successful, but, as with Saturn and similar operations, it does not necessarily change the entire organization. A more dramatic approach is essentially to shut down the existing organization and restart it with a whole new way of operating. There are, of course, incremental versions of the shutdown-restart approach in which over a relatively short period different systems in different parts of the organization are altered and redesigned so that, within a year or less, a totally new organization is created.

The incremental approach is less radical. It usually involves changing one system and then changing another, so that within a course of years a new organization has been created. Often this starts with structural change, moves to people change, and finally involves change in other key areas of the organization. This is probably the most common approach, but is it the most effective? It clearly is not as rapid as simultaneous change in all systems. The answer to this question, however, is unclear.

Change can be managed in a variety of ways, from purely top-down to highly participative. Democratic societies are built on the principles of high levels of involvement in the change process. The classic town meeting is perhaps the most extreme version; it often leads to slow change or even standoff and no change when there is no consensus. But when it does produce change, there is often high acceptance of and commitment to it.

CEO-led or top-down change often produces much quicker decision making but faces a significant challenge when it comes to implementation—that is, in enrolling the rest of the organization in the change. This type of change process must somehow answer the what's-in-it-for-me question for those who did not participate in the change decision. From a leadership point of view, top-down change requires dramatically different behaviors and orientations than participative change.

The field has developed a number of change technologies designed to help organizations move toward new ways of operating. In many respects, these are difficult to separate from the role of leadership in the change process because they either explicitly or implicitly make key assumptions about the leadership style of the organization. For example, large-scale community meetings aimed at producing change seem to assume that leaders want the involvement of people in the organization, and that the leader's role, to a substantial degree, is to lead the community toward a consensus about what the change should be. Change processes that focus more on the use of outside consultants typically align much more closely with a top-down leadership style and change initiation process.

The diagnosis-and-feedback approach is another piece of change process technology that assumes that a considerable amount can be learned from getting the opinions and inputs of individuals throughout the organization. It also tends to assume that individuals have good ideas about how the organization can be improved. Thus it aligns more with participative rather than top-down leadership styles.

It goes without saying that no single change process fits all situations, and that today's wide variety of change processes will expand further as more and more approaches are developed. In the chapters that follow, the specifics of several change processes are described and one main question addressed: What kind of leadership is required for a given change process to be successful?

Does Leadership Make a Difference?

Case studies often suggest a heroic model of the effective leader: one larger-than-life person comes into the organization and saves the day—he (in these studies they are predominantly male) is the knight in shining armor. But in reality the leader's success may depend on many others, including members of the top management team; the inherent complexity of large organizations usually requires the knowledge, skills, and abilities of more than one person. Even the best vision in the world will not make a difference unless the leader can achieve the buy-in and motivation of the rest of the organization to implement it. As the business world becomes more complex, the efforts of a single leader are likely to be less important then the coordinated efforts of a leadership team in conjunction with a motivated employee base. Often chance or luck plays into the leader's success as well. Yet invariably the heroic leader ends up with credit for a successful change. Some researchers refer to this as the "romance" of leadership;[18] it leads one to question whether leadership really matters.

It might be argued that the key role for the leader is setting context; he or she must create a culture that embraces the importance of change. The leader then needs to create an organization structure that will support the new vision. This might, for example, involve a team-based design to reduce centralization, hierarchy, and bureaucratization. The leader must select and hire top-notch people who have the skills necessary to bring the new vision to reality. If the vision involves globalization, for example, this might involve hiring or promoting people who have international experience. The leader must also create a reward system that encourages behaviors appropriate for the new vision. For example, if the vision requires more focus on the customer, then employees must be rewarded for actions that improve customer satisfaction. In other words, the leader's most important role may be to design an organization that supports the vision.

Developing Change-Agent Leaders

A final issue for this volume concerns how to enhance and expand the pool of executives and managers capable of orchestrating large-scale organizational change. As several chapters suggest, consultants can play a vital role. The experience of good consultants often spans numerous companies and industries, affording them a unique vantage point for learning about leading change. Each client is a laboratory where the consultant can gauge the impact of interventions, learning what works universally and what must be tailored to the context at hand. Along with that of academics, consultants' work affords them the opportunity to develop models and principles of change that may be applicable in many settings.

For organizational leaders, particularly those early in their careers, consultants can serve as guides and teachers. With fewer vested interests and less baggage, they are also in a good position to help managers challenge their own worldviews and routines. Yet the use of consultants must be approached with caution. Often they have only a superficial understanding of the situation at hand, not being a long-term member of the organization. Because they frequently move on to new opportunities before the change is completely implemented, they may assume more of a short-term perspective than executives and managers do.

In addition to consultants, leaders themselves can help develop the next generation of leadership talent. The CEO of Pepsico, Roger Enrico, created a leadership development program for very-high-potential young managers in which he mentored them through a specific change initiative.[19] Moreover, as we shall see in the case of Lucent Technologies, succession when orchestrated well can play a pivotal role in ensuring that leadership talent is passed on to future leaders. Henry Schacht, CEO of Lucent, worked closely with then-president Richard McGinn to help him develop the "right stuff" to become CEO.

Also, educational initiatives in recent years have shifted from simply attempting the transfer of knowledge toward action and intervention. In companies such as General Electric, and Philips, education is increasingly a tool to facilitate change.[20] Executives are now taught what leading involves and how they can be more effective leaders.[21]

Conclusion

We argue that intense global competition, rapid technological change, and international capital markets are creating more demand for change leadership than at perhaps any other time in history. These forces, combined with the complexity of new and more global organizational forms that span nations and unite organizations through alliances, joint ventures, and mergers and acquisitions, make the job of leadership increasingly difficult. No wonder it is popular to suggest that leadership is in short supply in most organizations. Moreover, we have a limited understanding of the role that leaders should play in making effective change a reality. This is the motivation for this book. In the chapters that follow, we discuss how leaders can help organizations change to meet the challenges of the twenty-first century.

Notes

1. Lawler, E. E. *The Ultimate Advantage: Creating the High-Involvement Organization.* San Francisco: Jossey-Bass, 1992.
2. Pfeffer, J. "Producing Sustainable Competitive Advantage Through the Effective Management of People." *Academy of Management Executive,* 1995, *9,* 55–69.
3. Mishra, K., Spreitzer, G., and Mishra, A. "Preserving Employee Morale During Downsizing." *Sloan Management Review,* 1998, *39,* 83–95.
4. Rousseau, D. M. *Psychological Contracts in Organizations.* Thousand Oaks, Calif.: Sage.
5. Bass, B. *Leadership and Performance Beyond Expectations.* New York: Free Press, 1985.
6. Bennis, W., and Nanus, B. *Leaders.* New York: HarperCollins, 1985.

7. Conger, J. A., and Kanungo, R. N. "Towards a Behavioral Theory of Charismatic Leadership in Organizational Settings." *Academy of Management Review*, 1987, *12*, 637–647.

8. Kotter, J. P. *A Force for Change*. New York: Free Press, 1990, pp. 8–9.

9. Kouzes, J. M., and Posner, B. F. *The Leadership Challenge*. San Francisco: Jossey-Bass, 1987.

10. Peters, T., and Waterman, R. *In Search of Excellence*. New York: Warner Books, 1982.

11. Tichy, N., and Devana, M. A. *The Transformational Leader*. New York: Wiley, 1987.

12. Conger, J. A., and Kanungo, R. N. *Charismatic Leadership in Organizations*. Thousand Oaks, Calif.: Sage, 1998.

13. Conger, J. A. *The Charismatic Leader*. San Francisco: Jossey-Bass, 1989.

14. Spreitzer, G. M., Kizilos, M., and Nason, S. "A Dimensional Analysis of the Relationship Between Psychological Empowerment and Effectiveness, Satisfaction, and Strain." *Journal of Management*, 1997, *23*(5), 679–704.

15. Lawler, E. E. *High-Involvement Management*. San Francisco: Jossey-Bass, 1986.

16. Galbraith, J. *Designing Complex Organizations*. Reading, Mass.: Addison-Wesley, 1973.

17. Pascale, R. *Managing on the Edge*. New York: Simon & Schuster, 1990.

18. Meindl, J. R., Ehrlich, S. B., and Dukerich, J. M. "The Romance of Leadership." *Administrative Science Quarterly*, 1985, *30*, 78–102.

19. Tichy, N., and Cohen, E. *The Leadership Engine*. New York: Harper-Business, 1997.

20. Conger, J. A., and Xin, K. R. "Executive Education: A Critical Level for Organizational Change." In S. A. Mohrman, J. A. Galbraith, and E. E. Lawler (eds.), *Tomorrow's Organization*. San Francisco: Jossey-Bass, 1998.

21. McCall, M., Lombardo, M., and Morrison, A. M. *The Lessons of Experience*. New York: Free Press, 1988.

The Leader's Change Handbook

Part One

Change Leadership in Action

Chapter One

A Success Story
The Case of Lucent Technologies
David A. Nadler

On October 21, 1995, AT&T caught the business world by surprise, announcing plans for the biggest voluntary break-up in commercial history. Within a year, the telecommunications giant would split itself into three independent corporate entities. AT&T would continue as the long-distance communications service company. NCR, the computer company AT&T had acquired and tried unsuccessfully to integrate a few years earlier, would be back on its own. And AT&T's systems, equipment, and technology operations would be grouped in a brand-new company soon to become known as Lucent Technologies, Inc.

Everyone understood what AT&T and NCR were all about. But Lucent was a different story. Rather than spinning off an existing entity, AT&T lumped together four of its least successful and least profitable businesses, throwing in a portion of the demoralized Bell Labs for good measure. Together, this amalgam of disparate operations would be cut off from the mother of all corporate mother ships, launched straight into the heart of the chaotic and hypercompetitive telecommunications industry, and expected to successfully compete as a $23 billion start-up with 130,000 employees around the globe.

The daunting job of managing the spin-off and leading the new company—one of the most awesome change management challenges in recent times—fell largely on the shoulders of newly named senior executives Henry Schacht and Richard McGinn. As a longtime AT&T executive, McGinn was an obvious choice for president and chief operating officer, but Schacht's appointment as chairman and chief executive officer caught many by surprise. He had served several years as an AT&T director, but the sixty-one-year-old retired CEO of Cummins Engine hardly seemed the logical choice to mold a new company capable of doing battle along the far frontiers of communications technology. In retrospect, the decision of AT&T's then-chairman Robert Allen to appoint Schacht as CEO and McGinn as COO was particularly astute, though at the time no one could have predicted just how effective the new team would become.

Now fast-forward to the fall of 1997. Two years have passed since AT&T's announcement. Schacht is in the process of passing the reins of leadership to McGinn, and Lucent is being widely acclaimed as one of the great success stories in the annals of American business, due in large part to Schacht and McGinn's adroit leadership.

The record is remarkable by any measure. Revenue growth has been solid—up 10 percent each year—while net income has risen dramatically. Through the first nine months of fiscal 1997, net income stood at $1.1 billion; third-quarter earnings per share had tripled year over year and topped analysts' projections by more than 30 percent. In the telecommunications marketplace, and in the business world at large, Lucent sped from zero to sixty in record time; in less than two years it had established a presence in the marketplace and the public consciousness, built a record of financial success, and attracted solid backing in the investment community. It had come to be regarded as a dynamic, successful, and growing company that compared favorably with its former parent AT&T.

All in all, it's a remarkable business success story, and one well worth close examination as a classic study in the leadership of large-scale and complex organizational change. Literally thousands of people contributed to Lucent's success, but the single most important factor was the leadership of the organization by its senior executives—and by Schacht and McGinn in particular. Consequently, there are important lessons to be learned from looking at how they led the company through a dramatic, successful and—in relative terms—remarkably short period of massive change.

First, a word about methodology. As a consultant to Lucent—and before that, to AT&T—the author worked closely with Schacht, McGinn, and the leadership team even before Lucent's formal creation, up through the present. In addition, Schacht agreed to sit down halfway through his tenure for an in-depth interview that allowed us to document some of his personal perspectives on what he was doing and why. As a result, we had the unusual opportunity to combine the insights gained through our own participation and close observation with the thoughtful reflections of the key principal at the center of the change effort. Together, these two views provide a comprehensive inside look not only at the actions that were taken to effect change, but the thinking that went into them.

With that perspective, we'll begin by briefly describing the situation Schacht confronted as he assumed leadership of Lucent, and then explain the series of critical actions that Schacht and McGinn took to shape and lead the company. Then we'll step back and consider some general lessons their experience offers to all those engaged in the management of change.

The Genesis of Lucent

In the early 1990s, AT&T found itself in an increasingly untenable situation. More and more, it was coming into direct conflict in the United States with many of the regional Bell operating companies and overseas with postal telephone and telegraph companies as they competed to provide the same communications services. Yet those same competitors were among the largest customers of AT&T's equipment and systems businesses.

In effect, AT&T was turning into a company in competition with itself. As deregulation progressed, particularly in the United States, it became clear to AT&T chairman Robert Allen that his company's systems and equipment businesses would be severely devalued unless they were freed to compete aggressively for business from other service providers. As a result, Allen made the difficult but strategically correct decision in 1995 to spin off the systems and equipment operations into a separate corporate entity. That new company, which eventually became Lucent Technologies, would develop, manufacture, distribute, sell, and support communications equipment, systems, and technology for information service providers, for enterprises, and for individuals.

Initially, Lucent was structured as follows (see Figure 1.1). The largest group was network systems, which had developed and provided equipment for information system providers, including switching, transmission, wireless and operating systems, and cable. Business communications systems focused on telecommunications systems, including PBXs, for corporate customers. Consumer products was responsible for a wide range of products including corded, cordless, and wireless phones. Microelectronics was involved in the development of microprocessors and chips for communications applications, both for Lucent and for other customers. Finally, the famed Bell Laboratories would continue to engage in cutting-edge science and technology.

In general, these businesses had exhibited lackluster performance for a number of years. From 1992 to 1995, as new leadership emerged in each of these businesses, significant turnarounds were accomplished. However, many critics would say, with some accuracy, that those improvements had merely started the process of raising performance to target levels. Moreover, these businesses were largely disconnected features of the AT&T corporate landscape. They hadn't operated as a single, cohesive corporate entity since they were part of Western Electric Corp. before the 1984 Bell System break-up.

As the various components of the new company were gathered together, it quickly became clear that there was no sense of identity. There was no strategy beyond adding up the financial results of the four businesses. Within the component businesses, each had developed its own culture and management style to address different challenges. Complicating matters even further, the business unit leaders felt limited commitment to the new enterprise. None had participated in the decision to create it. None had been asked for their opinion about joining it. And in some cases, the leaders clearly would have preferred seeing their own units individually spun off as stand-alone companies.

This was the situation confronting Henry Schacht in the fall of 1995 when he accepted the offer to come out of retirement to lead the new organization, and the situation facing Rich McGinn as he

Figure 1.1. Lucent Technologies Organization, 1996.

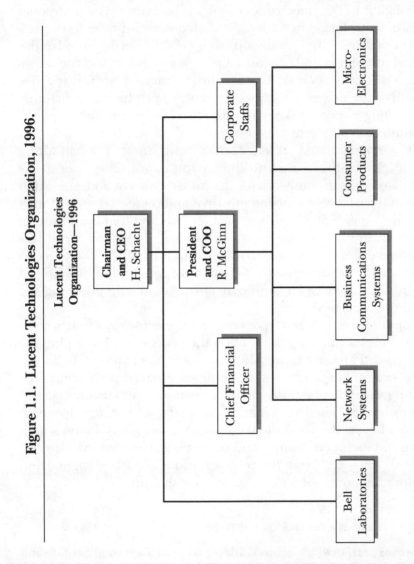

moved from being the operating head of a division of AT&T into the presidency of Lucent. Their immediate and obvious challenge was to separate the businesses from AT&T and meld them into a new corporate entity. That in itself would have been a huge responsibility. But the mechanics of the spin-off created an additional layer of complexity; in early 1996, Lucent would have to orchestrate a massive initial public offering (IPO) in order to raise the capital so essential to launching the new company. And the implication of that was clear: In very short order—within just a few months—the new company would have to produce a sufficiently compelling story to make it an attractive prospect to the financial community and potential investors.

Clearly, top management had to move simultaneously along two tracks: maintaining and improving continuing operations while laying the groundwork for the future. Schacht addressed that issue at the outset, identifying informal and somewhat unorthodox roles for himself and McGinn. Schacht realized that even though he'd served for years on the AT&T board, he lacked McGinn's longtime experience as a manager within the industry. So to a certain extent it made sense for Schacht to focus on the building of the institution while McGinn concentrated on strengthening the existing businesses.

But they both shared in developing the company's future strategy, with Schacht taking the lead on the process for developing the strategy and McGinn immersing himself in the content. To an unusual extent, the two men shared the external responsibilities for dealing with the press, the financial community, customers, and other outside audiences. What's noteworthy is the extent to which they eschewed the traditional CEO-COO division of labor, with a sharp split between strategy and operations, between "Mr. Inside" and "Mr. Outside." From the very beginning, Schacht designed and deployed a model for a genuine team at the top.

The Critical Elements of Change

In our experience, it's often difficult to get CEOs to articulate the precise ways in which they go about leading change. For one thing, CEOs by their very nature tend to be more oriented toward action than introspection; having made the decision to forge ahead in a given direction, they rarely have the inclination to pause and re-play the set of decisions they made along the way. And even if you could get them to stop and look back, most have a hard time dis-secting and describing what they did. By and large, these are ex-perienced executives who have reached the point where they're leading through instinct; most are hard-pressed to describe their specific strategies or techniques, because they don't think about what they do in those terms.

Henry Schacht is unusual on both counts. His approach to change management is clear, deliberate, and explicit. And perhaps because he came out of retirement after leading one successful change to take on another, he's had the chance to pause and re-flect on what worked and what didn't. Consequently, he took on his new duties at Lucent with some sharply focused ideas about how to proceed and what pitfalls to avoid.

Given that fortunate circumstance, we're able to draw heavily upon Schacht's own observations to explain what we consider to be the seven critical things he did to design, lead, and manage change at Lucent. As will quickly become clear, some were se-quential steps and others involved management techniques he and McGinn applied throughout the process.

1. Diagnosing the Need for Change

Given the tight deadlines Lucent faced as it prepared to go public, one might have expected Schacht to hit the ground running and never slow down. In reality, he did just the reverse. Although he first became involved with Lucent in the late fall of 1995, he didn't start his active work with the senior team until mid-January of 1996. During the intervening sixty days, he spent much of his time talk-ing to people, collecting data, gathering all kinds of information, and forming impressions of the appropriate way to approach the situation. Schacht explained:

> My advice to anybody who wants to be a change agent is to do the reverse of what everybody says. Everybody says, "Get in there and get busy." My answer is: stop. Figure out the lay of the land, what it is that needs to be done, and how you're going to be the leader. Figure out what the diagnosis is, and where you can participate.

Schacht went on to describe the importance of organizational diagnosis:

> The most fundamental issue about creating or managing change is an assessment of where you are. If you're going to be really successful, it has to be explicit, not implicit. Your assessment of the conditions in which you're operating has to be explicit, and your assessment of what to do has to be explicit.

> You've got to decide time frame, current status, current competence. You've got to decide what's the momentum, and what value added you bring as the new person. In other words, what is the nature of change that's required? You've got to start with a fundamental assessment.

Obviously, Schacht wasn't starting from square one; he had the advantage of having been an AT&T board member with a particular interest in the systems and equipment businesses for years. But he also knew there was a tremendous difference between board-level overview and on-the-ground perspective. So he very deliberately invested time in "getting the lay of the land"—figuring out what he and the company needed to do.

One element of his assessment concerned McGinn. Schacht's initial assessment confirmed Bob Allen's view of McGinn as an extremely competent and capable executive who was the obvious choice to be the CEO of Lucent over the long term. Given Schacht's age and McGinn's obvious qualities, Schacht decided right away to support that view of succession, explicitly assuming that McGinn would become the CEO. Consequently, Schacht insisted that he and McGinn not only work together closely in all areas of leadership, but that they be perceived as the team of "Henry and Rich." The idea was to quickly meld the two men as an inextricable unit, rather than drawing sharp distinctions in the eyes of the senior team and the organization at large. Therefore, although Schacht was the senior author of the assessment and the subsequent change strategy, most of the elements were the product of the Henry-and-Rich collaboration.

It was during this period that Schacht and McGinn concluded the company needed cohesion and direction, not emergency surgery. A few years earlier the situation had been markedly different, with some of the businesses in critical condition. But by the time Schacht arrived at Lucent, all were recovering—though hardly robust. They also concluded that the senior team was essentially the right one, that the individuals in key senior jobs were first-class executives. In fact, one of the new Lucent board members remarked that this was one of the strongest management teams he'd seen in his career. Therefore, the circumstances did not call for a CEO to walk in the first day and replace the senior team, shutter plants, and wipe out lines of business.

The problem was more subtle, though no less acute. With the IPO fast approaching, there was an immediate need to sell the idea of the new company as a single entity with a clear direction. But there was no story to tell; there was no strategy, no cohesion, no sense of identity that wasn't tied to AT&T. The impending split was creating confusion and a lack of confidence; people knew they'd be losing their affiliation with a rock-solid company and one of the world's best-known brands. They'd be losing what appeared at the time to be an unassailable core business—long distance service— that had effectively shielded the rest of the company from poor performance and periodic downturns.

Above all, careers spent within a massive corporation had robbed most managers of the sense that their destiny was in their own hands. No matter what happened, there was always some unnamed "they"—AT&T corporate management—who would make the tough decisions, provide resources, and protect them from disaster. And "they" were always convenient scapegoats for whatever went wrong.

All of a sudden, the security blanket was gone. This group of displaced managers, suddenly robbed of their identity and thrown together with others they didn't entirely trust, were supposed to convince Wall Street of their ability, confidence, and commitment to turn their fragile businesses into a world-class powerhouse. That was the leadership challenge that emerged.

2. Developing a Change Strategy

For Schacht and McGinn, the initial organizational diagnosis was a critical precursor to the next step: the development of a change strategy. In Schacht's view of change management, the first step is always essential to the second, because so many change leaders make the mistake of simply recycling the same strategy that worked at their previous company. That can be disastrous. Schacht readily acknowledged that the change strategy pursued at Cummins in 1971—or for that matter, the strategy that might have been employed at AT&T in the 1980s—would have crashed and burned at the Lucent of 1996. He put it this way:

> Do not assume that what's worked for you before will work again. One of the challenges of management is to assess all the techniques and tactics available in the "managerial kit bag." You've got to decide which ones are required and why.
>
> Think: What is it you're trying to do, what is the current topography, what do you need to do first? Of all the experiences you've had, of all the methodologies you've tried over the years, what is most likely to work here and why?

The principles underlying the approach couldn't be more basic: gather information, assess the situation, figure out what has to be done, decide what role you can play to add the most value, and lay out a sequence of steps to get started. Obviously, the hard part is doing it—and doing it in a way appropriate to the situation at hand, rather than falling back on stylistic approaches that all too easily can become a standardized bag of tricks.

Conceptually, Schacht and McGinn's strategy was surprisingly simple and straightforward. They started with the assumption that what looked like a spin-off from AT&T's perspective was, in fact, a start-up from Lucent's. That meant emphasizing a new corporate identity and constantly emphasizing the immense opportunities that lay ahead. It meant working in the short term to seize the "low-hanging fruit"—capitalizing on improvements in operational performance—while building a vision for the long term.

In practice, Schacht and McGinn used the IPO and the multi-million-dollar launch of the new name to build a sense of identity. As we'll shortly see, they developed a shorthand set of goals for operational improvement—the "five simultaneous equations." They began to mold the senior team by having its members work together on the new company's vision, values, and strategy. And they mobilized the company's enormous communications capability to send waves of carefully planned messages to the workforce at large.

Taken together, these moves were designed to swiftly demonstrate internal improvements and simultaneously build credibility with the outside world. The specific things they did, which we describe throughout the rest of this chapter, were all part of that simple overall strategy for change.

3. Developing and Sharing a Clear Vision

From the outset, Schacht and McGinn spent much of their time shaping and communicating a vision for Lucent Technologies. That process involved a delicate balancing act. On one hand, they sought to involve as many people as possible in the initial stages of developing and refining the vision. On the other hand, Schacht clearly had some strong ideas of his own—chief among them the primacy of creating and sustaining long-term shareholder value— and he fully intended that those ideas would be reflected in the company's vision (see Figure 1.2).

Almost as soon as Schacht and McGinn began involving the senior team in shaping the vision, they used the preparation for the IPO "road show" to hone and disseminate the same messages. Over time, a shared vision and shared sense of goals began to emerge. The vision continually underscored the notion of a single company working collectively to meet a set of high expectations and achieve best-in-class performance.

In one sense, Schacht and McGinn were intent on replacing the sense of loss over the split from AT&T with a surge of excitement about the challenges that lay ahead. Over and over, company

Figure 1.2. Lucent Technologies Mission.

Lucent Technologies Mission
To provide our customers with the world's best and most innovative communications systems, products, technologies, and customer support.
Powered by excellent people and technology, we will be a customer-driven, high-performance company that delivers superior, sustained shareholder value.
We make the things that make communications work

communications with employees during that period included the catch phrase "the opportunity of a lifetime." At the same time, leaders hammered away at the vision of a high-growth, high-performance company that was eager to take on the competition. To do that, the immediate performance challenge was encapsulated in what the leadership described as the five simultaneous equations—specific financial objectives involving criteria such as margins, tax rates, cost reductions, and the like. The role of the five equations was to define specific ways to demonstrate that the long-term mission was credible, understandable, and achievable. These weren't the ultimate goals; they were short-term objectives that set the stage for the more refined strategy that was to follow.

Schacht reflected on the importance of conveying that early vision:

> You have to be able to instill that general sense of shared vision and shared goals over a relatively short period of time, right at the beginning. Every signal counts—little signals, big signals, intentional signals, unintentional signals.
>
> That is part of getting changes in organizations—having common goals and common targets, and to repeat them over and over again. We start every session by saying, "What are we trying to do? We want to be best in class. What does that mean? We have to lift our growth rate and improve our financial performance substantially." And you just repeat that over and over again.

An important element in building the credibility of the vision was to get an early win, and the road show provided that opportunity. The question was: Can we go out and sell investors on this vision? As it turned out, Lucent's IPO was the most successful in the history of the U.S. financial markets, providing Schacht, McGinn, and their team with an important victory within the crucial first six months.

4. Building Processes That Broaden Participation

One of the key issues Schacht and McGinn identified during their diagnosis was the pressing need to create a shared sense of identity, both within the senior team and across the entire corporation.

Consequently, he and McGinn resolved that everything they did from that point on had to involve as much participation as possible. In Schacht's words,

> In order to create change, you've got to know where you're going, you've got to know why, and you've got to have buy-in. That's fundamental.
>
> I'm a great believer that if you don't have everybody on board, you're not going to get there. You're pushing the boat through the water sideways. You're far better off to get the boat turned around, get everybody pulling the oars, and then go like hell.

They began right away with the creation of the vision and the development of the investors' road show. At most companies, the road show is conducted by a small group of senior executives, rarely more than half a dozen. At Lucent, Schacht and McGinn appointed three teams to go out on the road at the same time, and made sure that key managers from the operating units were involved to get them used to talking about the entire corporation, not just their own businesses. Indeed, they very deliberately created structures to encourage participation, and used them to involve dozens of managers in developing the vision. The inner circle was the eight-member Business Council. The Executive Council, a group of seventeen people including key operating executives, did much of the most difficult work on the vision, sometimes in off-site sessions lasting several days. They finally took their work to the officers—the top sixty people in the company—who then went over the vision with their own staffs. The same participative process was used to develop first the corporate strategy and then, in Lucent's second year, to begin work on reshaping the company's operating environment. As Schacht explained,

> You start with the idea that it's "we." You really have to have understanding with broad rather than narrow groups. You have to have a shared vision, a shared sense of the external community, a shared commitment. You decide what is going to be a manageable group who will be your cohorts, and they become part of all of the decisions. You start through a process of team building with the key managers.

Schacht and McGinn had two goals in mind. The first was to create a shared sense of ownership and a common identity during Lucent's first critical months. Second, they understood the importance of engaging the full leadership team in all the processes essential to running the business. So they looked at participation in two ways: as a method of accomplishing specific tasks and, more broadly, as a fundamental approach to ongoing processes.

They specifically looked for ways to reinforce the sense of team identity by bringing senior people together in ways that would encourage them to talk and work with each other. They began holding Monday lunches where the members of the Business Council would regularly get together. They brought in a noted architect to redesign the executive offices, which were originally housed in cold, cavernous, and isolated suites set apart from the rest of the building. They took over space back in the labs and built a new cluster of executive offices—smaller, brighter and enclosed in glass, and with visitors' offices for the operating unit heads whose primary offices were located elsewhere. Their intent was to create a sense of openness and to stimulate opportunities for chance encounters and informal interactions among top executives.

In addition, Schacht took the unusual step of bringing together the board of directors and the senior executives to begin building their shared identity as a team. In the fall of 1996, he held a meeting in Florida for both the board and the seventeen–member Executive Committee, and invited all attendees to bring their spouse. In addition to working meetings and a major demonstration of new products, a dinner and dance were held—opportunities for people to spend informal time together—all orchestrated to meld the new team.

All those efforts were part of Schacht and McGinn's determination to get the new team to think in terms of "we" rather than "they." Certainly, the effort involved immense time and effort; there were times when people questioned the necessity of so much participation and so many meetings. But they never wavered from their belief that the benefits of broad participation would ultimately outweigh the costs. Schacht likes to contrast the typical American approach to decision making with the more collaborative Japanese approach:

We are very bright, very quick, very impatient. We make decisions quickly, then we execute. About halfway through the execution time we find out that most of the people don't have any idea what we're talking about, the people who have to execute don't have any idea how to get it done, and we have to loop back. We go through another decision-making process, get everybody on board, then we try it a second time and we finally get the damn thing done.

The Japanese drive you crazy. They spend enormous time making sure the decision's right, getting everybody to buy in. They keep going until everybody's all lined up, and then they go like hell and get it done. I think they save 30 to 50 percent of the time it takes us by getting everybody on board to start with.

5. Using the CEO's Role for Teaching and Coaching

In a sense, much of what Schacht, in particular, did during his two years was to conduct a series of tutorials for his top managers. In a variety of ways—private sessions, meetings both large and small— he consciously worked at helping people understand the business and their own roles within it. Without question, he was motivated in part by his knowledge that he would be there for only a limited period, and he saw part of his role as helping those who would remain after him to learn and grow professionally.

At one executive off-site meeting, for example, Schacht helped the group prepare for an upcoming board of directors meeting by spending nearly an hour explaining his theory of corporate governance, and describing the proper relationship between the board and the senior team. Afterward, people expressed their amazement at his unprecedented discussion, acknowledging that he had exposed them to issues they'd never even considered. When asked later why he had devoted so much time to the discussion, he simply responded, "They have to learn." And his teaching went beyond talking; he actively encouraged his executives to serve on other company boards so they could enrich Lucent with experiences gained elsewhere.

In hindsight, Schacht regularly employed four teaching techniques. First, he constantly made a point of putting issues in context, rather than just diving in. He often sounded like a professor reviewing the previous material before starting on a new chapter. Second, when he made a decision or took action he always explained the rationale behind it. Third, he regularly engaged in reflection; in other words, he'd make his people step back and consider why something had worked or why it hadn't so they could learn from the experience. Finally, he engaged in constant repetition—repetition that could occasionally seem maddening to his subordinates, who occasionally complained about it. But his repetition was conscious and purposeful, intended to drive home important lessons.

Schacht also understood that in order to learn, people had to believe they were operating in an environment that would occasionally allow them to fail and learn from their mistakes. He could be unyielding in his demands for superior performance, yet he avoided letting people feel personally embarrassed or degraded. He was both demanding and supportive, and in the process created a climate that fostered teaching, learning, and growth.

6. Understanding the Value of Symbolic Acts

Like other successful leaders, Schacht and McGinn demonstrated a deep appreciation of symbolic acts and the powerful role they can play in supporting large-scale change. Through personal gestures and sweeping decisions, they generated momentum, energy, and a sense that a new era had begun and there was no turning back.

Take the Bell Labs situation. For decades, Bell Labs had been the crown jewel of AT&T, arguably the world's most renowned research complex. In the years immediately preceding the spin-off, the crown had accumulated a little tarnish; spending on fundamental research had been flat for ten years, the once formidable torrent of innovations had slowed, and morale was sinking. So one of the new leadership's first decisions was to locate Lucent's corporate headquarters in Bell Labs' main facility in Murray Hill, New Jersey. Schacht explained:

> We could have gone anywhere—downtown New York, out in the woods somewhere. This isn't the most convenient place to be; it hasn't been fixed in years, it's depressing. But we wanted to send a

signal to the external world and internally that this was the heart of the place.

What else did we do? I decided we would spend one percent of sales on fundamental research, year in, year out. Rich and I spend half a day, every other week, in the laboratories. They'd never done that before. And we set up a venture capital company here. We said, "You don't have to quit because you're so frustrated you can't get your ideas to market."

On a more personal scale, Schacht and McGinn resolved early on to break with the AT&T corporate culture by being more informal and accessible. Both made a point of eating whenever possible in the company cafeteria, being seen in their shirtsleeves, and getting out on the road and meeting as many of their employees as possible. To reinforce their role as a team, Schacht insisted that McGinn always be present with him for press interviews; at one point early on, McGinn had to helicopter into Manhattan for an interview and photo shoot for the Sunday *New York Times*, because if he hadn't made it Schacht would have canceled the interview rather than allow himself to be photographed alone.

Some of the most memorable symbolism was conveyed through Lucent's ubiquitous advertising campaign, which bore much of the weight of introducing the new company to its customers, employees, the financial community, and the hordes of AT&T retirees who would become Lucent shareholders once the spin-off was completed. There were a lot of subtle messages to convey in a short period of time, Schacht noted.

First you have to get through all the clutter. It has to catch people's attention. It has to be in keeping with our values. It has to say forward-looking, modern, new, different, exciting—all that stuff. Second, we wanted to make a clean break from AT&T—therefore, a different color, a different look, nothing in the name to remind you of AT&T.

Indeed, by the spring of 1996, it was impossible to turn on the television or open a business publication without running across that easily identifiable red circle and the simple slogan, "We make the things that make communications work."

7. Managing Executive Succession

Unlike most CEOs, Schacht began his brief career at Lucent with a clear sense of his own professional mortality. As a consequence, he said, "We were into management succession the day I walked in here."

Given Schacht's age and the prevailing assumption that he would only remain for a few years—though no deadline was ever stated publicly—the situation could easily have dissolved into an ugly and counterproductive horse race, with ambitions and egos running amok. Instead, Schacht made it clear from the outset that McGinn was the uncontested heir apparent. As mentioned earlier, Schacht made a conscious decision to position McGinn as his partner, and actively prepared him and the rest of the senior group to assume control of the corporation upon his retirement. And he went out of his way to reassure McGinn that he wasn't on trial:

> We started off saying, "Rich, there is no alternative in this company to you to be the next CEO. My job is to do everything I can to make sure you are the next CEO. We're not going to hire somebody else to make this a horse race." And I told everybody else in the company, "Look, Rich is my guy. I'm here to help him lead this group."

Obviously, this was somewhat unusual, shaped by the circumstances of Schacht's age and personal goals. Nevertheless, some of the things he did are equally relevant to CEOs in more normal situations. Schacht went out of his way to avoid building a corporate structure that revolved around himself. From the very beginning, he viewed teaching and coaching as an essential part of his job, working closely with McGinn to help him become even more effective in areas such as building senior team identity and managing the board of directors. With succession never far from his thoughts, Schacht constantly looked for opportunities to leverage his strengths in ways that would build the institution and the leadership team, rather than making them increasingly dependent upon him.

Learning the Lessons of Lucent

Despite its initial success, it would be premature for Lucent Technologies to declare victory, as its leaders are well aware. No company in the dynamic telecommunications industry can reasonably think that its future is secure, given the swiftly changing competitive landscape and the rush of new technology. For Lucent, the shifting emphasis from voice-based switching to data networking presents some major challenges.

Moreover, any attempt to distill the lessons of Lucent must take into account a unique combination of circumstances. The first, obviously, is the spin-off situation itself—the rare opportunity to simultaneously choose new leaders, design new governance structures, and develop entirely new strategies for an existing multibillion-dollar business. The second unusual circumstance was the appointment of a new CEO with the express understanding that one of his priorities was to groom his successor to take over within a few short years. Finally, Schacht and McGinn had the good fortune to inherit a highly capable and diverse group of senior managers who had already been tested in some of AT&T's most competitive situations. As a result, the two leaders were able to avoid the trauma of deciding when and how to "pull the trigger" on unacceptable senior executives, a luxury enjoyed by few CEOs.[1]

Nevertheless, the Lucent case offers some important lessons that apply to practically any organization—particularly large ones—engaged in radical change.

The first has to do with the importance of leadership selection. In hindsight, Bob Allen's appointment of Schacht as CEO and McGinn as COO was a stroke of genius. The task of starting up this new $23 billion enterprise, including managing the separation, doing the IPO, building the team, and the rest would have been difficult for one person to accomplish and daunting for a brandnew CEO. Schacht's experience and natural orientation toward being a supportive teacher and coach, combined with McGinn's deep knowledge of the business and strong strategic skills, created an immensely successful team.

The second lesson involves the potential power of leveraging corporate identity and brand-building activities to create internal energy and support for change. One would be hard-pressed to find another situation in which the full range of internal and external communications techniques—everything from advertising and press relations to employee meetings, magazines, and videos—were so thoroughly coordinated to create clear, consistent, and reinforcing messages. From the very beginning, Schacht viewed Lucent's

130,000 employees as one of the target audiences for the company's massive external ad campaign. Too often, companies think of the their internal and external communications as separate functions with different missions. Lucent demonstrated the enormous potential of strategically employing them in concert with one another.

The third lesson involves the design and implementation of shared leadership. Lots of companies talk about it; few succeed. Certainly, not every company can duplicate every factor that led to Lucent's success on this score. But there are lessons that can be applied almost everywhere. The first is to make succession a legitimate topic of discussion and planning. In countless organizations the issue is off-limits and the CEO won't even discuss it with possible successors until the last minute. Second, top leaders need to think about their roles in nontraditional ways and divide their responsibilities according to their abilities and interests, rather than simply accepting established notions of what the CEO and COO are supposed to do. Finally, the leaders must use language, symbolism, and management processes to demonstrate the reality of "the team." Like Schacht and McGinn, they must seize every opportunity to show that they are a team in deed, not just word.

It's worth noting that well before Schacht's departure, McGinn was at work on a design for a second generation of shared leadership. Together with four other senior executives, he was reviewing various models for assigning primary and secondary responsibility within the new team for each of the major executive functions.

Change Leadership: From Theory to Practice

In previous work,[2] we advanced a theory of change leadership that includes three basic elements. In a sense, the successful launch of Lucent Technologies provides an unparalleled example of how the theory of change leadership translates into practice.

At the core of our concept is the ultimate leader of change—generally the CEO—who must demonstrate certain characteristics that set the "heroic" or "mythic" leader apart from those managers who simply maintain the status quo. Second, that heroic or mythic leadership has to be complemented by solid operational leadership, a role that's normally played by the chief operating officer. In the case of Lucent, McGinn clearly provided the operational leadership as he focused on building the business while Schacht concentrated on building the institution.

The final element is the creation of structures and processes that extend top leadership's vision and energy throughout the organization. At Lucent, Schacht and McGinn accomplished that through the use of formal governance structures—the Business Council and Executive Council, for example—and through their commitment to participative processes that built understanding and ownership of the vision, the strategy and the principles of a new operating environment.

All three elements are important, but the role of the top leader is the most crucial. In our previous work, we suggested that the popular notion of "charismatic" leaders falls far short of accurately describing the attributes common to successful leaders of change. Classic good looks, a dynamic speaking style, and bundles of charm don't hurt—but they have little to do with effective leadership. In our view, heroic leadership involves three essential characteristics:

- Envisioning: the ability to develop, articulate and communicate a clear vision of what the future will look like if change is successful
- Energizing: the ability to motivate large groups of people and infuse them with the leader's own sense of enthusiasm, excitement, and confidence
- Enabling: the ability to figure out how to provide people with the necessary support—structures, processes, resources, and rewards—and how to remove the obstacles standing in their way

Now listen to Henry Schacht's description of the role of leaders:

Leaders are here to raise sights; gain commitment; provide help, advice, and counsel; and establish a feedback mechanism that repeats the process. That's my four-step model of a leader—and if you think about it, that's how you get change.

The words are slightly different, but the underlying concepts are the same: envisioning, energizing, and enabling. It's worth taking a closer look at what Schacht means, because his model so closely describes the leadership roles we've seen repeated time and again at organizations where change is successful.

The role we describe as "envisioning" was at the heart of Schacht's approach to building Lucent from the ground up. As he said in 1996,

> The most important thing is to establish what it is that we're trying to do, as separate from AT&T, and how are we going to measure ourselves as a corporation rather than as four vertical, stovepipe organizations with Bell Labs loosely connected? What is it we want to do? We said: "We want to be world class. We want to be the best."

In light of the collective trauma created by the break with AT&T, the "energizing" role was particularly critical for Schacht:

> One of the most delicate issues here is to create the excitement about being on our own, without in any way disparaging AT&T, and countering what was going to be a cold wind we felt when we weren't part of AT&T. We were taking half of AT&T's people but only a quarter of the revenue; we had to figure out how not to scare these people half to death. So we kept pounding away at "opportunities"—we talked about opportunity, opportunity, opportunity—and it's worked.

The final element is "enabling," which Schacht contrasts with the popular technique of "exhortation":

> You can't just say "do it harder" without telling people why you think it's possible. Exhortation only gets you so far. You have to stop and say, "What are your alternatives? What's in the way? Here are some benchmarks that suggest we can do better in this area. Our competitors aren't magicians—we have the same set of capacities, and if we don't, let's get them. What's blocking you? How can I help? What ideas do you have?" That's what empowerment is all about.

In his brief but enormously successful tenure at Lucent Technologies, Henry Schacht, working closely with Rich McGinn, demonstrated what effective change leadership can accomplish. Together, they showed that large, complex organizations can indeed be changed and, when necessary, in a relatively short period of time. For those who stand on the bridge and are confounded by the complexity of change, the lesson from Lucent is clear: yes, you really can steer the battleship. It can be done, and done well. When pursued thoughtfully, energetically, and with total engagement at the top, change can succeed. The key is the role of the top leader—and there's no better description than Schacht's:

> It is not a "bully pulpit." It is all the techniques of team building in large, complex human organizations. It means working through complexities. It requires time, patience, willingness to compromise, unbending commitment to your colleagues, and an understanding that you can't get there unless your colleagues are with you and have the same sense of zeal that you have.

Notes

1. Nadler, D. A., and Nadler, M. B. "Performance on the Executive Team: When to Pull the Trigger." In D. A. Nadler and J. B. Spencer (eds.), *Executive Teams*. San Francisco: Jossey-Bass, 1997.
2. Nadler, D. A. *Champions of Change*. San Francisco: Jossey-Bass, 1997.

Chapter Two

Creating the Individualized Corporation

The Path to Self-Renewal at General Electric

Christopher A. Bartlett
Sumantra Ghoshal

There must be few companies that have not tried to reinvent themselves in some form over the past decade—some more than once. Yet for every successful corporate transformation there is an equally prominent failure. GE's dramatic performance improvement stands in stark contrast to the string of disappointments and crises that led to Westinghouse's demise; Asea Brown Boveri's ascendance to global leadership in electrotechnical businesses only emphasizes Hitachi's inability to reverse its declining fortunes; and Philips's gradual turnaround in recent years only highlights its own confused meanderings in the preceding ten years.

In the course of our research, we have studied more than twenty companies that have implemented innumerable programs intended to rationalize their inefficient operations, revitalize their ineffective strategies, and renew their tired organizations.[1] We have sought to understand why some made progress in the difficult and painful battle for transformational change while others only replaced the dead weight of their bureaucracies with change-program overload.

This chapter is an adaptation of Chapter Nine of Ghoshal, S., and Bartlett, C. A. *The Individualized Corporation.* New York: Harper Business, 1997.

In observing how the successful corporate transformation processes have differed from those that struggled or failed outright, we were struck by two distinctions. First, successful transformation processes almost always followed a carefully phased approach that focused on developing particular organizational capabilities in an appropriate sequence. And second, actual transformation only occurred when the structural reconfiguration was reinforced by real and enduring change in the behaviors of individuals within the organization.

This chapter sets forth a general process model describing how companies have evolved from traditional divisionalized hierarchies to more flexible, self-renewing organization forms we describe as "individualized corporations." We will illustrate how the sequential process by which the individual capabilities of entrepreneurship, learning, and self-renewal are built through the development and interaction of the company's behavioral context, its organizational processes, and its redefined individual competencies.

A Phased Sequence of Change

The problem with most companies that have failed in their transformation attempts is not that they tried to change too little but that they tried to change too much. Consider the events we observed over a nine-month period in one company. In the aftermath of a major restructuring, the new CEO embarked on a series of visioning retreats. One outcome was a senior-management–endorsed definition of the company's core competencies that was then handed to a task force to recommend how they might be more effectively developed and managed. Meanwhile, the newly appointed chief knowledge officer launched an initiative to help the company become a more effective learning organization. And in a separate but contemporaneous initiative, consultants were called in to help design a reengineering program.

Sound familiar? Although this scenario describes the activities at one particular company, it could have been another among many. In their desperate search for more effective organizational models, managers have launched a flurry of unconnected programmatic activities in almost random order. According to one survey, between 1990 and 1994 the average company committed itself to 11.8 of the 25 popular management tools and techniques listed—from corporate visioning and TQM programs to empowerment and reengineering processes.[2] Despite this widespread frenzy of activity, the study found no correlation between the number of tools a company used and its satisfaction with its financial performance. Little wonder that in many companies frontline managers are completely bewildered in the face of the multiple and inconsistent priorities being imposed on them.

In contrast, we found that the companies that were most successful in transforming themselves into more flexible and responsive organizations seemed to have much clearer understanding of what they were trying to achieve and pursued a sequence of actions that were extremely intense but comparatively simple. Although inevitably implemented in an intuitive manner and in a very company-specific way, when compared retrospectively the transformational paths of these successful organizations looked remarkably similar.

Building on the simple but powerful ideas that Jack Welch used to describe the series of changes he implemented at General Electric, we developed a model that seemed to capture the transformational experience of several of the companies we were studying, including Asea Brown Boveri (ABB), Motorola, Komatsu, AT&T, and Corning.[3] Our underlying assumption is that the performance of any company depends on the strength of each of its component units, as well as on the effectiveness of their integration. (The model applies equally to the integration of individually strong functional groups along an organization's value chain, the synergistic linking of a company's portfolio of business units, or the global networking of its different national subsidiaries.) We used this simple yet fundamental premise to define the two axes of the corporate renewal model represented in Figure 2.1.

As they face the renewal challenge, most companies find themselves with a portfolio of operations that can be represented by the circles in Figure 2.1. They may have a few strong independent units and activities represented by the tightly defined but separate circles in Quadrant 2. In addition, they usually have a cluster of better-integrated operations that are not performing well individually, as depicted by the looser, overlapping circles in Quadrant 3. And finally, most companies contain a large cluster of business units, country subsidiaries, or functional entities that don't perform well individually and are also ineffective in linking and leveraging each

Figure 2.1. Strength of Component Units.

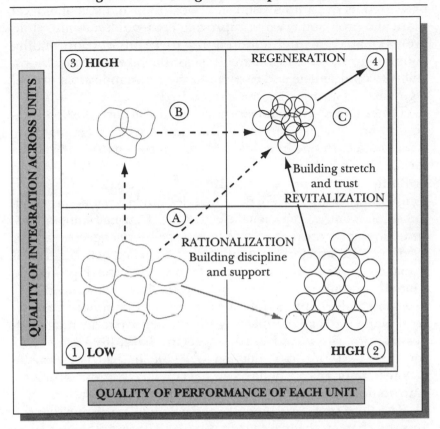

other's resources and capabilities. These units are illustrated by the ill-defined, unconnected circles in Quadrant 1.

Most of the activity underlying recent transformation efforts has aimed at improving performance on one or both of the two dimensions represented. The overall objective of the process has been to move the entire portfolio of entities into Quadrant 4, where individually strong units work together to create competitive advantage none of them could achieve independently.

Some companies—General Motors during the 1980s, for instance—tried to improve performance on both dimensions simultaneously—an approach represented by diagonal Path A. Though intellectually and emotionally appealing, this bold approach typically produces internal contradictions and complexities that block effective change. GM discovered this during the 1980s, when it pressured its five auto divisions to boost their individual market share and profitability while improving cross-unit synergies. However, as management discovered, the demands of coordinating body styling and chassis design often conflicted with the divisions' ability to differentiate and respond to their own individual market segments. Unsurprisingly, the effort failed.

Other companies' transformation efforts have pushed integration first, on the assumption that better synergy among units would help each one in its attempts to improve its individual performance. This change model, represented by Path B, was taken by Philips in the mid- and late 1980s. In a bold reorganization, company president Cor van der Klugt declared the company's consumer electronics, professional electronics, electronic components, and lighting businesses as "core interdependent" operations and tried to create structures and processes that would help them each manage their perceived interdependencies. However, it proved extremely difficult to integrate operations that were individually struggling with enormous internal difficulties. Even where they succeeded, the linkages connecting uncompetitive individual businesses primarily served to reinforce the liabilities of each. As corporate performance continued to decline in the late 1980s, the gallows humor among Philips managers held that "four drunk fat guys do not make an effective team."

The third transformational option, Path C, is the one that follows the changes that have taken place at ABB over the past eight years. In the first phase, ABB's CEO Barnevik stripped away much of the old bureaucratic superstructure to focus attention on the task of realigning the organization around the efficient operations of 1,200 frontline companies. It was at this stage that ABB energized hundreds of latent frontline entrepreneurs and gave them the mandate to build their businesses as if they owned them.

As the entrepreneurial engine of frontline units began to restart growth, Barnevik moved the company into the next stage of its transformation process, creating an integrated learning organization. In this phase, he focused the organization more intensely on the task of linking and leveraging the valuable resources and expertise that had been developed in pockets of entrepreneurial initiative throughout the company. Through such initiatives, ABB was able to combine products and technologies from dozens of its operating companies in Europe, Asia, and the United States in order to deliver a turnkey power plant project in India or China, for example.

By the mid-1990s, Barnevik was pleased with the progress that ABB had made, but knew the process was not complete. As it headed into the closing years of the century, ABB was entering into the self-regeneration phase of its transformation process. This was the stage in which the organization would have to learn how to balance the tensions and manage the paradoxes implicit in the new cooperate model. It required managers to strive for superior individual unit performance while capturing the corporate-wide benefits of cross-unit integration. Moreover, they had to do so in an organizational environment in which the hard-edge demands for operational efficiency were offset by the uplifting challenge of innovative expansion—a management model we described as "cooking sweet and sour." Like the first two stages, the revitalization phase would rest on the achievement of profound changes in the perceptions and behaviors of people in ABB.

To explore in more detail how this multiphased model is managed through changes to a company's hardwired strategy, structure, and systems, as well as to the softer elements of culture, values, and norms, consider the evolution of the most celebrated corporate transformation of our time: the rebirth of General Electric under Jack Welch's leadership. Even as most other highly diversified companies were breaking themselves up, Welch was proving that effective corporate management could add enormous value by improving the performance of individual businesses and achieving multibusiness synergies. In fact, his success in fundamentally redefining the way GE worked was widely recognized as the reason behind the company's 1,155 percent increase in market value in fifteen years.

GE is the appropriate company with which to illustrate the simple transformation model for several reasons. First, because it so clearly represented the old hierarchical corporate model, GE's commitment to becoming an individualized corporation is particularly powerful. Second, because Welch initiated these dramatic changes earlier than most, GE provides a better opportunity to observe the longer-term impact of the transformational process. And third, because it is such a well-known example, it presents us with an ideal opportunity to penetrate beyond the well-known story of strategic realignment and structural reconfiguration and observe some of the more subtle changes that made GE a benchmark for large-scale corporate transformation and Welch a model change leader.

Phase 1: Rationalization—Embedding Entrepreneurial Drive[4]

When he became CEO in 1981, Jack Welch inherited an organization that was widely regarded as one of the best-managed large industrial corporations in the world. This was the company whose creation of the strategic business unit (SBU) concept had provided a template for companies worldwide; its planning processes, long the standard in the industrial world, set the pace with the pioneering application of sophisticated strategic portfolio planning tools; and its development of group- and sector-level management to control the growing portfolio of SBUs also was widely imitated by large companies worldwide. In short, GE was the benchmark for large diversified corporations—the modern-day standard bearer for the professionally managed divisionalized hierarchy.

Furthermore, Welch took over the reins from Reg Jones, perhaps the most admired company leader in the country, a man *Fortune* magazine described as "a management legend." It would have been easy to stand on the legend's shoulders and refine the GE innovations that had become so widely accepted as leading-edge practice. But that was not Welch's style. Almost immediately, he began fretting that the company had too many underperforming businesses and too much organizational bureaucracy. Rather than building on GE's past accomplishments, Welch began restructuring the company's businesses, reconfiguring its organization, and redefining its management processes. Welch seemed to confirm *Fortune's* prediction that the GE board had chosen to "replace a legend with a live wire."

In an analogy he was to use repeatedly, Welch saw the need to base the transformation of GE not only on changes to its "hardware"—its existing business strategy, organizational structure, and management systems—but also to its "software," which he saw as the values, motivations, and commitment of its employees. Although he employed both elements in the rationalization process, it was clear that his years of training in the GE system gave him a strong early bias toward changing the hardware.

Changing the Hardware

Taking over in the midst of a recession and in a competitive environment in which Japanese companies were inflicting huge damage in many industrial sectors, Welch decided that his first priority was to focus attention on improving the operating performance and strategic competitiveness of GE's portfolio of businesses. His simple standard was to make each business number one or number two in its global market to achieve quality and performance that were "better than the best." To those who did not meet standards, he said, "Fix it, sell it, or close it."

It was a bold move that radically reshaped the company's strategic portfolio. During the 1980s, GE sold or closed businesses that had represented about one-quarter of the company's 1980 sales. In the same period it was selling off assets worth almost $10 billion, the company made acquisitions worth $17 billion to reinforce the competitive position of the number one and number two businesses it retained.

As the business-level organization began to grind into action under his new challenging strategic criteria, Welch became increasingly frustrated with the layers of hierarchy and the density of corporate staff that insulated him from the business leaders who were emerging. Gradually he began to strip away the structures that his predecessors had so carefully built. By 1985, sectors, groups, and SBUs had been eliminated and GE's once powerful two-hundred-person corporate planning staff had been decimated. "As we develop our strategies," said Welch, "I want general managers talking to general managers, not planners talking to planners."

As Welch pushed to reduce GE's nine levels of management to his objective of four, he explicitly discarded the old span-breaking theory that a manager should have no more than seven direct reports. Believing the right number to be ten, fifteen, or perhaps even twenty, Welch deliberately created on organization that forced his senior-level executives to delegate more and more.

The changes were designed to redefine the management roles and relationships that had became embedded in the old hierarchical model. In particular, Welch wanted GE's operating-level managers to develop their roles around what he defined as ownership, stewardship, and entrepreneurship of the company's portfolio of competitive businesses. To drive ownership, he delegated more responsibility and pushed decision making deeper into the organization; to encourage stewardship, he decentralized more assets and resources and challenged his managers to leverage the company's return on them; and to spark entrepreneurship, he encouraged those on the front lines to initiate more action and to take more risks.

But the organizational impact of these strategic and structural changes was as traumatic as it was dramatic. Between 1981 and 1984, GE's total workforce was reduced by over seventy thousand. In this environment of restructuring, delayering, and downsizing, many began to feel overloaded and stressed out. And to Welch's chagrin, his aggressive restructuring earned him the nickname "Neutron Jack."

Changing the Software

Like most managers of his generation, Welch had a strong bias for the traditional levers of strategy, structure, and systems to drive change. But as powerful as they were, he found them to be blunt instruments. Gradually, his perspective began to soften and broaden. "A company can boost productivity by restructuring, removing bureaucracy, and downsizing," said Welch in 1985, "but it cannot sustain high productivity without cultural change."[5]

By the mid-1980s, Welch's talk about number one and two businesses gave way to a passion to "combine the strength, resources, and reach of a big company with the sensitivity, leanness, and agility of a small company." It was an objective that demanded massive cultural change, but as Welch was to discover, managing behavioral context proved to be a much more subtle and difficult task than managing strategic content.[6] For one thing, it had to be approached in a much more gradual and sequential manner.

In the first-stage task of creating entrepreneurial drive, the bedrock element of the desired behavioral context was self-discipline, for it was this cultural norm that gave top management confidence to empower those on the front lines. By removing the layers of hierarchy that institutionalized the culture of compliance, Welch created an environment in which managers were required to set their own standards and evaluate their own performance. It was what he referred to as the mirror test: "Only you know whether or not the excellence is there," he told his operating managers. "Are you setting the standards of excellence? Are you demanding the very best of yourself?" Rather than just meeting the numbers, Welch wanted his managers to "face reality, see the world in the way it is, then decide for yourself how to act."

Even from his earliest days as CEO, Welch was building this cultural value at GE. Breaking with the GE tradition of framing strategies in detailed analyses and complex objectives, he set his operating-level managers the simple yet demanding challenge of making their businesses number one or number two in their global industry, then got out of the way.

As Welch discovered, however, a single-minded focus on tough targets and self-imposed discipline can leave the organization stressed out and exhausted. After reaching that point in the mid-1980s, Welch became more conscious of the need to soften his tendency to push the organization to what he himself described as "the point where it almost comes unglued." He had to supplement his focus on discipline with an equal emphasis on support.[7]

One key reason why frontline managers had become so overburdened and stressed out was that they had little or no experience in managing the resources or handling the responsibilities that had been pushed down to them. Recognizing this, Welch began to focus on ways he could support them in taking on their new tasks. He redirected the highly regarded Crotonville, New York, training facility from its traditional role of providing general management education and training to take on a more targeted agenda of designing and delivering company-specific organization development programs.

Equally powerful were the radical changes Welch made to GE's legendary strategic-planning and budget-development processes to become the basis for supportive discussion rather than forums for formal review. At a 1985 officers meeting, he asked each of his business managers to present their strategies in five one-page charts that defined the global market structure of their businesses, their key competitors' positions and expected actions, and their own business strategy and its expected impact. The subsequent give-and-take strategy discussions focused on how Welch and his key staff could help the business leaders achieve their objectives. It became an ongoing dialogue based on a five-page playbook and stood in sharp contrast to an annual exercise in reviewing and approving two-inch-thick plans in three-ring binders. Welch described his role in such discussions: "It is the business leader's job to create and grow new businesses. Our job in the executive office is to facilitate. Probably the most important thing we can promise our business leaders is fast action. When our business leaders call, they don't expect studies, they expect answers."

Gradually, Welch began to change management norms and practices, but always in a fairly controlled top-down manner that revealed his own history and experience as a manager who had cut his teeth on a classic hierarchy. It was only several years later that he really began to let go and, through the powerful process he called "Work-Out," allowed frontline employees to redefine the behavioral context. In a series of carefully defined forums, those working under the constraining and controlling structures and systems were given the opportunity to challenge their managers with their problems and proposals for change. Through this process, the norms of self-discipline and support were operationalized through hundreds of specific proposals and projects. After scores of such meetings throughout the company, empowerment developed real meaning, and discipline and support became embedded in the culture—or "the smell of the place," as we often called the emerging behavioral context.

Changing the Behaviors

A subtle but important change was occurring during these first few years of realignment of GE's structural hardware and cultural software. Consciously or unconsciously, Welch began shifting the management rhetoric and focus from a near obsession with structure and systems that impose direction and ensure compliance toward reliance on embedding changes in the attitudes and behaviors of individual organization members in order to build the desired change into day-to-day activities. And the behavior he was most trying to create within GE was a sense of entrepreneurial drive and initiative.

Heading up a company that was increasingly reliant on the motivations and self-initiated actions of hundreds and eventually thousands of people deep in the organization required Welch to focus much more intensely on human resource issues—employee development, management education, evaluation and reward systems, and so on. For example, twice a year he spent half a day with each of his fifteen business leaders reviewing the human resource potential within their operations and quizzing them on how they were developing the high-potential people.

He also wanted to signal clearly the kind of entrepreneurial behavior he sought by reinforcing it through the reward system. The company's predictable 3 to 4 percent salary increases, supplemented by 10 to 15 percent bonuses to most at senior levels, had clearly reinforced the old expectation of long-term loyalty, dependable compliance, and strong implementation skills, but Welch wanted to recognize and support different behavior. He started acknowledging true corporate entrepreneurs with salary increases in the 10 to 15 percent range, bonuses of 30 to 40 percent to many fewer managers, and stock options, which he began distributing to hundreds of effective frontline managers rather than reserving them for the top echelons.

In the end, the new structural framework and behavioral context he was creating was designed to do nothing short of redefine the basic relationship between the company and its employees. Welch explained, "Like many other large companies, GE had an implicit psychological contract based on perceived lifetime employment that produced a paternal, feudal, fuzzy kind of loyalty. That contract has to change. . . . The new contract is that jobs at GE are the best in the world for people willing to compete. We have the best training and development resources and an environment committed to producing opportunities for personal and professional growth."

This organization of highly disciplined frontline competitors armed with the training and resources to allow them to take on the world was a very different model than the classic divisionalized hierarchy that had defined management behavior and relationships for decades. Like many companies in the first stage of the transformation process, GE was going through a period that many described as "inverting the pyramid." By empowering and energizing those running the company's portfolio of businesses and focusing them outward on customers and competitors, this change represented a powerful first step toward building the new organization model (see Figure 2.2).

In the inverted pyramid, the fifteen viable frontline businesses became the company's basic structural unit, replacing the sectors and groups as the locus of power, and the behavioral context of embedded discipline and support supplanted imposed compliance and control, empowering those running the businesses to take charge. But as Welch and others discovered when they reached this stage, the transformation process was not yet complete. Some obstacles still blocked their way.

The first major problem derived from the fact that in the process of empowering those in the front lines, many senior-level staff and line managers (indicated by the dotted lines on Figure 2.2) were unsure of how to redefine their roles or reshape their relationships with the frontline entrepreneurs. In several transformation processes, these managers became the "layer of clay" that blocked further progress by trying to hold on to power. In some cases they even subverted frontline initiatives to do so. For the transformation to succeed, the senior-level managers' new roles had to be defined.

The second major limitation of the inverted-pyramid model was that each of the frontline entrepreneurs was focused on developing his or her own individual business opportunity. Even where customers, markets, or technologies overlapped, they had little incentive to cooperate. To remain viable, the company had to become more than a holding company for a portfolio of independent business, no matter how entrepreneurial they were individually.

Phase II: Revitalization—Developing Integrative Synergies

The primary focus of the first phase of GE's transformation process was on the restructuring, delayering, and downsizing activities and was designed to cut costs and enhance productivity. Less attention

Figure 2.2. Inverting the Pyramid for Frontline Empowerment.

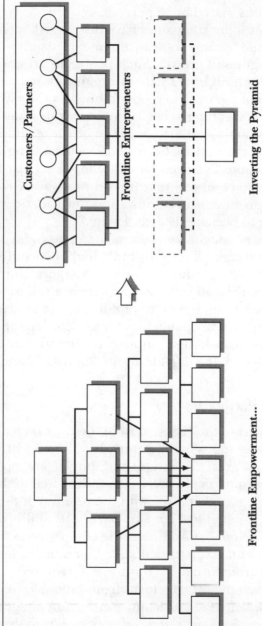

Customers/Partners

Frontline Entrepreneurs

Inverting the Pyramid

Frontline Empowerment...

was given to growth or expansion. Indeed, GE's sales increased by only 8 percent during Welch's first five years at the helm, while its operating profits soared by 58 percent.

The risk, as some companies have discovered, was that the organization could became so "lean and mean" that it was unable to restart the engines of growth. Such problems arise when a company downsizes itself into a state of organizational anorexia that not only leaves it too weak to rebound but also too psychologically obsessed with cost-cutting to begin looking for new ways to expand.

Welch was careful not to allow GE to be sucked into that downward spiral. By the mid-1980s, as he grew increasingly frustrated with the nickname "Neutron Jack," he made it clear both inside and outside the company that he did not want GE to become known as a lean-and-mean organization. Instead, he wanted managers to strive to became "lean and agile."

The agility he sought was achievable in part by an organization in which resources and responsibility had been shifted down to more-empowered frontline business managers. But, in Welch's view, it also required an organization in which resources, information, and expertise moved more rapidly and easily across internal and external structural boundaries. It was a concept he would later call "boundaryless behavior," another profound shift he achieved through changes in the organization's "hardware" and "software."

Changing the Hardware

By the latter part of the 1980s, most of the radical changes to GE's structures and systems had been made. The new stripped-down framework was a great deal clearer and simpler, and operating-level line managers in particular were responding well to the openness and freedom it gave them. Yet, with the removal of the group and sector levels, GE had lost a major part of its ability to integrate across organizational units. Unless the company was to operate in a fragmented and compartmentalized manner, some kind of replacement coordinative mechanisms were required.

As he moved the primary focus from rationalization to revitalization, Welch began to create more cross-unit integrative forums to allow business-level managers the opportunity to share resources and leverage ideas. His first step was to create a Corporate Executive Council (CEC) consisting of his three-man office of the CEO and the managers with direct responsibility for the company's business. For two days each quarter, the CEC gave the top-line managers the opportunity to grapple with common problems, share insights, and offer advice and assistance to each other on key problems and opportunities. For example, when the appliance business manager reported a major recall due to serious problems with compressors, his colleagues in the turbine and aircraft business were able to offer valuable technical support to solve the problem.

To push the opportunity for cross-unit integration deeper into the organization, Welch convened officers' meetings, which pulled together the top hundred managers. Again, he encouraged them to find ways to work together more effectively. The relationships soon extended beyond the CEC and officers' meetings, and individual managers began finding ways they could work together through internal sourcing (the plastics business increased its content in GE refrigerators to sixteen pounds a unit) or by working with common customers (as occurred in France when a joint venture in aircraft engines was able to help GE's medical business gain access to the government-controlled health care system).

Welch also wanted to dramatically redefine the role of the staff groups remaining at corporate headquarters "from checkers, inquisitors, and authority figures to facilitators, helpers, and supporters of operating-line managers." He wanted each staff manager to continuously ask, How do I add value? How do I help people on the line become more effective, more competitive?[8] Again, his objective was to create an organization in which "ideas, initiatives, and decisions could move quickly, often at the speed of sound—voices—where once they were muffled and garbled by being forced to run the gauntlet of staff reviews and approvals."

But although he was successful in creating a more open and supportive learning environment at the top levels of GE, it was only at the end of the decade that Welch succeeded in pushing the process deep into the organization. One of the most powerful tools was an integrative process called Best Practices. Begun as a corporate-staff–led analysis of high-productivity companies, the program's site visits to selected benchmark organizations were soon recognized as offering extremely powerful learning opportunities. To spread the learning through the organization, the company created a Best

Practices development program at Crotonville. Every month, a dozen people from each of GE's businesses would exchange views and experiences as they compared their own management approaches with the best practices they studied. It was in this stimulating and collaborative environment that cross-unit learning took firm root.[9]

One situation Welch liked to recount to inspire imitation involved GE's Canadian appliance company, which had successfully adapted the flexible manufacturing approach of a small New Zealand appliance maker. Welch told how two hundred managers and workers from the giant Louisville plant toured the Canadian operation to learn what they had done. After a series of Work-Out sessions, the U.S.-based team put plans in place to reduce the production cycle time of its appliances by up to 90 percent while increasing product availability. The achievements at Louisville were so impressive that it immediately became a popular internal best-practices destination for teams from other businesses, from locomotives to power-generating equipment. It was classic Welch—another inspirational story designed to spark widespread imitation.

Changing the Software

As important as the various informal structural overlays were in creating new channels and forums to permit the cross-unit integration so central to revitalization, Welch recognized that unless he could change the slow-moving bureaucratic culture, the cross-unit processes he had framed would never become effective. Over time, he continued to shift his attention from the hardware elements that had so preoccupied him in the early- and mid-1980s to focus most of his time on the software issues of GE's culture, values, and management style.

One of the strongest signals of this new emphasis came early in 1989, when Welch began to talk about the need for the company to develop a management approach based on speed, simplicity, and self-confidence.[10] These themes provided him with the means to expand on the behavioral context of discipline and support that he had begun to build earlier with contextual characteristics we describe as trust and stretch.

In the aftermath of downsizing and delayering, one of the key challenges for Welch personally and for the company in general was to rebuild a trust relationship with GE's somewhat traumatized employees. Welch knew that people would be willing to take risks only if they trusted top management. And only if they trusted each other would they be able to work together. Welch's new management values spoke directly to those needs. "Becoming faster is tied to becoming simpler," said Welch. "And on an individual and interpersonal level, this takes the form of plain speaking, directness, and honesty."

Through his widespread interactions with organization members, Welch personified this open, candid management style that he believed was the only way he could overcome the negativism and mistrust attached to his "Neutron Jack" reputation. He met tirelessly with GE employees, from his regular one-on-one reviews with business leaders to his no-holds-barred exchanges with more than five thousand managers a year at Crotonville sessions. He participated in Work-Out sessions, traveled tirelessly to visit GE facilities worldwide, and, above all, found every opportunity possible to communicate his message. In the process, he gradually earned not only the respect of his employees but also their trust.

The process took years. When Work-Out was first introduced, for example, many were suspicious that this was just another process designed to justify cuts and layoffs. It was Welch who immediately and unequivocally assured the organization that this was not so. By carefully controlling Work-Out sessions so they were not abused, Welch was able to use the process to create a new level of openness and understanding between employees and their bosses—albeit through the often uncomfortable process of directly confronting reality for the first time. Again, trust was being built.

In an environment characterized by fairness, where people learned to trust their bosses and their colleagues sufficiently to take risks, the other key element of a growth-supportive context is stretch.[11] Welch's notion of self-confidence addressed this need directly as he encouraged his managers to free themselves from the confines of their box on the organization chart, share information freely, listen to those around them, then move boldly. "Shun the incremental," he told them. "Go for the leap."

As the company moved into the 1990s, this notion became an increasingly important one for Welch, to the point where he believed that self-imposed stretch targets could drive the company's growth much more effectively than management-imposed budget numbers. He began to preach a belief that "budgets enervate, stretch energizes." He explained, "We used to timidly nudge the peanut along, setting goals to increase operating margin from 8.53 percent to 8.92 percent, for example. Then we'd engage in time-consuming, bureaucratic negotiations to move the number a few hundredths one way or the other. The point is, it didn't matter. Today, we challenge the organization with bold stretch targets, and trust that everyone will do as well as they can to achieve them. People come in with numbers far beyond what we would have asked for. It would kill accounting professors but it's real."[12]

Welch believed it was the power of this approach that allowed the company to break out of its long history of single-digit operating margins as it stretched for the 15 percent target set in 1991. In 1995, GE reported an operating margin of 14.4 percent, a little short of the objective but well beyond anything it could have achieved under the lowest-common-denominator negotiations that characterized the old budgeting process.

Changing Individual Behavior

Once again, Welch took his grand strategic objective of reigniting growth and his lofty organizational goal of creating more cross-unit learning and translated them into the changes they implied for the behaviors of individual GE employees. Building on the energy, focus, and drive that he had instilled in his managers in the earlier rationalization process, Welch shifted his attention in the revitalization phase to reinforcing a need for more self-confidence and collaboration.

"Boundaryless behavior" was the antiparochial, anti-incremental style required if GE was to integrate and leverage the pockets of entrepreneurial activity it had created so effectively in the early and mid-1980s. After years of work to change the internal norms, there was more than a hint of pride in Welch's 1996 declaration of "the demise of the 'Not-Invented-Here' syndrome within GE." By the mid-1990s, he was proudly recounting a long list of innovations and ideas that had been transferred across its businesses, driving growth and profitability throughout the company.

Like ABB, Komatsu, Corning, and other companies at this stage of their transformation process, GE had begun to develop a set of entirely new management roles and relationships. The organizational configuration that shaped them was also evolving with the inverted pyramid of the mid-1980s, starting to look more like an integrated network of entrepreneurial activities in the 1990s (see Figure 2.3).

If the first stage of the transformation process is focused on the task of releasing entrepreneurial hostages on the front lines of the organization, the second phase transforms middle- and senior-level managers into developmental coaches. Their key task is to stretch the individual entrepreneurs to become the best they can be and to create an open, trusting, and collaborative environment that facilitates boundaryless behavior.

Welch showed he was serious about this shift in the corporate culture at GE when he began talking about the consequence of being a "Type IV" manager—one who got results but did so without sharing the values of openness and collaboration.[13] Calling this "the ultimate test of our commitment to the transformation of this company," Welch began to remove these individuals, even when they met their financial projections.

As his senior managers began developing and supporting the ideas and initiatives of those in the front lines, and as GE developed an openness that encouraged collaborative behavior, Welch began to feel that the company was approaching the organizational objective he had set for it. GE was developing the soul of a small company within the body of a big one.

Phase III: Regeneration—Achieving Continuous Self-Renewal

Well into the 1990s, Welch seemed to recognize that what he had been working on for over a decade was more than just the major shakeup and realignment of a grand old company. It was the creation of a fundamentally different corporate model operating through a radically different management philosophy. And the more this new model was defined and developed, the clearer it became how delicate and vulnerable it was during its slow and painful birth process.

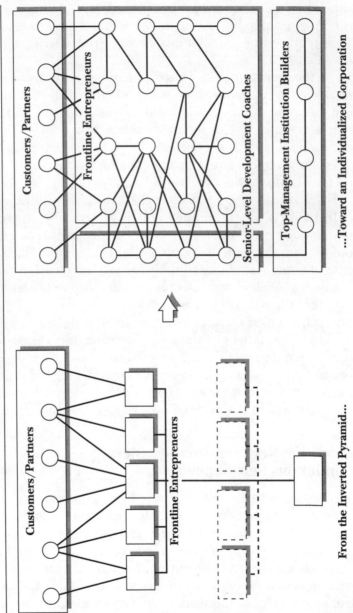

Figure 2.3. From the Inverted Pyramid
Toward an Individualized Corporation.

Customers/Partners

Frontline Entrepreneurs

Senior-Level Development Coaches

Top-Management Institution Builders

...Toward an Individualized Corporation

Customers/Partners

Frontline Entrepreneurs

From the Inverted Pyramid...

Compared to the clarity, stability, and certainty of roles and relationships in the old divisionalized hierarchic model, the operating environment being created in the new individualized corporation seems much riskier. Do those on the front lines have the skills and motivation to use the resources and responsibilities thrust upon them in an effective manner? Can senior-level executives step back from the take-charge behaviors that allowed them to achieve their current positions and take on a more supportive coaching role?

The greatest risk occurs when organizations in transition face some kind of major challenge or crisis. Most employees are not only exhausted from the protracted and profound change process, but they feel tentative and uncertain about their newly defined management roles. In such a stressful time, the natural inclination is to retreat into the comfort of the more predictable and stable old management model. Even with a well-designed multiyear change process, it is hard to change behaviors learned, practiced, and reinforced over a twenty- or thirty-year career.

The third stage of the transformation process must respond to that postchange letdown. The challenge is to create an internal environment that supports both individual initiative *and* team-based behaviors on a continuous basis. To achieve this objective, the new behavioral context and management roles must be reinforced long enough for the organization to gradually free itself from the embedded practices and conventional wisdoms of the past. Thus the final objective is to build the company as a self-renewing organization, something that Welch described in his vision for the new millennium: "Our goal is to build a GE that renews itself constantly, exhilarates itself with speed, and freshens itself through constant learning."

As Welch would readily acknowledge, however, GE has not yet achieved this final stage of self-generated, continuous renewal. However, he does recognize occasional glimpses of such behavior. Many of GE's traditional industrial businesses, for example, have injected a new lease of life into old operations by shifting their focus to selling services to supplement their traditional product-focused approach. GE Medical Systems began offering service contracts on hospital chains' medical equipment, including competitive products; Aircraft Engines supplemented its highly cyclical sales by signing engine maintenance agreements with major airlines; and Power

Generation is pursuing opportunities to operate and maintain power plants. Yet management understands that in order for such promising regenerative initiatives to become the rule rather than the exception, the company will need to continue to change its organizational software and hardware.

Changing the Hardware

The farther companies like GE evolve through their transformation processes, the more the hardwired, static structures recede to become little more than a general framework defining the overall configuration of the company's resources and responsibilities. Much more important in shaping the finer-grained management decision making and action is the portfolio of processes that increasingly define the workings of today's multidimensional and flexible organizations.

Elements of the new renewal process have already been put in place in the Best Practices programs that began decoupling managers from the comfort of their old ways of doing things, and even pushing them beyond the limits of internal cross-unit learning. By encouraging managers to seek out leading-edge practice wherever it may exist, Welch institutionalized a dynamic disequilibrium that is replacing the constant quest for fit and alignment with a model focused on embedding continuous challenge and stretch.

Although the shape of all the new process changes is not yet clear, some clues are appearing in the new challenges Welch is framing for the organization. He is identifying the need to raise quality standards yet another notch, and has pointed to Motorola as an inspirational benchmark; he has focused on the need for faster new-product introduction and has suggested that GE is some distance behind pace-setting companies like Hewlett-Packard and Toshiba; and he has thrown down the gauntlet in areas such as globalization, information technology, and service, which he defines as "the biggest growth opportunities in our history."

Yet, unlike many of his earlier highly specified programs and challenges, these latest key goals seem remarkably broad and underdefined, perhaps in an effort to create space for the individual business leaders and their teams to take the leadership on this next round. All the signs seem to point to the fact that Welch is creating the context for the process of self-renewal to take root.

Changing the Software

Having created a management model based on speed, simplicity, and self-confidence, Welch confirmed its importance by aggressively rewarding those who personified those values and removing those who were unable to manage this way. As the organization moved into the third stage of its transformation process, the challenge was to retain the dynamic tension that existed in a behavioral context characterized by stretch, discipline, trust, and support. Like most companies, GE had developed a system that had a strong bias toward hard-edged objectives and measures, and managers found it a great deal easier to develop and sustain the norms of stretch and discipline than to embed the values of trust and support.

Welch understood better than most the need to offset the constant hard-edged demands and pressures it took to create a truly competitive company with the softer-edged values that maintained energy and motivation among employees. He set high standards and stretching goals for his organization, but he also made sure there was constant celebration of the milestone achievements—even when the organization didn't quite make it, as in the case of 1995 operating margin of 14.4 percent. More fundamentally, even as he removed the barriers and guarantees that had long protected GE employees from the competitive reality of the outside world, he also offered them the comforting assurance that the company would give them the training and support to become the best they could be. By maintaining this ying-yang tension, Welch was able to redefine GE's relationship with its employees in a way that gave them the responsibility for ensuring the company's continued success.

Welch was learning that creating a self-renewing organization required management to cook sweet and sour—to offset the hard-edged context of discipline and support with the softer elements of stretch and trust. Only by building rationalization and revitalization into the ongoing flow of business operations could a company prevent the kind of accumulation of inefficiencies that result

in massive restructuring programs. And only through constant renewal can they stem the gradual atrophy of initiative and collaboration that stalls growth and requires jump-starting through
expensive revitalization initiatives.

Changing the Behaviors

To develop a truly self-renewing organization, companies must do
more than change the exhibited behaviors of key management
groups. They must ensure that such changes are rooted in the personal values and beliefs of all members of the organization. It was
this notion that ABB's new chief executive officer, Göran Lindahl,
described as his core task—to turn engineers into capable managers, and managers into effective leaders. "When we have developed all our managers into leaders," he explained, "we will finally
have a self-driven, self-renewing organization."

   That leadership model of behavior is most rapidly communicated if it is modeled effectively by those at the very top of the organization. Their ability to spend more time framing context and
less time defining content becomes a critical example for middle-
level managers who must learn to manage more through coaching
and supporting than by directing and controlling. And their ability
to see themselves not just as the chief strategists but also as the institution builders reinforces to those on the front lines that they
do not just work for a company; they also belong to an organization.

From Caterpillar to Butterfly

Managers of most large companies around the world have recognized the need to make some radical, even transformational
changes to their well-embedded organizational and management
models. Yet few have gone as far as GE in throwing off their familiar old ways; most have done little more than tinker at the margins.

   The problem is that their mind-sets are so dominated by structural and engineering models built into their traditional hierarchies that they try to bring about change by reconfiguring the
assets and reengineering the processes rather then focusing on
how to change individual motivations and interpersonal relation-

ships. Those who have successfully led their companies through transformational change have all discovered one central truth: no change will occur until people change.

But as the GE case illustrates, the voyage from a structural hierarchy to a self-renewing individualized corporation is likely to be long and painful. The metaphor of a caterpillar transforming itself into a butterfly may be romantic, but the experience is an intensely unpleasant one for the caterpillar. In the process, it goes blind, its legs fall off, and its body is torn apart to allow beautiful wings to emerge. We cannot deny the pain involved, but for companies that succeed, the wings they grow as they develop the new behavioral context will allow them to take flight as individualized corporations.

Notes

1. A full description of the research and findings are presented in Ghoshal, S., and Bartlett, C. A. *The Individualized Corporation.* New York: Harper Business, 1997.
2. Results are from the Bain & Co./Planning Forum survey reported in D. K. Rigby, "Managing the Management Tools." *Planning Review,* Sept.-Oct. 1994, pp. 20–24.
3. Jack Welch outlined the basic elements of his logic at a presentation at Harvard Business School in December 1992. It can also be inferred from the descriptions of change at GE in Tidy, M. N., and Sherman, S. *Control Your Destiny or Someone Else Will.* New York: Doubleday, 1993.
4. A more detailed account of the implied organization processes and management roles is provided in Ghoshal, S., and Bartlett, C. A. "Building the Entrepreneurial Corporation: New Organization Processes, New Management Tasks." *European Management Journal,* 1995, *13*(2), 139–155.
5. Welch, J. "Competitiveness from Within." Speech to GE employees, Feb. 1995.
6. A more developed description of the concept of "behavioral context" and the desirable elements we describe as discipline, support, stretch, and trust, see Bartlett, C. A., and Ghoshal, S. "Rebuilding Behavioral Context: Turn Process Reengineering Into People Rejuvenation." *Sloan Management Review,* Fall 1995, *37*, 11–23.
7. For more on the need to offset discipline with support, see Walton, R. "From Control to Commitment in the Workplace." *Harvard Business Review,* Mar.-Apr. 1985, pp. 76–84.

8. Tichy, N., and Charan, R. "Speed, Simplicity and Self-Confidence: An Interview with Jack Welch." *Harvard Business Review,* Sept.-Oct. 1989, p. 14.

9. For an expanded account of this process, see Stewart, T. A. "GE Keeps Those Ideas Coming," *Fortune,* Aug. 12, 1991.

10. Although presented in several internal speeches earlier, this theme was formally launched in Welch's presentation to GE's Annual Shareholders Meeting in Greenville, S.C., on April 26, 1989. See Welch, J. F. "Speed, Simplicity, Self-Confidence: Keys to Leading in the 1990s." Internal GE Executive Reprint.

11. For a more detailed study that has shown the positive influence that ambitious goals have on organizational climate and performance, see Gordon, G. G., and Di Tomaso, N. "Predicting Corporate Performance from Organization Culture." *Journal of Management Studies,* 1992, *29,* 783–798.

12. Videotaped interview with Jack Welch, conducted by Harvard Business School professor Joseph Bower, Sept. 1994.

13. Welch's first identification of "Type IV" managers occurred in 1992 when he raised the issue in GE's 1991 Annual Report. He revived the issue for further discussion and comment in the 1995 Annual Report.

Part Two

Setting Directions: Principles to Guide Change Leaders

Chapter Three

Mobilizing Adaptive Work
Beyond Visionary Leadership

Ronald A. Heifetz
Donald L. Laurie

We no longer live in a world where we have the right to expect authorities to know the answers. The adaptive challenges facing businesses demand not merely the application of expertise, but ongoing changes in the habits, attitudes, and values of people high and low in the workplace.

We may know this in one part of our brain, but the rest continues to operate as if the job of top managers were to provide decisive know-how. Indeed, in the crises and pace of our current age we look even more eagerly and expectantly for deliverance from on high. We fall into patterns of dependency that place impossible burdens on those at the top to pull the next rabbit out of the hat. And if their magic fails, we kill them off. Rarely do we blame ourselves for our unsuitable expectations.

We confuse ourselves in many ways when we analyze the practice of leadership, but especially when we equate leadership with authority. Every day we use the term *leader* to denote people who have authority or a following; we talk about the leadership of the gang, the mob, the organization, Congress, the nation. At some level, however, we know we confuse leadership with authority, because in the next breath we complain about the lack of leadership by many people in authority.

This chapter expands upon the work of Ronald A. Heifetz and Donald L. Laurie as presented in the *Harvard Business Review* article "The Work of Leadership" (January–February 1997). Reprinted by permission of Harvard Business School Press.

Exercising leadership requires distinguishing between leadership and authority and between technical and adaptive work. The first distinction provides a framework for developing leadership strategy given one's place in a situation, with or without authority. The second points to the differences between expert and learning challenges, and the different modes of operating that each requires. Clarifying these two distinctions enables us to understand why so many people in top authority fail to lead: they commit the classic error of treating adaptive challenges as if they were technical problems.

In confusing technical problems with the adaptive challenges we face in business and society, we look for the wrong kind of leadership. We call for someone with answers, decision, strength, and a map of the future: someone who knows where we ought to be going—in short, someone who can make hard problems simple. Instead of looking for saviors, we should be calling for leadership that summons us to face the problems for which there are no simple, painless solutions—the challenges that require us to learn new ways.

To develop an appropriate strategy for leadership that mobilizes adaptive work, we need first to clarify the nature of this classic error—to explain the difference between adaptive challenges and technical problems and the tasks of leadership and authority.

What Is Authority?

Authority is a bargain; people entrust authorities in exchange for service. Indeed, we can define *authority* as "power entrusted to perform a service." When people in authority meet expectations, their credibility and chances for promotion increase; when they do not, they risk their power and position.

Authority takes two forms: formal and informal. With formal authority comes the various powers of the office; with informal authority comes the power to influence attitude and behavior beyond compliance.[1] Formal authority is granted because the office holder promises to meet a set of explicit expectations (job descriptions, legislated mandates), whereas informal authority comes from promising to meet expectations that are often implicit (trustworthiness, ability, civility).

Take the case of an elected official. Before her election, a candidate focuses on increasing her informal authority—the respect, admiration, and trust of prospective constituents. Her hope is to transform that into the formal authority of office. Yet even after she gains office and the powers that come with it, she still has to monitor her informal authority, because it remains a critical source of leverage for mobilizing people. It determines not only her prospects for reelection but also her ability to influence fellow officials while in office.

Formal authority brings with it the powers of office, but informal authority brings with it the subtle yet substantial power to extend one's reach way beyond the limits of the job description. Formal authority changes in quantum jumps at discrete moments when formal mandates for action are given: swearing-in, hiring, firing, signing of legislation, issuance of a license. In contrast, informal authority changes constantly as one's general credibility and professional reputation rise and fall.

To the extent that practitioners and scholars tried in the past to distinguish between leadership and authority, they merely drew a distinction between two kinds of power: formal and informal authority. Leadership has commonly been associated with informal authority, denoting the ability to gain and deploy noncoercive power—that is, the power to persuade and inspire a following. As we shall see, however, both formal and informal authorities are saddled with expectations that constrain the exercise of leadership. Consequently, equating leadership with informal authority does little to help us develop strategies of leadership, whether with or without authority, to tackle our most important challenges.

Services Authorities Are Expected to Provide

Primate societies provide insight into the five vital social needs that authorities are expected to fulfill: direction, protection, orientation, conflict control, and norm maintenance. Although dominance structures among primates vary from fluid to rigidly hierarchical, dominant individuals across species serve many of these same social functions. Dominant animals take a prominent stance. They dominate the attention of the band; they sometimes reside in the spatial center of the group. By providing a central focus of attention, they often serve as reference points by which the other members of the band orient themselves. By keeping a watchful eye on the location and actions of central figures during the day's activities, they know roughly which direction to travel for food, what position to take in camp, whom to mate with, where to run for protection, and whom to look to for the restoration of order when a fight erupts.

For example, when a silverback gorilla walks at the head of the line through mountain forests, he directs the band toward food and water. When a leopard appears, he coordinates the protective response. When members of the band rest at midday and evening, they orient themselves according to where he places himself. Characteristically, nursing mothers stay close by. When conflicts over resources arise, a dominant individual steps in to restore social equilibrium. When norms are violated—for example, during pairing and mating—the silverback reinforces the norms.

Though these five social needs are served in a myriad of ways by authority systems in human organizations and communities, still these services must be rendered. They are essential to the viability of both simple and complex systems, from the family to the multinational corporation.

Indeed, the ability to create societies, from small bands of hunter-gatherers to large organizations, rests on the fundamental ability of humans to authorize one another to do different tasks. Without systems of authorization, we would have neither organization nor civilization. Without trusting one another with power, we atomize.

So it is no wonder that we come to identify leadership with authority in our everyday language and thinking. Every day we look to authorities to coordinate social processes and provide answers to problems and crises as they emerge. And much of the time, despite widespread cynicism these days, authorities deliver.

Distinguishing Between Technical and Adaptive Work

When the problem at hand falls within the know-how of those in authority, individuals in communities and organizations rightly depend on them for decisive direction. Consider hospital personnel in the emergency room. Without an explicit hierarchy of authority to orchestrate the actions of a medical staff needing to provide a swift and coordinated response, chaos would ensue. Someone takes charge, usually a physician, and all eyes turn to her for cues and instructions. Information flows to her from all other members of the staff: the one monitoring blood pressure, the one inserting the intravenous catheter and infusing medication, and the one monitoring the EKG. She provides direction; she provides a focus of attention that orients members of the team to their place and role; she stops any disruptive conflict that arises on the team.

The staff of an emergency room faces a kind of problem similar to many everyday situations. These problems are technical in the sense that we know already how to respond to them. Often they can only be accomplished with mastery and ingenuity. They are not easy, nor are they unimportant. Their solutions frequently save lives and require great organizational effort. Such problems are technical because the necessary knowledge about them already has been digested and transformed into a set of legitimized organizational procedures guiding what to do and role authorizations guiding who should do it.

In similar situations we reasonably turn to authority; in many social systems our authority structures and the norms they maintain govern thousands of problem-solving processes. Meeting a host of vital everyday problems, they are the product of previously accomplished adaptive work. Over the course of history, we have successfully faced an array of adaptive challenges by developing new knowledge and organizations with new values, purposes, beliefs, norms, and rules. Now that we have them, many of our problems have become routine; our expert systems already know how to respond. And because we know how to respond, the stresses generated by these problems are temporary. If a car breaks down a mechanic, an authority on fixing cars, is called in; if a child breaks his arm an orthopedic surgeon, an authority on fixing arms, sets the bone; if a social security check fails to arrive, a local politician is called to "work the bureaucracy" for her constituent. Similarly, if a company's marketing department is caught off guard when a competitor introduces a price cut, the vice president of marketing, or perhaps the company president, intervenes to correct the situation, perhaps by meeting the competitor's price.

For many problems, however, no adequate response has yet been developed. New adaptations are required: habits, attitudes, and values must change, and organizational roles, norms, and procedures have to be learned anew. And because social learning is required, the problem cannot be treated with the mind-set of a technical expert and distilled from the people with the problem.

Why not? Because the stakeholders are the problem. The locus of responsibility for problem solving must shift from those in authority to the people who have to do the changing.

In medicine, for example, a hard-charging overstressed executive may develop heart disease, and though he looks to his physician for a technical remedy, he often has to face adjustments in his life: in diet, exercise, work habits, and stress management. In these situations, the doctor's technical expertise allows her to define the problem and suggest solutions that may work. But merely giving the patient a technical answer does not help him. Her prescribing must actively involve the patient if she is to be effective. The patient needs to confront the choices and changes that face him; technical answers mean nothing if they are not implemented. Only he can reset the priorities of his life. He has to learn new ways, and the doctor has to manage the learning process in order to help the patient help himself. The dependency on authority appropriate to technical situations becomes inappropriate in adaptive ones. The doctor's authority still provides a resource to help the patient respond, but beyond her substantive knowledge she needs a different competence—the ability to help the patient do the work that only he can do.

Examples of adaptive work abound in business and public life: globalization, rapidly changing markets, mergers of disparate corporate cultures, the national debt, failing schools, crime, racial prejudice. These adaptive challenges demand learning and the widespread shouldering of responsibility if they are to be resolved. Mere authoritative response is not enough; no clear expertise, no single sage, no established procedure will suffice. To meet challenges such as these, we need to promote our adaptive capacities rather than expect authority to carry us through. We need to reconceive and revitalize the meaning of organizational citizenship.

These are the times for leadership, but ironically we instead look too longingly to authority for answers. Stresses build up and produce a sense of urgency. Yet problems that cause persistent distress do so because the system of accepted dependencies being applied to them cannot do the job. We look to our authorities for answers they can't provide.

What happens, then? Authorities, under pressure to be decisive, often fake the remedy or take action that skirts or avoids the issue. They succumb to widespread pressures to restore equilibrium, even if that means bolstering patterns of work avoidance. And though they may succeed in the short run to mollify discontent, they lose credibility, often irretrievably, as the problem festers over time into the next crisis.

Not only do we vent our frustrations at the authorities who were supposed to save the day, but also we perpetuate the vicious cycle by looking even more earnestly for someone new offering more certainty and better promises. We may rid ourselves of our current authorities with the false hope that if only we had the right leader our problems would be solved. But the pattern of inappropriate dependency goes unchanged.

The dependency on authority generated by distress has the special advantage of holding a social system together when other cultural constructs fail. Authority relationships become a critical feature of a holding environment. Mismanaged, however, such dependency discourages more adaptive social constructs and behavior. The biological pattern of dependency itself evolved not to enable a given troop to achieve new adaptations (for example, to venture into new ecological zones or address new kinds of challenges), but to enable the troop to function routinely within the ecological zone to which its particular set of social behaviors had adapted already. That is, the alpha male is not designed to invent new norms or role structures, but to direct, defend, and maintain order within the established routines. If a new kind of predator arrives on the scene, the troop will enact its procedure for routine predators and the alpha will valiantly attempt to fulfill his role, however unsuccessfully. Coalescing into a tight group so that no stray falls prey to a leopard brings devastation when the troop faces a man with an automatic rifle.

It makes sense to equate leadership with formal and informal authority in a world of technical problems in which expertise and well-designed procedures and norms suffice to meet the challenges we face. Authorities can realistically be expected to provide direction, protection, orientation, conflict control, and norm maintenance. Many organizations have thrived for long stretches of time in fairly stable environments due in large part to wise and expert authority.

But when progress requires changes in people's values, attitudes, or habits of behavior, when responsibility, pain, and initiative must be distributed widely, our unrealistic expectations of authority serve as constraints on the exercise of leadership. In the context of adaptive work, leadership often makes demands that frustrate people's expectations for easy answers.

A Strategy of Leadership with Authority

After a group of IBM division managers, each representing a different functional area within the company, presented a work plan to address a difficult problem that had cross-functional implications, an uncomfortable silence descended on the room. Although they had developed a six-step plan, assigned responsibility, and placed a due date next to each step, at the end of the three-hour meeting everyone in the audience knew they were not committed either to the work or to each other. One manager had more important functional priorities; another would not provide needed resources; still another would sabotage the initiative. Despite all their talk about cross-functionality, these middle managers delivered a plan that would never be implemented. It was completely transparent; this issue would not get resolved.

Such failures to resolve business problems happen every day. People bring to the table incompatible assumptions and competing perspectives. Managers are often convinced that their part of the truth is the whole truth.

In our work with large multinationals and small start-ups, we have seen the tendency to focus on the technical aspects of work required to solve a problem—that is, the work that either we know how to do because there are prescriptions for doing it, or for which we can hire experts to find the solution.

Yet management cannot solve strategic or operating problems without doing adaptive work—that for which no satisfactory response has yet been developed, no plan of action specified, no technical expertise found fully adequate. These are problems for which new adaptations are required and new organizational roles learned. In adaptive work, we must relinquish deeply held beliefs and learn new skills where old ones are insufficient.

Framing a business challenge in a way that looks at the strategic and adaptive challenges as parts of the same system is central to the work of executive teams. In our experience, too many executive teams do not know how to frame or work on integrated strategic and adaptive issues. They fail to ferret out people's underlying assumptions and understand the competing values that often are at stake. When the IBM executives devised their work plan, for example, they addressed the technical dimension of the problem. But when they left the room without raising questions about the collective commitment of the group to perform this work, they failed to address the adaptive challenge. At this critical moment, no one exercised leadership; their six-step plan neglected to identify the adaptive work and involve the people who would have to implement the changes.

Indeed, many senior executives fail to appreciate the trauma of change and the need to help people through the tough transition. But adaptive work can be achieved *only* by mobilizing the people with the problem to make painful adjustments in their attitudes, work habits, and lives. Clearly stated objectives, detailed work plans, equations, schematics, and PERT charts can prove useful, but such technical solutions are wholly insufficient in grappling with both the design and implementation of new processes. These require adaptive solutions.

In short, we believe that the prevailing notion that leadership consists of having a vision and aligning people with it is bankrupt because it continues to treat adaptive situations as if they were technical. Like a silverback gorilla in a stable environment, the authority figure is supposed to divine where we're going. Leadership is reduced to a combination of omniscience and salesmanship. Hard to define and even harder to resolve, adaptive situations demand the work and responsibility of managers and workers high and low. They are not amenable to solutions that company "leaders" issue from on high; instead, they require that everyone in the organization address the problems and opportunities they face.

We present five principles of leadership for mobilizing people to do adaptive work:

- Identify the adaptive challenge
- Regulate distress
- Maintain disciplined attention
- Give the work back to people
- Protect leadership below

These are interdependent. Managers cannot subscribe to one while excluding the others. They cannot say, "We will accept all but not give the work back to people," or "Fine, but we can't afford to protect dissidents." Adaptive work is difficult because it asks each manager to tackle business problems, hold people in their work, and be present for everyone as the work goes forward.

In practice, such work tends to be messy, but we suggest that effective leaders apply all five principles simultaneously, mobilizing people to adapt to such complex problems as rapidly changing socioeconomic trends and markets, overnight innovation from competitors, mergers across disparate corporate cultures and industries, new distribution channels, and the globalization of business. Confronting such challenges, people cannot merely look up to an authority for a ready-made solution; no one person, however prescient, has all the answers. It is the people themselves who have to adapt, for they are the problem. They must come to see that the answers to complex problems reside in their collective intelligence and skills.

Identifying the Adaptive Challenge

When Colin Marshall became chief executive of British Airways, he discovered that the airline faced more than the usual assortment of key technical problems such as selecting routes, cutting costs, choosing the correct mix of aircraft, buying new planes, and reimaging the fleet. He also found a number of adaptive problems, including a hierarchical organization in which functional loyalties inhibited communication across the business and people were focused internally rather than externally on the needs of customers. Having announced its ambitious goal to become "the world's favourite airline," Marshall had to mobilize 35,000 people—flight crews, reservationists, baggage handlers, caterers, schedulers, marketers, and many others—and rewrite the implicit rules of functional loyalty. Employees had to be weaned from their dependence on the boss to issue instructions. Recognizing that he had to break old habits of distrust and hardened patterns of noncollaboration, Marshall framed the problem as a set of questions: How do we create trust across functions imbued with a tradition of internal competitiveness? How do we break down the "silos" and work collectively to serve customers more responsively? He made clear that he alone could not solve the problem. Only the people deep within the organization could do this work.[2]

Unfortunately, authorities under pressure to deliver "leadership" all too often make the classic error of treating adaptive challenges as if they were technical problems. Proclaiming decision-making and problem-solving skills that have made them so successful, managers readily take responsibility for other people's problems and give them back ready-made solutions. Indeed, top managers gain authority in the first place because they take responsibility and solve problems with such aplomb. Managers rarely receive promotions for providing the leadership required to do adaptive work. Both the repertoire developed from past experience and the pressures of the moment dispose them to make the classic error.

We all—superiors and subordinates alike—have to change our expectations for dispensing and receiving definitive answers. In order to mobilize ourselves to do adaptive work, we have to shift our individual and collective modes of conceptualizing problems in the first place and learn how to distinguish the technical problems in a situation from adaptive challenges in it. Heart disease usually requires a change in habits and priorities, not just surgery.

When society's values change and markets respond with pressures that call for adaptive measures, leadership from a position of authority often requires going against the grain. Rather than fulfilling the expectation for answers, leaders have to frame and provide the tough questions; rather than protect people from an outside threat, they have to let people feel the pinch of reality in order to stimulate adaptation; rather than orient people to their current roles, they must disorient people so that new role relationships develop; rather than quell conflict, they have to draw the issues out; rather than maintain norms, they have to challenge "the way we do business," distinguishing those values and norms that must endure from those that should go. Table 3.1 outlines the shifts that adaptive situations require of authorities.

Leaders crafting strategy have technical expertise and tools available to understand future trends and discontinuities, identify opportunities, map existing competencies, and design the steering

Table 3.1. Adaptive Work Calls for Leadership.

Responsibilities	Situation	
	Technical or Routine	Adaptive
Direction	Authority defines problems and solutions	Authority identifies the adaptive challenge, frames key questions and issues and solutions
Protection	Authority shields the organization from external threats	Authority lets the organization feel external pressure within a range it can stand
Orientation	Authority clarifies roles and responsibilities	Authority disorients current roles or resists pressure to orient people in new roles prematurely
Controlling Conflict	Authority restores order	Authority exposes conflict or lets it emerge
Shaping Norms	Authority maintains norms	Authority challenges unproductive norms or allows them to be challenged

mechanisms to support the strategic direction. Those tools and techniques are readily available both within organizations and from a variety of consulting firms.

In many cases, however, seemingly good strategies fail to get implemented. And often the failure is misdiagnosed: "We had a good strategy, but we couldn't execute or implement it effectively." Actually, the strategy itself is often deficient. The failure to do the necessary adaptive work among the mix of key constituents in the strategy development process—high, lateral, and low—is symptomatic of the technical orientation of top managers. Managers frequently derive their solution to a problem and then attempt to sell some colleagues and bypass or sandbag others in the commitment-building process. Too often those leaders, as well as their top management teams and the consultants they hire, fail to tackle the adaptive dimensions of the challenge and ask themselves the key question: *Who needs to learn what in order to develop, understand, commit to, and implement this strategy?*

The same pitfall awaits many a business process reengineering plan. Although consultants and management have the know-how to do the technical work of framing objectives, designing new work flows, documenting results, and identifying the tasks people need to do, they often ignore the adaptive work needed to mobilize people to change their behaviors. Although these efforts aim to reduce costs by, say, 40 percent even as they increase customer responsiveness, it is estimated that as many as 70 percent of change initiatives fail to achieve their objectives.[3]

Many businesses risk extinction because they cannot learn quickly enough to adapt to the new adaptive challenge. Clearly, the first task of adaptation is to spot the challenge and identify its organizational implications.

The clients of KPMG Netherlands, the renowned accounting firm, came to see auditing as a commodity and negotiated substantially reduced fees. Client relationships of many years' standing grew radically shorter and considerably more expensive. It appeared that technology would change the work of auditors. Rather than a band of junior accountants following a large paper trail at year's end, a handful of people with access to financial databases could complete their sampling and gain deeper insights into their clients' expenditures.

At the same time, KPMG's operations-focused consulting business was not growing as fast as others in the industry. The future looked uncertain. In spite of those trends, KPMG had a record financial year in 1994, commanded its clients' respect, and stood as one of the best-managed companies in the Netherlands.

Ruud Koedijk, chairman of KPMG Netherlands, believed the company needed to rethink its future and develop a strategy to reinvent the firm, becoming "a class apart." With a new strategic architecture, KPMG would migrate from audit to assurance, from operations consulting to focusing on strategy and ambition, from process reengineering to helping clients develop and manage competencies, and from skill-based training to creating organizational learning (see Figure 3.1). Within this architecture, KPMG identified six major new business opportunities. All that was the good news.

The bad news came in the form of a question of self-doubt: Are we capable of doing this? KPMG's board acknowledged that the organization usually had problems accommodating change and often found it difficult to discover and exploit new possibilities. Powerful regional managers, in particular, resisted any change that threatened their units or the resources they controlled. One study of the corporate culture revealed that "as directors, we generally provide our people with very little room to use their creativity or carry out tasks beyond day-to-day work activities."[4] Each partner had his or her little kingdom, and the unstated rule was that no

Figure 3.1. Map of KPMG Netherlands' Changing Domain.

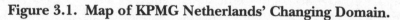

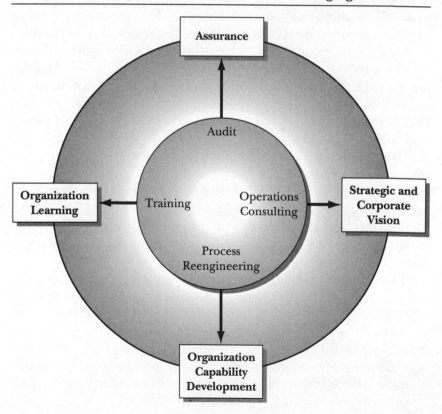

Assurance

Audit

Organization Learning

Training

Operations Consulting

Strategic and Corporate Vision

Process Reengineering

Organization Capability Development

one should trespass on another's turf. Accordingly, people either were unwilling or unable to collaborate with individuals from other units. Historically, the company had realized its success from the cumulative achievements of its individual partners; it was not a team of three hundred partners pulling together.

As strategy development proceeded, each individual felt more inclined to assert a favorite solution to a problem than listen to the underlying assumptions related to a competing perspective. At the same time, people avoided conflict; they simply did not want to discuss those far-reaching problems. Senior partners on the strategy integration team and cross-functional groups themselves grew more dysfunctional. Although the problem could be described, it became clear these good people did not know how to enter into or solve the systemic problems they faced.

To lead KPMG out of its dysfunctionality, Koedijk first had to mobilize his team to assess the environment and discern the nature of the threat: Did it represent a technical or an adaptive challenge? Would adjustments to basic routines suffice to sustain success, or would people throughout the company have to learn new ways of doing business, develop new competencies, and work collectively? Koedijk had to get people to grasp the difference between technical and adaptive work and shift modes of operating.

Second, he and his executive team had to identify the relevant community of interests and key stakeholders. What changes in whose values, beliefs, attitudes, or behaviors would promote progress on these issues? What would be the losses? Which units had to shift priorities, resources, and power?

Third, Koedijk and his team recognized that the initial conflicts were merely symptoms of distress that required adaptive solutions. Those superficial conflicts included issues such as procedures, scheduling, structure, and lines of authority. These seemed merely technical issues, but they were proxies for deeper conflicts in values and norms. Strategy development became part of the adaptive work because no sharp distinction could be drawn between developing the required strategic understanding of the issues and implementing the strategic change.

Fourth, at KPMG the executive team's competing values and norms impaired the capacity of the organization below to collaborate across functions and units. No one wanted to make any concessions. But the top team has to do its adaptive work; if it cannot present adaptive behaviors to emulate, the rest of the organization will languish.

Respect for conflict, starting at the top, allows people to learn from diverse perspectives. When each person defends a personalized and therefore partial view of the systemic challenges, then leadership is rendered ineffective. The organization loses any chance to harness creativity and rigorously assess the business environment.

Regulating Distress

People can learn only so much so fast when it comes to absorbing losses and taking on new responsibilities. We need to prioritize issues and structure the process. Experienced cooks know that they have to heat the pressure cooker properly so as to avoid an explosion. As depicted in Figure 3.2, every organization has a productive range of distress and a limit to its capacity to tolerate disruption. The leader's task is to hold people through a sustained period of disequilibrium during which they learn to achieve the new adaptation.

Figure 3.2. The Persistence of Disequilibrium.

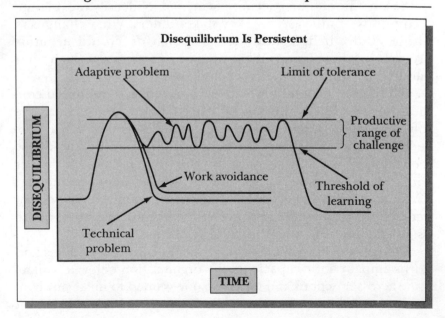

During his first two months as CEO of British Airways, Colin Marshall assessed the readiness of BA's top 160 managers to become more customer responsive. On what the British press called "the day of the long knives," Marshall fired sixty of those managers, convinced that they were neither ready nor willing to make the necessary adaptive changes. Predictably, the level of distress within the airline rose significantly.

People in authority often feel the pressure to protect others from painful adjustments. But leadership requires letting people feel the pinch of reality—sometimes even forcing them to. Otherwise they have little stimulation to take on adaptive work. When the chairmen of Ford, General Motors, and Chrysler went to Japan with President Bush in December 1991, it was not a field trip to learn from Toyota how to build better cars. They went seeking protection from Japanese competition, and they looked to the president to provide it. Of course, Bush was also expected to promote free market values. (Such conflicting expectations can make Presidents sick.)

Recognizing that few people undertake adaptive work if they don't have to, Colin Marshall first made it clear throughout British Airways that the adaptive pressures in the marketplace demanded adaptive responses within. Firing a large number of resistant managers delivered that message. But Marshall also had to have the personal credibility to persuade people that BA's distress was caused not simply by pressures from top management but by the market environment that posed new challenges for both the business and the people who constituted British Airways. Yesterday's technical solutions and norms were insufficient to enable the company to thrive in the future.

Second, Marshall needed to give people a reason to make sacrifices. "Why suffer?" they asked. As Marshall put it, "You have to get people to understand and believe in their work—giving people confidence to do the things they know need doing." Although people at BA were pessimistic and morale was low, Marshall perceived their deep loyalty to the company and their desire to see it succeed. "People want to work for a successful company," he said.[5]

Moreover, they want to work for a company that stands for something. Marshall generated a transformation that embodied new, explicit values that oriented BA personnel to serve customers, respect individuals, and work as team members across traditional business functions.

Marshall established this new orientation by identifying the disparity between the company's current operating norms and the values it had to adopt in order to become "the world's favourite airline." That diagnosis helped the people at BA recognize the changes in behavior they had to make. Performance reviews, for instance, became a fact of BA life. Marshall brought the top 150 managers together each quarter, at a minimum, to explain the ongoing changes, maintain commitment, focus on the next set of problems, set priorities, and foster openness across units. He used newsletters, videos, and other media to improve internal communications, and spoke frequently with the press—not only to establish new customer expectations but also to generate external reinforcement for the internal change. Employees thus found another reason to trust Marshall's commitment to change, and his public pronouncements legitimized their efforts to work adaptively in daily interactions with customers and colleagues.

As Marshall put it, "You have to let people know you are taking a real interest. You need to be visible—my way is to go around and meet people." Accordingly, Marshall listened to employees talk about their main concerns. He met with flight crews, sometimes showing up in the 350–person reservation center in New York, wandering around the baggage area in Tokyo, or visiting the passenger lounge in London or Moscow. Both customers and employees of BA began to feel some relief from the stress of change, for the mere physical presence of the senior authority figure reduces the sense of disorientation.

Third, Marshall had to pace the work. From the inside, it seemed as if everything at BA was being tackled at once. In fact, the strategic change took place over five years. Early on, Marshall and his executive team determined to shift BA's focus from internal functions to a strategy that emphasized customers. That change took place on many fronts, including working with the British government to privatize the airline, building a credible team of managers, mobilizing a highly fragmented organization, and defining new measures of performance and compensation. Information systems had to change as well. This unit played a particularly important role in managing the customer base and monitoring the performance of the business.

People in operations and functions, where formal rules and regulations had dominated thinking for years, felt the distress of change the most. In contrast, customer-oriented people scattered throughout the organization found the adaptive changes particularly refreshing. Indeed, some had been waiting a long time to take responsibility for doing the work that would warrant the slogan of "the world's favourite airline."

As illustrated in Table 3.1, every manager must regulate distress by attending to the social functions of authority: direction, protection, orientation, conflict control, and norm maintenance. The practice of leadership—mobilizing adaptive work—demands serving these functions differently from the way required by technical problems that lie within our organizational repertoire. That is, in adaptive situations a leader provides direction by articulating key questions, clarifying issues, and presenting facts (not by issuing directives). Likewise, a leader provides protection paradoxically by keeping people within an energizing discomfort zone, pacing their work, and sequencing the issues so that they can still be productive (not by sheltering them from threatening change). A leader orients people not to the old procedures and role relationships but to the realities that must drive the development of new ones. An adaptive leader surfaces and orchestrates conflict rather than squelching it, because conflict is the engine of creativity and learning. Finally, a leader mobilizing adaptive work gets people to distinguish those norms and values worth preserving from those that have become antiquated and dysfunctional.

Maintaining Disciplined Attention

Facing different tasks and responsibilities, people in an organization bring to their work diverse values, beliefs, and behaviors. That is as it should be. Innovation and learning are products of differences. No one learns anything new without encountering a different point of view. Yet adaptive work requires a context if it is to be coherent; for diversity to generate innovation, the innovators must have an orientation. Adaptive leaders, in other words, must maintain a disciplined attention on the central issues confronting the business. Otherwise the collaborative effort can fragment into petty rivalries and secondary concerns.

We asked Jan Carlzon, the legendary CEO of Scandinavian Airways (SAS), if he had difficulty with his senior team during adaptive change.

"Absolutely a problem," he replied. "People classify problems in relation to their own experiences. There are two basic types of managers: those who are creative and innovative, and those who need to control and follow the rules of the organization. Creative managers want the freedom to explore new areas; controllers want freedom from innovation. These two types have very different vocabularies. They hear what the other group says, but come up with very different interpretations. Getting these people to listen and learn from each other is one of the leader's most challenging tasks, bringing the conflict out into the open, helping them to understand each other's assumptions and positions. The leader has to guarantee the legitimacy of debate. People at this level learn their way to collective solutions by engaging in a debate and understanding each other's assumptions."

Jan Timmer, the former chairman of Philips Electronics, points to a similar dichotomy. "Top managers," he says, "fall into two camps: engineers and visionaries." Timmer describes as both intellectual and emotional the challenge of getting people to do adaptive work: "At the intellectual level, you need programs, milestones, and discipline. At the emotional level, you need each person to put heart and soul into the effort. Engineers see 'visions' as a waste of time. They have a bias towards 'fixing' the current critical problem. 'We're macho, tough, numbers guys,' they say, 'the other types really shouldn't be here!'" By definition, visionaries are more conceptual and have a sense of duty to shape the company for the longer term; they know they cannot do it if they control only today's operations.

"Fire the engineers and you get harmony and day-dreaming," Timmer warns. "Every business leader needs the cold shower of the engineering type's numbers. Eliminate the visionaries and you have a business oriented to financial and production controls, but often without a clear purpose or meaningful work. Control-oriented people are highly suspicious. If something can't be measured, it is not meaningful. The numbers people are much less at ease with discussions of how to satisfy the customer and mobilize everyone in the organization toward a common goal. The inevitable tension between the engineers and the visionaries seems to militate against complete consensus. My work as the leader is to help people understand the underlying logic of those competing perspectives and to move forward with the best possible decision."[6]

The dynamic tension and conflict, however, have to be actively orchestrated into a dialogue focused on the central issues—otherwise these issues generate work avoidance as the conflicts remain beneath the surface and are played out in reinforced turf boundaries.

When the conflict of values and viewpoints permeates the senior executive team, the entire company can experience the dysfunction and fail to do its cross-functional work. Paul Garwood, general manager of Lever Brothers Fabrics, faced such a challenge when his fabrics leadership team managed to increase earnings during his first two years of leadership. Although it was an increase, it was inadequate given the company's performance objectives. (That increase had been achieved in an oligopolistic market in which Lever is the number-two competitor and vulnerable to competitive moves by Procter & Gamble, the industry leader.) Significant market failures for two new products Lever introduced caused many people within the organization to lose confidence.

Garwood had already reduced costs, reengineered processes, and focused people on the details of the business to become profitable. Yet these activities kept senior managers focused on operating and control issues for about 95 percent of their time; there seemed to be no time to develop and implement a coherent strategy. Coupled with the uncertainty of executive changes at the board level, these restructuring activities caused managers to feel that this was a time to "keep your head down, plow through your own work, and not be too associated with different or potentially risky projects"—such as crafting strategic architecture.[7]

To persuade managers to devote more energy to setting strategy, Garwood first asked three members of the executive team to design a process to identify and eliminate time-consuming, lower-priority tasks. Next, he asked each member to submit on a card one task or activity that he or she could stop. Neither action led anywhere. At one stage, Garwood held a day-long meeting to explore the team's priorities and agendas. Not much happened. The work was never collectively pursued, and people did not hold each other accountable to create space for strategy development. For example, team members had intended to visit two leading-edge companies, in pairs, to determine the characteristics of innovative companies in the future. Because of their busy schedules, however, no one conducted any interviews.

In the traditional command-and-control style organization, quite nice and well-meaning people on the top team hesitate to bring difficult issues to the table. At Lever Brothers, they deferred to Garwood, tolerated distracting and disruptive behavior during meetings, often told jokes that diverted attention from real issues, and generally saw themselves as victims and second-class citizens.

Top managers at Lever colluded, perhaps unwittingly, in avoiding adaptive work. They failed to see conflict as a source of creativity and to recognize that their behavior threatened to lead them down the road to mediocrity. In short, the top team distracted itself from its work on the key strategic issues that would shape its future.

To maintain disciplined attention, Garwood needed to gauge the ripeness of the strategic issues, create a holding environment— a containing vessel—within which to orchestrate conflict and counteract work avoidance, and deepen the dialogue about Lever Brothers' future. He knew that his leadership required both presence and poise. In his personal conduct, Garwood himself had to hold steady to both his sense of priorities and his insistence that team members collaborate on solving the problems ahead. Fostering the team's sense of confidence became central to his work. But how?

First, in assessing the ripeness of issues, Garwood had to evaluate whether the team felt the sense of urgency, or whether only a few managers sensed it. A few managers felt that the team had to invest its time now to develop a strategic architecture, but most felt the priority was to achieve the stated goals for each year's operations. Recognizing that the issue was not yet ripe, Garwood faced the following decision: either take steps to generate a widespread sense of urgency, or let marketplace realities accomplish the ripening by introducing an unforeseen crisis.

Second, Garwood created a holding environment within which to accomplish these large-scale changes to the organization. A *holding environment* consists of any relationship in which one party has the power to hold the attention of another party and facilitate adaptive work. This applies to any relationship that has a developmental task or opportunity. The holding environment can generate adaptive work because it contains and regulates the stresses that work generates. For example, a friend who listens with empathy to a difficult story or who can tell a joke that fits the moment will provide respite and perspective that buffers distress. The friendship is a holding environment. Social structures and hopeful visions of the future during times of hardship reduce social distress: Franklin Roosevelt and the programs of the New Deal provided a holding environment for the nation during the Great Depression.

To create a holding environment for adaptive work on strategy development, Garwood invited twenty-five volunteers from different levels and functions to form a team of "explorers" to shape strategy. He asked the members to develop a set of shared assumptions about trends and discontinuities that would shape the future, identify opportunities, and determine the gap between Lever's current core competencies and those that would be needed to exploit future opportunities.

Garwood authorized these explorers to take three days a week for four months to complete their work. He gave them a separate open-plan work space and a budget for research, travel, and consultants. Most important, he allowed a different culture to emerge at Lever Brothers, one that valued ideas and dialogue, in contrast to the prevailing mode of hierarchy and control. Establishing these conditions created a collective confidence and coherent sense of purpose.

Third, because work avoidance on the top team was rampant, Garwood had to keep attention focused on adaptive issues. Team members wanted to engage in scapegoating, denial, reducing problems to technical terms, and attacking individuals rather than the perspectives they represented. These distracting behaviors occur frequently in the midst of adaptive work. When sterile conflict took the place of dialogue, Garwood had to step in and put the team to work on reframing the issues. He asked the questions that deepened the debate by unbundling the issues and keeping personal conflicts at bay. When team members took up cudgels to defend their own turf, Garwood had to plead the necessity of collaboration, the value of consulting one another and using each other as resources in the problem-solving process.

Not all managers actively try to avoid work. Although technical issues are compelling and legitimate, most managers feel ambivalent about pursuing adaptive work. Although we want to make progress on hard problems and live up to our renewed and clarified values, we also want to avoid the distress associated with adaptation. Millions of Americans wanted to reduce the budget deficit or pay down the national debt, but not with their tax dollars or with the loss of their benefits and jobs. So too do managers want the adaptive work to get done—they may even see it as a priority—but most find it difficult to sustain the losses to their way of doing business.

Garwood exemplifies the leader who has poise, the tolerance for uncertainty, frustration, and pain. His management team saw him shift from being buried in operating detail to helping them develop an ambition and a strategy for the business. Raising tough questions without becoming too anxious himself, he presented a model of behavior to employees, colleagues, and customers, who observed his verbal and nonverbal cues of equanimity. If in his body language or tone of voice he had instead communicated uneasiness, he would have communicated a lack of confidence in the process. By containing his anxieties, he communicated that the stresses of the work itself were containable and embodied disciplined attention.

Giving the Work Back to People

The story of Scandinavian Airways shows how Jan Carlzon coordinated the adaptive process by giving the work back to people. In fact, Colin Marshall had the opportunity to observe Carlzon's experience at SAS and to adapt many of his management ideas.

In the growth markets of the 1960s and 1970s, airline companies seemed to have it all. An abundance of customers, favorable tariffs for national companies, and price controls provided a stable environment for steady growth. Yet by the early 1980s, signs of change began to appear. Airline deregulation in the United States foreshadowed the lifting of favorable tariffs and price controls. The previously increasing customer pool began to wane. The oil crises of the 1970s severely cut profit margins. These changes meant the end of the gentlemen's game airline executives had traditionally played. Airlines began to play rough as they competed for each other's customers.

After seventeen years of profits and growth, SAS sustained $30 million of losses in 1979 and 1980. Carlzon saw those losses as a sign of something very different from poor cost control or flabby middle management. To him they signified fundamental changes in the industry. Rather than responding to losses in the usual way— looking for specific sources of waste and inefficiency—Carlzon began a campaign not only to keep old customers but to win new ones from other airlines. For Carlzon, that meant SAS had to become much more responsive to customers' needs. Thus, in 1981 he implemented a strategy for adaptive work aimed at promoting leadership at the front line and across the boundaries between divisions within SAS.

Meeting the needs of customers in a highly competitive environment presented both technical and adaptive challenges. These challenges had some technical components that were amenable to routine response: Carlzon could rely on market research to assess general patterns of need and set general market strategy. Should SAS go after the vacationing traveler or the business traveler? What schedules would meet those needs? What routes of travel were in greatest demand?

Yet adaptive problems surfaced in the analyses of particular customers, who came in all shapes and sizes, all ages and incomes. In other words, particular customers looked not a thing like the average customer profiled by market research. Carlzon knew that SAS had to acquire a new approach to gathering information about customers in order to appeal to their specific needs.

So Carlzon turned his company on its head, giving much greater latitude for decision making about customer needs to people on the front line. Middle and senior management would support the front line instead of controlling it. Carlzon's reasoning was elegant and simple: the front-line people knew the most about the needs of individual customers. Ticket agents, baggage handlers, and flight attendants were in the best position to discover the needs of real people.

Apart from having critical information about their customers, people on the front line were in the optimal and often only position from which to respond to customers' needs. They had to take action. There was no time to go up the line for permission to act when the customer was standing right in front of them waiting. Front-line employees had to define and solve problems in fifteen seconds or so while customers were in direct contact with the company. Carlzon called these encounters "moments of truth."[8] SAS would succeed or fail each day during those 140,000 moments of truth when customers would be won or lost.

To accomplish this adaptive work, Carlzon needed to give the work back to people. He wanted ticket agents and others close to customers to take responsibility for making costly decisions on the spur of the moment if they saw the need. The front-line employees had to be able to take financial risks on behalf of the customer. As senior executives diagnosed overarching trends of the market— economic patterns, regulatory policies, the actions of competing companies—front-line workers diagnosed the specific situations in the market.[9] Sometimes a new pattern of customer need emerged at the front line for which an organizational response was necessary—a new policy, a change in organizational structure, or a shift in the allocation of resources. In such cases the ticket agent would report the need to middle management and mobilize the organization to respond adaptively. In short, the ticket agent would lead the organization from below.

Each individual in the organization had special access to information that came from his or her vantage point. Each saw different needs and opportunities to fulfill. Although front-line workers might not be able to assess changes in European politics that would lead to airline deregulation in Europe during the 1990s, neither could senior management best assess information from front-line workers that indicated a need for systemic change. That was the job of middle managers. But even the most astute middle manager could not see the faces of individual customers and have intimate knowledge of their needs. That was the job of the front-line employee.

In many organizations, developing widespread responsibility-taking is a central feature of achieving a new adaptation. At SAS, letting the front line take the initiative of defining and solving customer problems meant reorienting much of management from a control to a support mind-set, thereby establishing new norms and values for people throughout the organization.

Carlzon built widespread acceptance of the new approach by spending up to 50 percent of his time during the first two years communicating directly in large meetings and indirectly through workshops, brainstorming sessions, learning exercises, public media exposure, brochures, newsletters, and a variety of symbolic acts; he redesigned the pretentious executive dining room, for example. Finally, having identified the adaptive challenge, he saw that his leadership task had to be educative in the broad sense. He had an overall business strategy that oriented people, but he also had a host of questions requiring innovation across boundaries throughout the organization.

To manage the disequilibrium, Carlzon bolstered the holding environment, the organizational space in which the conflicts and stresses of adaptive work take place. Carlzon put it this way: "Before, leaders used to be authoritarian [command and control]; now their emphasis is on vision, strategy, and skilled people everywhere. The leader communicates strategy and objectives, and so the people take over. The leader is no longer engaged in the act of managing the business himself, but creating an atmosphere and establishing the values so people can do their work."[10]

In addition to establishing orienting values and a norm of front-line responsibility-taking, Carlzon strengthened the containing vessel by bolstering his authority. To strengthen his formal authority, he made sure that his board of directors understood the magnitude of the change and the cost. He included them. In his first year, when the company was losing $20 million a year, Carlzon asked the board to invest $50 million more in improvements, even though he could not guarantee or predict how much revenue the proposed changes and marketing investments would bring in. He needed their commitment and full authorization. Unlike many leaders, Carlzon consulted openly and frequently with his board. That strengthened his formal hand.

The holding environment also depends on relationships of informal authority derived primarily from trust. If trust in Carlzon had been weak, he would have had to reduce the pressure, perhaps by slowing down the change process. But because the degree of trust was high, Carlzon could afford to turn up the heat by introducing tough challenges more quickly. Trust provided a critical resource, and he had to tend to it fastidiously.

To strengthen his informal authority, Carlzon made himself a pervasive personal presence, meeting with and listening to people intently inside and outside the organization. He wrote a book to explain his values, philosophy, and strategy. "If no one else read it, at least my people would," he said. Moreover, he generated trust by trusting others—by decentralizing authority. "The key is to prepare people's mind-set and let them discover the problem. You won't be successful if people aren't carrying the recognition of the problem and the solution within themselves."

Perhaps most critically, Carlzon strengthened the holding environment by developing collective self-confidence. As he said, "People aren't born with self-confidence. It comes through success and experience and the environment. Even the most self-confident people can be broken. The most important role of the leader is to create confidence among people. Look at authority figures in a public organization. Do they punish mistakes? Do they do nothing? The result is inefficiency. How to build a management system related to the responsibility and the authority you give away is the real challenge."[11] It does not work to demand that people give good service, but then fix severe limits on the resources they need to provide those services.

The purpose of the holding environment is not to eliminate stress but to regulate and contain it so that it does not overwhelm anyone. Eliminating stress altogether is counterproductive, for it removes impetus for adaptive work. The leader's major task is to maintain a tolerable level of stress that helps mobilize people's responsibility-taking. The example of Jan Carlzon at SAS demonstrates how productive such a holding environment can be.

Protecting Leadership Below

When Ruud Koedijk and Paul Garwood engaged one hundred and twenty-five people, respectively, in the strategy creation process, they gave voice to people below and throughout the organization. The same thing occurred when Colin Marshall launched an initiative to make British Airways more customer-responsive.

In these strategy projects, leaders established a temporary structure that allowed the architects and explorers to work. Authority figures were expected to operate as part of the team and, by and large, did. Ideas and dialogue became the standard by which contributions were measured. Openness became the norm, so much so that people agreed that they could be open in strategy development in ways not possible in their working groups, where they had to have the right answers, avoid mistakes at any cost, and be operational—where they could not exhibit curiosity, reflection, or insight. People felt pulled in two directions. In their strategy work they collectively stretched themselves; in their operational work they felt like individual units of production performing tasks in a highly controlled environment. The new cultural norms by which strategy development was recognized and treated as adaptive work clashed with the still-dominant norms by which all challenges, adaptive and technical, were treated like technical problems.

In the new culture of BA, front-line people were encouraged to take responsibility for and act on behalf of the customer. At both BA and SAS, this adaptive change created a revolution. The airlines created new classes of service, improved food-service and check-in procedures, lost fewer pieces of luggage, made special concessions for elderly and handicapped passengers, and provided all customers with more rapid and user-friendly solutions. People in each airline felt listened to, empowered to act, and responsible for improving service and performance. They began finding their work more meaningful and enriching. And management saw its role as encouraging, supporting, and guiding the work, not controlling it.

This is the foundation of an organization willing to experiment and learn. It is a necessary precondition for growing the business, not just managing its cost-to-revenue ratios. In contrast, whistle-blowers, creative deviants, and other such voices routinely get silenced in the traditional command-and-control organization. Because these people generate disequilibrium, those in power believe that the easiest way to restore equilibrium is to neutralize them. For example, the engineers who had feared that the O-rings on the Challenger space shuttle could not withstand the January frost were fired after the tragedy.

The voices from below might not be eloquent or articulate. After all, people speaking beyond their authority usually feel self-conscious, and sometimes they generate too much passion in order to gear themselves up for speaking out. Of course, that often makes it harder for them to communicate effectively. They pick the wrong time and place; they neglect proper channels of communication and lines of authority. But buried inside a poorly packaged interjection may lie an important intuition that needs to be heard. Tossing it off for its bad timing, lack of clarity, or unreasonableness can eliminate potentially important information and discourage a potential leader in the organization. Adaptive work cannot rely on "normal" people alone.

One manager, call him Michael, listened when his seniors encouraged people in a large manufacturing company to look for problems, speak openly, and take responsibility. Believing in their sincerity, Michael once raised an issue that was too hot to handle. Swept under the carpet for years, the issue of the CEO's pet project was tacitly acknowledged in the company, but Michael knew that maintaining this investment could damage or derail key elements of the company's strategy. He raised the issue directly in a meeting with his boss and the CEO. He provided a clear description of the problem, a representation of the competing perspectives on the issue, and a summary of the consequences of continuing to operate the project.

The CEO squelched the discussion. He reinforced the positives of his pet project. He then asked Michael if he had discussed this with a particular task force—which he knew would shield him from this kind of challenge. Michael had not. The CEO then handed the problem over to Michael's boss. The issue was not up for discussion.

When Michael and his boss left the room, his boss's disapproval became apparent. Why hadn't Michael discussed this with him before speaking to the CEO? The boss attacked Michael personally: "Who do you think you are, with your holier-than-thou attitude?" The subject was closed.

Michael had greater experience and expertise than either the CEO or his managers in this area, but they expressed not one bit of curiosity about it, made no effort to investigate Michael's reasoning, and had no sense that he was behaving responsibly with the best interests of the company at heart. The climate in the room had shifted from a friendly, everything-is-going-fine mood to a chilly don't-ever-bring-that-up-again atmosphere.

The CEO and Michael's boss quashed the potential leader below. Clearly, authority figures are constrained from exercising leadership, not only by their own blind spots but also by expectations from key stakeholders to keep the ship on an even keel. They must rely on others in the organization to spot and raise questions that indicate, early on, an adaptive challenge. Yet they have to provide cover to people who point to the internal contradictions of the enterprise. These individuals often will have latitude to provoke rethinking that people in authority do not have.

When an authority figure feels the urge to glare at or otherwise silence someone, he or she has to stop for the moment. That urge to restore the group's equilibrium is understandably quite powerful, and it happens fast. But an authority figure intent on leadership has to get accustomed to delaying the impulse and ask, "What really is this person talking about? Is there something we're missing?"

Conclusion

Focusing management teams and front-line workers on adaptive change is among the leader's most difficult tasks. Most of the problems facing top management are highly interrelated strategic or operating issues and adaptive challenges that need to be viewed as systems problems. Engaging key managers with different styles and agendas in the work is necessary to create understanding, generate commitment, and solve complex problems.

Adaptive challenges have no ready solutions. They require that people collectively apply their intelligence and skills to the work only they can do. This requires unlearning the habits of a managerial lifetime, new learning to meet challenges where current skills are insufficient, and the capacity to explore and understand the competing values at stake.

Leading adaptive change requires a learning strategy. To learn the way forward, each manager facing an adaptive challenge must ask who needs to learn what and how. The work begins by framing the challenge and effectively holding the people with the problem as they think together, engage their conflicts and differences, and learn from each other. For this, a leader must be ready with good questions and the willingness to sustain uncertainty.

Notes

1. For discussion of the distinction between formal powers and informal influence, see Neustadt, R. E. *Presidential Power and the Modern Presidents: The Politics of Leadership from Roosevelt to Reagan.* (3rd ed.). New York: Free Press, 1990.
2. Personal communication with D. Laurie, Oct. 23, 1992.
3. Hammer, M., and Champy, J. *Re-engineering the Corporation: A Manifesto for Business Revolution.* New York: Harper Business, 1993.
4. Personal communication with D. Laurie, 1992.
5. Personal communication with D. Laurie, Oct. 23, 1992.
6. Personal communication with D. Laurie, Nov. 23, 1992.
7. Personal communication with D. Laurie, Feb. 8, 1996.
8. Carlzon, J. *Moments of Truth.* New York: HarperCollins, 1987, pp. 1–2.
9. Carlzon, J. *Moments of Truth.* New York: HarperCollins, 1987, p. 25.
10. Personal communication with D. Laurie, Aug. 24, 1992.
11. Personal communication with D. Laurie, Aug. 24, 1992.

Chapter Four

Leading Change
The Eight Steps to Transformation
John P. Kotter

Over the past decade, I have watched more than a hundred companies try to remake themselves into significantly better competitors. They have included large organizations (Ford) and small ones (Landmark Communications), companies based in the United States (General Motors) and elsewhere (British Airways), corporations that were on their knees (Eastern Airlines), and companies that were earning good money (Bristol-Myers Squibb). Their efforts have gone under many banners: total quality management, reengineering, right-sizing, restructuring, cultural change, and turnaround. But in almost every case the basic goal has been the same: to make fundamental changes in how business is conducted in order to help cope with a new, more challenging market environment.

A few of these corporate change efforts have been very successful. A few have been utter failures. Most fall somewhere in between, with a distinct tilt toward the lower end of the scale. The lessons that can be drawn are interesting and will probably be relevant to even more organizations in the increasingly competitive business environment of the coming decade.

The most general lesson to be learned from the more successful cases is that the change process (see Table 4.1 at the end of this chapter) goes through a series of phases that, in total, usually require considerable time. Skipping steps creates only the illusion of speed and seldom produces a satisfying result. A second lesson is that critical mistakes in any phase can have a devastating impact, slowing momentum and negating hard-won gains. Perhaps because we have relatively little experience in renewing organizations, even very capable people often make at least one big error.

Error 1: Not Establishing Enough Sense of Urgency

Most successful change efforts begin when certain individuals or groups start to look hard at a company's competitive situation, market position, technological trends, and financial performance. They focus on the potential revenue drop when an important patent expires, the five-year trend in declining margins in a core business, or an emerging market that everyone seems to be ignoring. They then find ways to communicate this information broadly and dramatically, especially with respect to crises, potential crises, or great opportunities that are very timely. This first step is essential because just getting a transformation program started requires the aggressive cooperation of many individuals. Without motivation, people won't help and the effort goes nowhere.

Compared with other steps in the change process, phase one can sound easy. It is not. Well over 50 percent of the companies I have watched fail in this first phase. Sometimes executives underestimate how hard it can be to drive people out of their comfort zones. Sometimes they grossly overestimate how successful they have already been in increasing organizational urgency. Sometimes they lack patience: "Enough with the preliminaries, let's get on with it." In many cases executives become paralyzed by the downside possibilities. They worry that employees with seniority will become defensive, that morale will drop, that events will spin out of control, that short-term business results will be jeopardized, that the stock will sink, and that they will be blamed for creating a crisis.

A paralyzed senior management often comes from having too many managers and not enough leaders. Management's mandate is to minimize risk and to keep the current system operating. Change, by definition, requires creating a new system, which in turn always demands leadership. Phase one in a renewal process typically goes nowhere until enough real leaders are promoted or hired into senior-level jobs.

Transformations often begin, and begin well, when an organization has a new head who is a good leader and who sees the need for major change. If the renewal target is the entire company, the CEO is key. If change is needed in a division, the division general manager is key. When these individuals are not new leaders, great leaders, or change champions, phase one can be a huge challenge.

Bad business results are both a blessing and a curse in the first phase. On the positive side, losing money does catch people's attention. But it also gives less maneuvering room. With good business results, the opposite is true: convincing people of the need for change is much harder, but you have more resources to help make changes.

But whether the starting point is good performance or bad, in the more successful cases I have witnessed, an individual or a group always facilitates a frank discussion of potentially unpleasant facts about new competition, shrinking margins, decreasing market share, flat earnings, a lack of revenue growth, or other relevant indices of a declining competitive position. Because there seems to be an almost universal human tendency to shoot the bearer of bad news, especially if the head of the organization is not a change champion, executives in these companies often rely on outsiders to bring unwanted information. Wall Street analysts, customers, and consultants can all be helpful in this regard. The purpose of all this activity, in the words of one former CEO of a large European company, is "to make the status quo seem more dangerous than launching into the unknown."

In a few of the most successful cases, a group has manufactured a crisis. One CEO deliberately engineered the largest accounting loss in the company's history, creating huge pressures from Wall Street in the process. One division president commissioned first-ever customer-satisfaction surveys, knowing full well that the results would be terrible. He then made these findings public. On the surface, such moves can look unduly risky. But there is also risk in playing it too safe: when the urgency rate is not pumped up enough, the transformation process cannot succeed and the long-term future of the organization is put in jeopardy.

When is the urgency rate high enough? From what I have seen, the answer is when about 75 percent of a company's management is honestly convinced that business as usual is totally unacceptable.

Anything less can produce very serious problems later on in the process.

Error 2: Not Creating a Powerful Guiding Coalition

Major renewal programs often start with just one or two people. In cases of successful transformation efforts, the leadership coalition grows and grows over time. But whenever some minimum mass is not achieved early in the effort, nothing much worthwhile happens.

It is often said that major change is impossible unless the head of the organization is an active supporter. What I am talking about goes far beyond that. In successful transformations, the chairman or president or division general manager, plus another five or fifteen or fifty people, come together and develop a shared commitment to excellent performance through renewal. In my experience, this group never includes all of the company's most senior executives because some people just won't buy in, at least not at first. But in the most successful cases, the coalition is always pretty powerful in terms of titles, information and expertise, reputations, and relationships.

In both small and large organizations, a successful guiding team may consist of only three to five people during the first year of a renewal effort. But in big companies, the coalition needs to grow to the range of twenty to fifty before much progress can be made in phase three and beyond. Senior managers always form the core of the group. But sometimes you find board members, a representative from a key customer, or even a powerful union leader.

Because the guiding coalition includes members who are not part of senior management, by definition it tends to operate outside the normal hierarchy. This can be awkward, but it is clearly necessary. If the existing hierarchy were working well, there would be no need for a major transformation. But as the current system is not working, reform generally demands activity outside of formal boundaries, expectations, and protocol.

A high sense of urgency within the managerial ranks helps enormously in putting a guiding coalition together. But more is usually required. Someone needs to get these people together, help them develop a shared assessment of their company's problems and opportunities, and create a minimum level of trust and communication. Off-site retreats for two or three days are one popular vehicle for accomplishing this task. I have seen many groups of five to thirty-five executives attend a series of these retreats over a period of months.

Companies that fail in phase two usually underestimate the difficulties of producing change and thus the importance of a powerful guiding coalition. Sometimes they have no history of teamwork at the top and therefore undervalue the importance of this type of coalition. Sometimes they expect the team to be led by a staff executive from human resources, quality, or strategic planning instead of a key line manager. No matter how capable or dedicated the staff head, groups without strong line leadership never achieve the power that is required.

Efforts that don't have a powerful enough guiding coalition can make apparent progress for a while. But, sooner or later, the opposition gathers itself together and stops the change.

Error 3: Lacking a Vision

In every successful transformation effort that I have seen, the guiding coalition develops a picture of the future that is relatively easy to communicate and appeals to customers, stockholders, and employees. A vision always goes beyond the numbers that are typically found in five-year plans. A vision says something that helps clarify the direction in which an organization needs to move. Sometimes the first draft comes mostly from a single individual. It is usually a bit blurry, at least initially. But after the coalition works at it for three or five or even twelve months, something much better emerges through their tough analytical thinking and a little dreaming. Eventually, a strategy for achieving that vision is also developed.

In one mid-size European company, the first pass at a vision contained two-thirds of the basic ideas that were in the final product. The concept of global reach was in the initial version from the beginning. So was the idea of becoming preeminent in certain businesses. But one central idea in the final version—getting out of low value-added activities—came only after a series of discussions over a period of several months.

Without a sensible vision, a transformation effort can easily dissolve into a list of confusing and incompatible projects that can take the organization in the wrong direction or nowhere at all. Without a sound vision, the reengineering project in the accounting department, the new 360–degree performance appraisal from the human resources department, the plant's quality program, the cultural change project in the sales force will not add up in a meaningful way.

In failed transformations, you often find plenty of plans and directives and programs, but no vision. In one case, a company gave out four-inch-thick notebooks describing its change effort. In mind-numbing detail, the books spelled out procedures, goals, methods, and deadlines. But nowhere was there a clear and compelling statement of where all this was leading. Not surprisingly, most of the employees with whom I talked were either confused or alienated. The big, thick books did not rally them together or inspire change. In fact, they probably had just the opposite effect.

In a few of the less successful cases that I have seen, management had a sense of direction, but it was too complicated or blurry to be useful. Recently, I asked an executive in a mid-size company to describe his vision and received in return a barely comprehensible thirty-minute lecture. Buried in his answer were the basic elements of a sound vision. But they were buried—deeply.

A useful rule of thumb: if you can't communicate the vision to someone in five minutes or less and get a reaction that signifies both understanding and interest, you are not yet done with this phase of the transformation process.

Error 4: Undercommunicating the Vision by a Factor of Ten

I've seen three patterns with respect to communication, all very common. In the first, a group actually does develop a pretty good transformation vision and then proceeds to communicate it by holding a single meeting or sending out a single communication. Having used about .0001 percent of the yearly intracompany communication, the group is startled that few people seem to understand the new approach. In the second pattern, the head of the organization spends a considerable amount of time making speeches to employee groups, but most people still don't get it (not surprising, as vision captures only .0005 percent of the total yearly communication). In the third pattern, much more effort goes into newsletters and speeches, but some very visible senior executives still behave in ways that are antithetical to the vision. The net result is that cynicism among the troops goes up while belief in the communication goes down.

Transformation is impossible unless hundreds or thousands of people are willing to help, often to the point of making short-term sacrifices. Employees will not make sacrifices, even if they are unhappy with the status quo, unless they believe that useful change is possible. Without credible communication, and a lot of it, the hearts and minds of the troops are never captured.

This fourth phase is particularly challenging if the short-term sacrifices include job losses. Gaining understanding and support is tough when downsizing is a part of the vision. For this reason, successful visions usually include new growth possibilities and the commitment to treat fairly anyone who is laid off.

Executives who communicate well incorporate messages into their hour-by-hour activities. In a routine discussion about a business problem, they talk about how proposed solutions fit (or don't fit) into the bigger picture. In a regular performance appraisal, they talk about how the employee's behavior helps or undermines the vision. In a review of a division's quarterly performance, they talk not only about the numbers but also about how the division's executives are contributing to the transformation. In a routine Q&A with employees at a company facility, they tie their answers back to renewal goals.

In more successful transformation efforts, executives use all existing communication channels to broadcast the vision. They turn boring and unread company newsletters into lively articles about the vision. They take ritualistic and tedious quarterly management meetings and turn them into exciting discussions of the transformation. They throw out much of the company's generic management education and replace it with courses that focus on business problems and the new vision. The guiding principle is simple: use every possible channel, especially those that are being wasted on nonessential information.

Perhaps even more important, most of the executives I have known in successful cases of major change learn to "walk the talk." They consciously attempt to become a living symbol of the new corporate culture. This is often not easy. A sixty-year-old plant manager who has spent precious little time over forty years thinking about customers will not suddenly behave in a customer-oriented way. But I have witnessed just such a person change, and change a great deal. In that case, a high level of urgency helped. The fact that the man was a part of the guiding coalition and the vision-creation team also helped. So did all the communication, which kept reminding him of the desired behavior, and all the feedback from his peers and subordinates, which helped him see when he was not engaging in that behavior.

Communication comes in both words and deeds, and the latter are often the most powerful form. Nothing undermines change more than behavior by important individuals that is inconsistent with their words.

Error 5: Not Removing Obstacles to the New Vision

Successful transformations begin to involve large numbers of people as the process progresses. Employees are emboldened to try new approaches, to develop new ideas, and to provide leadership. The only constraint is that the actions fit within the broad parameters of the overall vision. The more people involved, the better the outcome.

To some degree, a guiding coalition empowers others to take action simply by successfully communicating the new direction. But communication is never sufficient by itself. Renewal also requires the removal of obstacles. Too often, an employee understands the new vision and wants to help make it happen. But an elephant appears to be blocking the path. In some cases, the elephant is in the person's head, and the challenge is to convince the individual that no external obstacle exists. But in most cases, the blockers are very real.

Sometimes the obstacle is the organizational structure: narrow job categories can seriously undermine efforts to increase productivity or make it very difficult even to think about customers. Sometimes compensation or performance-appraisal systems make people choose between the new vision and their own self-interest. Perhaps worst of all are bosses who refuse to change and who make demands that are inconsistent with the overall effort.

One company began its transformation process with much publicity and actually made good progress through the fourth phase. Then the change effort ground to a halt because the officer in charge of the company's largest division was allowed to undermine most of the new initiatives. He paid lip service to the process but did not change his behavior or encourage his managers to change. He did not reward the unconventional ideas called for in the vision. He allowed human resource systems to remain intact even when they were clearly inconsistent with the new ideals. I think the officer's motives were complex. To some degree, he did not believe the company needed major change. To some degree, he felt personally threatened by all the change. To some degree, he was afraid that he could not produce both change and the expected operating profit. But despite the fact that they backed the renewal effort, the other officers did virtually nothing to stop the one blocker. Again, the reasons were complex. The company had no history of confronting problems like this. Some people were afraid of the officer. The CEO was concerned that he might lose a talented executive. The net result was disastrous. Lower-level managers concluded that senior management had lied to them about their commitment to renewal, cynicism grew, and the whole effort collapsed.

In the first half of a transformation, no organization has the momentum, power, or time to get rid of all obstacles. But the big ones must be confronted and removed. If the blocker is a person, it is important that he or she be treated fairly and in a way that is consistent with the new vision. But action is essential both to empower others and to maintain the credibility of the change effort as a whole.

Error 6: Not Systematically Planning and Creating Short-Term Wins

Real transformation takes time, and a renewal effort risks losing momentum if there are no short-term goals to meet and celebrate. Most people won't go on the long march unless they see compelling evidence within twelve to twenty-four months that the journey is producing expected results. Without short-term wins, too many people give up or actively join the ranks of those people who have been resisting change.

One to two years into a successful transformation effort, you find quality beginning to go up on certain indices or the decline in net income stopping. You find some successful new product introductions or an upward shift in market share. You find an impressive productivity improvement or a statistically higher customer-satisfaction rating. But whatever the case, the win is unambiguous. The result is not just a judgment call that can be discounted by those opposing change.

Creating short-term wins is different from hoping for short-term wins. The latter is passive, the former active. In a successful transformation, managers actively look for ways to obtain clear performance improvements, establish goals in the yearly planning system, achieve the objectives, and reward the people involved with recognition, promotions, and even money. For example, the guiding coalition at a U.S. manufacturing company produced a highly visible and successful new product introduction about twenty months after the start of its renewal effort. The new product was selected about six months into the effort because it met multiple criteria: it could be designed and launched in a relatively short period; it could be handled by a small team of people who were devoted to the new vision; it had upside potential; and the new product-development team could operate outside the established departmental structure without practical problems. Little was left to chance, and the win boosted the credibility of the renewal process.

Managers often complain about being forced to produce short-term wins, but I've found that pressure can be a useful element in a change effort. When it becomes clear to people that major change will take a long time, urgency levels can drop. Commitments to produce short-term wins help keep the urgency level up and force detailed analytical thinking that can clarify or revise visions.

Error 7: Declaring Victory Too Soon

After a few years of hard work, managers may be tempted to declare victory with the first clear performance improvement. Although celebrating a win is fine, declaring the war won can be catastrophic. Until changes sink deeply into a company's culture, a process that can take five to ten years, new approaches are fragile and subject to regression.

In the recent past, I have watched a dozen change efforts operate under the reengineering theme. In all but two cases, victory was declared and the expensive consultants were paid and thanked when the first major project was completed after two to three years. Within two more years, the useful changes that had been introduced slowly disappeared. In two of the ten cases, it's hard to find any trace of the reengineering work today.

Over the past twenty years, I've seen the same sort of thing happen to huge quality projects, organizational development efforts, and more. Typically, the problems start early in the process: the urgency level is not intense enough, the guiding coalition is not powerful enough, and the vision is not clear enough. But it is the premature victory celebration that kills momentum. And then the powerful forces associated with tradition take over.

Ironically, it is often a combination of change initiators and change resistors that creates the premature victory celebration. In their enthusiasm over a clear sign of progress, the initiators go overboard. They are then joined by resistors, who are quick to spot any opportunity to stop change. After the celebration is over, the resistors point to the victory as a sign that the war has been won and the troops should be sent home. Weary troops allow themselves to be convinced that they won. Once home, the foot soldiers are reluctant to climb back on the ships. Soon thereafter, change comes to a halt and tradition creeps back in.

Instead of declaring victory, leaders of successful efforts use the credibility afforded by short-term wins to tackle even bigger problems. They go after systems and structures that are not consistent with the transformation vision and have not been confronted before. They pay great attention to who is promoted, who is hired, and how people are developed. They include new reengineering projects that are even bigger in scope than the initial ones. They understand that renewal efforts take not months but years. In fact, in one of the most successful transformations that I have ever seen, we quantified the amount of change that occurred each year over a seven-year period. On a scale of one (low) to ten (high), year one received a two, year two a four, year three a three, year four a seven, year five an eight, year six a four, and year seven a two. The peak came in year five, fully thirty-six months after the first set of visible wins.

Error 8: Not Anchoring Changes in the Corporation's Culture

In the final analysis, change sticks when it becomes "the way we do things around here," when it seeps into the bloodstream of the corporate body. Until new behaviors are rooted in social norms and shared values, they are subject to degradation as soon as the pressure for change is removed.

Two factors are particularly important in institutionalizing change in corporate culture. The first is a conscious attempt to show people how the new approaches, behaviors, and attitudes have helped improve performance. When people are left on their own to make the connections, they sometimes create very inaccurate links. For example, because results improved while charismatic Harry was boss, the troops link his mostly idiosyncratic style with those results instead of seeing how their own improved customer service and productivity were instrumental. Helping people see the right connections requires communication. Indeed, one company was relentless, and it paid off enormously. Time was spent at every major management meeting to discuss why performance was increasing. The company newspaper ran article after article showing how changes had boosted earnings.

The second factor is taking sufficient time to make sure that the next generation of top management really does personify the new approach. If the requirements for promotion don't change, renewal rarely lasts. One bad succession decision at the top of an organization can undermine a decade of hard work. Poor succession decisions are possible when boards of directors are not an integral part of the renewal effort. In at least three instances I have seen, the champion for change was the retiring executive, and although his successor was not a resistor, he was not a change champion. Because the boards did not understand the transformations in any detail, they could not see that their choices were not good fits. The retiring executive in one case tried unsuccessfully to talk his board into a less seasoned candidate who better personified the transformation. In the other two cases, the CEOs did not resist the boards' choices, because they felt the transformation could not be undone by their successors. They were wrong. Within two years, signs of renewal began to disappear at both companies.

There are still more mistakes that people make, but these eight are the big ones. I realize that in a short chapter everything sounds a bit too simplistic. In reality, even successful change efforts are messy and full of surprises. But just as a relatively simple vision is needed to guide people through a major change, so a vision of the change process can reduce the error rate. And fewer errors can spell the difference between success and failure.

Table 4.1. Eight Steps to Transforming Your Organization.

---

1. Establishing a Sense of Urgency
   - Examining market and competitive realities
   - Identifying and discussing crises, potential crises, or major opportunities

2. Forming a Powerful Guiding Coalition
   - Assembling a group with enough power to lead the change effort
   - Encouraging the group to work together as a team

3. Creating a Vision
   - Creating a Vision to help direct the change effort
   - Developing strategies for achieving that vision

4. Communicating the Vision
   - Using every vehicle possible to communicate the new vision and strategies
   - Teaching new behaviors by the example of the guiding coalition

5. Empowering Others to Act on the Vision
   - Getting rid of obstacles to change
   - Changing systems or structures that seriously undermine the vision
   - Encouraging risk taking and nontraditional ideas, activities, and actions

6. Planning for and Creating Short-Term Wins
   - Planning for visible performance improvements
   - Creating those improvements
   - Recognizing and rewarding employees involved in the improvements

7. Consolidating Improvements and Producing Still More Change
   - Using increased credibility to change systems, structures, and policies that don't fit the vision
   - Hiring, promoting, and developing employees who can implement the vision
   - Reinvigorating the process with new projects, themes, and change agents

8. Institutionalizing New Approaches
   - Articulating the connections between the new behaviors and corporate success
   - Developing the means to ensure leadership development and succession

---

Chapter Five

Breaking Away

Executive Leadership of Corporate Spinoffs

Donald C. Hambrick
Kristin Stucker

Although a great deal has been written about managing in the face of discontinuities, the vast majority of such literature has focused on adapting the organization to external jolts, such as technological, regulatory, or market changes. But discontinuities also can emanate from within the firm. An increasingly common organizational shift is the one that occurs when a subunit is spun off from a parent company, instantly becoming an autonomous entity with none of the constraints—or support—of the parent. Some recent spinoffs have been very visible, such as AT&T's spinoff of its equipment business (named Lucent Technologies) and computer business (NCR) and 3M's spinoff of its storage device businesses (Imation). These prominent spinoffs, however, are only the tip of the iceberg. According to Securities Data Corporation, as confirmed by a major investment bank, there were 137 major spinoffs between 1986 and 1990, 168 between 1991 and 1995, and 39 in 1996 alone.[1] Clearly, spinoffs represent a dramatically expanding phenomenon, a logical outgrowth of the well-documented trend for corporations to reduce domains to a coherent set of businesses that exploit yet reinforce their central competencies.

There is a widespread myth that spinoffs always have happy endings, yielding large increases in shareholder wealth through the liberation of assets from clumsy or burdensome parents. Certainly, some well-known cases perpetuate this myth. For instance, in its first thirteen months as an independent company Lucent Technologies outpaced the Standard and Poor 500 by 57 percent. (See Chapter One for a detailed account of the Lucent story.) But less well known are the spinoffs that fail. For example, Aviall, an aircraft maintenance business spun off in 1993 from Ryder, the truck leasing company, lost about 50 percent of its market value in its first year of independence; after three years it still had only about half its initial value even as the stock market was up about 40 percent.

So, contrary to widespread belief, spinoffs are not a sure-fire way to enhance shareholder value. Indeed, as we shall elaborate, about half of all spinoffs underperform the market—many by more than 50 percent. Although some do exceedingly well, spinoffs are occasions of simultaneous opportunity and peril. They can go on to great success or dismal collapse, but usually they do not end up in between as simply moderate performers.

If a spinoff is a high-risk, high-reward juncture for a business, what should spinoff executives do to successfully navigate this transition? The purpose of this chapter is to address this question, attempting to improve understanding of the managerial actions associated with postspinoff performance. We present preliminary conclusions from an extensive, multistage research project on spinoffs.[2] As will be seen, our proposals adopt a broad conception of the spinoff executive's (particularly the CEO's) responsibilities and challenges. Spinoffs succeed or fail depending on executive attention to external and internal constituencies, substantive decisions *and* symbolic initiatives, strategy *and* the organization, and change *and* continuity. That is, spinoffs are arenas calling for leadership in a total sense.

Background on Spinoffs

Spinoffs are distinctive as managerial situations for two interrelated reasons. First, a spinoff amounts to instant independence. A business that had been part of a larger firm is all of a sudden on its own—with its own board, investors, and assets. It has none of the encumbrances—or resources—of the parent. It faces the direct glare of external scrutiny. Other forms of ownership transition—such as being sold by one parent to another or having a large investor buy a major stake in a firm—are also jarring and noteworthy, but spinoffs are alone in their abrupt conferral of autonomy to an established business.[3] These are situations in which managerial discretion is sharply—and purposely—enhanced.

Second, and an ironic complement to the instant autonomy of spinoffs, is the fact that their performance prospects and their needed courses of action are largely dependent on the conditions they faced under their parents. Spinoff executives do not face a blank slate. The ways in which their parents managed or mismanaged them set the stage for potential improvements. Parents impose policies, wittingly or unwittingly, that may help or retard the subunit. Parents instill cultural imprints in their subunits, and these imprints affect the way the spinoff needs to be managed.[4] Moreover, the stature of the subunit and the way it was perceived within the parent firm provide a social milieu that affects managerial outlooks and behaviors in a spinoff.

On the one hand, then, spinoff executives are on their own, with no parental constraints or resources. But on the other hand, their opportunities for improvement lie in a deep understanding of the benefits and liabilities they drew from their parents. These two points are central to the development and presentation of our guidelines for spinoff executives.

The Logic of Spinoffs

A spinoff is a distribution of shares in a subunit on a pro rata basis to parent company shareholders. A spinoff typically begins with a public announcement of the parent's intention to spin off the subunit. Several months later, the transaction is consummated through the distribution of shares in the new company to existing parent shareholders. The shareholders are then free to hold their shares in the new independent company or sell them.

Spinoffs differ from other forms of divestitures—particularly the more common sale of a business to another corporation—in important ways. If they meet certain IRS requirements (and most do), spinoffs are done on a tax-free basis. Also, they yield no inflow of capital either to the parent or the spinoff.[5] Spinoffs are the only type of divestment that results in a new, publicly traded company. Finally, and of central importance here, spinoffs grant complete strategic and operational authority to the spinoff's management team—a group that is initially selected by the parent.

Among the various reasons a parent would opt to spin off a subunit, three are especially prevalent. First, the parent may believe that the operating performance of its core business will improve if the subunit is no longer part of the company. This could be the case if the subunit requires a disproportionate amount of capital or managerial attention. For example, it has been widely reported that one of the reasons Pepsi-Cola lost so much ground to Coca-Cola during the early 1990s was the distraction posed by Pepsico's very challenging restaurant chains. By spinning off its restaurant operations, Pepsico hopes to be able to redouble its efforts against Coke.

Second, the parent may believe that the subunit will be able to achieve better operating performance on its own. For instance, AT&T concluded that its equipment business could derive far more revenues from other telephone companies if those customers knew they were not supporting AT&T. Hence, Lucent was spun off. Similarly, the parent may be motivated to conduct a spinoff if it realizes that the key success factors for the subunit differ from those for the parent's other businesses. Additionally, if the parent believes that managers will act more in line with shareholders if they face the direct scrutiny of a board of directors and public disclosure of their results, it is likely to execute a spinoff.

Third, the parent may believe that, quite apart from any improvements in operating performance, the stock market will place a higher valuation on the parent and the subunit once they are split apart. This could occur because each firm comes closer to being a "pure play," with a more attentive following by security analysts and greater appeal as a potential takeover candidate. Fisher-Price's spinoff from Quaker Oats was prompted by management's recognition that investors in food stocks do not necessarily want to subject themselves to the wide fluctuations of the toy market. Three years later, Fisher-Price had doubled its stock price, and it was taken over by Mattel, a more appropriate match.

Evidence of the Merits of Spinoffs

To what extent are the objectives of conducting a spinoff achieved, on average? A comprehensive review of the literature on spinoffs is beyond our scope, but some key themes can be reported. The vast majority of empirical inquiries into spinoffs focus on the movement of the parent corporation's stock price at the time of spinoff announcements. These studies generally find a positive abnormal return in the several days prior to announcement and a further positive effect immediately upon announcement.[6] However, these upward ticks are not always sustained. In a recent study of 167 spinoffs between 1985 and 1995, Wruck and Wruck[7] found that the average parent's abnormal stock returns were significantly positive (2.35 percent) on the day of spinoff announcement, but that over the ensuing twenty days the returns were significantly negative (–2.47 percent), more than wiping out the one-day gain.

Research on the longer-term performance of parents (without their spun-off units) is sparse but suggests a favorable pattern. One study found that parents experience a 27 percent abnormal return over the two years following spinoffs.[8] However, removing those cases in which the parent had become a known takeover target caused the significant pattern to disappear. Wruck and Wruck found that parents had abnormally high returns for the first year following their spinoffs, but not beyond that. Overall, then, there is some indication that parents perform better without their spun-off subunits.

The evidence regarding the performance of the spinoffs themselves is more mixed. It appears that during the first few months of trading, spinoffs have negative abnormal returns[9] due both to a general unease about some of the new firms' prospects and the tendency of large institutional investors to sell their shares because the new firms do not meet the requirements of their portfolios. But it is in the next stage that the seemingly wondrous side of spinoffs reveals itself. Cusatis, Miles, and Woolridge,[10] for instance, found a 25 percent abnormal return to spinoff firms over the first two years of trading. With findings like these, it is not surprising to see magazine articles with titles such as "Pick Your Moment and Catch a Rising Spinoff."[11]

Puncturing the Myth: Perils and Opportunities Facing Spinoffs

Although spinoffs, on average, perform well in the first two or three years of their independence, a given one is not ensured of doing so. This becomes strikingly clear if we turn again to Wruck and Wruck's findings. The mean returns for the spinoffs they studied (net of the market's overall performance) were an enticing 22 percent during the first two years of independence. However, the median returns were –3.4 percent, indicating that actually slightly more spinoffs lagged the market than outpaced it. But just because this median is close to zero does not necessarily imply that most spinoffs experience such a return. Indeed, the facts are quite to the contrary: the lowest-performing quarter of Wruck and Wruck's sample lagged the market by a remarkable 52 percent or more, whereas the highest-performing quarter exceeded the market by 54 percent or more.

In our own analysis, we find the same tendency toward extreme postspinoff performance. For a sample of eighty-eight spinoffs conducted in the years 1990 to 1993, we find that the mean shareholder returns (again, net of the market) are 35 percent over the first two years of independence.[12] And, in line with Wruck and Wruck, we find a median return of close to zero: 7 percent. To shed more light on the degree to which spinoffs deliver extreme results, we generated a comparison sample of eighty-eight firms and examined their returns over the same two-year period as the spinoff sample.[13] We find that this comparison sample also has a median return (net of the market) of close to zero: –1 percent. However, the standard deviations of the two groups differ appreciably—134 percent for the spinoffs, 53 percent for the comparison group. This pattern of extreme performance is further highlighted when we examine the histograms of the two-year returns for the two groups, as shown in Figure 5.1. Whereas two-thirds of the comparison sample had two-year returns within 50 percent (plus or minus) of the market's, only slightly more than one-third of the spinoff sample were within this band. Nearly one-third of the spinoffs had performance that differed from the market—positively or negatively—by 100 percent or more.

It is clear that a spinoff is a consequential juncture for a business. There is a disproportionately great chance that the spinoff will do very well or very poorly, but relatively little chance that it will perform neutrally. As we might expect, independence presents both opportunity and peril. Freedom from a parent can bring exhilaration, entrepreneurship, and much-needed corrections. Or it can

Figure 5.1. Two-Year Market-Adjusted Returns of Spinoff and Comparison Firms.

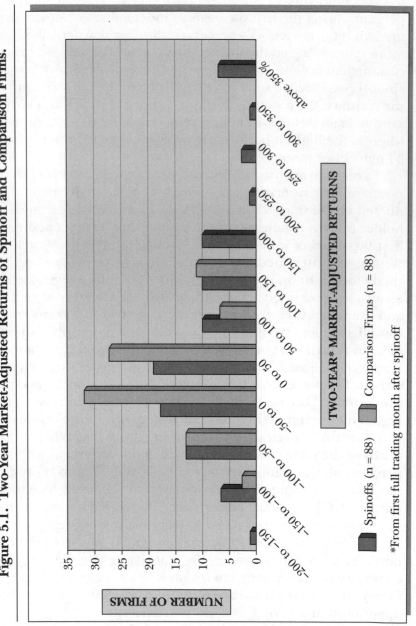

bring chaos, an identity crisis, severe shortages of needed resources, and—ironically—overcorrection.

Effective Management of Spinoffs

If spinoffs tend to become either big winners or big losers, the obvious and most important question to ask is, what factors affect the outcome for a given spinoff? Unfortunately, very little research has been conducted to explain variance in postspinoff performance. The few inquiries that have been conducted have focused primarily on such "givens" as the relative size and relatedness of spinoffs to parents, but with mixed results in explaining spinoff outcomes.[14] Our interest, however, is in managerial action: What should parent and spinoff executives do to increase the likelihood of spinoff success? Based on our research, we have identified seven major managerial guidelines that distinguish the most successful spinoffs from the least successful. Figure 5.2 summarizes these guidelines and their underlying rationales.

The first five guidelines derive from the opportunities and perils associated with a business that is abruptly on its own:

1. Assemble the required executive talent to meet expanded challenges.
2. Inject as much ownership incentive into the organization as possible.
3. Establish and communicate a clear vision.
4. Demonstrate reliability and legitimacy with key stakeholders.
5. Straighten out and strengthen the core business before embarking into new domains.

The final two guidelines build on the conditional context of spinoffs—the fact that their opportunities for improvements depend on the benefits and liabilities they drew from their parents:

6. Make changes proportional to the parent's mismanagement of the subunit.
7. Be artful in symbolically distancing the new company from its former parent.

Figure 5.2. Framework for Executive Leadership of Spinoffs.

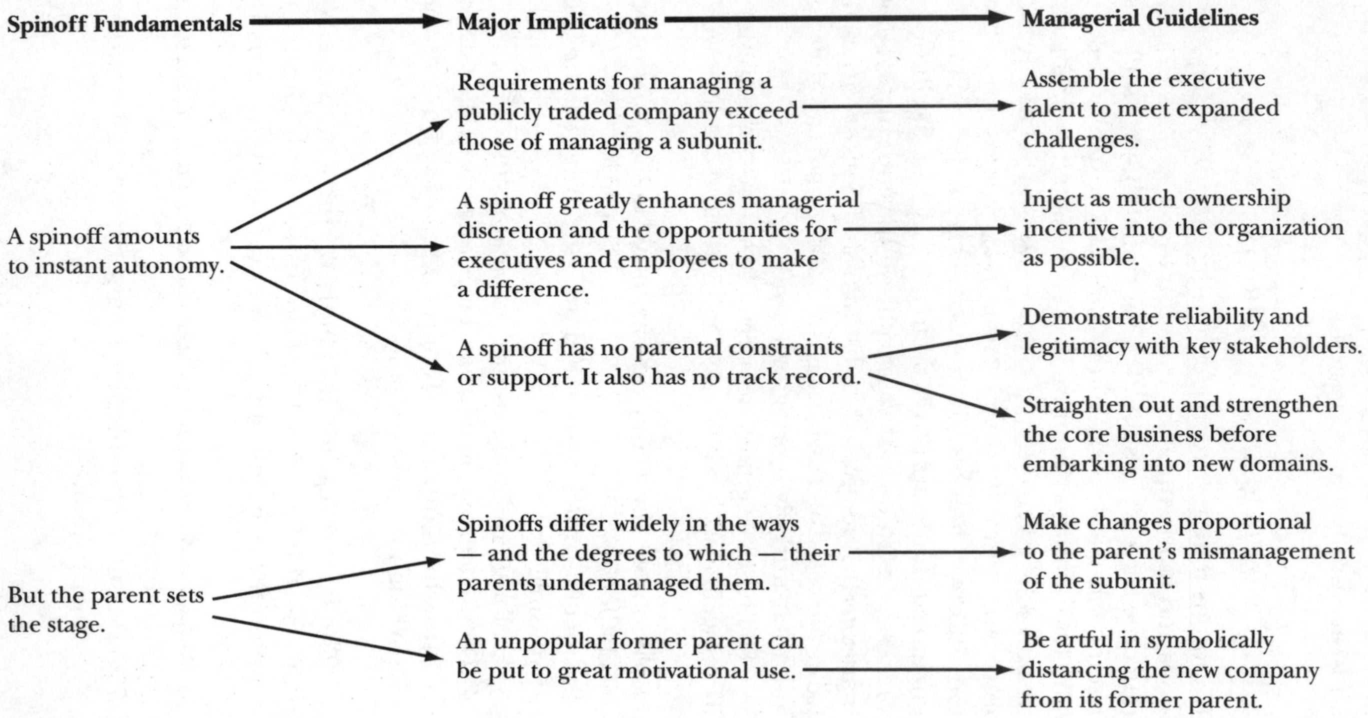

Spinoff Fundamentals	Major Implications	Managerial Guidelines
A spinoff amounts to instant autonomy.	Requirements for managing a publicly traded company exceed those of managing a subunit.	Assemble the executive talent to meet expanded challenges.
	A spinoff greatly enhances managerial discretion and the opportunities for executives and employees to make a difference.	Inject as much ownership incentive into the organization as possible.
	A spinoff has no parental constraints or support. It also has no track record.	Demonstrate reliability and legitimacy with key stakeholders.
		Straighten out and strengthen the core business before embarking into new domains.
But the parent sets the stage.	Spinoffs differ widely in the ways — and the degrees to which — their parents undermanaged them.	Make changes proportional to the parent's mismanagement of the subunit.
	An unpopular former parent can be put to great motivational use.	Be artful in symbolically distancing the new company from its former parent.

Thus our proposals span the realms of both substantive and symbolic managerial action; they are concerned both with external and internal constituencies, and they highlight a difficult tension between stability and reliability on the one hand and change and innovation on the other.

Assembling the Required Executive Talent

A corporate division that suddenly becomes a publicly held corporation typically needs executive capabilities well beyond those it possessed as a subunit. Even if the management team of the subunit were delivering satisfactory results, its members may well be in over their heads when the business becomes a stand-alone company. As a public corporation, the spinoff must deal with an array of challenging external forces, including the investment community, banks, regulatory bodies, and the press. And its executives can no longer look upward to corporate for advice and support, because they now *are* corporate. In our research, we have identified two major executive vulnerabilities in businesses that are slated to be spun off: the CEO position and senior staff positions (such as in finance, legal, human resources, and information technology).

The CEO of a publicly held corporation has responsibilities that far outweigh those of a subunit general manager. These responsibilities—particularly in dealing with investors, security analysts, the press, and other external parties—require knowledge and aptitudes that the general manager may not possess and may not be able to develop promptly. Some incumbent general managers are able to take on these expanded responsibilities with success, but many are simply not equipped for the new, broader challenges. We spoke with one CEO appointed after the board ousted his predecessor, who had overseen a two-year halving of the spinoff's stock value. The previous CEO, who had been generally effective as divisional manager, was vastly underprepared for the complexities of leading a publicly traded corporation. He badly mismanaged relations with the company's investors and creditors; and, with no experience in dealing with a board of directors, he withheld critical information that might have allowed some important corrections. Eventually the banks turned off their faucets, the board became fully apprised of the situation, and the new CEO was brought in to try to save the company.

A striking proportion of the most successful spinoffs have had new CEOs who were purposely selected for their qualifications to lead the newly public firm. When Pacific Telesis spun off its cellular telephone business AirTouch, its CEO, Sam Ginn, moved over to AirTouch and drew on his wealth of experience in dealing with investor groups, regulatory bodies, and the press—all to the great benefit of AirTouch. When AT&T spun off Lucent, it selected the renowned former CEO of Cummins Engine (and AT&T board member) Henry Schacht to be chairman and CEO of the new company, and paired him with Richard McGinn, who had been vice president of AT&T Network Systems (a major part of what became Lucent), as president. The results have been outstanding (see Chapter Two).

Sometimes the subunit general manager will make a superb chief operating officer in the new firm but needs to be complemented by another executive from the parent who has a strong financial or external orientation. For example, when CPC International recently announced the spinoff of its corn refining business, it appointed Samuel Scott, a widely admired executive in the industry who had headed the business under CPC, to be chief operating officer and president. It teamed him with a chairman-CEO, Konrad Schlatter, who had been CPC's highly regarded chief financial officer. He has the intensive understanding of the financial and legal communities that is so critical for publicly traded firms—especially new ones that need to quickly attract followings and develop reputations.

The second area where new executive talent is often needed is in senior staff positions. From our observations, there are two interrelated reasons why incumbent managers in staff areas may often not be adequate for their counterpart positions in the spunoff firm. The first has to do with the heightened need for first-rate technical and professional expertise in a publicly traded independent corporation, as compared to a division of a company. Again, divisional subunits are largely buffered from dealing with some of the most complex financial, legal, and human resource issues. Moreover, although part of a larger corporation, subunit staff executives are typically complemented at headquarters by far more

seasoned professionals who can help solve many complex technical issues. Once the unit is spun off, these complex issues become
more prevalent, yet the sophisticated resources at corporate are no
longer available. The new company might choose to outsource
some staff work, but even the decisions about outsourcing and the
management of those relationships require expertise that often exceeds the capabilities of the incumbent subunit executives.

It is humanly uplifting to think about the exhilaration, motivation, and drive that a group of divisional executives might experience when the business they run is set free. Across the board,
CEOs we interviewed and surveyed emphasized the feverish energy
surrounding the initial period of independence. But motivation
does not equate to horsepower. Thus we strongly caution against
the blanket assumption that subunit managers should run the new
independent entity. In fact, the working hypothesis should be that
some replacements—perhaps including the top person—may be
very warranted.

Injecting Ownership Incentive into the Organization

A primary reason for doing a spinoff is to expose an organization's
executives and employees to the rigors and rewards of the financial markets. The rigors inevitably are present: a spinoff receives
no subsidies, its performance is transparent and no longer hidden
within financial statements of the multibusiness firm, and vigilant
investors vote every day with their buy and sell orders. These are
rigors indeed and are thought to stimulate aggressive shareholder-
minded behavior by spinoff managers.

However, it is vitally important to include the rewards part of
this formula. A great benefit of focused, independent enterprises is
that they allow high-powered incentives[15] in ways that larger, more
diverse enterprises do not. High-powered incentives exist when individuals' contributions have a clear effect on unit performance
and they are rewarded for that performance, primarily through
ownership opportunities.

The most effective spinoffs are those that provide high-powered
incentives, primarily through equity opportunities. Senior executives should receive a substantial portion of their compensation in
the form of stock options or restricted stock grants. Similarly, other

employees should be encouraged to participate in employee stock-ownership programs or other vehicles for injecting ownership incentives throughout the organization.[16]

Spinoff firms are always smaller than the companies they were a part of, and about half are less than a quarter the size.[17] Reduced size significantly enhances the ability of individuals to make a difference and, in turn, increases the logic of paying them for overall company performance. One CEO we interviewed said there is a "different chemistry" in a smaller firm that enables employees to feel a greater sense of ownership. He emphasized that the smaller size has made a difference in his spinoff's ability to align management, shareholder, and employee interests. Whereas an executive at the parent firm might have owned twenty thousand shares and not felt an impact on the organization, that same manager in the spinoff would own more than 1 percent of the firm and know that he was making a big difference. Although their financial involvement or exposure had not changed, managers in the spinoff had greater incentives to operate in shareholders' interests as a result of being big fish in a small pond.

The focused, independent firm has the virtue of an incontrovertible performance metric—something perhaps lacking under its former parent—and must capitalize on that. Moreover, a central part of the formula for spinoff success is to harness and heighten the motivation associated with independence. At a minimum, this means turning anxiety in a positive direction; at another level, though, it means accentuating an already positive outlook and energy.

Establishing and Communicating a Clear Vision

As a newly independent entity, no longer part of a larger enterprise, a spinoff can easily confront an identity crisis: If we're not part of Company X anymore, then what are we? Who are we? What do we stand for? These types of questions will be asked explicitly or implicitly by employees at all levels; unresolved, they can lead to disorientation and wasted human energy. Accordingly, the spinoffs that perform best are those in which the top executives commit themselves to establishing and communicating a clear vision of the new company's mission, objectives, and values.

At Cytec, the industrial chemicals spinoff from American Cyanamid, top executives devoted an enormous effort to crafting and communicating the new company's vision and values. They involved a wide range of employees in the development process, and then they convened groups at all levels and used other media as well to explain and illustrate the new ideology ("First we will be the best, then we will be the first."). At Alliant, the defense system spinoff from Honeywell, there was similarly a major emphasis on clarifying the new company's vision. In this case, the employees were doubly uncertain of the company's viability and direction because of their separation from long-time parent Honeywell and the depressed condition of the defense marketplace. Senior management put in place an extensive communications and organization development effort, however, and were able to clarify how the split from Honeywell would be beneficial and how the new Alliant intended to distinguish itself as a premiere defense systems provider.

Naturally, the communication of vision and values cannot consist only of words. It must also occur through concrete deeds—the day-in, day-out actions taken by senior management. There must be a consistency of message that emanates from large decisions, as well as from small, mundane behaviors. At Cytec and Alliant, as well as Praxair, Gardner-Denver, and other highly successful spinoffs we have examined, senior executives placed a major emphasis on rapidly creating and reinforcing a vision and set of values for the newly independent company.

Demonstrating Reliability with Key Stakeholders

A blue-chip parent confers important legitimacy and credibility to its subunits. For example, being part of the lustrous 3M Corporation is a very valuable calling card for all its business units, opening up many doors on favorable terms. However, once a unit is on its own, such as 3M's Imation spinoff, it must quickly establish new legitimacy in the eyes of its key constituencies, including the investment community, creditors, suppliers, distributors, and the press. All these parties will look for early signs that the new company has the requisite resources, capabilities, and staying power for sound business operations. Spinoffs that cannot provide such evidence will be at a sharp disadvantage in their business dealings, setting off a downward spiral of doubtful legitimacy, slippage in support from stakeholders, even less legitimacy, and so on.

As part of its demonstration of legitimacy, it is essential for the spinoff to have a board of directors that will help convey credibility. It is especially important to enlist as board members the senior executives of highly respected firms and prominent figures in the financial community. Although having mere "celebrity directors" who can bring no substantial expertise or time to the affairs of the spinoff is not called for, it is essential that the board convey reassurance and, if possible, prestige. For example, the CEO of Eastman Chemicals, a spinoff from Kodak, expressly ruled out having "marquee names" on the board for fear that they would not or could not participate actively in board affairs, but instead assembled a group of eight distinguished outside directors, including six CEOs of other prominent, respected companies and two other individuals with strong ties to the financial community.

Additionally, it is crucial for the spinoff to be very selective in the professional service firms it engages. The spinoff's auditing firm, external counsel, and stock transfer firm, for instance, should be selected not only for their substantive expertise but also for the important symbolic or representational roles they fulfill. Because the identity of these service firms is a matter of immediate public record, their reputations attach themselves to their clients, conveying some measure of credibility and reassurance of stability. New spinoffs must be very mindful of the prestige of the professional service firms they enlist, which vary widely. In one case, a spinoff CEO whose former parent company was undergoing intensive audits purposely chose a different Big Six accounting firm—in his eyes, the one with the greatest reputation for caution and thoroughness—as a means of disassociating the new firm from the troubled parent and to signal strength.

As a new, unknown, untested firm, the new spinoff also may need to mount a significant public relations and identity campaign, enlisting the services of a high-quality PR firm. This can be useful not only in influencing the investment community, but also for energizing other stakeholders, including employees, about the strength and prospects of the new firm. Lucent Technologies, which launched a multimillion-dollar advertising campaign to develop brand awareness and a company identity, has been rewarded in part because of these efforts. In stark contrast, Airtouch Communications' management felt that the publicity surrounding the spinoff was sufficient and so did not undertake its own PR campaign. Even though its operating performance has been solid, the company has met with considerable coolness from the stock market, in part, we believe, from its inattention to communicating a clear identity.

In short, spinoff managers must carefully monitor the impression they give to potential investors and analysts, as well as to other constituencies. Newly traded firms, often viewed skeptically, can help establish their legitimacy by bolstering themselves with highly respected board members and professional service firms and by forcefully communicating their vision and identity.

Straightening Out and Strengthening the Core Business

Although a spinoff may be energizing, it is also organizationally stressful. Therefore, it is critically important to stabilize and strengthen the core business before attempting strategic expansions. Moreover—to repeat a theme—it is essential that the spinoff quickly demonstrate its reliability and stability to stakeholders, showing that it can operate effectively on its own. To do so, the spinoff needs to attend to its existing domain—its current products and markets—by improving market penetration, quality, and efficiency before taking on whole new endeavors.

In some cases, this first step to strengthening the existing business may involve actually *reducing* the scope of activities, getting rid of the least productive assets and cleaning out the underbrush as a precursor to new growth. In our survey research, we found that high-performing spinoffs (those with two-year shareholder returns that exceeded their industry sectors) differed from low-performing spinoffs in their emphasis on consolidation in the first year of independence: the high-performing spinoffs had engaged in less expansion of their product lines, less expansion of their asset bases, and less expansion of their workforces (all differences significant at $p < .05$). What is additionally remarkable is that the executives in high-performing spinoffs also indicated that their philosophy of refocusing continued beyond the first year. They reported, for instance, that in their second year of independence they had engaged in less expansion (than low-performing spinoffs) of their work-forces and their assets. Thus, it appears that the task of strengthening the existing business—before expanding the product-market domain—is not accomplished in a matter of weeks or even months, but rather may require substantial effort for a year or more.

The spinoff of Cytec, an industrial chemicals business, from American Cyanamid is a case in point. Prior to the spinoff, the business had been involved in a wide array of segments ranging from cutthroat commodity products, such as nitrogen fertilizer, to highly specialized but tiny categories, such as liquid light sticks. Cytec's CEO, Darryl Fry, emphasized a new strategy of "lopping off" these two tails and instead focusing on a limited set of segments that met the dual criteria of being inherently attractive and in line with Cytec's competencies. Cytec's recommitment to this narrower set of businesses meant that its efficiency improved greatly. In Cytec's first year of independence, overall sales were up only negligibly (reflecting some advances in its core segments, net of major withdrawals from other segments), but net income went from a large loss to a profit and the stock price doubled.[18]

Alliant Techsystems, a military munitions supplier, was spun off from Honeywell because Honeywell was no longer interested in the defense industry. Toby Warson, who had been in charge of Honeywell's United Kingdom operations, was brought in to run the new firm. Although Alliant's prospects at this point were poor, Warson felt that he would have a lot of leeway to make necessary changes at an independent company and so accepted the challenge. He consolidated an unwieldy organizational structure, cut employees by 20 percent, and reduced unnecessary layers of management. Then and only then did he consider adding products and generating new areas of business. Over Alliant's six years of independence, the firm has consistently outperformed its defense industry peer group as well as the overall market, due in great part to Warson's initial emphasis on fixing the core enterprise first.

We do not mean to imply that new spinoffs should entirely avoid entrepreneurial activities such as pursuing new products and new markets. However, for the vast majority of spinoffs, such initiatives should follow consolidation and stabilization. First and fore-most, spinoffs must demonstrate their viability. Early failures, or even minor stumbles, can cause severe damage to stakeholders' confidence in the new firm. And because product-market expansion is inherently risky, it is generally not a prudent course for a new spinoff. Fortunately, however, as at Cytec and Alliant, there are usually improvements that can be made in the new enterprise that do not entail early major risks. As we shall now see, knowing how much change to inject into the business is one of the most essential judgments required of spinoff executives.

Making Proportionate Changes

Facing the fresh breeze of independence and feeling the need to show their stand-alone capabilities, spinoff executives are sorely tempted to make many changes quickly. However, the amount and direction of change needs to be carefully calibrated to match the degree to which the subunit was undermanaged or mismanaged by the parent. In some cases few changes will be warranted, and the spinoff executives must recognize this and show restraint. In other cases, as we noted with Alliant, an array of organizational changes will be highly useful. And in still other cases a combination of both organizational and radical strategic alterations are called for.

It is essential to recognize that not all spinoffs are done in an attempt to improve operating performance in the spinoff business. Some spinoffs are intended primarily to improve the performance of the parent's other businesses, and some are prompted by the hopes that higher stock valuations (for either the parent or the spun-off business) will be accorded for already high levels of operating performance. If a spinoff fits one of these profiles, its executives should try to avoid making unnecessary changes that could actually weaken an already strong performer and that additionally could expose the company to risks of early stumbles, which spinoffs cannot afford.

When are major changes most warranted? The most obvious case is when the business has been performing poorly—either absolutely or within its industry. The worse the performance, the greater the need for changes on all fronts—qualifying as a classic turnaround situation. (It is worth noting that very few spinoffs are severe, chronic underperformers, as such businesses would be met with disastrous initial reactions from the stock market. When a parent wishes to divest a severely troubled business, it almost always sells the unit to another corporation or to an investor group specializing in turnarounds.)

Significant changes are also warranted if the parent had been imposing policies or constraints that were unsound for the business, causing it to perform below its potential. Sometimes these policies are overt, such as requirements for prompt capital payback or strict adherence to company-wide pay programs when these are simply at odds with conditions facing the business. But often intrusions by parents are more subtle and elusive to detect. For example, Darryl Fry, the CEO of Cytec, commented on how the parent American Cyanamid's philosophy about R&D was a drain on its business:

> Cyanamid emphasized basic research in all areas. This approach worked well on the agricultural side, so the decision was made to drive it through the entire company. It was a disaster in chemicals. We spent 3 percent of sales in the chemicals business in "discovery research." One of the first things I did when I went to chemicals was have someone do research on exactly how many new molecules discovered in the world of industrial chemicals over the last twenty-five years had more than $50 million in sales today. We guessed there might have been six to ten, or maybe more. There were a lot in Medical and Agriculture. It turned out that in the chemicals business the answer was zero. Not one. The last one was Cyanoacrylate, which formed the basis for Loctite (the active ingredient in Super Glue), but that was more than twenty-five years old.[19]

In the thin-margin industrial chemicals business, American Cyanamid's norm of spending 3 percent of sales on discovery research was severely damaging. Once on its own, Cytec stopped this spending and put more money into process technology, which was far more appropriate for its business context. A parent like Cyanamid may imprudently impose not just one policy or norm but dozens or even hundreds. Thus a spinoff may allow numerous important corrections to be made.

In our research, we have concluded that the likeliest condition for a parent to have imposed imprudent policies is the one represented by American Cyanamid and Cytec, in which the spun-off business is moderately similar to the parent's core business. If the parent and the subunit are greatly dissimilar, the parent is likely to have recognized the dissimilarity and managed the subunit at arm's length, allowing considerable autonomy. This is not to say that the parent will have allowed the subunit to achieve its full potential, but it is relatively unlikely that the parent will have injected many decisions that affected the configuration and practices of the subunit. At the other extreme, if the parent and subunit business are highly similar, it is relatively unlikely that the parent's policies will have been seriously unwise or unsuited for the subunit. (There is of course the possibility that the parent is not very adept even at managing its core businesses!) But in the middle condition—when the parent thought it ought to know a lot about how to run the subunit but in fact did not—the likelihood of a history of unwise parental intrusion is greatest. In turn, the needed postspinoff changes in such situations may be abundant.

Another condition prompting the need for considerable change in the spinoff firm is when the subunit had been operationally interdependent with other parts of the parent firm—say, sharing resources or engaging in a buyer-supplier relationship. It is likely that such interdependence would have led to a great deal of parental intrusion into the subunit, as part of its attempts to harmonize relationships or adjudicate disputes between the units. Moreover, once such a subunit is spun off, there is a void where a relationship had existed. This void might constitute a genuine loss (say, if another unit had been sharing its technological developments), or it might be a boon (as when another unit marketed the company's products halfheartedly). In either case, changes are needed and warranted.

In our research, we have found that the most fruitful and pivotal changes in spinoffs are typically organizational rather than strategic. That is, effective spinoff executives are those who act vigorously on their understanding of the administrative breakthroughs that can be achieved by a business that is on its own. These include changes in reward systems, controls and measures, information and communications flows, and decision processes. It is in these areas that parent firms can have particularly adverse effects on their subunits by injecting bureaucracy, homogenization, and incrementalism. Airtouch CEO Sam Ginn echoed this conclusion when he told us, "My philosophy of management hasn't changed, but my ability to execute it has." At Pacific Telesis—even as its CEO—Ginn's ability to implement new ideas was limited by a large bureaucratic organization that was resistant to change.

One of the chief objectives of many spinoffs is to liberate the subunit from the organizational shackles of a parent. The sixty-four respondents to our survey seemed to show this understanding. They were asked, "If you could do it over, what would you emphasize as needed changes in the first year of the spinoff?" Of numerous items presented (encompassing products, markets, capital structure, workforce, and so on), the three highest-rated items by far were these:

1. Alter reward system
2. Realign organizational structure
3. Alter performance review system

Thus, looking back and learning from their successes and failures, these spinoff executives recognized the major opportunities for organizational improvements after life in big, diverse, cumbersome parent firms.

In sum, spinoff executives should embark upon changes only in proportion to the need for them. The need is generally greatest when the business has been a poor performer, when the parent's business and the spinoff business are moderately similar (drawing unwise intrusions by the parent), and when the spinoff has been interdependent with other of the parent's businesses. The most promising changes are in organizational practices, more so than in strategy.

Being Artful in Distancing Spinoff from Parent

One of the major opportunities facing spinoff executives is to motivate and catalyze their organization by symbolically putting the parent in the past, verbalizing and accentuating how much better the business can perform without it. Indeed, heaping disdain on a vilified former parent can be very motivational for the organization, particularly if the subunit had not been well regarded within the parent firm.

For example, accounts from Cytec executives indicate how their industrial chemicals business was seen within American

Cyanamid: "the poor folks," "dregs," "dirty bathwater," "dog," "black sheep," and "third-class citizens." Darryl Fry, Cytec's CEO, took advantage of the residue of these feelings by emphasizing how Cyanamid's structure had been conservative and bureaucratic, inwardly focused and wasteful. He dedicated his top management team to crafting a vision and values statement that set Cytec apart from the Cyanamid mentality; he purposely picked a spartan headquarters building in a blue-collar part of New Jersey, in contrast to the opulent campus headquarters of Cyanamid. Cytec's top executives—even though all long-term Cyanamid employees—became convinced that they were mavericks.[20] That is, the former parent was set up as a villain to be proven wrong or inept.

It may only be in extreme circumstances that as much symbolic distancing from the parent can occur as did at Cytec. Even then, the distancing needs to be done carefully, and perhaps differently for internal parties than for external parties. External constituencies may value the reassurance and reminder that the spinoff has its roots in a larger, well-established enterprise and, by extension, is reliable and legitimate. So, for instance, Lucent Technology's massive advertising campaign emphasized its AT&T origins. Similarly, Imation made clear that it had been part of the 3M family. These identity campaigns were primarily for external consumption, to develop broad awareness about these new companies. By contrast, the rhetoric and positioning used internally was aimed primarily at accentuating the gulf between the parent and the new business. For example, within a matter of a few weeks after independence Lucent managers at all levels came to realize the motivational benefits in ridiculing the AT&T bureaucracy—but only internally, because AT&T is Lucent's biggest customer. The difference in external and internal messages reflects that symbolic distancing from the parent must be done artfully.

Conclusions

Spinoffs are becoming more and more common. And, as we have reported, they tend to become big winners or big losers, with sizable stakes hanging in the balance. In this chapter we have drawn upon our research to set forth major guidelines for helping parent and spinoff executives navigate this risky transition. We have taken a positive, affirmative approach, proposing what managers should do. But, after talking with executives and analysts as well as studying the sagas of numerous spinoffs, we can also voice the prevailing pitfalls encountered by spinoffs—highlighting what *should not* be done.

Spinoff executives must not think of themselves as unbridled entrepreneurs, at least not at the outset of the spinoff. Their actions need to acknowledge the new company's lack of legitimacy; early stumbles can be fatal. Actions must be geared to the degree and type of underperformance the unit suffered under its parent. Very often, restraint is most called for. Spinoff executives do not face clean slates.

Conversely, spinoff executives must not think that the only thing that has changed is that their business is now publicly traded. We have seen evidence of this no-big-deal mentality, and when it occurs the results are usually catastrophic. Although technically a spinoff is merely a change in ownership control, this new status poses an array of accompanying opportunities and risks. Effective spinoff executives will recognize and address the new complexities of autonomy, the challenges of securing resources that were once provided by the parent, and the motivational potential of independence. A spinoff is not simply a financial reshuffling. It is a vibrant arena for executive leadership on a host of fronts.

Notes

1. These data are for U.S. spinoffs only. Spinoffs occur in other countries as well, and are especially becoming more popular as a means of corporate restructuring in Western Europe.

2. To this point, we have surveyed available literature, identified a definitive sample of spinoffs conducted between 1985 and 1996, conducted interviews with twenty executives in spinoff firms, and conducted a survey of executives in forty-one spinoffs that occurred between 1990 and 1993. The sixty-four survey respondents allow quantitative insights into executive actions in spinoff companies, which complement the qualitative interview data. As next steps, we intend to continue our data collection (particularly adding data on concrete company characteristics and changes from annual reports and other public filings). We then will integrate the data we have obtained from multiple sources to examine in depth how spinoff contexts differ in the managerial actions they elicit, as well as the effects of those actions on performance. This chapter primarily is intended

to provide guidance to managers who head up spinoffs. Parent firm executives who are preparing subunits for spinoff may also find these ideas helpful. Additionally, we hope our insights will be useful to investors and analysts who need to assess the prospects and progress of spinoffs, and of course to scholars of executive leadership.

3. Management buyouts bear some similarities to spinoffs, but because of their high debt levels do not allow as much managerial autonomy or discretion.

4. To qualify as a tax-free spinoff under IRS guidelines, the business must have been part of the parent firm for at least five years. Thus, some amount of cultural imprinting is likely to exist.

5. Some spinoffs, however, are preceded by initial public offerings (IPOs), which serve a dual purpose: raising additional capital for the spinoff and providing parent and spinoff executives an advance indication of stock market interest in the new firm.

6. See, for instance, Kudla, R. J., and McInish, T. H. "Divergence of Opinion and Corporate Spinoffs." *Quarterly Review of Economics and Business,* 1988, *26*(2), 20–29; Miles, J. A., and Rosenfeld, J. D. "The Effect of Voluntary Spin-Off Announcements on Shareholder Wealth." *Journal of Finance,* 1984, *38*(5), 1,597–1,606; Slovin, M. B., Sushka, M. E., and Ferraro, S. R. "A Comparison of the Information Conveyed by Equity Carve-Outs, Spin-Offs, and Asset Sell-Offs." *Journal of Financial Economics,* 1995, *37,* 89–104; Rosenfeld, J. D. "Additional Evidence on the Relation Between Divestiture Announcements and Shareholder Wealth." *Journal of Finance,* 1984, *39*(5), 1,437–1,448; Seward, J. K., and Walsh, J. P. "The Governance and Control of Voluntary Corporate Spinoffs." *Strategic Management Journal,* 1996, *17,* 25–39.

7. Wruck, E. G., and Wruck, K. H. "Codependent No More? How Spinoffs Affect Parent and Spinoff Firms' Performance." Working paper, Harvard Business School, 1996.

8. Cusatis, P. J., Miles, J. A., and Woolridge, J. R. "Restructuring Through Spinoffs: The Stock Market Evidence." *Journal of Financial Economics,* 1993, *33,* 293–311.

9. Brown and Brooke, 1993.

10. Cusatis, Miles, and Woolridge, 1993 (see note 8).

11. Dunkin, A. "Pick Your Moment—And Catch a Rising Spinoff." *Business Week,* May 13, 1996, p. 156.

12. This figure does not include four extraordinary outliers whose two-year market-adjusted returns were in excess of 1,000 percent.

13. For each firm in the spinoff sample, a comparison firm from the same index group assigned by Bloomberg was randomly selected. For instance, the comparison firm for Alliant Techsystems, a munitions

spinoff from Honeywell, was randomly drawn from the Standard and Poor's Small Aerospace and Defense Index Group. Both the sample and the comparison firms' performance were adjusted for the S&P 500 performance for the two-year postspinoff period, beginning with the first full trading month.

14. See, for example, Cusatis, Miles, and Woolridge, 1993 (see note 8); Woo, C. Y., Willard, G. E., and Daellenbach, U. S. "Spin-Off Performance: A Case of Overstated Expectations?" *Strategic Management Journal,* 1992, *13,* 433–447; and Wruck and Wruck, 1996 (see note 7).

15. Zenger, T. R., and Hesterly, W. S. "The Disaggregation of Corporations: Selective Intervention, High-Powered Incentives, and Molecular Units." *Organization Science,* 1997, *8*(3), 209–222.

16. Careful execution of an employee stock ownership plan, however, should be a reflection of managerial foresight rather than just a knee-jerk, token effort. One new spinoff was eager to reverse the parent's lack of employee participation programs. On the first day of independence, management gave each employee one share of stock with a one-cent quarterly dividend. With stagnant performance, it continued mailing out three thousand one-penny checks every quarter—a huge waste of badly needed resources and the source of Dilbert-like derision from employees. In contrast, Lucent gave all employees one hundred stock options valued at $44 each (and not exercisable until 1999), which was enough to rivet everyone's attention to company performance and their role in achieving it.

17. Forty-seven percent of spinoffs in our 1990–1993 sample were traded on a one-to-four (or more) basis, so that shareholders received one share in the spinoff for every four (or more) shares they held in the parent.

18. Roper, S. P., and Wruck, K. H. "Sink or Swim? Cytec Industries Spin-Off." Harvard Business School case 9–897–053, 1996.

19. Roper and Wruck, 1996 (see note 18), p. 5.

20. Roper and Wruck, 1996 (see note 18).

Part Three

Taking Action: New Strategies for Transformation

Chapter Six

Leading Learning and Learning to Lead

An Action Learning Approach to Developing Organizational Fitness

Michael Beer

> *There are no great men. There are only great challenges*
> *that ordinary men like you and me are forced by*
> *circumstances to meet.*
> ADMIRAL WILLIAM F. "BULL" HALSEY[1]

Leading, changing, and learning are virtually synonymous. One cannot contemplate dramatic change occurring within an organization without the exercise of some leadership. The leader must mobilize organizational members to understand the nature of the adaptive challenge and engage them in a process by which the organization does its adaptive work. And an organization does not change fundamentally without significant reorientation and learning by its leaders and members. Without learning, the attitudes, skills, and behavior needed to formulate and implement a new strategic task will not develop, nor will a new frame by which selection and promotion decisions are made.

In this chapter I argue that the leadership of change is too often thought to require the acts of a single heroic individual, frequently a new CEO or general manager. He or she is thought of as the source of vision and energy for change. Heroic leadership brings with it, however, several unintended and undesirable by-products. Such leaders are not told if their ideas are invalid or unimplementable, they do not receive feedback about how they contribute to the ineffectiveness of the organization, they create dependent or counterdependent subordinates, solutions they develop fail to encompass diverse perspectives, and they create unrealistic and unachievable goals.[2-5]

By playing a dominant heroic role, leaders also prevent the development of leaders at multiple levels in the company. Such a wide distribution of leadership is essential if a company is to renew itself continuously in response to rapid change in its environment, something that is essential in today's competitive world.[6]

Why, despite the many negative consequences of heroic change leadership, has it become the dominant model? Historically, frame-breaking changes are most often brought about by CEO succession or wholesale replacement of the top team.[7] It is not clear, however, to what extent this pattern is conditioned by the relatively low skills of senior executives in promoting an organizational learning process and by a cultural context that does not value, and may even prevent, learning. Some evidence exists that a small number of high-performing firms are able to anticipate environmental shifts and achieve frame-breaking organizational transformations without replacement of the CEO or wholesale replacement of key executives.[7,8] These firms possess the capability to learn from their own experience, and their nonheroic leaders appear to be skilled in leading that learning process. What of those firms, however, that do not possess this capability? Are they doomed to move from crisis to crisis and heroic leader to heroic leader? Or can their leaders learn to lead a transformation that will both improve immediate performance and create the cultural context needed for continuous adaptation?

Intervention theory and method has not focused sufficiently on the possibility that strategic change can be motivated by a carefully designed action learning process that confronts the fit between strategy, organization, and leadership behavior. Such a process could guide CEOs or business unit managers in leading frame-breaking changes in their respective organizations, at the same time developing their leadership skills and transforming the organization's capability to learn. Nor have such methods been used to learn about the deep barriers that appear to block existing leaders from preventing their own demise and that of their organization.

Of course, such an action learning process would have to be powerful. That power can, I will argue, be obtained from an organizational conversation—a dialogue between the top team (also referred to later as the leadership team) and lower-level people concerned with implementing the strategic task of the organization. The dialogue would have to provide valid data about how well strategy, organization design, organizational capabilities, and leader behavior fit each other.[9-14] And that data would have to be subjected to a rigorous analysis of and reflection about inevitably emotional issues that block leaders from fitting their behavior to strategically driven organizational requirements.[3, 15]

Lacking the capacity for an open dialogue and rigorous analysis of how leader behavior fits strategy and organization, it is inevitable that fundamental transformations in corporations occur only after financial crisis leads to the replacement of the CEO and his top team. Although this appears inevitable given present leadership skills and social technology, the economic and human cost of waiting until a crisis creates a revolution are sufficiently high to warrant a search for an alternative to the heroic leadership model we argue dominates the landscape of change.

Using the lens of an action learning process called Organizational Fitness Profiling, which fosters an organizational conversation between the leadership team and key actors at lower levels, I propose that a far less heroic model of organization change is possible. If institutionalized, it offers corporations the possibility of developing the very leadership skills they now lack while developing the capability for organizational learning needed to manage in a dynamic environment.

An action learning approach to change such as Organizational Fitness Profiling is also more consistent with reality that only a very limited number of leaders possess the will and skill needed to transform their business. To avoid the cost of ever-increasing turnover of CEOs and their top teams, a need exists for an institutionalized process for change that can guide leaders and from which they can learn. That process would have to foster a valid dialogue between leaders and followers about how leader behavior and the instruments of their leadership—organizational design and management process—shape organizational effectiveness. If that process were the norm, defensive routines could not and would not prevent the transparency organizations require for ongoing learning. The results would be both organizational change and leadership development.

The Myth of Heroic Leadership

In an era of intense global competition, demanding standards of performance by capital markets, and rapid technological change, the will to lead change and the skill to do so are in great demand. It is not surprising, therefore, that the short supply of great leaders who can create dissatisfaction, inspire, motivate, and develop urgency has become apparent to researchers of managerial behavior. Kotter reports that, when asked, managers overwhelmingly say their organization has too many managers whose skills are to plan, organize, and control and too few who can unleash energy, the "force for change."[16, 17]

As the competitive environment has continued to intensify, change has increasingly become synonymous with heroic leadership. CEOs such as Jack Welch of General Electric, Jan Carlzon of SAS, and Lee Iacocca of Chrysler have been heralded by academics and the business press as models of effective leadership to be emulated by others. Nadler, in Chapter One of this book, describes Henry Schacht's leadership of Lucent Technology's transformation from a subsidiary of AT&T to a successful independent company. Dissatisfied, strong, visionary, urgent, focused, inspiring, tough, demanding, disciplined, intense, and passionate are among the adjectives used to describe the personal attributes required by managers who hope to lead their companies from the brink of failure to the high road of success. Change leadership is increasingly being portrayed as an inherently personal affair in which the leader provides the will and skill the organization requires to move through a discontinuity in its environment. Consider the words of Intel CEO Andrew Grove as he equates his experience in managing the crisis in memory chips, faced by Intel in the early 1980s, with a movie image.

> Managing, especially managing through a crisis, is an extremely personal affair. Many years ago, in a management class I attended,

the instructor played a scene from the World War II movie *Twelve O'Clock High*. In this movie, a new commander is called in to straighten out an unruly squadron of fliers who had become undisciplined to the point of self-destruction. On his way to take charge, the new commander stops his car, steps out and smokes a cigarette, while gazing off into the distance. Then he draws on the last puff, throws the cigarette down, grinds it out with his heel and turns to his driver and says, "Okay Sergeant, let's go."

Our instructor played this scene over and over to illustrate a superbly enacted instance of building up the determination necessary to undertake the hard, unpleasant, and treacherous task of leading a group of people through an excruciatingly tough set of changes—the moment when a leader decides to go forward, no matter what.

I always related to this scene and empathized with that officer. Little did I know when I watched that movie that I would have to go through something similar in a few year's time. But beyond experiencing this crisis personally, the incident that I am about to describe [the memory chip crisis] is how I learned with every fiber of my being what a strategic inflection point is about and what it takes to claw your way through one, inch by excruciating inch. It takes objectivity, the willingness to act on your convictions and the passion to mobilize people into supporting those convictions. This sounds like a tall order and it is.[18]

Having taught *Twelve O'Clock High* many times, I found compelling Grove's comparison of General Savage, the movie's hero, to the CEO who must lead a transformation. *Twelve O'Clock High* is indeed an idealized example of how an individual can change the standard of performance in an organization singlehandedly and mobilize its energy to master a difficult and dangerous task. Savage embodies the qualities of a charismatic *and* instrumental leader.[5] He personally mobilizes energy through his determination, vision, modeling, and communication. And Savage manages to foster change through the skillful use of structure, selection of lower level leaders, symbols, the reward (promotion and demotion) system, and training. These induce, shape, and reinforce the behavior needed to succeed at the task.

I have often used the film as an example of best practice in leading change. Savage's leadership of change is consistent with a number of ingredients of effective change about which I have written:

for example, the importance of creating dissatisfaction with the status quo, changing behavior by focusing on the task, fostering learning by doing instead of classroom training or other human resource programs, a clear model or vision of the future state, and the importance of using the change process to develop or replace key actors in the organization.[6,19]

Yet the idea that these key ingredients of change can be developed only by strong heroic leaders does *not* match with my experience or research—crises like that faced by Savage notwithstanding. Few leaders whom I have studied or with whom I have consulted were charismatic and heroic.[6] Indeed, it is not clear that the rhetoric about heroic leaders reflects what really goes on behind the scenes.

Even in a time of war, General Savage found it necessary to develop a top team (an adjutant and operations officer) to inform and support him in his efforts to lead a change in the Wing's effectiveness. He had to seek support from pilots who rebelled against his stern tactics and threatened him with an investigation by the Inspector General. And the film ends with his mental breakdown, despite some successful efforts to develop allies. In the end he was the lonely hero who led the change against all odds. He owned the decisions and their consequences—the death of pilots he sent on difficult missions, the stress of flying missions himself, and his inability to share his feelings about all this with others.

Despite Andrew Grove's use of General Savage's character to describe what it takes to lead strategic change, in other parts of his book Grove paints a far less heroic picture of how he led change. He used the knowledge and views of other managers to develop a better understanding of the competitive problem facing Intel and he promoted a widespread debate among his managers to help him and them understand the challenge. These steps led him to develop his convictions and created support in the organization. And he reports that the change from a memory to a microprocessor business had already begun to occur through a multitude of manufacturing capacity allocation decisions made at lower levels in the organization. In effect, Intel began the transformation from memories to microprocessors well before top management could articulate that vision. Grove strongly implies that his awareness of the strategic challenge facing Intel came considerably after that awareness had penetrated the periphery of the company. He states that CEOs are often the last to know what is happening in far-flung markets or in diverse parts of the organization, and he recommends debate and participation to inform and move the CEO to recognize the need for change.

Could it be that the desire of CEOs to appear competent and in control has biased their report of what it takes to lead change? Is it equally likely that employees' need for strong leadership makes it difficult to ascertain exactly how much of the force for change comes directly from the CEO rather than through interaction with and learning from others? A burgeoning literature and a good deal of empirical evidence suggests that managers, the media, and academics alike may be making a fundamental attribution error when they construe that a decline or increase in organizational performance is due to leadership. According to Meindl, Ehrlich, and Dukerich, this "romanticized conception of leadership results from a biased preference to understand important but causally indeterminant and ambiguous organizational events and occurrences in terms of leadership."[20]

Consider the case of Don Rogers, a relatively new general manager in Corning's Electronic Products Division with whom I consulted many years ago.[21] Rogers successfully led an organizational transformation as measured by changes in behavior and performance. Yet, unlike Savage, he embodied few heroic qualities. Though he was tall, smart, outgoing, and very bright, he was also new in his job, had never been a general manager, was uncertain about why his division was experiencing interfunctional conflict and poor performance, was seen as not tough enough by subordinates, avoided conflict, and did not have a diagnosis or a vision.

To offset these liabilities Rogers formed a new top team with which he felt he could work. He engaged me as a consultant and accepted a lot of feedback about his organization and his leadership. He was even willing to have his own deficiencies as a leader exposed to all salaried employees in a presentation to them. Rogers was far from the strong, certain, and fully competent leader we are told is needed to transform an organization.

When I teach the Corning cases, I am always struck by how critical senior executives discussing the case are of Rogers's leadership. Not finding a hero, they assume that the organizational and cultural changes Rogers is sponsoring will fail. Rogers is simply not as demanding and confronting as the heroic model of change leadership suggests. In classroom discussions, senior executives often conclude that he must be replaced. They rarely see that Rogers and his people were embedded in a new structure and management process from which they were learning by doing and that this learning takes time.

Students are dumbfounded to discover that the organizational changes Rogers led actually succeeded in transforming the organization and its performance. He used his top team to articulate a clearer strategy; he allowed himself to be influenced by the voice of employees about problems and by new ideas about how to redesign the organization. These succeeded in transforming the behavior of the leadership team and that of other employees. And Rogers and his team learned to use themselves more effectively to rally others in the organization. Students are even more amazed to learn that Don Rogers became the president of Corning a few years later. He had led learning but in the process also learned how to lead.

The case of Don Rogers at Corning exemplifies a vast majority of organizational change efforts. Rogers's lack of skill and uncertain will is quite similar to that of many business leaders. The cry to replace nonheroic Rogers is also typical. The recommended action for any performance problem is almost always to change the leader.[22] It is rarely to develop a process of change from which leaders can learn. Yet in reality executives rarely have the mythical heroic qualities of General Savage or Jack Welch. As Merck CEO Ray Gilmartin has observed, there are no great men and women.[23] Moreover, as discussed in the introduction to this chapter, heroic leadership prevents the development of the organization and its people, particularly lower-level leaders. A careful study of Jack Welch would show that his demanding tough-guy approach early in the change had to be supplemented with a second people-and-learning-oriented approach to change embodied in the GE "Work Out" program. John Reed had to follow his top-down revolution in Citibank's back room in the 1970s with a "people program."

If heroic leaders are not widely distributed in the population nor capable of developing effective organizations, we need a better and generalizable model of strategic transformation. And we need to develop processes for change that simultaneously transforms the organization and develops the leadership qualities of its managers. The story of Don Rogers suggests that change leadership need not and does not typically depend on a single leader. It can emerge from a partnership between leaders and organizational members, as Intel CEO Andrew Grove suggests, though the leader may need the help of a consultant or specified change process (or both) from which the organization and the leader can learn.

In the last decade Russell Eisenstat and I have been engaged in developing a partnership process for leading continuous change. Our premise was that leadership is best thought of as a high-involvement action learning process, not the sole responsibility of a single person. Agenda setting, networking, inspiring, motivating, and mobilizing commitment to action have been conceptualized as the job of the general manager.[24, 25] Given the scarcity of leaders and the undesirable by-products of heroic leadership, we wondered why these same tasks could not be accomplished by a partnership between organizational leaders and members. Such a process would mobilize energy for change while modeling and developing the participative leadership style that enables high-performing firms such as Hewlett-Packard, for example, to manage revolutionary change without wholesale replacement of its leaders.[7, 26, 27] Leaders are not born; they develop through a process of apprenticeship— learning by doing. In a world where there is a scarcity of competent leaders to guide managers in becoming change leaders, a carefully designed and highly specified process in which the acts of effective change leadership are embedded is needed.

The process Russell Eisenstat and I developed came to be called Organizational Fitness Profiling.[28, 29] We have learned from its application what blocks strategic change and we have tested and evolved our initial understanding of what a guided change process that simultaneously changes organizations and develops its leaders might look like.

The Organizational Fitness Profiling Process

In 1988 Eisenstat and I were engaged by the top management of Becton Dickinson (BD), then a $1.5 billion global medical technology company, to help the company develop greater capability to implement strategy. The company's call for help was prompted by difficulties they were having implementing a new "Transnational Organization" emerging from the work of Bartlett and Ghoshal.[30] One of the company's principle corporate strategies was to drive its products worldwide where the company's existing medical products were in higher demand then in the more mature U.S. market. The transformation to a transnational organization proved to be far more challenging than management anticipated.[31] Laying lateral worldwide teams, led by U.S. division presidents, over strong country organizations in Europe and several other parts of the world ran into substantial difficulties. Transnational Management, it turned out, was not the only place where the organization was not aligned with the strategic vision laid out by Becton Dickinson CEO Ray Gilmartin. Several other corporate strategies were blocked by poor coordination between business units and between the corporate marketing and R&D organizations. Top management was also dissatisfied with the capacity of divisions to implement their own strategies.[32]

Gilmartin and many of his key executives had been strategy consultants earlier in their careers. The company had developed excellent strategy, employing a process called Strategic Profiling. That process, facilitated by trained line and staff managers, requires the top team to confront a series of questions about the business and its environment. The questions represent commonly accepted analytic frameworks required for good competitive analysis and strategy formulation.[33] When we were approached by Becton Dickinson about how to solve its strategy implementation problems, the idea of developing a parallel process that would motivate change in the organization and its leaders immediately sprang to mind.

Gilmartin, who had just taken over as president in 1988, became convinced that managers at Becton Dickinson lacked the will or skill to lead a high-involvement change process that would align organizational design, culture, and behavior with the organization's strategic imperative. We were intrigued by the possibility of developing a process that would guide the CEO and business unit general managers in realigning their organization with strategy. Several decades of research, theory, and practice had established that strategy implementation requires that the organization "fit" the environment and the firm's chosen strategy.[9, 11, 13, 34, 35]

Developing an organization aligned with new and emergent strategies would require leadership. A hero-centered model of change leadership would, however, have required the overnight replacement of many of BD's senior executives. This was not an option at BD any more than in many other situations. First, BD's strategically oriented top management was better at analysis then leading strategic change. Therefore, it could not easily discern deficiencies in change leadership among the division managers. One has to possess leadership attitudes and skills to see them in others. The orientation and skills of division managers, therefore, reflected top management's own orientation and skill. Even if top management could discern ineffective leaders and unaligned organizations, it could not quickly replace all the divisional presidents short of a crisis. Such an action would jettison vital business knowledge and relationships, be perceived as unfair, destroy trust, and unsettle the organization in a major way. Nor could new divisional presidents with mastery of the business be found quickly and attracted to BD easily. Even if such executives were available, their capacity to lead would be significantly impaired by a cultural context that did not value, support, or reinforce effective leadership and radical organizational change.

Becton Dickinson faced the problems of many corporations that are short of leaders with change management skills. Short of a new heroic CEO and a totally new executive team, the capacity to lead change cannot be obtained quickly or easily. Convinced by a large stream of research on the inadequacy of education and training programs, these capabilities, we thought, could not be developed in a massive educational effort.[6, 36, 37] Learning to lead had to be a by-product of leading change.

Organizational Fitness Profiling, the process that emerged, is an action learning process by which a leader and his or her top team can assess how well organizational behavior and design and their own behavior as leaders fit the strategy and values espoused by them. Simon has argued that all organizations have nonprogrammed decision processes by which purpose and goals are defined and the organization is designed and redesigned. He suggests that decision-making processes like these depend heavily on judgment, intuition, and creativity, but that they can be enhanced through heuristic problem-solving techniques.[38] Fitness

Profiling attempts to provide the decision-making context, valid data, and a heuristic problem-solving technique that will enhance decisions typically blocked by defensive routines and normally made in an ad hoc, unsystemic, unsystematic manner.[39]

An external or internal consultant facilitates the process. Depending on his or her expertise, the profiler, as the consultant is called, may also act as a resource to the top team on questions of strategy, organizational design, and change. A detailed manual provides less expert managers and consultants with the underlying theory of the process, step-by-step guidelines for how they can move through various phases of the process, and a heuristic framework for making organizational design decisions. The process incorporates a number of steps described below:

> A two-hour preliminary discussion with the general manager to gain commitment begins the process. It is followed by a half-day orientation and contracting meeting with the top team, which must demonstrate conviction that there is a business case for change and make a joint go or no-go decision. In a one-day meeting, which follows, the top team develops a consensus statement of its goals, strategic task, and values.

An eight-person employee task force (ETF) one or two levels below the top is selected by the top team. The top team as a group nominates one or two people in each organization who are among the best performers, perceived by the team and others to be objective, capable of confronting the top team with difficult issues, and who will be trusted by other employees to maintain the confidentiality of their views. Top team members have to agree on the employees finally selected.

Employees are told that the organization is undergoing an examination of its capability to implement strategy.

Over the course of a day, the ETF receives the statement of goals, strategy, and values from the general manager, and then selects for interviews between eighty and one hundred employees in their organization one or two levels below the top team. This preserves the anonymity of interviewees. The sample of employees includes some in other organizational units who are involved in implementing the target organization's strategy—for example, a sales force, international subsidiary, or internal customer for its product or service. Within the target organization the task force selects employees from every function. Task force members usually know exactly who these employees are. In some instances external customers have been selected to be interviewed.

Task force members are trained in basic interviewing methods, interview each other for practice, and reflect on their experience in the context of the interviewing principles they were given. The results of these practice interviews are included in the final data set analyzed later. In this way task force members have a voice in the process as individuals but can retain the stance of reporters when they feed back the data to the top team.

Over two or three weeks, confidential interviews are conducted by the ETF with employees in the sample selected. Each task force member interviews people outside their function or department. Interviewees are provided the statement of strategy and asked: Do you agree with the strategy? What are the organization's strengths and barriers to implementing the strategy? Additional probes may also be developed by the task force. These may reflect questions that the top team would like answered—for example, about the quality of teamwork between functions they identified in their one-day strategy meeting as key to implementation. Usually the task force also adds questions that reflect their hypotheses about key barriers. Typically, however, 80 percent of the relevant data is obtained in answer to the broad questions about the strategy, and about strengths and barriers to its implementation.

Simultaneously, the consultant interviews the top team with the same questions the task force is using in its interviews. But he or she also asks the following questions: How effective is your top team? What is your perception of the leader's role in helping or hindering the team from being effective?

After completing the interviews, the ETF spends a day analyzing the data it has collected and organizing it into key themes. Using their interview notes, ETF members are asked to nominate the three strengths and barriers that most interviewees mentioned. The task force is advised to screen out issues that were mentioned by only one or two interviewees. A final consolidated list is created by dropping issues that have not appeared on the list of most task force members or by consolidating similar issues.

The next step in the process is an Organizational Fitness Profiling meeting, which lasts three days. Day one begins with an introduction and norm setting for an open, nondefensive, fact-based dialogue. The idea that good communication includes advocacy and inquiry is introduced.[39]

Task force members, *acting as reporters,* feed back their findings by sitting around a table facing each other while the top management team sits in a U-shaped arrangement around the task force. This arrangement, known as a "fishbowl," enables the task force members to talk among themselves while the top team listens. They discuss what they heard in their interviews about each of the key themes into which they organized their data the previous day. Though names of interviewees are withheld to preserve confidentiality, the function, business unit, or department from which the viewpoint comes is not, unless of course naming the unit would identify the source. The fishbowl takes between four and six hours. A rich picture of the organization emerges.

Because one of the objectives of Fitness Profiling is to enable the leader and the top team to explore their effectiveness as a leadership team, the task force departs following its report. This also enables a more efficient process in moving through the remaining agenda of the Fitness Profiling meeting.

Although the objective of forming a partnership between the top team and lower levels is not served by excluding the task force, experience suggests that the top team must work on its own development before establishing a partnership with the task force, something that happens at a later step in the process. However, to establish some connection between the top team and lower levels at this early stage, task force members call the people they interviewed immediately after they leave. They describe the receptivity of the top team and the quality of communication, but do not reveal the substantive issues they raised.

During the late afternoon of the first day, the consultant feeds back findings from interviews with the top team. In most instances their views of organizational strengths and barriers are identical to that of employees. However, they have far better data about the dynamics in their team. Facilitated by the consultant, a discussion of these dynamics follows and major issues are engaged. If this discussion goes reasonably well, as it has in virtually all instances, it sets the stage for a productive discussion in the remainder of the meeting.

On day two, the top team performs a diagnosis using a systemic organizational model (Figure 6.1). The diagnosis focuses on the

Figure 6.1. Organizational Fitness Model.

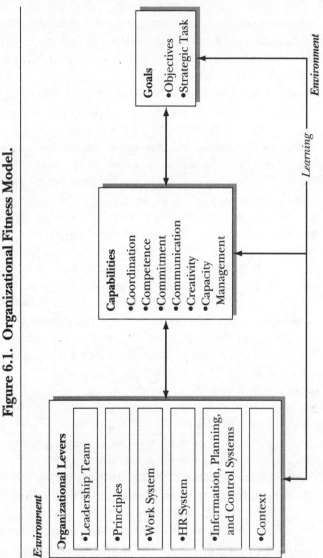

leadership team as well as the organizational design—structure and roles, human resource system, the information and control system, and principles and values.

On day three, a broad vision of the future state is developed with regard to the leadership team, principles and values, and organizational design; design teams are formed to sharpen the redesign of the organization. Participants reflect on the meeting and what they have learned about their organization, employees, and selves.

Later, the top team meets for a day with the ETF to review its work, receive critique, work through differences, and reformulate the change plan. The leadership team follows up by informing the whole organization about planned change through town meetings.

The top team reviews the work of the design teams and authorizes implementation, and the Fitness Profile is repeated periodically to assess progress and to continue change and learning.

The design of the Organizational Fitness Profiling process reflects several normative assumptions about how organizations can transform themselves into more effective institutions. Organizational effectiveness is a process of mutual adaptation between competitive realities, leader values and behavior, existing people and culture, and organizational design.[9, 11-13] Because managers who can lead this process of mutual adaptation are in short supply, as argued earlier, corporations would be well served to institutionalize a planned process that exposes gaps in fit between strategy, organizational behavior, organizational design, and leadership behavior. Such a process requires valid data about the tensions between espoused strategy and values and enactment within the organization. That data is widely distributed in the organization. It needs to be collected, analyzed, and made discussable in a systematic manner so that a vision of the future state can be created.[40]

Human defensiveness, however, makes it very easy for managers to avoid the tough strategic and behavioral issues that block better fit. The process should, therefore, enable leaders to learn about gaps between their espoused theory of the business and organization and their theory in use.[3, 15, 39] And the process should specify the leadership behavior required to change the organization. This enables unskilled change leaders to move through the change process and learn through enacting it. The learning comes from doing and the doing reveals gaps between requisite and actual leadership assumptions, skills, and behavior. The metaphor we have used is that of bicycle training wheels: the process guides and supports, prevents crashes, and develops confidence.

Of course, like any developmental process, Fitness Profiling is also an evaluation process. It provides an assessment of organizational fitness and leadership capability. Managing the tensions between development and evaluation is one of the major challenges in implementing and institutionalizing this process.

Many organizational change efforts violate the assumptions underlying the Organizational Fitness Profiling. The result is new organizational arrangements and practices that fail to achieve their potential.[6, 37, 41] Becton Dickinson's top management found it difficult to implement the structure of Transnational Management because the diagnosis and action plans did not incorporate an explicit discussion of organizational behavior and culture, the leadership team, and the CEO's own behavior and assumptions. Indeed, a Fitness Profile of Becton Dickinson conducted with the CEO and his top team surfaced a number of hidden leadership and organizational issues and their underlying assumptions.[32]

The organizational conversation about hidden issues and the contention and actions that follow can, we argue, serve as the force for change when the general manager has the will to lead change and learn from the process. Organizational Fitness Profiling operationalizes the process of inquiry, discussion, diagnosis, debate, and action that several other authors in this book (Pascale, Heifetz and Laurie, Quinn and Snyder) would agree is an essential ingredient in adaptive work—the work managers must do to reconceptualize their organization and themselves in the light of changing circumstances.

Six Hidden Barriers That Reveal a Nonheroic Model for Leading Change

Fitness Profiling is an open-ended inquiry process. Members of the employee task force commissioned to collect data present interviewees with the goals and strategy developed by the top team and ask the following question: What are the strengths of the organization, and what barriers do you see to implementing this strategy?

A content analysis of the data collected by task forces across many different organizations at the corporate and business-unit level yielded an alternative, nonheroic view of what it takes to lead an effective organization and change it. Task forces consistently identified six significant and interdependent elements of leadership that were in dangerously low supply in their organization. An ineffective leadership process and the lack of skills to enact it prevented the organizations, they reported to top management, from implementing and reformulating the new strategy top management had said was essential for success.[29] Task forces identified the following barriers:

- *Unclear strategy and conflicting priorities:* Employees had not heard the strategy articulated previously, it did not make sense to them, or the priorities of various functional departments were inconsistent with each other and the articulated strategy.
- *An ineffective top team:* Employees perceived lack of cooperation and agreement at the top. Members of the top team met infrequently; when they met the agenda was filled with administrative rather then strategic issues. Consequently decisions were made one-on-one between the general manager and subordinates. They did not come out of group deliberations. General managers perceived that top team members approached problems with a functional rather then general management perspective.
- *A top-down or laissez-faire leadership style by the general manager:* The leader dominated the top team or went around them to gather information and give direction. Or the leader did not engage the top team sufficiently to confront and resolve conflicts between them and their departments.
- *Poor coordination and teamwork across key interfaces:* Functions, business units, or geographically dispersed entities whose close coordination was needed to implement the strategy efficiently and effectively were making decisions without consulting each other.
- *Poor vertical communication:* Lower levels did not feel top management was communicating their vision and strategy clearly or forcefully. They, in turn, could not be honest with the top team about business problems or perceived organizational

barriers to implementing the strategy including management's own behavior.

- *Inadequate management and leadership skills and development throughout the organization:* Key managers below the top team were perceived by employees to lack management and leadership skills. They were perceived as narrow, parochial, and insufficiently motivated by the objectives of the organization as a whole. This was often attributed to an inadequate career development system. Managers felt stuck and undervalued.

Considered singly these leadership and organizational deficiencies are not new. What was striking to us, however, was that they often were a syndrome: if one was present, the others almost always were too. In a word, that syndrome might be labeled ineffective management or leadership.

The barriers are interdependent and mutually reinforcing. Good coordination, the organizational behavior needed to implement or change virtually anything in the organization, is clearly dependent on an effective leadership context. There has to be agreement on strategy and priorities. To have agreement at the top, the leadership team must be effective—its members must be capable of debating with each other and the leader and be capable of coming to a unified view of strategy and organization.[27, 42] To have an effective top team and effective coordination, the general manager had to engage the organization through his top team as opposed to going around them and driving change personally. Forcefulness in pushing process, not content, was important, however; laissez-faire leaders who did not engage their team in constructive debate were equally ineffective. The three barriers that emanate from the top are themselves interconnected and mutually reinforcing. Teams may be ineffective because of the leader's behavior. Conflicting priorities are a function of an ineffective team. Leaders go around their top team if they lack the will or skill to engage their team in the constructive conflict needed to shape a team and a vision.

What made it hard for organizations to engage these barriers were the last two barriers. These seemed to moderate the depth, pervasiveness, and length of time an organization was mired in the syndrome. Low quality and frequency of communication between the top team and key managers, one or two levels below them, caused two problems. Lower levels often did not know, understand, and sometimes agree with the strategy. And they found it virtually impossible to communicate with the general manager and the top team about how behavior at the top was causal to the difficulties the organization was experiencing. At Becton Dickinson, for example, it was the CEO's singlehanded and dominant role in the strategic management process as well as ineffective teamwork between domestic divisions, R&D, corporate marketing, corporate supply chain management, and the International Division that made it difficult to implement the corporate strategy.[32]

Employee task force members in almost all organizations were both eager to participate and anxious about their assignment. They were energized by the opportunity to help straighten out the organization, but they were concerned about having a candid communication with the top about the real problems they knew existed. Would they embarrass and hurt top management? Would this hurt their acceptance or career prospects? Many task forces started their feedback to the top team with the phrase "don't shoot the messenger." Their words and behavior reflected the barrier of poor vertical communication with which almost all top teams were presented. Without good upward communication, however, top teams had been unable to learn about their ineffectiveness until they were confronted in the profiling meeting.

The last barrier, inadequate leadership and management skills and development throughout the organization, seems to be both a result and a cause of the organization's inability to change. In all the companies, the new management paradigm that they were attempting to adopt was a lateral team organization—worldwide strategy teams at Becton Dickinson, or new product development or business teams in various other organizational units. A team-based organization demanded more leaders with far better skills. These skills did not exist because ineffective top teams did not typically have open and frank conversations about the capabilities and potential of managers in their respective organizations; talking candidly about managers reporting to peers might damage relationships with them. Moreover, ineffective top teams did not possesses leadership skills to assess and develop leadership in lower-level managers. Nor were members of ineffective top teams ready to transfer their best managers to other parts of the organization for development. And they did not delegate responsibility. Lower-level managers, in turn, did not take leadership responsibility for changes they thought necessary. Anxiety about upward feedback by managers on task forces helps explain why lower-level managers are reluctant to risk leading change.

The picture that emerges from this analysis is far from the ideal of heroic leadership. Indeed, the barriers cannot be overcome by strong heroic leaders; in many cases they are the ones who create the barriers. Instead, effective leadership of change requires a process that embodies inquiry, decision making, and action within the top team, between functions, and between the top team and lower levels. For this to occur, constructive conflict and mutual influence must dominate these relationships. Empowerment, the new paradigm many companies want to enact, is impossible without it. And without empowered managers, the general manager is left no alternative but heroic leadership.[22] Open dialogue about substantive business and organizational design issues is not enough, however. The dialogue also has to include examination of process and behavior—"what is really going on in this organization and why."[43, 44] We found that without this dialogue the organization and its managers could not learn about the pattern of organizing and leading that was blocking their effectiveness. As with Don Rogers at Corning, the willingness of leaders to be vulnerable seems far more important than heroic leadership.

Consider a top management team that instituted cross-functional teams to develop new products. A year after teams had been put in place, top management had failed to learn from them that their own behavior violated their espoused theory of organization and management. According to team members, top managers were still making decisions. Teams were simply executing; as team members put it, "we are go-fors." Team members had not found a way to tell top managers that their behavior was not consistent with the change they claimed to champion.

Virtually all change initiatives—attempts to change strategy, structure, systems, staff (through better selection and training), culture, and leadership itself—are blocked by the inability to surface, diagnose, and act on an ineffective leadership process represented by the six barriers. In other words, the hard or soft aspects of the organization cannot be realigned in any fundamental way with a new strategic direction without engaging and overcoming the six leadership barriers. Avoiding the barriers through a series of change initiatives that disconnect hard from soft and rational from emotional does not work either. These programmatic efforts result in cynicism and low commitment, the enemies of change.[6] What appears essential is an action learning process such as Organizational Fitness Profiling.

Overcoming the Hidden Barriers

Can a carefully crafted action learning process such as Fitness Profiling help managers, with uncertain will or skill, to lead change and learn from leading? In particular, does Profiling expose the hidden barriers to leading change? Does the process enable the mutual adaptation of strategy, organizational design, organizational capabilities, and leadership behavior? Can leaders learn to lead from enacting a highly specified process in which are embedded the elements of leading strategic change? Does the process sustain leadership will and skill to lead an organizational learning process?

The answers to these questions that follow are based on our analysis of the Fitness Profiling process and its outcomes in many different organizations. Profiles were conducted at levels ranging from CEO to business-unit manager and in several cultures as diverse as Japan, continental Europe, and South America. The quotes included come from two organizations.[32, 45]

Did Organizational Fitness Profiling
expose hidden barriers and motivate change?

As the discussion of hidden barriers indicated, Profiling succeeds extremely well in raising and opening for discussion typically undiscussable issues of leadership behavior and effectiveness. Survey results at Becton Dickinson, where the process has been applied widely, clearly showed that top teams and task force members thought this happened.[46, 47] We know of no instance where the Employee Task Force has not been able to obtain honest data from organizational members or where the fishbowl method has not enabled them to deliver between 90 and 95 percent of the data.

Occasionally, individual feedback for members of the top team are smoothed a bit, but the essential message gets through. Moreover, a longitudinal study of one company undergoing Fitness Profiling confirmed that the data surfaced and issues engaged were valid, fundamental, and vital to corporate competitiveness. Issues fed back by a corporate task force to a CEO and his top team in 1988 continued to be the focus for organizational change initiatives led by his successor in 1995. Consider the following description of Profiling by a division president:

> Fitness Profiling allowed us to discuss the undiscussable: it got things on the table that would have taken me years. Getting feedback from the employees is indispensable, and putting it into a strategic context is important. We were there to discuss behaviors that were consequential; it wasn't personal. We discovered things that would help us succeed or that were preventing us from succeeding. They were strategic issues, such as delivering the goods and services to our customers better than our competitors. Once we decided it was strategic, we had to fix it or suffer the consequences; no one is willing to suffer the consequences of gradual loss of competitive position.

The key to success of the feedback process lies in management's selection of its best people, in the fact that task force members are reporters of others' views, and in the fishbowl method itself. The fishbowl enables task force members to speak to each other and as a group—much less threatening than making an individual presentation and speaking for yourself. Because the issues are raised in the context of business strategy, personal feedback is not taken personally, so to speak. Indeed, the report of the task force covers all facets of the system—leadership and organizational behavior as well as harder issues of strategy, structure, and systems.

The feedback also has a very powerful effect on leaders, particularly when the leader has been in the organization for some time and the data reflects his or her leadership. The data is received by general managers as an appraisal of their leadership and stewardship and it motivates them to act. Because feedback comes from their own employees, it has face validity and obligates general managers to act. And task force members are powerfully motivated and affected by the experience. In one organization that has institutionalized Fitness Profiling, being selected to be on the task force is coveted. Consider the reports of a general manager and a top team member.

Division President

I had known that there were some serious issues in the division that needed to be addressed. But when these problems were spelled out in detail to me and my staff by a group of employees, the situation took on a whole new light.

Some of the task force feedback directed at me and my staff was pretty hard to swallow. Frankly, I am not sure I would have taken it as seriously as I did if those remarks had been coming from a group of outside consultants. Instead, it is very difficult to ignore tough feedback when your own people are the ones giving it.

The work that the employee task force did was extremely impressive. They operated much like a professional consulting firm, except unlike consultants they were a part of the organization and knew it inside and out. I think they worked so well together because they believed in what they were doing.

Top Team Member

I was taking a lot of notes, but all I could think of the whole time was, how did it get this bad? The discussion between the top team and how we worked together was even more painful. The whole thing was easily the worst day of my career. In my room that night I was considering writing a resignation letter, until I realized that Scott probably couldn't accept it. It hit me that we were in up to our necks now and there was no turning back.

Does the process enable mutual adaptation of strategy, organizational design and capabilities, and leadership behavior and values?

An assessment of organizational changes resulting from Profiling indicates that the answer to this question is yes. In some instances deficiencies in the strategy itself were voiced by the task force and acted on by the top team. In virtually all instances, organizational design—particularly structure, business and decision-making processes, and accompanying roles and responsibilities—has changed.

At Hewlett-Packard's Santa Rosa Systems Division (SRSD), for example, task force data about conflicting strategies and priorities pursued by two departments endangered the implementation of the division's emerging systems strategy. As a result of Fitness Profiling, the top management team was able to engage in an open discussion of why the conflict existed. It discovered that the cause was a complex interaction between a number of elements in the organization's social system—the general manager's assumptions about the best process for decision making at the top, the organization's design (particularly the allocation of decision rights), different assumptions about strategy and how to organize the business, and interfunctional and interpersonal conflicts—that emerged from an organization design that promoted conflicting strategies. This discovery led to the design of a matrix organization in which business managers would be responsible for ensuring coordination of all functions. It also resulted in the redesign of the management process within the top team and a redefinition of roles, decision process, and norms within the top team and within business teams.[45] Consider the following views by a participant in the process, a production manager speaking a year after the Profiling:

> What was really important was that we really understood what the process was trying to do—that is, align the different parts of the organization. I think that the alignment we now have after the reorganization is both accurate and necessary for us to become an effective organization. In the small systems business that we have, there is no way of getting around the [new] matrix structure. In the past there was no clear level of top management responsibility and ownership for key decision making. . . . That is something that is vital for strategic success of SRSD, and it is something that the matrix is able to provide.
>
> Back before the profiling process, the morale of SRSD's employees was at an all-time low. There weren't too many people that thought we had a prayer as a new division. But the reorganization really lifted people back up and energized us to start moving to where we thought we needed to go as a systems business.

Does Fitness Profiling develop a more
effective leader and leadership team?

As the discussion of hidden barriers indicates, virtually all leaders and top teams received feedback about the role they played in blocking the organization from adapting to new strategic realities. Because these issues were placed in a strategic context, leaders and their teams were motivated to deal with them. All leadership teams targeted change in the content and process of their management work—usually budgeting more time for strategic issues. Of course, these changes were gradual and only regular use of Profiling could give members of the organization confidence that the top team was still open to and struggling with change. Consider the observations of a task force member two years after the Profile.

> Our top team has taken some big strides in becoming more effective. Scott [the general manager] looks to be taking more control of the reins and becoming the kind of leader the division needs. He and his staff will sit down as a group now and talk strategy where before they would have only talked about administrative detail. But they are still not where they want to be as a team. They still seem to be having a tough time getting together and really coming to agreement over some tough and pressing issues. I think people in SRSD wanted an overnight change in the top team's behavior. But, realistically, most good teams are not made in a day. They will have to work at it.

Though personalities did not change, of course, CEOs and general managers did change their roles, time allocation, and approach to the job. For example, one CEO altered the dominant role he played in the strategic management process of the firm, enabling sector presidents to take responsibility for running their businesses. A division manager stopped going around his top team to direct and intimidate lower-level managers. In some cases Profiling motivated general managers to take action on subordinates they had long known to be ineffective.

How could the perception of leadership effectiveness change without a change in the leader or his or her personality? When effectively and consistently implemented, Fitness Profiling transformed the six barriers into emerging strengths. Lower levels had influence over top team behavior, and improving effectiveness at the top—tackling strategic issues and communicating decisions with one voice—gave lower levels confidence in their leaders. A more unified top team translated into a perception of stronger leadership by one general manager, for example, even though his less than charismatic leadership style had not changed. And CEOs and general managers felt they had learned a lot about leadership from engaging in Fitness Profiling. As one general manager said, "I have learned more about leadership through this process than I have in my whole career."

The fact that task force members were the best and most credible employees and were conversing face to face with the top team made it difficult for leaders to ignore the feedback. General managers understood that if they did not respond to the feedback they would lose credibility as leaders. Future change initiatives, they knew, would be accompanied by cynicism.[6]

There was a considerable difference, however, in the amount of leadership development that took place as a result of Fitness Profiling. New CEOs and general managers were generally more open to learning. They had fewer strongly held assumptions about the job and how it should be carried out. Moreover, the barriers new general managers were confronted with were not of their own making. Consequently they were less defensive. This is not to say that established general managers did not work hard to overcome the organizational and managerial problems they discovered through Profiling. They were highly motivated to do so initially, but their lack of perseverance over time caused some to allow the change process to atrophy. They and their organizations changed to some extent, but not as deeply and long-lastingly.

The most important ingredient for learning how to lead change is the openness of the manager to learning, which depends on readiness to be vulnerable, which in turn is a function of differences in individual leaders and in the norms of their corporation. For example, less controlling and more secure individuals were more likely to learn from Fitness Profiling. Companies and bosses that valued winning, being in control, appearing competent, and staying away from emotionally laden issues were less likely to encourage managers to learn about their leadership capabilities.[39]

These findings suggest that organizations wanting to foster ongoing organizational and personal learning will have to institutionalize an action learning process such as Fitness Profiling. In these companies, general managers would review with high management what they learned about their organization, their top team, and themselves. And they would become accountable for progress in transforming barriers into organizational strengths. The formal process of inquiry and action would force organizational and leadership development. The next section discusses some factors that we found enabled or prevented institutionalization of Fitness Profiling.

> Does Fitness Profiling sustain the will
> and skill of managers to lead
> an organizational learning process?

There is little doubt that Fitness Profiling was successful in enabling an organizational conversation about normally undiscussable barriers to realigning strategy, organization design, organizational capabilities, and leadership behavior. In all instances a valid and systemic agenda for change was set.[47] Some organizations have gone through three iterations. One company successfully applied Profiling in some fifty different branches as part of a strategic realignment of its eleven-thousand-person field sales and service organization. A division of Hewlett-Packard has applied Profiling four years in a row, each time developing a new agenda for organizational change.[45]

Not all organizations have persevered, however. Perseverance seems to depend on the belief of the CEO or general manager that Fitness Profiling helped them improve their performance and that of their organization. That in turn is, of course, a function of how strong the need for assistance was at the time Profiling was first undertaken. When Fitness Profiling was perceived to have been instrumental in improving the organization and its performance, it came to be valued and was adopted as a core process for action learning from which all change initiatives will emerge. Consider the perceptions, one year after Profiling, of the general manager of Hewlett-Packard's Santa Rosa Systems Division that has adopted Fitness Profiling as an organizational learning process over a four-year period.

> In my mind, I believe that the new SRSD organization had a lot to do with our success over this past year. Granted, with the economic

situation improving we still would have probably done better than previous years even if we hadn't gone through the profiling process. But chances are we would not have been able to capitalize on the potential of this past year without the organization that was properly focused on achieving the right goals.

The willingness of business unit leaders or CEOs to institutionalize Profiling also depended on their commitment to partnership and open inquiry—the principles underlying action learning. We discovered that general managers and corporations varied in their commitment to these principles. For example, the CEO of a company that had applied Profiling widely was convinced the process had helped him and his division managers set an agenda for change. He was far less comfortable, however, with the concept of partnership and insisted that the role of leaders was to decide. He used the military model of leadership to support his contention. Not surprisingly, he rejected the operational embodiment of partnership, the recommendation that task forces should be involved after Profiling to help management implement change. Another senior executive in the same company, who had managed to avoid using Profiling, offered the following observation: "I have two concerns about the process: a diffusion of accountability—now the team is accountable, not the general manager; [and] delays in decision making, given the need to create consensus. When the chips are down, it is an individual that is responsible to the shareholders—one individual is responsible. Once you get this in place, it is a new religion. You can't take away that responsibility for results. It is religion that the group own it, and the group makes decisions."

In psychodynamic terms, we believe that these executives—in our experience many senior executives—have a great deal of difficulty making themselves vulnerable to subordinate feedback given their assumptions that leaders should appear competent and in control.[4, 39]

In the company that applied Fitness Profiling widely, we observed an approach-avoidance attitude developing toward Profiling. Most executives acknowledge its instrumentality in realigning the organization with strategy, but appeared threatened by the values of open communication and partnership. In a classroom discussion with the top fifty executives of the firm, most agreed that Fitness Profiling was essential because it dealt with the business and identified a change agenda needed to compete. Beyond that, they were of two minds. Speaking as strategists, which many of them were, they recognized that Profiling identified vitally important barriers to strategy implementation. As human beings, however, they spoke of how negative and painful it was. The discussion revealed an inner battle between their need to defend their concept of themselves as strong and competent for psychological and political reasons, and their obligation as intelligent, analytic, and rational strategists to align the organization with strategy.

These reactions in a company committed to Profiling suggest that heroic assumptions about leadership make it difficult, though not impossible, for executives to learn about partnership and open inquiry from their experience with Fitness Profiling. For example, the CEO who was uncomfortable with partnership not only continued his commitment to Fitness Profiling but used it early in his tenure as the CEO of another much larger company.

Conclusions

Fitness Profiling has proved to be a powerful tool for both organizational and personal learning. Indeed, that is its distinctive feature. The process identifies needed adaptation in strategy and organization that all managers know are essential while also exposing them to personal and usually defended assumptions about how to manage, lead, and change organizations. The potential for mutual adaptation of hard organizational and soft personal and cultural issues reduces the risk of programmatic change. It also promises to develop leaders and the cultural context for further leadership and organizational development.[6] For this combination to work, leaders must, however, be willing to use Fitness Profiling as a continual, if occasionally painful, foil for learning.

It is unlikely, however, that Fitness Profiling would be successful in an organization facing a severe crisis such as imminent bankruptcy, a merger, or uncertainty about the general manager's future. Under these circumstances management would not be receptive to learning. Time pressures and concern about firm and career survival would prevent developing the partnership and trust so essential for the sustained implementation of an action learning process such as Fitness Profiling.

Learning to Lead by Leading Learning: Breaking Through the Paradox

In this chapter we argue that the heroic model for leading change is inaccurate, limiting, and inherently costly. The hidden barriers to strategy implementation and reformulation consistently cited by employee task forces during Fitness Profiling suggest that the essential ingredient for strategic reorientation are not heroic leadership but a leadership *process* that embodies the values of partnership and inquiry. That process molds the leader and his top team into an effective unit. It links the top team with lower levels on whom they depend for strategy implementation and information about the validity and implementability of the strategy. Only with such a process can the leaders of an organization do the following:

- Develop as a top team capable of constructive conflict and unity in strategic decisions, particularly resource allocation
- Inform lower levels with one voice of the direction in which the organization should go
- Learn from lower levels about organizational arrangements and their own top team behavior that may block implementation and reformulation of organizational strategies
- Learn from lower levels about environmental discontinuities they see in their interaction with that environment
- Energize the organization for continuous change and learning

A carefully specified action learning process such as Fitness Profiling can guide unskilled leaders through the hard analytic *and* soft emotional issues that inevitably surround strategic change. It can be the training wheels for learning to lead organizational learning.

The duality of leading and learning presents a paradox, however. Managers in high-performing and adaptive organizations—Hewlett-Packard, for example—are most receptive to partnering with employees in an organizational learning process and most likely to embrace and effectively institutionalize an action learning process.[26, 45] In these companies the values underlying Fitness Profiling are already likely to be present: emphasis on people, participation, partnership, and process, not just profits. But managers in lower-performing and less-adaptive companies, which are most in need of a well-specified action learning process, are less likely (our findings suggest) to institutionalize an action learning process. The very values that block them from being high-performing adaptive companies prevent them from adopting an action learning process that reveals deep-rooted barriers.

Overcoming this paradox requires courageous leaders willing to learn about their assumptions and values regarding leadership, management, and change. Otherwise their organizations may be doomed to go from crisis to crisis and from one heroic leader to another. We have found a number of general managers who have or develop that courage as they discover the limitations of their own assumptions and skills. More will be needed if average companies are to be transformed into high-performing adaptive ones.

A paradigm shift in management thinking about leadership and organization development is needed. Such a shift would encourage skeptical managers to adopt action learning processes such as Fitness Profiling as a core method for organizational and leadership development. Senior executives might want to reconsider the millions of dollars they spend on consultants to shore up inadequate change leadership skills, educational programs to develop those skills, or recruiters to find great change leaders. They might want to consider spending a far smaller sum on institutionalizing an action learning process. By establishing norms of partnership and inquiry, they will establish a learning culture that also develops leaders. By requiring general managers to lead a learning process, they will quickly identify leaders who can and will learn how to lead fundamental transformation. Under these circumstances, a process such as Fitness Profiling becomes both a development and an assessment tool. Managing the tension between these two potentially opposing aspects of the process will not be easy, of course.

Institutionalizing a specific organizational learning process provides a company with a core strategic management process. It constitutes an integrated systems approach to change; it connects hard and soft strategy with style, structure, and staffing. Most importantly, it is the vehicle for changing the cultural context that blocks mediocre firms from becoming high-performance organizations capable of continuous adaptation.

Paradigm shifts do not occur quickly or easily. They require a few innovative CEOs and corporations to demonstrate a new model of organizational learning that will allow organizations to survive and prosper in the twenty-first century.

Notes

I am grateful to Russell Eisenstat, an equal partner in the action research described in this chapter, for his comments on an earlier version of this chapter.

1. I am indebted to Dr. David McConnell for alerting me to this quote attributed to Halsey and spoken by James Cagney in the film *The Gallant Hours*. According to *Respectfully Quoted: A Dictionary of Quotations Requested from the Congressional Research Services*, edited by Suzy Platt, the authenticity of the quote cannot be verified.
2. Argyris, C. *Interpersonal Competence and Organizational Effectiveness.* Homewood, Ill.: Doresy Press, 1962.
3. Argyris, C. *Overcoming Organizational Defenses.* Reading, Mass.: Allyn & Bacon, 1990.
4. Hirschhorn, L. "Leaders and Followers in a Postindustrial Age: A Psychodynamic View." *Journal of Applied Behavioral Science,* 1990, *26,* 529–542.
5. Nadler, D. A., and Tushman, M. L. "Beyond the Charismatic Leader: Leadership and Organizational Change." *California Management Review,* 1990, *32,* 77–97.
6. Beer, M., Eisenstat, R. A., and Spector, B. *The Critical Path to Corporate Renewal.* Boston: Harvard Business School Press, 1990.
7. Virany, B., Tushman, M. L., and Romanelli, E. "Executive Succession and Organization Outcomes in Turbulent Environments: An Organization Learning Approach." *Organizational Science,* 1992, *3,* 72–91.
8. Brown, S. L., and Eisenhardt, K. M. "The Art of Continuous Change: Linking Complexity Theory and Time-paced Evolution in Relentlessly Shifting Organizations." *Administrative Science Quarterly,* 1997, *42,* 1–34.
9. Miles, R. E., and Snow, C. *Organization Strategy, Structure and Process.* New York: McGraw-Hill, 1978.
10. Argyris, C. "Strategy Implementation: An Experience in Learning." *Organizational Dynamics,* 1989, *18*(2), 5–15.
11. Beer, M. *Organization Change and Development: A Systems View.* Santa Monica, Calif.: Goodyear, 1980.
12. Tushman, M. L., Newman, W. H., and Romanelli, E. "Convergence and Upheaval: Managing the Unsteady Pace of Organizational Evolution." *California Management Review,* 1987, *29,* 1–15.
13. Nadler, D. A., and Tushman, M. L. *Strategic Organizational Design.* Homewood, Ill.: Scott, Foresman, 1988.

14. Tushman, M. L., and O'Reilly, C. A. III. *Winning Through Innovation.* Boston: Harvard Business School Press, 1997.

15. Argyris, C., and Schon, D. *Organizational Learning II: A Theory of Action Perspective.* Reading, Mass.: Addison-Wesley, 1996.

16. Kotter, J. P. *The Leadership Factor.* New York: Free Press, 1988.

17. Kotter, J. P. *A Force for Change.* New York: Free Press, 1990.

18. Grove, A. *Only the Paranoid Survive.* New York: Doubleday, 1996.

19. Beer, M. "Leading Change." Case study, Harvard Business School, 1991.

20. Meindl, J. R., Ehrlich, S. B., and Dukerich, J. M. "The Romance of Leadership." *Administrative Science Quarterly,* 1985, *30,* 78–102.

21. Beer, M. "Corning Glass Works: The Electronic Products Division." Cases A, B, and C. Case study, Harvard Business School, 1975.

22. Cohen, A., and Bradford, D. *Power Up: Transforming Organizations Through Shared Leadership.* Forthcoming.

23. Personal communication. Gilmartin observed this at the time he was CEO of Merck. Earlier he was CEO of Becton Dickinson, where he sponsored the development of Organizational Fitness Profiling described later in this chapter.

24. Kotter, J. P. *The General Manager.* New York: Free Press, 1982.

25. Kotter, J. P. *Leading Change.* Boston: Harvard Business School Press, 1997.

26. Beer, M., and Rogers, G. "Human Resources at Hewlett Packard." Cases A and B. Case study, Harvard Business School, 1995.

27. Eisenhardt, K. M., Kahwajy, J. L., and Bourgeois, L. J. III. "How Management Teams Can Have a Good Fight." *Harvard Business Review,* July-Aug. 1997, pp. 77–87.

28. Beer, M., Eisenstat, R. A., and Biggadike, R. "Developing an Organization Capable of Strategy Implementation and Reformulation: A Preliminary Test." In B. Moingeon and A. Edmondson (eds.), *Organizational Learning and Competitive Advantage.* London: Sage, 1996.

29. Beer, M., and Eisenstat, R. A. "The Silent Killers: Overcoming Hidden Barriers to Organizational Fitness." Working Paper 97–004, Harvard Business School, 1996.

30. Bartlett, C., and Ghoshal, S. *Managing Across Borders: The Transnational Solution.* Boston: Harvard Business School Press, 1989.

31. Biggadike, R. "Research in Managing the Multinational Company: A Practitioner's Experiences." In C. Bartlett, Y. Doz, and G. Hedlund (eds.), *Managing the Global Firm.* London: Routledge, 1990.

32. Beer, M., and Williamson, A. D. "Becton Dickinson." Cases A, B, C, and D. Case study, Harvard Business School, 1991.

33. Porter, M. E. *Competitive Advantage: Creating and Sustaining Superior Performance.* New York: Free Press, 1985.

34. Lawrence, P. R., and Lorsch, J. W. *Organization and Environment.* Boston: Harvard Business School Press, 1967.
35. Lawrence, P. R., and Lorsch, J. W. *Developing Organizations: Diagnosis and Action.* Reading, Mass.: Addison-Wesley, 1969.
36. Fleishman, E. A., Harris, E. F., and Burt, H. E. *Leadership and Supervision in Industry.* Columbus, Ohio: Ohio State University Bureau of Educational Research, 1955.
37. Schaffer, R. *The Breakthrough Strategy: Using Short-Term Success to Build the High Performance Organization.* Cambridge, Mass.: Ballinger, 1988.
38. Simon, H. A. "Decision Making and Organizational Design." In D. S. Pugh (ed.), *Organization Theory.* England: Penguin Books, 1984, pp. 202–224.
39. Argyris, C. *Knowledge for Action.* San Francisco: Jossey-Bass, 1994.
40. Walton, R. W. "A Vision Led Approach to Management Restructuring." *Organizational Dynamics,* 1986, *14,* 5–16.
41. Hall, G., Rosenthal, J., and Wade, J. "How to Make Reengineering Really Work." *Harvard Business Review,* Nov.-Dec. 1993, pp. 119–131.
42. Eisenhardt, K. M. "Making Fast Strategic Decisions in High Velocity Environments." *Academy of Management Journal,* 1989, *32,* 543–576.
43. Schein, E. H. *Process Consultation: Its Role in Organization Development.* Reading, Mass.: Addison-Wesley, 1969.
44. Schein, E. H. *Organization Culture and Leadership.* San Francisco: Jossey-Bass, 1985.
45. Beer, M., and Rogers, G. "Hewlett Packard's Santa Rosa Division: The Trials and Tribulations of a Legacy." Cases A, A1, A2, A3, A4, B, B1, B2, and B3. Case study, Harvard Business School, 1997.
46. Beer, M., and Eisenstat, R. A. "Developing an Organization Capable of Implementing Strategy and Learning." Working Paper 95–037, Harvard Business School, 1994.
47. Beer, M., and Eisenstat, R. A. "Developing an Organization Capable of Strategy Implementation and Learning." *Human Relations,* 1996, *49,* 597–619.

Chapter Seven

Advanced Change Theory
Culture Change at Whirlpool Corporation
Robert E. Quinn
Nancy T. Snyder

In the global economy, organizations are under pressure to adapt or experience dire consequences. Despite this pressure, they continually struggle and often fail. In Chapter Three, Heifetz and Laurie gave us a clue why by differentiating between technical and adaptive challenges. A technical challenge is one in which the necessary expertise and a credible technique somewhere exist; authority needs only to find it and mandate it. In contrast, the adaptive challenge has no existing solution, and meeting it includes the difficult problem of changing human behavior: "Adaptive work can be achieved only by mobilizing the people with the problem to make painful adjustments in their attitudes, work habits, and lives."[1] As Bartlett and Ghoshal point out, although changing behavior does not come easy to large organizations, it is the key to achieving patterns and processes of self-renewal.[2] Such an accomplishment requires a redefinition of what it means to lead.[3]

Experience suggests that most authority figures, indeed most all of us when we take the role of change agent, fail in our attempts to get others to "make painful adjustments in their attitudes, work habits, and lives." One reason is that our implicit and unexamined theory of action comes out of the technical worldview. In trying to bring change in human systems, we follow two unspoken propositions:

1. Employ rational persuasion—that is, tell people why they should change.
2. If they do not comply, employ coercion—that is, force them to change.

From the parent seeking to get the resistant teenager to do homework to the CEO trying to implement a vast organizational turnaround, this two-step theory is enacted over and over in society. The results are usually disappointing. In this chapter we introduce a set of notions designed to increase the number of alternatives that can be employed in efforts to change human behavior. We first review three well-known strategies for change and then introduce a new one, Advanced Change Theory (ACT).

The foundations of ACT were first proposed by Quinn, Brown, and Spreitzer.[4] Their work emerges from the examination of Chin and Benne's classic 1969 paper on organizational development, "Three General Strategies for Effecting Change in Human Systems,"[5] which articulates three general change strategies: empirical-rational, power-coercive, and normative-reeducative. But Quinn, Brown, and Spreitzer cite behaviors exhibited by particularly transformational change agents, such as Gandhi and Martin Luther King Jr., that are unaccounted for by those three general strategies. The authors therefore elaborate a fourth: empowering-self modification strategy, or Advanced Change Theory.

In the first part of this chapter we review the original three strategies and then present ACT. In the second part we recount the history of a corporate-wide cultural change effort at Whirlpool. In the final section we do a retrospective analysis of the Whirlpool experience, focusing on ways in which elements of ACT were enacted.

Advanced Change Theory

The word "advanced" is used because ACT is not cognitively available to most people who are trying to bring change in human systems. It is the most complex and least observable general strategy for effecting change—least observable because it is less frequently employed than other strategies and, when employed, is enacted outside the paradigmatic assumptions of the normal observer. That is, it transcends the normal assumptions of self-interested, transactional exchange that permeates both implicit theories of social action and the formal theories of social science. Furthermore, ACT focuses on the confrontation, facilitation, and creation of emergent reality. The logic of action is more paradoxical than linear and the view of social reality is based on moral-relational rather than political-technical assumptions. In short, ACT requires the change agent to employ a high level of cognitive, behavioral, and moral complexity. To explain ACT, here is a brief account of the original three strategies.

The Three Strategies of Chin and Benne

The Empirical-Rational Strategy. The objective of the empirical-rational strategy is to alter the behavior of the change target so that it comes into alignment with established knowledge or fact. It involves the information transfer from change agent to change target, and the generation of knowledge, information, or intellectual rationales for action that serve as the levers for change. People, the change targets, are assumed to be embedded in ignorance and superstition; nevertheless, they are assumed to be rational and likely to follow their self-interest once it is revealed to them. Hence the job of the change agent is to persuade rationally, to disseminate expertise, to emphasize content knowledge. In daily discourse, this is probably the single most employed strategy. Whenever we act as an expert (parent, teacher, consultant, executive) and seek to change behavior by instructing or telling the change target, we are employing this general strategy.

The Power-Coercive Strategy. The objective of this is to alter the behavior of the change target so that it comes into alignment with established or formal authority. It assumes that individuals are embedded in hierarchical relationships of a formal or informal nature, and that people with less power comply with the plans, directions, and leadership of those with greater power. The change agent is a social strategist who seeks to create authority through law and policy, or by exercising coercive power in support of the desired change. In doing so the change agent manipulates an implicit or explicit set of sanctions designed to obtain compliance. Like the empirical-rational strategy, this one is regularly applied in daily affairs and often is the second resort if the simple instruction of the change target fails to bring results; often the two strategies are combined.

The Normative-Reeducative Strategy. The objective here is to align behavior with negotiated outcomes. This strategy assumes that individuals are embedded in transactional social relationships and that all parties have power. Change targets need to be committed to change outcomes. Because people are culturally determined—that is, driven by multiple social stimuli while embedded in complex networks—change processes must be both rational and affective. Change involves process as well as content. It is possible that collaborative, open discussion of issues in the relationship can lead to reeducation or value change. Here the change agent is a facilitator who focuses on the interactional process and seeks to fashion win-win outcomes. Although these ideas are better understood today than when Chin and Benne wrote about them, they are still not as widely employed as the first two strategies. This strategy is often seen as counterintuitive, risky, and time-consuming. It also necessitates a high level of interpersonal skill.

An Introduction to Advanced Change Theory

In ACT the objective is to bring both the change agent and change target into alignment with currently changing reality. Given the past-centered cognitive structures that we carry around, this is a formidable objective that involves deep change or transformation. ACT assumes that people are inherently free but tend normally to choose the path of least resistance. In doing so, they lose vitality and become caught in externally determined patterns. This eventually leads to feelings of disempowerment. To engage present reality, people must be empowered. This cannot happen within the existing hierarchical categories and rules that have emerged from past interactions. The change target must be attracted to choose transformational tasks by feeling simultaneously challenged and supported. Telling (empirical-rational), coercing (power-coercive), or even participating (normative reeducative) strategies are insufficient to bring such results. Here, as in the normative-reeducative approach, the change agent and the change target are in a relationship, but the change agent does not target the relationship directly. Rather the change agent seeks to change the relationship by changing self. Through the confrontation of one's own self-deceptions, the change agent models walking at the edge of chaos by stepping outside the comfort zone and letting go of control. At the personal level, the change agent then experiences an elaboration of cognitive complexity, gains vision, experiences increased personal congruence and self-esteem, transcends the external system of sanctions, and feels increased concern for the change target. The change agent emerges from this process, in the words of Joseph Campbell, "both empowered and empowering to the community."[6] That is, the process simultaneously increases the discipline, vision, expectation, and sensitivity of the change agent.

Moving forward with normally conflicting characteristics, the change agent sees the organization not only as a technical and a political system, but also as a moral system. Committed to the common good of the system, the change agent is willing to ignore normal external sanctions and behave in unconventional ways that attract attention and commitment. This attracts the change target into the personal change process that results in the transformation of the change target. In this process the change agent is a role model who works with the change target in a process of cocreation. At the individual level, cocreation results in a new person; at the collective level, a new culture.

In their original paper Quinn, Brown, and Spreitzer provide an appendix that identifies thirteen principles of ACT. Each is illustrated by a quote from three practitioners of the transformational self-modification strategy: Jesus Christ, Mohandas K. Gandhi, and Martin Luther King Jr. Following is a restatement of these.

The Assumptions of Advanced Change Theory

1. *Assumptions of relationship: alignment with changing reality requires relationships of inclusion, openness, and emergent community.* In ACT, the change agent recognizes that, over time, positive processes such as articulation, routinization, formalization, and organization are followed by negative processes such as stagnation, denial, deception, and manipulation and alienation. The change agent strives to move self and others from assumptions and strategies of hierarchy to assumptions and strategies of inclusion, openness, and

emergent community. This particularly emphasizes assumptions of equality in relationships.

> The princes of the Gentiles exercise dominion over
> them. . . . But . . . whosoever will be great among you, let
> him be your minister.
>
> Jesus (Matthew 20:25–26)

> In the orthodox army, there is a clear distinction between
> officer and private. In a non-violent army, the generals
> are just chief servants—first among equals.
>
> Gandhi[7]

> Nonviolent resistance does not seek to defeat or humiliate
> the opponent but to win his friendship and understand-
> ing. . . . The aftermath of nonviolence is the creation of
> the beloved community, while the aftermath of violence
> is tragic bitterness.
>
> Martin L. King Jr.[8]

2. *Assumptions of purpose: to establish an emergent community, a change agent must put the pursuit of the common good ahead of self interest.* In ACT, the change agent recognizes that in normal relationships all individuals will pursue self-interest and, in so doing, preserve the existing patterns and processes of equilibrium. In contrast, the change agent operating according to ACT envisions a higher pur- pose and pursues it at personal cost, making the attainment of the common good and the self-interest of the change agent one and the same.

> This is my commandment, That ye love one another, as I
> have loved you. Greater love hath no man than this, that
> a man lay down his life for his friends.
>
> Jesus (John 15:12–13)

> The present plan for securing self-rule is not to attain a po-
> sition of isolation but one of full self realization and self-
> expression for the benefit of all.
>
> Gandhi[9]

> I still have a dream. It is a dream deeply rooted in the American dream that one day this nation will rise up and live out the true meaning of its creed—we hold these truths to be self evident, that all men are created equal.
>
> Martin L. King Jr.[10]

3. *Assumptions of resistance: to maintain alignment with changing reality and with the common good, a change agent focuses on internal sources of resistance, continually seeking to reduce self-deception and personal hypocrisy.* In ACT, the change agent assumes that all people let conscience and responsibility diverge, but the change agent does not focus on ignorance, weaknesses, or resistance in the change target. Instead the change agent begins with a disciplined examination of personal motives, continually seeking to reduce his or her own hypocrisy and self-deception. Because the divergence of responsibility and behavior is a regularly occurring event, the quest for personal integrity is continuous.

> He that is without sin among you, let him first cast a stone at her. . . . [And they . . . being convicted by their own conscience, went out one by one . . .]
>
> Jesus (John 8:7–9)

> Modern organized artificiality . . . cannot have any accord with true simplicity of heart. Where the two do not correspond, there is always either gross self-deception or hypocrisy.
>
> Gandhi[11]

> It is a method which seeks to implement the law by appealing to conscience of the great descent majority who through blindness, fear, pride, or irrationality have allowed their consciences to sleep.
>
> Martin L. King Jr.[12]

4. *Assumptions of influence: in influencing others, the change agent first models the courage and discipline of self modification, the resulting integrity then serves to influence others by attracting them into a relationship, or*

community, of mutual support and exploration. In ACT, the change agent assumes that rational persuasion and political leverage are of limited potential in bringing about deep personal change and building emergent communities. The change agent therefore seeks first to increase his or her own moral power so as to model courage and "attract" the change target into a relationship of self-exploration, commitment, and growth.

> Thou hypocrite, cast out first the beam out of thine own eye, and then shalt thou see clearly to pull out the mote that is in thy brother's.
>
> Jesus (Luke 6:42)

> The function of violence is to obtain reform by external means; the function of passive resistance, that is "soul-force," is to obtain reform by growth from within; which, in turn is obtained by self-suffering, and self-purification.
>
> Gandhi[13]

> The words I spoke to God that midnight are still vivid in my memory. I am here taking a stand for what I believe is right. But now I am afraid. The people are looking to me for leadership, and if I stand before them without strength and courage, they too will falter.
>
> Martin L. King Jr.[14]

5. *Assumptions of empowerment: by transcending self-deception and personal hypocrisy, the change agent empowers and frees the self from the controlling sanctions within the existing social system.* In ACT, the change agent assumes that the highest forms of freedom and power do not come from increased technical knowledge or higher formal position. Every social system evolves a set of both positive and negative sanctions to maintain patterned behavior. These lead to the formation of a paradigmatic assumption set that traps people in an existing reality. The only way to free one's self from past perspectives is through personal transcendence of self-deception and hypocrisy. When this occurs, the change agent becomes free of the sanctions in the existing system, and better sees the changes necessary for the common good of the people in the original system.

When Jesus therefore perceived that they would come and
take him by force, to make him a king, he departed again
into a mountain himself alone.

John 6:15

Every man has to obey the voice of his own conscience, and
be his own master by seeking the Kingdom of God from
within. For him there is no government that can control
him . . .

Gandhi[15]

First, we must unflinchingly face our fears and honestly ask
ourselves why we are afraid. This confrontation will, to
some measure, grant us power. We shall never be cured
of fear by escapism or repression, for the more we attempt
to ignore and repress our fears, the more we multiply
our inner conflicts.

Martin L. King Jr.[16]

6. *Assumptions of enlightenment: in freeing self from external sanctions
through personal modification, the change agent obtains increased understanding, enlightenment, or vision about direction and strategy.* In ACT,
the change agent assumes that rational analysis will tend to begin
with assumptions from within the existing system. New vision is
achieved by abdicating equilibrium and control and moving to the
edge of chaos, that is, by entering the behavioral state of bounded
instability one engages and enacts the process of emergence. In
this paradoxical state, one gains increased knowledge of self and
environment. New and more powerful visions or strategies become
available.

But when they deliver you up, take no thought how or what
ye shall speak: for it shall be given you in that same hour
what ye shall speak.

Jesus (Matthew 10:19–20)

History teaches us that men who are in the whirlpool . . .
will have to work out their destiny within it; but I do not

submit that those who are still outside its influence . . .
should be helped to remain where they are.

Gandhi[17]

Heraclitus argued that justice emerges from the strife of opposites, and Hegel . . . preached a doctrine of growth
through struggle. It is both historically and biologically
true that there can be no birth and growth without pains.
Whenever there is emergence of the new we confront the
recalcitrance of the old.

Martin L. King Jr.[18]

7. *Assumptions of volition: the change agent's increased understanding
and personal empowerment result in increased reverence for the potential
and the volition of the change target.* In ACT, the change agent assumes that the existing system is evolving toward increasingly hierarchical and transactional assumptions. In such assumption sets,
the change target tends to be looked upon with mistrust, as an object to be manipulated and controlled. In ACT, the change agent's
experiences with victory over the old self result in the emergence
of a new, more complex, and more aligned self. This process stim-
ulates great sensitivity to others. The empowerment of self leads to
a belief in the positive potential in all others. The change agent's
experience also gives rise to an acute awareness that people cannot be empowered by another, but can only empower themselves.
This can only happen through the exercise of choice. The change
agent sees the change target as a person, not an object, and continually honors the volition and potential of the change target. In
ACT there is always a reverence for the target's freedom of choice
and a striving to eliminate the natural tendency in the change
agent for manipulation and control. The change agent strives to
clarify values and purify motives, to provide a role model, to attract
and inspire.

If ye continue in my word, [then] are ye my disciples indeed; And ye shall know the truth, and the truth shall
make you free.

Jesus (John 7:31–32)

> Instead of bothering with how the whole world may live in
> the right manner, we should think how we ourselves may
> do so. . . . If . . . one lives in the right manner, we shall
> feel that others also will do the same, or we shall discover
> a way of persuading them to do so by example.
>
> > Gandhi[19]

> If our words fail, we will try to persuade with our acts. We
> will always be willing to talk and seek fair compromise,
> but we are ready to suffer and even risk our lives to be-
> come witnesses to the truth.
>
> > Martin L. King[20]

8. *Assumptions of motivation: given the high respect for the volition of the change target, the change agent seeks to inspire growth by attracting the change target to engage in noble tasks of service for the higher good of the community.* Without ACT, the change agent assumes that exist-ing systems will develop strategies of motivation designed to obtain compliance with existing norms. In contrast, the change agent in ACT believes that the greatest good will come to the community when the change target is experiencing significant personal growth. Empowerment does not result in loss of control for the larger system. It results in increased commitment, courage, and confrontation of the hypocrisy in the larger system. The empow-erment of the individual ensures the empowerment of the greater system. The primary motivational process for initiating this process is inspiring and attracts the change target to risk self-modification and empowerment.

> [And he saith unto them,] follow me, and I will make you
> fishers of men.
>
> > Jesus (Matthew 4:19)

> If you surrender yourself, body, soul, and mind, and give
> yourself up to the world . . . the treasures of the world are
> at your feet, not for enjoyment, but for the enjoyment of
> service, only yours for that service.
>
> > Gandhi[21]

Let us not seek to satisfy our thirst for freedom by drinking
from the cup of bitterness and hatred. We must forever
conduct our struggle on the high plane of dignity and
discipline. We must not allow our creative protest to de-
generate into physical violence.

Martin L. King Jr.[22]

9. *Assumptions of causality: the change agent recognizes the change target's need for relationship and assumes that change happens as a nonlinear process of mutuality and cocreation that further requires continued
integrity and increasing trust.* In ACT, the change agent does not
assume a linear model of cause and effect in which change is imposed on the target. Instead the agent and target are in relationship. They are mutually linked in the enactment of an emergent
system. As the change agent models the reduction of personal integrity gaps, the emergence of a new and more aligned self results
in an increased sense of self-esteem and an increased capacity for
love and support. The modeling of personal change, the increased
vision, and the provision of interpersonal support increase the
probability that the change target will choose self-modification.
The eventual transformation of the change target, in turn, alters
the relationship and therefore the change agent. Deep change
happens not through telling and coercing but through trust, relationship, and cocreation.

For I have given you an example, that ye should do as I have
done to you.

Jesus (John 13:15)

We shall never be able to raise the standard of public life
through laws. Only if the lives of leaders . . . are perfect
will they be able to produce any effect on the people they
lead. Mere preaching will have no effect.

Gandhi[23]

The universe is so structured that things do not quite work
out rightly if men are not diligent in their concern for
others. . . . All life is interrelated. All men are caught in

an inescapable network of mutuality, tied in a single gar-
ment of destiny. This is what John Donne meant.

Martin L. King Jr.[24]

10. *Assumptions of strategic vision: the change agent's efforts in self-
modification and empowerment result in increased cognitive complexity and
the ability to see larger governing rules or seemingly paradoxical relationships.* In ACT, the change agent does not assume that the easily observable means-ends relationships in the explicit or existing system
are the foundation of an effective change strategy. Such means-
ends theories lead to preservation of equilibrium rather than transformation. In personal transformation the change agent not only
frees self from the existing sanctions but also sees the system from
a more complex view, a view that includes paradoxical relationships
or deeper governing rules. In walking at the edge of chaos, the
change agent experiences the interpenetration of opposites and
the process of synthesis or emergence. In undergoing such a process, the change agent develops a more elaborate understanding
than the understanding available to those who choose to live within
the existing sanctions.

> Whosoever shall seek to save his life shall lose it; and whoso-
> ever shall lose his life shall preserve it.
>
> Jesus (Luke 17:33)

> Every fast was . . . an educative process, a method of teach-
> ing him about himself, and of reaching out into the ab-
> solute where the ordinary values of life were no longer
> applicable. . . . [I]t was necessary to devise an entire sce-
> nario, to develop complex and subtle maneuvers, and to
> gain precarious insights into a world which was not other-
> wise knowable.
>
> Said of Gandhi[25]

> Not ordinarily do men achieve this balance of opposites. . . .
> But life at its best is a creative synthesis of opposites in
> fruitful harmony. The philosopher Hegel said that truth

is found neither in the thesis nor the antithesis, but in an emergent synthesis which reconciles the two.

Martin L. King Jr.[26]

11. *Assumptions of behavior: freed from the influence of the existing sanction system, and holding a more complex or paradoxical world view, the change agent engages in unconventional behaviors that distort routines, capture attention, and move the system toward the edge of chaos.* In ACT, the change agent does not engage in the conventional behavior patterns of people in his or her role. Instead the change agent models surprising behaviors. These increase the attention of observers and the credibility of the change agent. They destabilize the system and make it sensitive to small acts. Such acts may not have made an impact under conditions of stability but they lead to transformation under conditions of bounded instability.

If I then . . . have washed your feet; ye also ought to wash one another's feet.

Jesus (John 13:14)

Inevitably, because he was dealing with morality, Gandhi was led into paradoxes. He was never more paradoxical than when he argued that the English should be permitted to remain in India as administrators and policemen, but they must abandon their commercial ventures . . .

Said of Gandhi[27]

When my home was bombed in 1955 in Montgomery, many men wanted to retaliate, to place an armed guard on my home. . . . Had we become distracted by the question of my safety we would have lost the moral offensive and sunk to the level of our oppressors.

Martin L. King Jr.[28]

12. *Assumptions of determination: the change agent assumes that altered internal states determine altered external states.* In ACT, the change agent does not assume that micro behavior is always determined

by macro behavior. Nor is it assumed that systemic change only happens through top-down efforts. Instead it is assumed that under conditions of bounded instability, individual people can transform the organization. What matters is the being state. If the change agent is aligned with emergent reality, has courage, vision, and purity of motive in service of the collective good, then change can flow from the individual to the collective, from the bottom to the top.

> [Why could not we cast him out? And he said unto them,] This kind can come forth by nothing, but by prayer and fasting.
>
> Jesus (Mark 9:28–29)

> By purifying himself and subjugating the flesh he would increase the powers of the soul and thus acquire the strength to dominate events. The strength of the soul grew in proportion as the flesh was subdued, and from the absolutely pure soul there flowed out in ever-widening circles a power that was ultimately invincible. He was perfectly serious in the belief . . .
>
> Said of Gandhi[29]

> Almost at once my fears began to pass from me. My uncertainty disappeared. I was ready to face anything. The outer situation remained the same, but God had given me inner calm. . . . I knew now that God is able to give us the interior resources to face the storms and problems of life.
>
> Martin L. King Jr.[30]

13. *Assumptions of action: the change agent is a self-authorizing person with a bias for action and enactment under uncertainty.* In ACT, the change agent does not put the highest premium on analysis, planning, and linear execution. Instead there is a trust in emergent processes and a bias toward self-authorizing action. Action experiments are seen as a trial-and-error process that gives rise to effective learning. Courage and risk taking are central. Failure is an expected part of the learning process. To walk the edge of chaos

one must be willing to engage in action learning. Because of action learning, the change agent's authority does not come through secondary authority or position. It comes from within, a function of experience and deep wisdom.

> For he taught them as [one] having authority, and not as
> the scribes.
> > Said of Jesus (Matthew 7:29)

> I know that in embarking on non-violence I shall be running what might be termed a mad risk. But the victories of truth have never been won without risks, often of the gravest character.
> > Gandhi[31]

> In any nonviolent campaign there are four basic steps:
> (1) collection of the facts to determine whether injustices are alive, (2) negotiation, (3) self-purification, and (4) direct action. We have gone through all of these steps in Birmingham.
> > Martin L. King Jr.[32]

Reactions to ACT

A frequent reaction to ACT is to recognize its inherent power but then to discredit its practicality by arguing that leaders such as Jesus, Gandhi, and King were heroic and that ordinary people could never apply such a theory of practice. A similar argument is that ACT is the stuff of social movements and could never be applied in a business organization; the real world is transactional and ACT is simply too idealistic to be of value. But Quinn, Brown, and Spreitzer devote considerable space to showing ordinary people engaging in the extraordinary act of transforming a relationship or organization. Although such transformation is far less frequent than incremental adjustment, it does occur. Indeed, adaptive challenges, as discussed early in this chapter, are appearing with increasing frequency and they require behavioral transformation. When behavior is transformed, some aspect of ACT is in play.

Whenever an organization of any kind goes through a transformation, the leader of the process is engaged in leading an emergent social movement. This concept is so counter to the norms and language of daily practice that the story is almost always retold as a case of brilliant strategy formulation and implementation. The linear story is necessary to "look intelligent," but seldom reflects the true, nonlinear, emergent nature of what happened.

To more fully explore and understand the nature and applicability of ACT, we now turn to an account of cultural change effort in a large organization. The intervention was not originally designed to follow the principles of ACT. In fact, some key actors were unfamiliar with ACT. Others were in the process of trying to formulate it. After the following account, we do a retrospective analysis looking for manifestations of ACT and for situations in which it might have been applied. The objective is not to demonstrate evidence of effectiveness or of some kind of causality, but to further our understanding of ACT and determine its potential application in the intervention process.

The Culture Change Effort at Whirlpool

Whirlpool Corporation is headquartered in Benton Harbor, Michigan. With $10 billion in sales, it is the world's largest manufacturer and marketer of home appliances. Today it is a global company that operates in 140 countries with sixty thousand employees. The process of globalization began in 1989 under the direction of chairman and CEO David Whitwam. He started by initiating a joint venture with, and then acquisition of, Philips home appliances in Europe. The company has since expanded into Asia, Eastern Europe, Africa, and South and Central America. Between 1988 and 1994, the company maintained an intense focus on creating value for the shareholder. During the five-year period ending in 1994, Whirlpool grew from twenty-nine thousand employees to thirty-nine thousand, from sales of $4.306 billion to $7.949 billion, and from a stock price of $24~ to $501/4.

In 1995 the company experienced a number of difficult challenges, including unforeseen currency devaluations in Europe, raw materials price increases, a refrigeration new-product launch that took more capital than expected, and the continuation of losing more money than planned in the Asian start-up. The pressures from these challenges resulted in problematic behavior patterns that highlighted the fact that the company had lost one of its most important assets: the integrative culture it had developed from being a midwestern American company for so many years.

Previously, that culture had provided clear norms and operating values to guide people in times of difficulty or uncertainty. But by 1995 it was becoming clear that the integrative benefits of the traditional Whirlpool culture were disappearing. Two events, one broad and the other narrow, particularly seemed to signify this. The first was the adoption of an unrealistic planning process in which the executive committee—composed of the eight senior officers—stretched the organization too far by setting unrealistic targets and by saturating the action agenda with an escalation of global initiatives, both of which weighed down local operations. The second and more narrow event had to do with eliminating eight marketing employees; as a result of the downturn of 1995, a marketing executive had targeted them. Uncharacteristic to Whirlpool's norms, the departing employees were treated most poorly. The termination of one occurred on his twenty-fifth anniversary with the company; all eight were escorted to their cars by security. This story circulated the globe in twenty-four hours and was retold frequently for several months.

Getting Started: Conceptualizing and Designing the Culture Change Process

As Whitwam became aware of the loss of cultural integration, he committed to reestablishing it. He often stated that "creating a global, high-performance culture is the most important thing I will do in my tenure as CEO." The changes he proposed were based on two important principles: first, that culture change starts with telling the truth; and second, that culture change depends on personal change by those leading it. The steps toward culture change included an audit to understand the present culture, a series of senior leadership culture conferences with intact work groups in business regions, a global conference of all top leadership teams from around the world, manager-conducted workshops for every employee, and meetings about values and behaviors led by department managers that featured discussion by all employees.

Step 1: The Culture Audit

Before the first senior workshop, the company conducted a culture audit. A team of interviewers met with five hundred employees in twenty countries. The interviewees ranged from senior leaders to blue-collar workers. The results suggested that although employees were very committed to the company, many serious problems existed: change overload, globalization that had reduced emphasis on key values, communication that seemed restricted to formal one-way presentations with a marked decline in real dialogue, too much hierarchy, questions about implementation of the global strategy, strained interpersonal relationships, unclear priorities and accountabilities, business focus mainly on short-term and financial matters, undervalued diversity, too much pretense, and a loss of balance between quality of work life and personal life.

Step 2: Senior Leadership Conferences

Work began on a series of workshops consisting of eight work groups and four hundred senior leaders over the course of one year. The first workshop was with the executive committee, the top eight officers of Whirlpool. A chairman's council workshop, for the next-highest twenty-five officers, followed. Workshops were then held at Whirlpool's regional business headquarters in the United States, Brazil, Italy, Hong Kong, India, and Thailand.

The executive committee workshop began by each member telling a story about past personal change. The group then worked on describing the preferred culture. In a third exercise, the members gave each other feedback on personal behaviors that helped and hindered moving the company toward the preferred culture. As a result of the feedback, the senior leaders agreed to keep personal journals to reflect on the personal behavior changes they intended to make.

The chairman's council workshop had particular impact. This was the first time this group had ever met face to face. The workshop began with an exercise designed to explore Whirlpool's past culture and values. For this purpose a Whirlpool museum was designed and participants were asked to interpret and retell the history of the company. This resulted in considerable insight about the existence and power of the past culture and had an integrating effect on the many people who had recently joined the company. In a surprising moment, the group rejected the executive committee's workshop output and decided to use existing Whirlpool values with the major revision of adding "respect" to the list alongside integrity, teamwork, learning to lead, and spirit of winning. Once comfortable with their conclusion, the group's members requested that the CEO meet with them and react to their recommendations. This interaction turned out to be a transformational moment: the risk of confronting the CEO galvanized the group and its commitment to the culture change effort. Members characterized the CEO interaction as "walking on thin ice."

Next they worked through issues that were keeping them from creating the preferred culture. They had a discussion around their feelings of exclusion from the central decision-making process in Whirlpool. Each felt excluded for a variety of reasons: the color of their skin, their mother tongue, the function they represented, the area of the business they came from, their newness to Whirlpool, their geographic location in the world. In the end, the group members had an epiphany: If they—as senior leaders—felt excluded, how did the people who work for them feel?

The workshop generated substantial results. There was a new perception of the CEO and the changes he was trying to make at a personal level. In witnessing his struggle, each participant committed to his own personal change. There was an ominous sense of how hard it would be to try to change the culture and how much it would demand from everyone. In retrospect, one year later, the CEO stated that "[the chairman's council workshop was] the high point and maybe the most powerful event. If I think back to the executive committee meeting we had in March, it was more superficial. The executive committee was not at that point engaged emotionally with the culture change effort; the chairman's council was. It was, for me, the most powerful experience I had in all of the workshops."

The regional workshops mirrored the chairman's council workshop. Each workshop lasted three days, was led by the executive committee and chairman's council members, and was attended by the CEO. Although the regions differed substantially in strategy and tactics, the issues that emerged from each were similar. Two of the most general issues were a resounding appreciation of the past culture and values of Whirlpool, and the collective realization that in 1995 internal management behaviors made most of the external challenges more difficult than they needed to be.

Step 3: The Naples Senior Leadership Conference

Every year the top 140 leaders of Whirlpool meet in January in Naples, Florida. As the 1997 meeting approached, a major issue concerned Whitwam: it was clear that 1997 and 1998 would be difficult years that would include painful cost reductions. For this reason, many senior people wanted Whitwam to put the implementation of the culture process on hold. They argued that talking values while practicing cost reductions would make everyone look like a hypocrite.

As Whitwam proceeded, he introduced a bold design for the Naples conference. He started by asking three industry analysts to provide an honest external view of Whirlpool. This ran the risk of alienating the participants and destroying the spirit of the conference. It did turn out to be brutally honest, and it did have a splintering effect as participants searched for explanations and excuses. Instead of resolving the tension by taking on his normal authority role, Whitwam chose the role of facilitator, opening dialog and surfacing conflicts. This role change was striking to the participants and noted as a dramatic change in Whitwam. By the end of the three days, the top management was more focused than at any time in recent history.

Step 4: High-Performance Culture Workshops for All Employees

This constituted the largest intervention in the history of the company. The objectives of the design included increased awareness of Whirlpool's history, a better understanding of the business plan, understanding of and commitment to the values, and the generation of a personal value-based action plan. At the time of this writing the workshops were being initiated.

Step 5: Value Challenge Meetings

Throughout the year, meetings were held encouraging people to challenge the values and discuss inherent trade-offs. The 140 senior leaders around the world were asked to conduct at least one multilevel challenge meeting on each of the five values: respect, integrity, teamwork, learning to lead, and spirit of winning. Using the intranet, the global results were reported to the entire company.

The Application of Advanced Change Theory: A Retrospective Analysis

Earlier we reviewed the basic assumptions of ACT and pointed out that ACT implies enormous personal accountability on the part of each individual. We noted that this can lead to two rationalizations: first, that ACT could be enacted only by heroic figures, not normal humans, and second, that ACT is unrealistic because it cannot be enacted in transactional settings such as corporations. Then we reviewed the history of Whirlpool's culture change effort. Here it might be useful to clarify the roles of the authors in the change process. Quinn was an external consultant who worked closely with Snyder, the chief learning officer for Whirlpool and internal director of the High-Performance Culture (HPC) process who closely witnessed the day-to-day change process. Quinn was also present for most of the major events described here.

Following is a retrospective analysis of the Whirlpool effort. Our purpose is to ground our understanding of ACT with actual examples and illustrate that ACT is in fact enactable in the world of business. It takes the form of an interview with the two authors of this chapter.

ACT begins with the assumption that to revitalize and find meaning in a world that is hierarchical and therefore losing alignment with present reality, it is necessary to create a community of inclusion, equality, and openness. In what way was Whirlpool having these problems of misalignment with reality and how did the culture effort embody equality and inclusion?

SNYDER: When you look at the issues of equality and inclusion, many stories come to mind. For eighty-five years, Whirlpool has been a very structured place to work. Along the way people were classified into hierarchical categories and these classifications created in-groups and out-groups. For example, one of the most divisive categorizations made in North America was the distinction between exempt and nonexempt employees. This has created enormous conflict and dissatisfaction. For example, we at Whirlpool have a forum where world-class speakers in management are invited to speak to a management club. Nonexempts are not allowed to join the management club. To most, this seems ridiculous, but it has been going on for twenty years. There are many examples of this kind of stratification. The culture initiative created a constructive forum where people could talk about these issues. We talked, for example, about the "PowerPoint Culture." That is code for lack of two-way dialogue. In recent years, there was no way to challenge ideas or assumptions. This is one reason why the plan for 1995 was so out of touch with reality. No one dared to tell the truth. There was a shield that prevented us from being honest with each other. The culture initiative opened up the dialogue and people began to feel that they could discuss real issues in a meeting room. Now a change is occurring. Recently, for example, I went to a meeting of one of the regional businesses. In that meeting some very difficult issues needed to be raised. One vice president started his comments by stating, "In the spirit of HPC, I think we are having a monologue instead of a dialogue." His statement had immediate impact. Suddenly the communication pattern went from a top-down monologue to a group of equals confronting each other over real issues.

QUINN: The capacity for discussion is important. This is a company that has been shaken by globalization and stretch effort. It has been taken out of a comfortable Midwestern mind-set, and over a five-year period people have been expected to perform beyond anything they could have previously imagined. At first the success was exhilarating. After five years, however, all slack was removed—both in material resources and in human energy. As these processes unfolded, there was less and less time for dialogue, and the PowerPoint Culture became more and more dominant. Results were emphasized over relationships, and, paradoxically for the actors, results soon deteriorated. This fact became undiscussable. As a consequence, people felt increasingly excluded. They were not part of the decision-making process.

So here was a company facing ever-more-complex global stimuli, facing ever-increasing pressure for financial performance, and a simultaneous shrinking capacity for meaningful internal dialogue and sense making. This combination had to result in a loss of alignment with presently emerging reality. Whitwam was the one who first realized this. His insight stimulated the HPC initiative. Quickly following Whitwam were a handful of vice presidents who realized that they had to change to get on board and that this change had to be very visible. I think of one vice president who did not have staff meetings or even talk to the people around him. He held an

HPC event and struggled to model the new behavior. He then asked for help to keep it going. His people were astonished and supportive. They still talk about it.

SNYDER: The culture initiative has also created community. One indication of this is that there is a new language. Two years ago you never would have heard terms like emotion, feeling, spirit, inclusion, relations, or even culture. If you used such language you would have been considered soft. I think the change started with Whitwam. I can remember times in meetings where he would use terms like culture, or nurture, and I would look up in surprise. Two years ago he never would have used the terms. I am not a language expert, but I think this introduction of new language has given us vehicles to talk about what we are feeling. We now have norms that make it all right to use these terms. It is permissible to reflect feelings and discuss them. I recently sat in a meeting with a mid-level manager who talked about the emotion and energy she wanted to create in her organization. Those words would not have been uttered one year ago.

QUINN: In summary, the company was getting increasingly disconnected from reality. The intervention created dialogue and the opportunity for people to take more equal roles and honestly communicate while still holding their formal places in the hierarchy. A new language helped in a number of ways to value and examine relationships as well as results. Whitwam's role modeling was a very important factor in the process but equally important was the modeling that was occurring at every level of the organization.

ACT assumes that the most important resistance is not within the change target but in the change agent, and that the change agent must continually seek to eliminate self-deception and reduce integrity gaps. Has that happened at Whirlpool?

SNYDER: I think self-deception is a serious problem in all human beings and all organizations. Yet we are making some progress. I think of a recent meeting with the top 140 people that was intended to address some difficult business proposals. In the meeting, Whitwam referred to the previous meeting with this group and some feedback he had received. In the previous meeting Whitwam indicated he was pleased with the second quarter results. People in the audience did not think it was a good quarter and felt bad about the results. In the feedback, some people told him that his statement appeared disingenuous. Now that would have never happened in the past. What was even more striking was Whitwam's reaction. He called each person who gave him that message and openly explored the issue!

This is my interpretation, but I believe he was checking his own integrity and self-deception issues. Think about it. Here we have people willing to risk telling the chairman that he is being self-deceptive, the chairman then actively explores the issue with them, then he reports on it in the next meeting. That is real culture change. Suddenly an undiscussable issue is discussable. There was openness, listening, learning, and exploration and closing of an integrity gap.

Despite this event we still have a long way to go in all parts of the organization. The role of formal feedback may prove important. Previously, no one asked for, or expected, meaningful feedback. We had an appraisal process but it was pretty constricted. As part of the culture initiative we introduced 360-degree feedback, but, more importantly, we structured it around the values. People are now being evaluated by supervisors, peers, and subordinates on whether they are demonstrating the values in their daily behaviors. Initially, people were very skeptical and hesitant to engage in the process. They really did not trust that it was anonymous and there was cynicism about whether it would really result in change. To help overcome this, it was communicated that Whitwam was going through the process. In addition to getting subordinate feedback, he had asked members of the board of directors to evaluate him on his demonstration of the values. At the time of this interview he is setting up the follow-up process so that when leaders receive their feedback, they will share it with their work groups and other peers to enlist their help in their personal change process. Whitwam plans to be the first to share his feedback with all of us. Recently the whole top management team in North America brought their 360 results and shared them in a workshop. Given the excitement that was generated, the process cascaded down to additional levels. There was one member in this group to whom people never gave feedback. He seemed too far gone. Having him share his feedback and ask his colleagues for help in living the values was a dramatic event for the group.

ACT assumes that the change agent's effort in self-modification and empowerment results in increased cognitive complexity and the ability to see larger governing rules or seemingly paradoxical relationships. They also engage in unconventional behaviors that distort routines, capture attention, and move the system toward the edge of chaos. Were there any examples of this?

SNYDER: I am reminded of the Naples senior leadership meeting, and Whitwam's invitation to the three analysts to give an honest external view of the company. That was high risk. He had no idea what they would say. I remember when he told me he was going to do this, I was scared to death. I refer to that session, which turned out to be a landmark event, as "first truth," because it was really the first meeting I remember where a message of that magnitude was not controlled.

I think of another example. Mike Thieneman was recently appointed as the new head of North America. This is the third-biggest job in the company. After just a few days on the job, he sent out a letter to everyone in his region that spelled out how he wanted to work. In the letter he requested no PowerPoint overheads be used in his meetings. He also indicated that he wants everyone to contact him directly if they have a problem or idea. The letter sent a positive shock wave. People are still talking about it. In an interview for our internal newsletter, Mike said that his hobbies are gardening and woodworking and that the first thing in his life is his family. I have never seen this kind of disclosure at Whirlpool. He recently dressed up like a wizard on Halloween and visited everyone on every floor. These are unconventional behaviors and they send the message, "Hey, something different is happening. I had better pay attention."

QUINN: There was something else very important about the Naples meeting. The analysts were stunning. In fact, I have never witnessed such a brutal assessment in any other company. They were challenging everything about the past, present, and future of the company, and doing it in a way that no internal person ever could.

What was particularly impressive to me was the role that Dave took after the analysts finished. At that moment of extreme challenge, nearly any CEO would have felt obliged to regain control by taking on an authority role. Given Dave's behavior in the past, this seemed a sure bet. Yet he resisted the predictable pattern and became a group facilitator. This was clearly an unconventional behavior and everyone noticed and commented on it. Instead of grasping for control he chose to trust the process, to open the honest exploration of the issues. This is the process of letting go of control, walking on the edge of chaos, and trusting that a new and better order will emerge. Such individual behavior becomes an attractor to the larger system, pulling it toward the edge of chaos where new structures can emerge.

At Naples, Dave allowed an emergent system to come forward, one that was more aligned with present reality. He was literally changing himself and the company at the same time. Dave and those senior managers were cocreating the future. Yet it is interesting to note that it got darker before it got lighter. For nearly a day and a half people were disoriented. Many commented that they had never seen the top group so fragmented. Yet Dave did not waver. I watched him very closely in the facilitator role, and he got better as time went on. For two days he let the natural process unfold. He trusted the emergent process and it worked. At the close of the week everyone, including Dave, was exhilarated.

Now here are three key questions: Why did he invite the analysts in? Why did he take the facilitator role? And why was he able to stick with it? I believe the answers are embedded in several previous events, particularly the chairman's council when it challenged Dave and he engaged in an honest dialog. That resulted in a dramatic change. Dave has described how moved he was by the council members' new level of commitment and their willingness to accept leadership responsibility. I believe as that process unfolded, Dave learned about the power of the emergent process. His cognitive complexity increased, he was able to see and understand new patterns. He had a greater vision and he employed that vision to design a most unconventional Naples program. It might even be said that he designed a paradoxical intervention. He built commitment by introducing intense criticism. In the end he increased control by letting go of control. I think that each time one of us lets go of control and approaches the edge of chaos, trusting the emergent system to arise, it does arise and our vision and capacity are greatly increased. I think this happened to Dave at several points in the process and again at Naples.

SNYDER: In regard to the paradoxical notion, I think of an event at the chairman's council. At the end of the workshop, we divided the participants into groups of four and gave them time to have private meetings with Whitwam. In one of those sessions, two of the members told him that they had thought about the culture change initiative and they had concluded that they could not support it. This was out-of-the-box honesty. What would the normal person do at that point? I believe most senior people would have told these two people to get on board or get out. Whitwam's reaction was surprising. He decided to spend time with them. He took a mentor role with the intention of helping them make a decision that was best for them and best for the company. He did not tell them what to think or do; he helped them make the right decision. In the end, one left the company and one stayed. That was new and unconventional behavior leading to the cocreation and emergence of two different but correct strategies for two unique individuals.

When I think of increased cognitive complexity and paradoxical behaviors, I also think of the controversy that we got into when we proposed to introduce the culture change at the same time we were introducing massive cost reductions, including layoffs. To nearly everyone these two initiatives seemed incongruent and ill-advised. Yet Whitwam would not let go. I think he intuitively realized that it was the ideal time. Bob, you helped articulate the notion when you presented in Naples. You argued that the culture changes in the same way it emerges, in dialogue under uncertainty. You claimed that the best way to change a culture is to enact the values when it is inconvenient to do so. Walking the talk in hard times would be the most powerful intervention of all. I think that articulated what Dave was feeling in the first place. For the rest of us, although it was undeniable logic, it was frightening responsibility. It meant we had to treat the values as a reality and discipline ourselves to a standard we were not sure we could live up to. It also made it clear that in arguing with Dave we were involved in an act of collective self-deception. That is, we were implicitly saying, "Do not introduce the values, people will expect us to behave with integrity and we do not want that responsibility, it is too high a standard." In other words, "In these hard times we need the freedom to go on not living the values."

ACT assumes that the pursuit of self-interest reinforces the existing equilibrium. In contrast, the change agent articulates and pursues a vision of common good at a personal cost to the change agent. Modeling the courage for personal change and increased integrity creates a situation in which others are attracted into a relationship of trust, exploration, and change. Did this occur at any point in the process?

QUINN: We already indicated several instances of vision, modeling, and attracting. These three behaviors were clearly part of the process. Modeling the courage for personal change was important throughout. It was a point of discussion from the very outset. Whitwam has always been a strong, directive, and results-oriented leader. Yet when I think about our early meetings with him, we saw a very reflective, sensitive, concerned person. In the early planning stages, however, I think he saw the culture change process as something we were supposed to "do to them." When I first raised the point that culture change begins with personal change, he was pretty suspicious. Then we had the second and third meetings, and with each meeting it was easier to talk about the principle of personal change. He gradually understood and bought in. After the chairman's council he was really committed to it. He recently told me he is using a journal to write down his reflections. He says that before almost every act he asks himself not only what the likely result will be, but also "Am I behaving according to the Whirlpool values?" He is a person who is genuinely reflecting on who he is.

SNYDER: There is a fascinating thread in all of this. I think he started to understand that he had to sacrifice long-held patterns for the good of Whirlpool, and he had to do all of this publicly. I think he could go through this change very privately, but he chooses to do it publicly. He talks about it with every group he meets, what he is working on, what is working, and what isn't. And when he does this, I find myself thinking: If he can do this in front of all of us, why can't I? I think that almost everyone that watches him is confronted with this thought. So I find myself doing the same kind of things he has done. I do it with people who work for me sharing my journey and asking for help. It is like he is either inspiring or shaming me into it. I am not sure which.

QUINN: I think you are really talking about the essence of ACT. In the chairman's council he got up one time and really engaged himself with the group, tried to listen and interact with them. The reaction was almost exhilaration in the room; you could feel it. There was something happening and they knew it was real. Later he would reflect that this experience had the greatest impact on him of all of the workshops. Whenever he dared to go to the edge of chaos, they could not help but go with him. He became an attractor. He was truly attracting them into new behaviors. I remember a senior officer making a comment at the end of the day in a session: "Dave Whitwam is asking me for help and I have no choice but to respond. He has been self-sufficient for all of these years. When he makes an honest plea for help, I find it irresistible." Later this very leader employed the same strategy with his group. He made himself vulnerable. He asked for help. He exposed a side of himself that his group had not seen. They had a very positive reaction. His people have told that story over and over.

SNYDER: I have a quote from a recent interview I did with Dave, and I think it speaks volumes about commitment to the common good and what it takes to successfully pursue the common good:

> Sooner or later, every leader comes to understand how little power he or she really has. I will take you back to when this was just a North American business. A person could get things done continuously, consistently. As we became more complex and the environment more intense, it became impossible to get things done through the force of leadership. Everything in my mind has always been so clear and logical. I felt, if we just do what we know how to do every day, this thing will work. I had this grand scheme and grand design and grand vision and I thought I could articulate it and get people lined up. It did not happen. It absolutely did not happen. I think that I had to come to grips with the fact that it is not enough for me to be committed, to have a plan and understand where we are going. I realized I had to get everyone engaged and committed.

QUINN: I find that statement very moving. It captures a core change in a very intense man. He came to understand that to achieve the results he was so intensely pursuing, he had to let go of control. He could only achieve those results by tending to the values and relationships in the company. He never lost his focus on results. He pointed out time and time again that the culture effort was about high performance, not relationships for the sake of relationships, but high performance and significant results. Whenever a person pushes self outside of the comfort zone in the pursuit of the common good, people respond. They may respond because they are inspired or shamed, but they do respond.

In summary, there are several points worth making. First, Whitwam has undergone some very impressive changes. He is, however, still the same man. I suspect we could interview anyone close to him and they would have a list of his shortcomings and failings. Second, many other people have also made important behavioral changes in leading the culture effort. This includes you, Nancy, the executive vice presidents, and numerous others. Third, this effort is not a panacea. If Whirlpool has a spectacular record in 1998 and 1999, we would be crazy to claim that it was the outcome of the culture change effort. The culture is only one of many important variables. Likewise, if the business struggles in 1998 and 1999, it will not be a demonstration that the culture effort was ineffective. Finally, this entire process is very fragile and it could disintegrate any time. It will take a committed, long-term effort to make it successful over time.

Summary and Conclusion

In this chapter we outlined the assumptions of Advanced Change Theory. We reviewed a major change effort in a major corporation. We provided a retrospective analysis of the change effort. In the analysis we attempted to show how the assumptions of ACT were enacted. The purpose was to further understanding of ACT and to show how real people in real organizations might enact it. We hope that this statement and illustration of ACT will help researchers to more deeply penetrate the phenomenon of transformation and help change agents more effectively execute the phenomenon of transformation.

Notes

1. Heifetz, R. A., and Laurie, D. L. "Doing Adaptive Work: The New Task of Change Leaders." In J. A. Conger, G. M. Spreitzer, and E. E. Lawler (eds.), *The Leader's Change Handbook: An Essential Guide to Setting Direction and Taking Action.* San Francisco: Jossey-Bass, 1998.

2. Bartlett, C. A., and Ghoshal, S. "Creating the Individualized Corporation: The Path to Self-Renewal at General Electric." In J. A. Conger, G. M. Spreitzer, and E. E. Lawler (eds.), *The Leader's Change Handbook: An Essential Guide to Setting Direction and Taking Action.* San Francisco: Jossey-Bass, 1998.

3. Pascale, R. T. "Leading from a Different Place: Applying Complexity Theory to Tap Potential." In J. A. Conger, G. M. Spreitzer, and E. E. Lawler (eds.), *The Leader's Change Handbook: An Essential Guide to Setting Direction and Taking Action.* San Francisco: Jossey-Bass, 1998.

4. Quinn, R. E., Brown, M., and Spreitzer, G. M. "The Empowering Self Modification Strategy: a Fourth General Strategy for Effecting Changes in Human Systems." Working paper available from the authors, 1998.

5. Chin, R., and Benne, K. D. "General Strategies for Effecting Changes in Human Systems." In W. G. Bennis, K. D. Benne, and R. Chin (eds.), *The Planning of Change: Readings in Applied Behavioral Sciences.* New York: Holt, Rinehart and Winston, 1969.

6. Campbell, J. *The Hero with a Thousand Faces.* New York: Bollingen Foundation, 1949.

7. Iyer, R. *The Essential Writings of Mahatma Gandhi.* England: Oxford University Press, 1990, p. 257.

8. King, C. S. *A Testament of Hope: The Essential Writings and Speeches of Martin Luther King, Jr.* (J. M. Washington, ed.). New York: Harper-Collins, 1988, p. 7.

9. See note 7, p. 53.

10. See note 8, p. 219.

11. See note 7, p. 108.

12. See note 8, p. 148.

13. See note 7, p. 90.

14. See note 8, p. 509.

15. See note 7, p. 92.

16. See note 8, p. 511.

17. See note 7, p. 89.

18. See note 8, p. 135.

19. See note 7, p. 182.

20. See note 8, p. 103.

21. See note 7, p. 122.

22. See note 8, p. 218.

23. See note 7, p. 411.

24. See note 8, p. 122.

25. Payne, R. *The Life and Death of Mahatma Gandhi.* New York: NAL/Dutton, 1969, p. 557.

26. See note 8, p. 491.
27. See note 25, p. 223.
28. See note 8, p. 57.
29. See note 25, p. 557.
30. See note 8, p. 509.
31. See note 25, p. 385.
32. See note 8, p. 290.

Chapter Eight

Leading from a Different Place

Applying Complexity Theory to Tap Potential

Richard T. Pascale

Over the past century, four useful templates have emerged in our quest to understand leadership. Complementary in many respects, each has a distinct bias. The *traits*-based view focuses on the behavioral attributes of leaders; the *situational* approach emphasizes the social context that calls forth particular types of leadership; the *contingency* approach combines these first two and prescribes the match of traits for particular situations. The *transaction* model investigates leadership as a negotiation in which followers confer authority in exchange for benefits.[1]

These distinctions unquestionably have shed light on the topic. But like the scholarly research on what makes jokes funny, dissecting leadership into categories loses something that is unfathomable in the whole. Leadership continues to fascinate us. Its paradoxes beckon for insight that always seems to elude our grasp.

A recent field of scientific inquiry, Complex Adaptive Systems, affords a new angle on the subject. The primary virtue of this work is that it looks holistically at the relationship both among an organism's component parts and between it and its environment. The Complexity view of leadership builds on the situational and contingency models. It goes further, however, by asserting that social systems contain latent (or emergent) properties. The primary task of leadership is to create a context that calls forth and taps this emergent potential. Gandhi, for example, gave expression to latent nationalism in India. Leaders of the American Revolution catalyzed unarticulated strivings for representative forms of government. More recently, a number of less historically celebrated figures have catalyzed, or at least permitted, an emergent trend away from Marxist governments and centralized economies. The "idea whose time has come" is all about emergence.

Harvard's Ron Heifetz has contributed to our understanding of leadership a perspective that dovetails with the general principles of Complexity. He observed that social systems react to disequilibrium by attempting to restore stability. If they are facing a clear-cut problem for which a prior solution has been devised, the system prevails intact. But when the problem faced has no known solution (in Heifetz's terminology, an "adaptive" problem), attempts to restore equilibrium often result in suppressing troubling factions, denial, or diverting attention to easier issues while the underlying problem grows worse.

Leaders often unwittingly compound their difficulties when facing an adaptive problem. This results from a conditioned reflex over an executive's career: authority is gained by taking a problem off others' shoulders and carrying them until a solution is found.

Authority restores and maintains equilibrium in a social system. Unfortunately, this becomes counterproductive in the face of an adaptive challenge. Heifetz observes that leaders often seek to reaffirm authority by quick fixes, moving on an issue too quickly and preempting followers from sharing the stress, understanding the full dimensions of the adaptive problem, and coming forward with solutions from the ranks. This work generates anxiety. Followers often turn to authority as a bulwark against the associated uncertainty and risk. Heifetz asserts, "The essential work of leadership is to resist these claims and, instead, (1) confront members with the reality that the [adaptive] challenge cannot be dealt with by the traditional repertoire, but rather that all must seek the answers together, (2) regulate distress such that the social system is drawn sufficiently out of its comfort zone, yet does not become dysfunctional, and (3) manage avoidance mechanisms that may arise to avoid adaptive work (such as scapegoating, looking to authority for the answer and so forth)."[2] Ultimately, if the social system is to succeed, emergent solutions must be generated to meet the challenge at hand.

Complex Adaptive Systems

The term Complex Adaptive Systems (Complexity for short) is used to label the developing theories of how the living world works. This is not, to be sure, a universal theory of everything. But the work has identified principles of great generality that are common among living entities—amoebae and ant colonies, bacteria, beehives and bond traders, ecologies and economies, you and me.

The origins of the work on Complexity began at New Mexico's Santa Fe Institute in the mid-1980s among a number of distinguished scientists (including two Nobel laureates) with backgrounds as diverse as particle physics, microbiology, archeology, astrophysics, paleontology, zoology, botany, and economics.[3] These individuals were drawn together by similar questions that lurked at the shadowy frontier of their respective fields. Wishing to stalk this enigmatic kernel, the National Science Foundation underwrote a series of symposia. These founding workshops revealed that all the assembled disciplines shared, at their core, building blocks composed of many, many agents. These might be molecules, neurons, a species, customers, members of a social system, or networks of corporations. Further, these fundamental systems were continually organizing and reorganizing themselves, all flourishing in a boundary between rigidity and randomness, and all occasionally forming larger structures through the clash of natural accommodation and competition. Molecules would form cells, neurons would cluster into neural networks (or brains), species would form ecosystems, individuals would form tribes or societies, consumers and corporations would form economies. These self-organizing structures give rise to emergent behavior, a straightforward example of which is the process whereby prebiotic chemicals combined to form the extraordinary diversity of life on earth. Self-organization and emergence are two sides of the same hand of life.

The science of Complexity has yielded four generalizable propositions that have relevance to leadership:

1. As a general rule, Complex Adaptive Systems are at risk when in equilibrium. Equilibrium is a precursor to death.[4]
2. Complex Adaptive Systems exhibit the capacity of self-organization and emergent complexity.[5] Self-organization arises from

intelligence in the remote clusters (or "nodes") within a network. Emergent complexity is generated by the propensity of simple structures to generate novel patterns, infinite variety, and, often, a sum that is greater than the parts—again, as with the escalating complexity of life on earth.

3. Complex Adaptive Systems surf at the edge of chaos when provoked by a complex task.[6] Bounded instability is more conducive to evolution than either stable equilibrium or explosive instability. One important implication of this principle is that a Complex Adaptive System, once having reached a temporary peak in its fitness landscape (such as a company during its golden era), must then "go down to go up"—that is, moving from one peak to a still higher peak requires it to traverse the valleys of the fitness landscape. In cybernetic terms, the organism must be pulled by competitive pressures far out of its usual arrangements before it can create substantially different forms and arrive at a more evolved basin of attraction.[7]

4. One cannot direct a living system, only disturb it.[8] Complex Adaptive Systems are characterized by weak cause-effect linkages. Phase transitions (or "gateway events") occur in the realm where one relatively small and isolated variation can produce huge effects. Alternatively, large changes may have little effect.[9] This phenomenon is common in the information industry. Massive efforts to promote a superior operating system may come to naught whereas a series of serendipitous events may establish an inferior operating system—such as MS-DOS—as the industry standard.

Leadership in a Complex Adaptive System

Let us examine the relevance of these four propositions through the lens of two real-life applications. Two unlikely institutions—Royal Dutch Shell ($130 billion in annual revenues, 105,000 employees in 130 countries) and the United States Army ($60 billion operating budget, 600,000 soldiers and civilians deployed around the globe)—provide the grist for our inquiry. Leaders at both institutions have embraced the principles of Complexity and pioneered their application in practice.

Disturbing Equilibrium in the U.S. Army

As suggested by the first principle of Complexity, a paradox besets every organization: social systems in disequilibrium seek stability. Yet without periodic instability, complacency renders them unable to adapt when the environment suddenly changes. Such were the perils facing the U.S. Army following the catastrophic setbacks in Vietnam. Many in its ranks sought to retrench around the military's tried and true formula. Illustrative was the institution's handling of the Volunteer Army. When Congress ended conscription following Vietnam, the Army regarded this change as an inconvenient modification to a factor of production. The Army requested, and received from Congress, a higher pay package to attract volunteers. This was seen as the only major adjustment necessary. The Army did not reckon with the difficulty of attracting the *right kind* of volunteers nor with the possibility that they would need to be motivated and led in a different fashion than conscripts. The result? Within three years, the Army found itself an extension of the U.S. criminal justice system; judges were offering first-time offenders the choice of jail or "volunteering" for the Army. By 1979, disciplinary problems were rampant. Surveys showed that 30 to 40 percent of soldiers engaged in drug use.[10]

Reluctantly, several senior leaders became convinced that the culture had to be pried loose from the iron grip of tradition. Instead of downplaying the growing crisis (as a means of falsely reassuring the troops that all was well), these leaders began to dramatically raise the stress level. They startled the ranks with an array of challenges so daunting that few could retain their equanimity. The "military model" was increasingly called into question—even heretically characterized as ballast that must be jettisoned in pursuit of necessary change.

Former Chief of Staff Gordon R. Sullivan describes this transition:

> Following Vietnam, it became evident to many that the Army
> needed to reinvent itself. We had to circumvent our traditional
> training institutions and create a whole new experimental domain
> where entire regiments of 3,000 soldiers (from privates to generals)

were confronted with a devastating introduction to modern warfare. In this environment, our usual doctrine for fighting and methods of leading often failed. This was the wake-up call and it served to boost the Army to a whole new level. Yet, even with the successes of the Gulf War, the requirement for continuous renewal has been unrelenting. Desert Storm was the first Information Age war. It was fought and won with smart weapons and by knocking out the Iraqis' communications system. The paradox of war in the Information Age is one of managing massive amounts of information and resisting the temptation to overcontrol with it. The competitive advantage is nullified when you try to run decisions up and down the chain of command. Every platoon and tank crew has real-time information on what is going on around them, the location of the enemy, and the nature and targeting of the enemy's weapons system. Once the commander's intent is understood, decisions must be devolved to the lowest possible level to allow these front-line soldiers to exploit the opportunities that develop. As the eighth-largest army in the world today, we must punch above our weight. We can do this by combining the best technology with an organization that is agile enough to exploit it.[11]

Shell and the Status Quo

Shell likewise found itself in the grip of the perils of its hundred-year history.[12] The cumulative effect of tradition, the cumbersome momentum of $130 billion in annual revenues, 105,000 predominantly long-tenured employees, and operations dispersed across 130 nations around the globe left Shell vulnerable. Profits continued to flow, but fissures were forming beneath the surface. From 1992 to 1995, a full 50 percent of Shell's retail revenues in France fell victim to the onslaught of the European hypermarkets and a similar pattern was emerging in Germany and the United Kingdom. Elsewhere in the world, new competitors, global customers, and more savvy national oil companies were demanding a radically different approach to the marketplace.

In 1996, Steve Miller, then fifty-one, was appointed Group Managing Director of Shell's Worldwide Oil Products business. With this appointment, he became a member of Shell's Committee of Managing Directors—the five senior leaders who consider and develop objectives and long-term plans for the Group. Over the previous two years, the company had been engaged in a program to transform the organization. But neither the massive reorganization, traumatic downsizing, nor thousands of man-hours spent in senior management workshops had much to show for all the effort. Shell's earnings, although solid, were disappointing financial analysts who expected more from the industry's largest competitor. Employees registered widespread resignation and cynicism. And the operating units at the "coal face" (Shell's term for its frontline activities in the 130 countries where it does business) saw little more than business as usual.

For Miller, Shell's impenetrable culture was especially worrisome. The Downstream Business (composed of dozens of product lines from fuels to lubricants to asphalt, and operations stretching from supply and trading to manufacturing and marketing) accounts for 37 percent of Shell's assets. Among the several businesses in the Shell Group's portfolio, Downstream faced the gravest competitive threats. Having observed the underwhelming progress of Shell's previous efforts to enroll and transform its many layers of management (one layer at a time!), Miller was convinced that it was essential to reach around the resistant bureaucracy and involve the front lines of the organization. This is a formidable task given the sheer size of the operation. For example, Shell's forty-seven thousand filling stations employ hundreds of thousands of people, mostly part-time attendants, and cater to approximately ten million customers every day. Having an impact on marketplace behavior for an operation of this scale could not, Miller believed, be driven by the centralized dictates of headquarters. In the language of Complexity, he believed it necessary to tap the emergent properties of Shell's enormous distribution system. He saw this system not as a resistant mass governed by apathy and inertia, but as a fertile organism that needed encouragement to, in his words, "send green shoots forth." Miller is succeeding at what few imagined possible.

Let us examine his approach to leadership within the context of Complex Adaptive Systems. Commencing in mid-1996, Miller reallocated more than 50 percent of his calendar to work directly with front-line personnel. Miller states:

Our Downstream Business transformation program had bogged down largely because of the impasse between headquarters and the operating companies [Shell's term for its highly independent country operations]. The tried and true solutions, perfected in a period of relative equilibrium, simply weren't working. But the forces for continuing in the old way were enormous, extending throughout the organization. We're overseeing the most decentralized operation in the world, with country chief executives that had, since the 1950s, enjoyed enormous autonomy. This had been part of our success formula. Yet we were encountering a set of daunting competitive threats that transcended national boundaries. Global customers—like British Airways or Daimler Benz—wanted to deal with one Shell contact, not with a different Shell representative in every country in which they operated. We had huge overcapacity in refining, but each country CEO (motivated to maximize his own P/L) resisted the consolidation of refining capacity. These problems begged for strategic optimization at a regional level.

Shell had tried to transform this organization using the social engineering approach: directives were issued at the top and driven through the organization one layer at a time. "It was like the old game of telephone that we used to play when we were kids," said Miller. "You'd whisper a message to the person next to you, and it goes around the circle. By the time you get to the last person, it bears almost no resemblance to the message you started with. Apply that to the sixty-one thousand people in the Downstream Business across the globe and I knew we couldn't transform our company that way. The linkages between directives given and actions taken are too problematic." What made sense to Miller was to broadly engage the members of the organization in the challenges Shell faced and to fundamentally alter the conversation. Organizations are networks of conversations—via memos, e-mail, reports, procedures, what people say to each other, and what they say silently to themselves. Miller believed it essential to change this conversation to unleash the emergent possibilities.

Miller's executives in the operating companies were saying that centralization would only bog them down. "They were partly right," he acknowledges. "These are big companies. Some earn several hundreds of millions a year in net income. But the alternative wasn't centralization—it was a radical change in our Downstream culture from top to bottom such that we could come together in appropriate groups, solve problems, and operate in a manner which transcended the old headquarters versus field schism. What initially seemed like a huge conflict has gradually melted away. This occurred, I believe, because we applied a whole new paradigm of leadership and change."

Miller's solution was to cut through all the layers and barriers of the organization, put senior management in direct contact with the people at the grassroots level, foster many, many initiatives, overwhelm the old order, create a whole new conversation and sense of urgency. The first wave of initiatives spawned other initiatives. In Malaysia, for example, Miller's pilot efforts with four initiative teams (called Action Labs) have proliferated to forty. "It worked," he states, "because the people at the coal face usually know what's going on. They see the competitive threats and our inadequate response every day. Once you give them the context, they can do a better job of spotting opportunities and stepping up to decisions. In less than two years, we've seen astonishing progress in our retail business in some twenty-five countries. This represents around 85 percent of our retail sales volume and we have now begun to use this approach in our service organizations and lubricant business. For example, by the end of 1997 the French operating company had regained initiative and achieved double-digit growth, and return on capital and market share."

Harnessing Self-Organization and Emerging Complexity

Living organisms, as described by the second principle of Complexity, have the ability to self-organize and generate higher levels of sophistication from simpler building blocks. Miller's methods add considerably to our practical understanding of what it takes to lead a Complex Adaptive System. Building on the earlier-noted principles of Complexity, on a marketing model developed by Columbia's Larry Seldon, and on initial process design help from University of Michigan's Noel Tichy, Miller and his colleagues at Shell tapped into the intelligence in the trenches and channeled it into a tailored marketplace response. Shell's methodology is as revolutionary in sharpening the cutting edge of sales and marketing as was Toyota's Total Quality program in honing efficiency in manufacturing.

Miller states, "We needed a vehicle to give us an energy transfusion and remind us that we could play at a far more competitive level. The properties of self-organization and emergence make intuitive sense to me. The question was how to release them. Larry Seldon's model gave us a sharp-edged tool to identify customer needs and markets and to develop our value proposition. This, in effect, gave our troops the ammunition to shoot with—analytical distinctions to make the business case. Shell has always been a wholesaler. Yet the forecourt of every service station is an artery for commerce that any retailer would envy. Our task was to tap the potential of that real estate and we needed both the insight and the initiatives of our front-line troops to pull it off. For a company as large as Shell, leadership can't drive these answers down from the top. We needed to tap into ideas that were out there in the ranks—latent but ready to bear fruit if given encouragement."

Shell's methods look pedestrian at first glance. Miller began bringing six-to-eight-person teams from a half dozen Operating Companies from around the world into wave after wave of intense "retailing boot camps." The first five-day workshop introduced tools for identifying and exploiting market opportunities. It also included a dose of the leadership skills necessary to enroll others back home. Participants returned ready to apply the tools to achieve a breakthrough in such areas as doubling net income in filling stations on the major north-south highways of Malaysia, or tripling market share of bottled gas in South Africa. As the first group went home, six more teams would rotate in. Over the next 120 days the first batch used the analytical tools to sample customers, identify segments, and develop a value proposition, then returned to the workshop with a tentative business plan. At the close of this second workshop, each "action lab" sat with Miller and several of his direct reports in a "fishbowl" to review their business plans while the other teams observed the proceedings from the perimeter. Peer pressure and learning were intense. Then the teams went back to the field for another sixty days to put their ideas into action and returned for a follow-up to analyze the breakdowns and breakthroughs. Miller continues:

> Week after week, team after team, my six direct reports and I and our internal coaches reached out and worked directly with a diverse cross section of customers, dealers, fifty-year-old shop stewards, and young and mid-level professionals. And it worked. Operating Company CEOs, historically leery of any "help" from headquarters, saw their people return energized and armed with solid plans to beat the competition. The grassroots employees who participated in the program got to touch and feel the new Shell—a far more informal give-and-take culture. The conversation down in the ranks of the organization began to change. Guerilla leaders, historically resigned to Shell's conventional way of doing things, stepped forward to champion ingenious marketplace innovations, such as the Coca-Cola challenge in Malaysia—a free Coke to any service station customer who is not offered the full menu of fore-court services. Sounds trivial but it increased volume by 15 percent. Best of all, we learned together! I can't overstate how infectious the optimism and energy of these committed employees was on the many managers above them. In a curious way, these front-line employees taught us to believe in ourselves again.

The insights of Complexity are not revolutionary per se. But they represent a whole new paradigm when contrasted to the social engineering model prevalent at Shell. As executives move up in organizations, they get farther away from the work that goes on in the field—and the insidious part of this out-of-touchness is largely invisible. Directives from the top become more and more abstract. There is a tendency to rely on relatively mechanical cause-and-effect linkages—such as head-count controls, operational expense targets, pay-for-performance incentives, and so forth—to drive the business. These are the tie rods and pistons of the social engineering model. Complexity Theory doesn't discard these useful devices but it starts from a different place. The living systems approach *begins* with a focus on the intelligence in the nodes. It endeavors to ferret out what this network "sees," what stresses it is undergoing, and what is necessary to unleash its potential. This is the engine of a Complex System. Other support elements (such as controls and rewards) are orchestrated to *draw on* this potential, not to *drive down* solutions from above.

Self-Organization in the U.S. Army

The manner in which the Army harnessed self-organization[13] and emerging complexity requires a trip to the desert. The crucible for the earlier-noted source of revolution in military thinking was the National Training Center (NTC), arguably the most powerful leadership development and organizational change experience on the planet. The Army maintains three such centers—one at Fort Polk, Louisiana, for training smaller units for peacekeeping, insurgency, and guerilla warfare (the facility includes towns and villages populated with impromptu actors who play the role of innocent civilians, hecklers, and demonstrators), a second at Fort Irwin, California, for mechanized warfare (which encompasses nearly a million acres of rugged terrain in the Mojave Desert), and a third hybrid facility in Germany.

Let's observe the NTC process in action at Fort Irwin. Each afternoon, the Brigade Commander receives his assignment: penetrate enemy defenses, perhaps, or defend the sector against a superior force. Inside crowded command tents, thirty to forty staff officers and senior fighting unit commanders study the situation and endeavor to hammer out a winning strategy. By late afternoon these intentions begin to filter out to three thousand soldiers dispersed across many square miles of rugged terrain. Tank crews and platoons are briefed, minefields laid, artillery and helicopters coordinated, reconnaissance initiated. At midnight both friendly and enemy probes get under way.

By dawn, the day's battle is in full swing. The "enemy," the 11th Armored Cavalry Division, is permanently stationed at Fort Irwin. These soldiers know the terrain, behave unpredictably, and almost always devastate the unit in training. And it is all recorded. Perched on mountaintops, powerful video cameras zoom in on the hot spots. An elaborate laser-based technology precisely tracks when and where each weapon is fired, electronically disabling any fighting unit that is hit. Audio tapes record communication and confusion over the voice net. By 11 A.M., the battle's outcome has been decided. Within ninety minutes, the respective Observer-Controllers begin to pull each combat team together near a piece of terrain that had been pivotal to its part in today's battle.

This critical part of the learning design is called After Action Review (AAR). As we zoom in on the AAR in progress, a company team of two platoons involving two tanks, four armored personnel carriers, and an HMMV (the modern version of a jeep) have pulled into a tight circle in the shade of a desert outcropping. The crews lean back against tank treads, a flip chart slung over the HMMV antenna. The fighting is in its fifth day. Exhaustion is evident. The Observer-Controller has created a "sand table" in the ground—a miniature of the terrain in which this unit was annihilated in today's battle. He asks a tank gunnery sergeant to come forward to position the company's armor on the sand table and explain his understanding of their mission:

> *Sergeant:* Our overall mission was to destroy the enemy at objective K–2.
> *Observer-Controller:* Why was this important? And do you know what your tank's particular role was in all of this?
> *Sergeant:* I'm not sure.
> *Observer-Controller:* Can anyone help?

A trickle of comments gradually builds into a flood of discussion. Through the unfolding it becomes evident that only the lieutenant in charge understood the rationale behind the mission. Individual armored units were not coordinated and each had not concentrated on a particular sector of fire. Nor had they grasped that their main task together was to drive the enemy column away from a weak point in the defenses into a zone where they were within range of other friendly tanks and artillery.

Key learning points for tomorrow are recorded on the flip chart. Each soldier leaves with a picture of what he was in the middle of that he could not see. Each has contributed to this composite understanding, bolstered by video clips and hard data on the engagement that the Observer-Controller provides. Day after day, key themes are reinforced: Everyone needs to understand the big picture. Everyone needs to *think*. Always put yourself in the shoes of an uncooperative enemy. Prepare to the level where you are not surprised by surprise. Put hierarchy aside, foster self-criticism, and learn to work as a team.

States Brigadier General Leon La Porte, former commander of the NTC, "I learned more in the NTC in fourteen days than I had learned in the previous fourteen years of my career. Before the NTC, we used to kid ourselves. The training was highly subjective. But the NTC experience leaves no room for debate. Day after day, you are confronted with the hard evidence of discrepancies between intentions and faulty execution, between what you wanted the enemy to do and what he actually did. The NTC trains you *how* to think, not what to think. It prepares you for the fast pace and unforeseeable events of Information Age warfare."[14]

Surfing the Edge of Chaos

The third principle of Complexity focuses our intellectual microscope on bounded instability. It is in this domain, close to the edge of chaos, where social systems are stressed, become unfrozen, and subsequently experiment and learn. Previous descriptions of Shell and the Army have portrayed the careful orchestration of stress toward this end. A soldier's field experience at the NTC is intensified by grueling days, harsh physical conditions, sleep deprivation, and engagement after engagement with a superior enemy. The task of the Observer-Controller is to create a context for the exhaustion and failure: get the big picture, apply your intelligence, execute reliably *and* improvise appropriately to exploit the local situation. Leaders at all ranks are particularly challenged by the experience. Most come from a tradition of giving orders and imposing control—a strategy that does not work well given the velocity of modern warfare and the accuracy of modern weapons. Those in leadership positions discover that their units do best when they act as a communicator of broad intentions, as teacher, coach, and facilitator. Deep learning takes place when the old beliefs (and the social order in which they are embedded) are unfrozen. The edge of chaos is where unfreezing occurs in a living system.

Surfing the edge of chaos, moving from a temporary peak in the fitness terrain through a valley of emotional and performance inadequacy toward a goal of higher attainment is much harder to stage in industry than in the desert of the NTC. Shell's approach was to assemble compelling data on worrisome competitive trends, immerse country teams in these harsh realities against the backdrop of its aspiration to be number one (or a strong number two) in every market in which it operates, and provide the teams with tools to identify opportunities and to close the gap in the marketplace.

Many corporations have used what appear to be similar approaches with disappointing results. Shell's success derives from several fine points in the design. First, Miller and his top team performed major surgery on their calendars and reallocated approximately half of their time to teaching and coaching wave after wave of country teams. When the lowest levels of an organization are being trained, coached, and evaluated by those at the very top, it both inspires and stresses everyone in the system (including bosses who are not present). Second, the design, as we have seen, sent teams back to collect real data for 120 days (all while carrying their current job). Pressure to succeed, long hours both during the workshops and back in country (where these individuals continued to carry their regular duties along with project work) achieved the cultural unfreezing effect. Participants were resocialized into a much more direct, informal, and less hierarchical way of working. Says Miller:

> One of the most important innovations in changing all of us was the fishbowl. The name describes what it is: I and a number of my management team sit in the middle of a room with one Action Lab in the center with us. The other team members listen from the outer circle. Everyone is watching as the group in the hot seat talks about what they're going to do, and what they need from me and my colleagues to be able to do it. That may not sound revolutionary—but in our culture it was very unusual for anyone lower in the organization to talk this directly to a managing director and his reports.
>
> In the fishbowl, the pressure is on to measure up. The truth is, the pressure is on me and my colleagues. The first time we're not consistent, we're dead meat. If a team brings in a plan that's really a bunch of crap, we've got to be able to call it a bunch of crap. If we cover for people or praise everyone, what do we say when someone brings in an excellent plan? That kind of straight talk is another big culture change for Shell.[15]
>
> The whole process creates complete transparency between the people at the coal face and me and my top management team. At

the end, these folks go back home and say, "I just cut a deal with the managing director and his team to do these things." It creates a personal connection—and it changes how we talk with each other and how we work with each other. After that, I can call up those folks anywhere in the world and talk in a very direct way because of this personal connectedness. It has completely changed the dynamics of our operations.

It is important to note that Miller portrays a very different model than was prevalent at Shell. His "design for emergence" generated hundreds of informal connections between headquarters and the field, resembling the parallel networks of the nervous system to the brain. This is in contrast to the historical model of mechanical linkages analogous to those that transfer the energy from the engine in a car through a drive train to the tires that perform the work.

Learning to Disturb, Not Direct, a Complex System

Consistent with the fourth principle of Complexity, both the Army and Shell have self-consciously undertaken to shift their traditional style of leadership. In each case, the old way was a variation on command and control. In today's fast-changing environment, both believe that leaders must intuitively sense and cultivate the emergent possibilities in their organizations. Shell's Steve Miller puts it this way:

A successful company depends on leadership. But we need a different definition of leadership and a different approach to providing it. In the past, the leader was the guy with the answers. Today if you're going to have a successful company, you have to recognize that no leader can possibly have all the answers. The leader may have a vision. But the actual solutions about how best to meet the challenges of the moment have to be made by the people closest to the action—the people at the coal face.

Change your approach to leadership and you change the way a company runs. The leader becomes a context setter, the designer of a learning experience—not an authority figure with solutions. Once the folks at the grassroots realize they own the problem, they also discover that they can help create and own the answer—and they get after it very quickly, very aggressively, and very creatively, with a lot more ideas than the old-style leader could ever have driven from headquarters.

A program like this is a high-risk proposition, because it goes counter to the way most senior executives spend their time. I spend 50 to 60 percent of my time at this and there is no direct guarantee that what I'm doing is going to make something happen down the line. It's like becoming the helmsman of a big ship when you've grown up behind the steering wheel of a car. This approach isn't about me. It's about simple, well-taught marketing concepts, combined with a strong process design, that enable front-line employees to think like businesspeople. Top executives and front-line employees learn to work together in partnership.

People want to evaluate this against the old way which gives you the illusion of "making things happen." I encountered lots of thinly veiled skepticism: "Did your net income change from last quarter because of this change process?" These challenges create anxiety. The temptation, of course, is to reimpose your directives and controls even though we had an abundance of proof that this would not work. My six direct reports differ widely in personality. Most of them would never have chosen this approach to transforming the downstream culture. Yet today, all are effective in this mode and see its merits over the old approach.

There's another kind of risk to the leader from a program like this, and that's the risk of exposure. You're working very closely and intensely with all levels of staff, and they get to assess and evaluate you directly. Before, you were remote from them; now, you're very accessible. If that evaluation comes up negative, you've got a big-time problem.

Finally, the scariest part is letting go. You don't have the same kind of control that traditional leadership is used to. What you don't realize until you do it is that you may, in fact, have more control— but in a different fashion. You get more feedback than before, you learn more than before, you know more through your own people about what's going on in the marketplace and with customers than before. But you still have to let go of the old sense of control.

Miller's words testify to his reconciliation with the weak cause-and-effect linkages that exist in a living system. When leadership is exercised through a design for emergence, it never assumes that a particular input will produce a specific output. It is more akin to the study of subatomic particles in a bubble chamber. The experimenter's design creates probabilistic occurrences that take place within the domain of focus. Period. Greater precision is neither sought nor possible.

The Army, likewise, gives testimony to an approach that embraces the humbling truth that good leaders disturb more than direct. The trick, of course, is to realize that not just *any* disturbance will do. The type of disturbance sought is one that focuses attention and cultivates sufficient stress to evoke leaderlike behavior at all levels. Guerilla leaders come forward with ways to contribute to the larger whole.

It would be overdrawn, of course, to assign all of the Army's progress to its radical shift in leadership philosophy alone. How the Army has achieved and sustained its extraordinary transformation may be attributed to a number of factors including far-higher-quality soldiers—one outcome of a volunteer Army. But insiders and external observers agree that the shift in leadership approach fostered by the NTC has been a critical part in it all coming together. Since its inception, the Army's six hundred thousand men and women have rotated through its programs one and a half times, and most of the Army upper-, middle-, and senior-level officers and NCOs three times. Brigadier General W. (Scott) Wallace, former commander of the National Training Center, observes, "The National Training Centers and the After Action Review have democratized the Army. They have instilled a discipline of relentlessly questioning everything we do. Above all, this has resocialized three generations of officers to move away from a command-and-control style of leadership to one that takes advantage of distributed intelligence. It has enabled us to learn that we can never become too wedded to our script for combat and to remain versatile enough to exploit the 'broken plays' that inevitably develop in the confusion of battle."[16]

Sustaining the Gains from Complexity

Recent innovations within the Army and Shell provide face validity for the four principles of Complexity. But given the organic nature of Complex Systems, how does an organization *sustain* the ability to transform itself ongoingly?[17] It seems like a contradiction in terms.

Shell and the Army have aspired to build this capability by cultivating core disciplines. These are transformed into mindful practices and, where appropriate, into routines (such as the AAR), measurements, rewards, and values. All serve to keep these institutions perpetually off balance. The disciplines are woven into the fabric of the Army's National Training Center experience and Shell's Action Lab process. There are seven of these core disciplines, and all are important to sustained success over time.

1. Intricate Understanding of the Business

An organization's members do best when line-of-sight understanding bridges the gap between overall strategy and individual performance. This is harder than it seems. On the one hand, the Army's troops need to understand the principal aims of each engagement ("move to establish contact but don't precipitate an all-out fight" or "block the enemy at this line but don't commit to a counterattack") and how it fits into the larger strategic context. On the other hand, soldiers need to be firmly proficient in responding to what is required of them in a given situation.

The first requirement—to convey the big picture to the small unit—is easy to overlook in the heat of preparing for battle. In the AAR close-up described earlier, we saw how the lieutenant commanding the armored unit had neglected to carry it out and how his men then failed to achieve the goal of which they were unaware. To carry out the second requirement, the Army has borrowed a concept from the Total Quality Movement and distilled all the various facets of a military action down to three: the key *tasks* involved, the *conditions* under which each task may need to be performed, and the acceptable *standards* for success. For example, at a range of two thousand yards, hit an enemy tank moving at twenty miles per hour over uneven terrain at night with an 80 percent success rate. Soldiers are trained to meet these standards so they can be counted on to deliver when the situation arises.

Shell has devoted considerable energy to this discipline. The initial workshop introduces a business model using Shell's aggregate Downstream Business as the practical example. While participants are learning the model, they are absorbing the broad outlines of Shell's Downstream strategy (that is, commander's intent). When the Action Labs return to their host country, they collect detailed data by talking to customers, suppliers, other Shell employees, and even competitors. These facts are used to build a business plan that exploits a local opportunity, yet fits within the larger strategic context. As these plans are built from the ground up, relatively junior employees gain a solid grasp of the linkage between broad strategic intentions and operational factors on which they can have an impact and that are keys to execution and ultimate strategic success.

2. Uncompromising Straight Talk

The After Action Review is predicated on a frank exchange among soldiers as they sort through the confusion of battle and figure out where things went wrong. This will not occur if people are showing deference to their superiors or holding back for fear of hurting someone's feelings. As we noted earlier, Observer-Controllers are skilled at using objective data to point the finger, fostering healthy give and take and creating a safe environment for candor.

Shell's "fishbowl" was a crucible for straight talk (Miller's earlier quote suggests how quickly one is found out trying to smooth over problems in the face of public scrutiny). Paralleling the Army's AARs, the Action Lab workshops used the data collected from field interviews to challenge subjective opinion. During fishbowl sessions, tough questions were asked about a presenting team's business plan both by reviewing executives and one's peers (during the peer-challenge phase of the process).

3. Managing from the Future

The Army's mantra "Be All You Can Be" is much more than a recruiting slogan. It has been used to challenge every element of the institution—soldiers, technology, Logistics Command, and Signal Corps—to stretch itself. Being all you can be is not a destination to be reached but a mind-set to manage from.

Organizations often "use up" their future, and this is precisely what happened to the Army after the high-water mark of the Second World War and to Shell in the 1980s. Once the members of an organization believe they have *reached* the future, they begin to codify their past successes. Overuse of an institution's winning formulas leads to drift and the loss of vitality. Since the early eighties, a succession of the Army Chiefs of Staff have introduced ever more demanding visions to draw the Army away from the seductive pull of complacency. In the early nineties, it was "Reinvent the Army for Information Age Warfare." Currently the challenge is to prepare for the radical changes of the digital battlefield.

The discipline part of relating to the future is all a matter of perspective. Are you standing in the present trying to pull the leaden past toward a future goal, or standing in the future as an inevitability and managing the present from the future? Steve Miller inherited a wholesale Downstream Oil Business that had used up its future. As long as Shell saw itself primarily as a commodity wholesaler, it was submerged in a rear guard action, losing share to hypermarkets and other aggressive competitors. When Miller defined Shell's future as a retailer, he was asserting that Shell's size and talent would enable it to be the dominant contender. The Action Labs were predicated on a "jump-into-deep-water-and-learn-how-to-swim" approach to retailing (that is, acting as if they were already in the future as a retailer and dealing with obstacles as they arose) rather than planning a careful transition from present wholesaler to future retailer. Action Labs were challenged to reinvent an entire market segment with Shell as a retail player. Headquarters staff and country teams were brought together to redefine entire businesses. Based on these initiatives, the previously fragmented Aviation, Marine Fuels, Bitumen, and Bottled Gas segments are becoming worldwide businesses. Once Shell's role as a retailer was accepted as an inevitable future, a stream of appropriate innovations flowed forth.

4. Harnessing Setbacks

NTC participants know from the outset that they are fighting an enemy far tougher than any they are likely to meet in the field. Observer-Controllers remind them daily that their maneuvers are not about winning but about learning. Harnessing setbacks is a matter of recontextualizing failure, treating breakdowns as a source of future breakthroughs. But this requires considerably more self-discipline than most managers realize. Human beings are hard-wired to react adversely to mistakes by blaming themselves (guilt or shame), others (finger-pointing), or bad luck (resignation and fatalism). Day after day, Observer-Controllers extol the benefits of "controlled failure" until every soldier learns to embrace setbacks as windows to learning.

This discipline was reinforced at Shell both in the fishbowl and during the phase of the training experience where Action Labs returned for an autopsy of breakdowns. Throughout the process, participants were reminded that if they are not encountering obstacles and failures, they are probably not pushing the envelope. Coaches and facilitators continually emphasize the value of failure as a stimulus for learning.

5. Inventive Accountability

The tasks, conditions, and standards in Discipline 1 create the benchmarks of acceptable performance. Soldiers are trained to meet or exceed these benchmarks so that their units can count on them in combat. But there is more to it than that. Close battles are won by exploiting the enemy's broken plays. Mastery of a combat assignment requires not just replicable skills but also the capacity to improvise. Observer-Controllers single out and reward creative acts of initiative that are built on a solid platform of proficiency.

When Shell's Action Labs return from the "greenhouse" of their training experience to the "jungle" of their own operating company, many obstacles stand in the way of successful execution. Teams are strongly encouraged to improvise—being accountable to achieve the milestones established but realizing that innovations on the court will often gain an advantage that was unforeseen when the original plan was presented.

6. Understanding the Quid Pro Quo

Surfing the edge of chaos and the disciplines that allow this to happen make huge demands on people. Organizations must ensure that their members receive commensurate returns. Once upon a time, institutions like Shell or the Army were like ocean liners. Anyone fortunate enough to secure a berth cruised right through to disembarkation at retirement. In return for loyalty, sacrifice, and the occasional aggravating boss, members enjoyed implicit or explicit job security.

We have now witnessed a decade of continuous job attrition in which companies have downsized, delayered, reengineered, and outsourced. The Army has discharged six hundred thousand soldiers from a high of 1.2 million during the Gulf War. Worldwide, Shell has reduced its ranks by 55,000 people since 1980.

Understanding the quid pro quo is a demanding discipline. A genuinely transformational employment contract has four levels, three more than the reward and recognition that was once considered adequate. The second level is employability—the training and skills that enhance people's marketability when it's time for them to move on. Valuable as this may be over the long run, it is nevertheless overrated as an incentive. Enhanced employability does not necessarily give incentive to the creative commitment and enthusiasm that organizations like Shell and the modern army require. Employees cannot be altogether bought or enticed. Transactional employment contracts typical of many kinds of credentialed experts and specialists have not demonstrated high correlation with a committed and loyal workforce.

All this points to a third factor: the requirement for a sense of meaning in the work strong enough to generate intrinsic satisfaction. And there is a fourth ingredient as well: employees must know that they understand where the enterprise is going and have some say in shaping its destiny. At Shell, front-line employees are having a real say in the company's destiny not only through their dialogue with the company's top executives but by having a major role in fashioning the market offerings through which Shell can compete successfully. In the Mojave Desert, the personal commitment evident in the After Action Reviews is fueled, in part, by a shared perception that defending their country is important work. And further, even the lowest-ranking soldier has a hand, day after day, in altering the Army's culture and ultimately its shape as an institution.

7. Relentless Discomfort with the Status Quo

The After Action Review is based on the notion that people can improve—in most cases dramatically—on everything they do. Observer-Controllers continually reinforce the notion that AAR

disciplines can be applied elsewhere to other activities, and a protocol like AAR does tend to get under a person's skin. Soldiers
carry the ideas back to their home bases. Once internalized, the
discipline of relentless discomfort begins to reveal itself as a repeated, gnawing question: How can we do this still better (faster,
cheaper)? Is there a radical new approach we haven't thought of
yet? Day in and day out, all through the Army, the AAR format and
disciplines are employed to critique performance and make improvements. Soldiers and employees at every level begin to see acceptable performance is a threshold condition, not a ceiling.

Shell struggles to turn its current episodic commitment to retail breakthroughs into a vigorous daily discipline. Among their
benchmarks is USAA, long a top performer in the insurance industry. USAA has adopted a practice it calls "painting the bridge,"
meaning that the task is never completed but restarts as soon as it's
finished. Briefly, an independent team of fourteen organizational
experts starts at one end of USAA and works its way to the other,
one unit at a time. Their mission is to work with departmental
teams in questioning everything they do. Is the role they perform
necessary? Can it be streamlined, improved, merged with another
unit? Can it be eliminated? Not surprisingly, people in the company have ambivalent feelings toward this once-every-two-year reg-
imen. But it reliably delivers improvements and, equally important,
reinforces USAA's unending effort to become a better company.

From Social Engineering to Designs for Emergence

Twenty years ago, who would have imagined that a program of war-
fighting simulations and After Action Reviews would have transformed the U.S. Army and made it a benchmark of change studied
by large corporations and governments around the world? Similarly, who at Shell would have imagined that a managing director
and his team would reallocate 50 percent of their time to work with
front-line employees, or that a simple model of Action Labs could
be perfected and replicated—and in turn spawn hundreds of initiative teams throughout this huge company—eventually achieving a critical mass for change.

The ways appear outwardly different. But they share the common principles of Complexity and are bolstered by disciplines that

sustain the vitality of a living system. The Army and Shell have both found ways to tap the distributed intelligence within their organizations and vastly strengthen the linkages between senior executives and front-line employees. The action learning environment has brought to the fore a new generation of leaders who might otherwise have been tuned out and turned off. Finally, and most surprisingly, the followers, in a well-orchestrated process, become powerful teachers for senior executives and, through their commitment and enthusiasm, have actually made believers of those in the jaded ranks above. By relocating initiative, redefining leadership, and forging a new relationship with failure, Shell and the Army are harnessing the potential of Complex Adaptive Systems—not a bad formula in a world where ongoing reinvention may be the most important capability for future success.

Notes

1. For a brief treatment of this literature, see Heifetz, R., Sinder, R., Jones, A., Hodge, L., and Rowley, K. "Teaching and Assessing Leadership." *Journal of Policy Analysis and Management*, 1989, *8*(3).
2. Heifetz, R. Lecture to National Security Fellows, Kennedy School, Harvard University, Cambridge, Mass., Aug. 14, 1996.
3. For an entertaining treatment of this inquiry, see Waldrop, M. M. *Complexity*. New York: Simon & Schuster, 1992.
4. Kauffman, S. *At Home in the Universe*. New York: Oxford University Press, 1995, p. 21; see also Hamel, G., and Prahalad, C. K. "Strategic Intent." *Harvard Business Review*, May-June 1984, pp. 63–76.
5. See Kauffman (note 4), p. 205. Also see Holland, J. H. *Hidden Order*. Reading, Mass.: Addison-Wesley, 1995, p. 3.
6. See Kauffman (note 4), p. 230; see also Gell-Mann, M. *The Quark and the Jaguar*. New York: Freeman, 1994, p. 249.
7. See Kauffman (note 4), p. 230; see also Gell-Mann (note 6), pp. 249–268.
8. See Gell-Mann (note 6), pp. 238–239; see also Holland (note 5), pp. 38–39.
9. See Holland (note 5), p. 5.
10. See Pascale, R. "The United States Army: Change or Transformation?" Unpublished case study, 1994.
11. Pascale, R. Interviews with General Gordon Sullivan, Washington, D.C., Apr. 4, 1994.
12. Pascale, R. Field notes at Royal Dutch Shell in London, The Hague, Kuala Lumpur, and Rio de Janeiro, Oct. 1995 through Feb. 1998.

13. Pascale, R. Field notes with the U.S. Army, Apr. 1994 through Feb. 1995.
14. Pascale, R. Interviews with General Leon J. Laporte, Fort Irwin, Calif., Feb. 13, 1995.
15. Pascale, R. Interviews with Steve Miller in London, The Hague, and Houston, Tex., Oct. 1997 through Feb. 1998.
16. Pascale, R. Interviews with General W. (Scott) Wallace, Fort Irwin, Calif., Feb. 13, 1995.
17. These disciplines are developed at greater length in Pascale, R., Millemann, M., and Gioja, L. "Changing the Way We Change." *Harvard Business Review,* Nov.-Dec. 1997, pp. 135–139.

Chapter Nine

Leading Corporate Transformation

Are You Up to the Task?

Robert H. Miles

A variety of corporate transformation challenges currently confront executive leaders across all industries, sectors, and geographies. I recently gave a speech in New York City to senior executives attending a conference sponsored by the Conference Board and the Drucker Foundation. The audience consisted of two hundred senior executives from virtually every type of organization. To open the presentation I asked everyone who was working in or with an organization undergoing fundamental transformation to stand. All arose. Then I asked for those to remain standing who believed their executive leaders had done all that was required to ensure that fundamental change would indeed be achieved without exposing their organization to unacceptable risk. Only three executives stood their ground.

The ability to orchestrate the fundamental process of transformation in complex organizations has become the ubiquitous challenge of executive leadership in our time. Moreover, the cycle time of corporate transformation is becoming shorter and shorter. During the 1980s, pioneering CEO Jack Welch could usher in a new phase of corporate transformation at GE every five to six years. Now, because of the ever-increasing pace of competitive foment and business discontinuity across all industries, executive leaders are expected to fundamentally refresh, reenergize, and relaunch a new phase of transformation in their organization about every two, not more than three, years. As management thought leader Peter Drucker warned during the same conference, "theories of the business won't last long. Every few years you'll have to sit down and think through the theory of the business, very critically."[1] And Bill Gates, founder and head of powerful Microsoft Corporation, was recently quoted as saying, "We're always two years away from failure!"[2]

To master the new pace, transformation leaders have to get it right the first time. They can't wait for early successes to hatch before the rest of the organization catches on. They have to hit the beaches simultaneously on all fronts. They no longer have the luxury of gradually cascading new ideas and expectations down through the organization. They have to greatly enrich and accelerate the processes of learning within the organization. And they have to quickly engage all employees, obtain their commitment, and enable them to lead at their own levels.

All this must be accomplished in a new context: the Age of Dilbert. People at all levels have become highly skeptical about all new management initiatives after a decade and a half of cost reduction, portfolio pruning, industry consolidation, outsourcing, and downsizing. They've seen it, done it, and have the T-shirts and plastic knickknacks all over their work spaces to prove it. The only thing that has a chance of working now is something comprehensive enough to fire all cylinders of human engagement and that may quickly be translated into immediate job requirements at all levels, beginning at the top.

This essential task of executive leaders requires a robust, field-tested approach that can be adapted to meet a variety of corporate transformation challenges, executive leader types, and organizational skill sets. This chapter is about such an approach: a general framework for orchestrating corporate transformation. It covers a number of levers that executive leaders have at their disposal to launch and guide such an undertaking. The approach is based to a large extent on my twenty years of assisting executive leaders as they struggled to rise to these difficult, variable, and highly visible occasions of corporate transformation.

Critical Tasks of Transformation Leaders

Successful corporate transformation leaders share a few fundamental attributes. First, they know how to create and sustain the enormous amount of energy required to launch and accelerate transformation. Everyone in the organization must not only understand the new direction and the need for it, but also be effectively engaged and substantially accountable for it at their own job level before they will release energy to support it.

Second, they use vision to lead. Transformational change, in contrast with incremental change, requires projection into a dimly lit future. It involves the creation of goals that stretch the organization beyond its current comprehension and capabilities. Therefore, the launch of corporate transformation necessitates the creation of a simple, compelling vision of a desirable future state—one that can only be fully defined with sustained movement of the organization to it. This is difficult to understand by individuals accustomed to incremental change as a way of life. But visionary leadership is the essence of successful corporate transformation.

The third essential ingredient of successful transformation leadership is a total system perspective. This seeks to boldly move the organization from an initial state to a vision state, not by advancing piecemeal but through the simultaneous articulation of all major elements of the whole organization.

This need for holism leads to the fourth essential attribute of successful corporate transformations: embedment in a systemic implementation process. The total system approach to change and the large magnitude of change implied by a visionary aspiration require a sustained process of organizational learning and an orderly orchestration of all of the pieces in order to make a safe passage to the vision state.

The tasks that the transformation leader—indeed, leaders at all levels in the organization—must perform in order to achieve successful transformation without exposing the corporation to unacceptable risk are summarized in the general framework (see Figure 9.1). Such leaders must generate energy to launch and sustain

Figure 9.1. Framework for Leading Corporate Transformation.

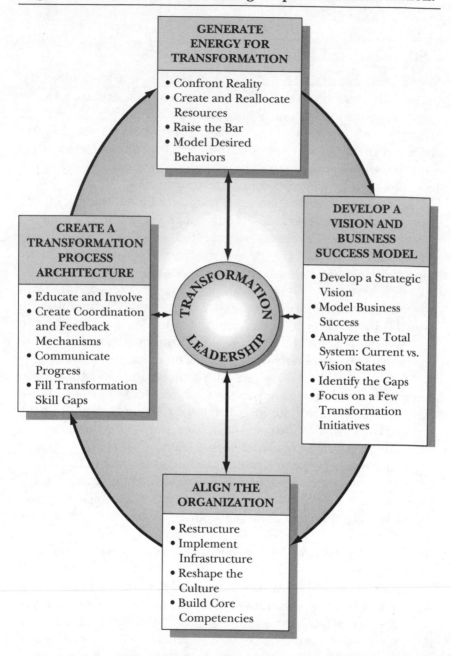

Source: Miles, 1997,[12] p. 6. Used by permission of Jossey-Bass Inc., Publishers.

the process of corporate transformation. They must develop a vision of the future. They must align the organization to the vision. And they must create a transformation process architecture to orchestrate the passage from current to vision state. Any attempt at corporate transformation that falls short on one or more of these leadership tasks will fail.

Generating Energy for Transformation

Launching and sustaining a successful process of corporate transformation requires the generation of enormous energy. There are four major levers available to transformation leaders for creating such energy. Leaders must be able to confront all levels of the organization with reality. They must be able to create and reallocate resources. They must raise and redirect the standards of performance. And they must encourage leaders at all levels to model required new behaviors. In addition, such leaders must emphasize the appropriate mix of these levers given the nature of the specific corporate transformation challenge they face.

Confronting Reality

Individuals do not invest their energy in support of a corporate transformation until they are sufficiently dissatisfied with the status quo and adequately informed about the magnitude and direction of change that is required. Therefore, the first step in generating energy for a corporate transformation effort is to create opportunities for employees at all levels to confront reality. The other aspect of confronting reality is the articulation of a vision of the future for the organization. Usually not much can be done to elicit the search behaviors required for this step until people are sufficiently informed about the current reality—both the current state of the organization and the information that must be obtained from various stakeholders and constituencies.

Many executive leaders wait too long to rigorously examine how reality is changing in their business. In some industries change comes slowly; in others change is dramatically imposed from outside with entrants offering new technologies, substitute goods, or alternative materials. The only way to successfully respond to either condition is to be constantly proactive in the process of confronting the realities surrounding the business. The earlier and more constant or routine such a confrontation process is for an organization, the more likely its people are going to recognize the need for change and still have at their disposal the resources to make the necessary transformation in order to restore and maintain competitive excellence.

External benchmarks may hasten the creation of energy for change when, in the absence of such data, things might appear to be going very well. Executive leaders often are lulled into continued reliance on outmoded strategies simply because things continue to improve. Without accurate, up-to-date benchmark data on leading competitors and best-in-class peers, such improving companies might not realize until too late that their rates of progress and levels of achievement fall well below competitive standards. Executive leaders in one of my client firms, for example, were quite pleased with the improvements they had made in scrap reduction until they discovered that even after sustained focus on the problem and measurable improvement, their scrap rate still was twice that of their toughest competitors. After digging deeper into the approaches used by their competitors they found even greater differences between the manufacturing processes they employed and those of their competitors. Apparent improvement can create a sense of progress even when its cause, if continued, will lead to a competitive performance crisis.

A second important lever for confronting reality is industry trend analysis. In addition to gauging where an organization stands relative to customers, competitors, and best-in-class peers, successful corporate transformations account for major industry trends that might reinforce or potentially disrupt current competitor advantages and patterns of industry rivalry. The leadership of IBM during the late 1970s and early 1980s forged ahead with its traditionally successful commitment to mainframe computing, dismissing major industry trends that favored alternative forms of computing. The Big Three U.S. automakers missed the turn to smaller, more fuel-efficient automobiles. Failing to appreciate the trend in the personal computer business, Apple Computer continued to go it alone, refusing to license its operating system, and as a result ceded the de facto industry standard to the Wintel platform, which combines Microsoft's Windows software with Intel's hardware. The predictable result is reminiscent of the victory of the VHS over the allegedly superior Betamax videotape format a decade and a half earlier.

Failure to track and interpret the meaning of important industry trends is a major reason why firms succumb to the so-called "paradox of success." Therefore, an important device in the toolkit for confronting reality is an ongoing process for scanning the business environment for discontinuities that have the potential for upsetting traditional patterns of competitive rivalry.

A third important component of confronting reality is the diagnosis of internal strengths and weaknesses of the organization. Such a preliminary analysis examines the capabilities, competencies, and culture of an organization relative to what is required to pursue a competitively successful vision state. All organizations have strengths and weaknesses that pertain to a particular performance situation or set of strategic objectives. Getting some of these obstacles to corporate transformation on the table as soon as possible, rather than waiting for a full total system analysis of the entire firm, helps speed people's recognition of the need for change and orients them to major areas requiring improvement.

All of these devices for confronting reality are legitimate tools. Their effects in generating energy for a corporate transformation effort are enhanced to the extent that they are applied in advance of crisis and performance decline. In other words, the confrontation of reality is best practiced as an act of proactive leadership, rather than as a result of having reality inflicted upon the organization. Such effects are also substantially enhanced to the extent that broad involvement of employees from different functions and levels is encouraged by leaders in the earliest stage of reality testing. The sooner large numbers of employees are exposed to credible information about the causes and consequences of current or potential business performance shortfall, the quicker massive levels of energy will be released into the corporate transformation process.

Creating and Reallocating Resources

Another important part of helping people in organizations let go of the past and begin to move to a future state is the creation and reallocation of resources. For many years business scholars have referred to these as "slack" resources—resources above and beyond those required to run the day-to-day operations of the business and plan for its future that may be devoted to supporting and reinforcing the transformation efforts that must take place at organizational and human levels.[3]

Leaders in crisis organizations facing a revitalization challenge must devote considerable effort at the front end of their transformation to the *creation* of resources. Individuals' resistance to change builds in direct proportion to the magnitude of the gap they perceive between the level of effort expected of them as part of the transformation process and the resources available to get the job done. Often this initial resource-generating step involves closing and consolidating peripheral or underperforming operations, trimming employee payrolls, reducing corporate staff overhead expenses, and suspending or deferring programs so that current operations can generate more cash to be redeployed to the launch of the corporate transformation process. Leaders attempting to revitalize their organizations also need to seek new external resources as they launch their transformation process. They often do this by increasing their debt burden or placing additional stock in the market, often on unfavorable terms because of their strained performance condition. When Lee Iacocca took over Chrysler Corporation in 1978, a government bailout was needed to avert bankruptcy and provide the company with new resources to launch the corporate transformation process.

In contrast, transformation leaders facing the challenge of a currently successful organization need to focus more on *reallocating* their existing resources. As they put significant and visible investments into the launch of their corporate transformation process, they powerfully signal that something major, new, and different is about to happen. As they begin to reallocate substantial resources away from businesses and activities that are not compliant with the new vision and direction toward those that are on the new critical path, they further reinforce the sense of commitment to change and clarify its meaning and direction. Moreover, when employees see resources diverted from deeply troubled business operations or ineffective staff functions and invested in activities and competencies that are more tightly aligned with the new vision, they become reassured that leadership is indeed "walking the new talk," and they feel enabled to proceed in the new corporate direction, especially if they are on the receiving end of these resources.

For example, at General Electric during the early 1980s under Jack Welch, the creation of slack resources was not so much a problem as was the reallocation of existing resources to the corporate transformation effort. When Welch began the transformation of General Electric in 1981, the company had a $2 billion cash balance. However, much of the company's resources were being allocated to businesses that were not financially attractive and did not fit Welch's vision for the future of the company. So the initial transformation issue was less one of resource creation than one of resource reallocation. Businesses that did not fit the vision had to fix, sell, or close themselves, and resources that would otherwise be consumed by these ill-fitting businesses were reallocated to enhance productivity and automation initiatives and to fuel capital investments in businesses that offered greater promise for achieving Welch's lofty vision of being first or second in their chosen global markets.[4] Although longtime employees did not like to see large, traditional parts of this revered company closed or sold, they were given some assurance by the new resources they received that the remaining GE portfolio was receiving healthy investments of resources that would better position them to achieve the stretch goals they had received as part of the corporate transformation initiative.

Raising the Bar

Another primary tool for generating energy to support a corporate transformation effort is to "raise the bar" for performance. Transformation leaders have the prerogative of altering the mix and elevating the level of performance expectations in their organization. The more substantial the shift on both dimensions, the more energy those held accountable will devote to searching for behaviors that will help them perform better. Put another way, if performance expectations change only modestly, as in many incremental improvement initiatives, those affected are not very motivated to risk trying new behaviors and approaches. Instead, they tend to work harder using the methods that have led them to success in the past, and to drive the people under them to work faster, come in earlier, and stay later.

Changes in performance expectations that represent stretch goals cannot be mastered by relying on old approaches and techniques. Under stretch performance goals, people are compelled to assume the risks of reinventing the way they get their job done. Such goals cause people to proactively search for new and different ways to perform their jobs. They more eagerly seek out best practices and they more readily engage in experiments and pilot projects because the risks of not pushing the envelope far outweigh those of failing to meet the new performance expectations. Stretch goals at the individual job level that have a clear line of sight to the organization's primary transformation initiatives are particularly useful in getting the corporate mountain to move without too much delay.

Modeling Desired Behaviors

Of all the levers for generating energy to launch and sustain a corporate transformation effort, the tangible, observable modeling by leaders of the new, desired behaviors is the most important.

There are different levels of leadership in a corporate transformation effort. Once leaders get beyond resistance to the needed changes, they may adopt a number of stances in support of a transformation effort. They may grant permission for people to engage in the required new behaviors. They may actively encourage others to make the necessary changes. They may take on the responsibility for managing the change process, ensuring that various initiatives are properly sequenced and coordinated. Or they may assume the role of transformation leader by taking the point position by personally role modeling the required new behaviors.

If you think of a transformation process as a parade, leaders may sit in the reviewing stands and salute as the band marches by, they may be in the parade, or they may become the drum major at the head of the parade. Successful transformations require lots of drum majors, and virtually every key leader in the organization, starting at the top, must become a walking and talking hyperbole of the behaviors and attitudes required to reach the vision state if the transformation is going to be successful. If even a few leaders at the top are unable or unwilling to assume this leadership stance, hundreds and sometimes thousands of people below them will be stifled in their attempts to make the changes and assume the risks necessary to support the corporate transformation effort.

In addition to rising to the occasion of corporate transformation, leaders must also demonstrate commitment to and simultaneously achieve and sustain success along two primary dimensions: business performance and culture change, as illustrated in Figure 9.2.

Successful corporate transformations are launched and sustained when leaders at all levels, especially those at the top, are successful in optimizing business performance and culture change initiatives. Conversely, maximizing one at the expense of the other undermines transformation. Indeed, many failed transformations may be characterized by very specific new *performance* expectations without very specific *behavioral* expectations or vice versa.

Figure 9.2. Transformation Leadership Matrix.

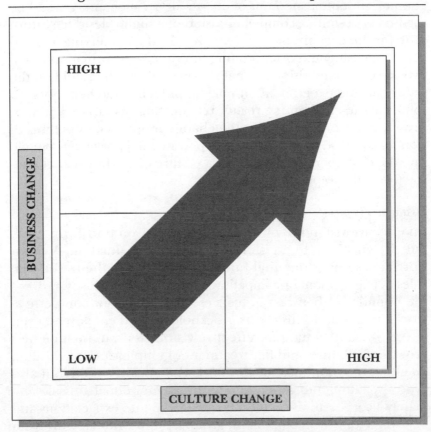

It is important to articulate, operationalize, measure, and take actions based on this leadership matrix if true transformation is to be realized. Ultimately, those who deliver business results in a manner inconsistent with the vision must be removed. Those who succeed in adopting the new vision-aligned behaviors but fail to achieve the required performance results should be placed, if possible, where they are able to generate business results that clear the elevated performance bar. Otherwise the skeptics in the organization will be encouraged to step up their attempts to undermine the transformation.[5]

Developing a Strategic Vision and Business Model

Successful corporate transformations do not derive from the creation of substantial amounts of energy alone; such energy must be focused on a simple, compelling vision of a highly desirable future state for the organization. Indeed, in addition to serving as a target for focusing and orchestrating multiple transformation initiatives, a compelling vision can help people release their hold on the status quo and experiment with new approaches and behaviors. To some extent, confronting reality, reallocating resources, and raising the bar *push* people into the change mode. A compelling vision, in contrast, has an equal but opposite effect of *pulling* people into the change mode by creating a picture of the future that is attractive and compelling.

Strategic Visioning

An effective vision not only helps a corporation transform itself, but also enables it to transform its competitive situation. A vision worth pursuing is one that fundamentally alters the traditional rules of engagement or competitive rivalries in an industry, redraws the boundaries between industries, or creates new competitive space.[6] It appeals to customers, stockholders, and employees. Even in the direst of situations, effective visions tend to include new growth possibilities and fair treatment of employees. In addition, an effective vision must be not only strategically sound, but also evocative enough to generate widespread emotional appeal. Ultimately a corporate vision must be translated into expectations and behaviors for every component, group, and individual. Only from massive alignment with the vision does corporate transformation take its energy and direction.

Modeling Business Success

A business success model is an absolutely essential companion to a simple, compelling vision of the future organizational state if successful corporate transformation is to be achieved. Just as it is impossible at the beginning of a quantum corporate transformation to specify in great detail all aspects of the future vision state of an organization, so too is it impossible to lock the trajectory of a transforming company into a rigid, predetermined business plan. But the necessary indetermination of such a plan under conditions of quantum change in no way diminishes the need to have a business success model that is grounded in solid external benchmarking data and that reveals what needs to transform in strategic and financial terms as the change process unfolds toward the vision state. So what is a success model and how does it work?

A business success model is both an articulation of strategic intent and a forecast of business results for an enterprise as a whole. Strategic intent reveals how the enterprise is going to create and sustain competitive advantage. It represents the nexus between customer needs and market trends on the one hand, and core competencies of the corporation on the other.[7] The forecast of business results projects how important dimensions of financial performance move over time from whatever the current reality is to eventually meet the business's stated long-range financial objectives of sales, profitability, asset utilization, productivity, and so on. Sometimes these forecasts are expressed as a series of annual projections of key business and financial indicators. Other times they are expressed as alternative future business scenarios.

Once developed at the corporate level, business success models may be constructed at any organizational level, down to individual strategic business elements and functional departments. The forecasts they contain illustrate a progression from the current situation of financial performance to the desired financial objectives associated with the future vision state.

Business success models and functional road maps are subject to change as the company moves toward its vision state. They must be updated to reflect changes both in the external environment and in the internal operating characteristics of the organization. They must also undergo modification as a company transitions from one phase to another in its transformation journey. Despite the need to update and adapt the business success model as circumstances change, such a model is essential during a corporate transformation because it makes concrete what the organization has to do in business terms—strategic and financial—in order to reach the vision state. Such a model may also serve as the basis for estimating likely performance outcomes along the way, such as future profitability level, stock price, market valuation, or market share, which can serve as powerful motivators for launching, gauging, and sustaining a corporate transformation process over a long period.

The process of visioning as a lead element in corporate transformation has come under criticism even as it has become more common. This criticism is warranted in many cases where lofty conceptual visions of desired future states are developed in the absence of either comprehensive and credible external benchmarks about customers, competitors, and market trends or sound business success modeling. If long-range organizational visions are built on wishful thinking and coupled with only a short-term financial plan, the consequence is all too predictable. Hope rises in the organization because of the compelling features of the new conceptual vision, particularly when large numbers of people have been involved in shaping it, but the real focus remains on quick financial fixes. Not too long afterward, a pervasive state of cynicism emerges because of the widely perceived disconnect between lofty visionary thinking and internal pressure for immediate business results.

What is needed to avoid this disconnect is a robust business success model that includes a clear statement of strategic intent grounded in market, customer, and competitor realities and in organizational capabilities, as well as a year-by-year financial forecast that shows how the business results are likely to evolve as the transformation progresses toward the vision state.

Analyzing the Total System

The next step in charting the course of a corporation's transformation is to identify the few important initiatives along which the fundamental changes needed in the organization will unfold. The vision state must be translated into an organization design that will uniquely support it. This step requires a total system framework or template that combines and configures the formal and informal elements of the organization to a state of tight "fit" with the vision.[8] Such a total system analysis not only identifies the major transformation initiatives, but also lays the groundwork for realigning the internal context of the organization to support the journey toward the vision state.[9]

To be effective, a total system analysis of current and future organizational states must incorporate several considerations. First, the framework must be comprehensive of all the major elements of the organization design. Yet it must do so as parsimoniously as possible. Reliance on too few design elements or levers oversimplifies the task of implementing the vision through organization design. Inclusion of too many design elements burdens the analytical and implementation process and risks confusion from overlap and redundancy.

Second, there has been a tendency among Western, especially American, managers to focus most of their implementation efforts on the more formal, objective, intellectual, analytical elements of organization, such as strategy, structure, and infrastructure, to the relative neglect of elements that are distinctly more informal, subjective, emotional, and processual. Today's era of fundamental or discontinuous change—of corporate transformation—not only requires major changes in the formal elements, but also fundamental alterations in people skills and orientations, management style, and organizational values and competencies. Such bold interventions into the softer elements of organization design require different leadership and facilitation skills than do the ones that engage strategy, structure, and infrastructure.

Third, the total system perspective reminds us that it is critical to make simultaneous changes across all dimensions of the organization. Corporate transformations move at a pace requiring simultaneous changes, one that denies the possibility of allowing people and organizational culture and competencies to evolve into alignment without direct and often dramatic intervention. Indeed, the cycle time of change needed to rise to a major market opportunity or challenge these days has been reduced dramatically, making the ability to orchestrate simultaneous organizational change a distinctive competitive advantage.

Fourth, the total system approach requires not only that all elements of the organization be configured to uniquely support movement to the vision, but that they be closely aligned to reinforce each other. All elements of the organization are interdependent in their effects on organizational performance and behavior. Big changes in one or a few elements without corresponding changes in the others tend to create chaos, as important design features begin to pull the organization in different directions. Therefore, under conditions of corporate transformation in which fundamental change is required, it is not advisable to proceed in the redesign of the organization in a sequential manner. The challenge is to move boldly on all fronts simultaneously.

Finally, considerable "tuning" of the organization using the total system approach is necessary to arrive at a point at which all elements of the organization are mutually reinforcing and internally consistent. Often this tuning takes place as a series of moves from the current organizational state to the desired vision state as the necessary processes of human skill building and organization development occur along the journey. Thus, an effective total system design template is one that can serve as a guide to the orchestration of major changes in all of the elements of organization over time as the corporation transforms to the vision state. Without such a framework it may not be possible to take the current organization apart and orchestrate its movement to the vision state without exposing it to unacceptable risk.

The total system framework that I have developed from practice and from other leading practitioners in corporate transformation is shown in Figure 9.3. The definitions for each element of the template are summarized in Table 9.1.

The template is centered around the vision that is the object of a corporate transformation effort. Surrounding the vision are the key formal and informal elements of organization design. Among the formal design levers are strategies, structure, and infrastructure; in general these are easier to diagnose and alter because they are more readily observed and measured. The informal design levers include people as well as organizational culture (values and management style) and competencies. These are considerably more difficult to alter in a short period of time and are

Figure 9.3. Total System Framework: Two Major Axes.

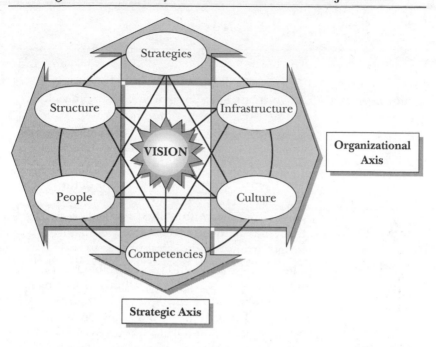

Source: Miles, 1997,[12] p. 37. Used by permission of Jossey-Bass Inc., Publishers.

generally more elusive in diagnosis because of their subjectivity. As part of conceiving and orchestrating transformation, however, the subjective elements are just as important as the more objective ones.

The total system framework may be divided into two major axes. Anchoring both axes is the vision. The vision, in turn, must be translated into what the corporation needs to put in place to operationalize it: the *strategic axis,* which consists of corporate strategies and competencies. The vision also needs to be translated into how it is going to be implemented: the *organizational axis,* which includes structure, infrastructure, people, and culture. All successful corporate transformations begin with the articulation of a vision, typically followed first by the initial specification of the strategic axis and then by the organizational axis.

Table 9.1. Total System Framework: Definitions.

Organizational Design Elements	Definitions
Vision	The purpose and mission of the organization and the supporting business success model.
Strategies	The primary bases upon which an organization allocates resources to differentiate itself from competitors, create customer value, and achieve exemplary performance in order to realize its vision.
Structure	The formal structural arrangements of the organization that delineate its basic units of authority and accountability and the "overlays" that regulate the interdependencies that the formal arrangements create.
Infrastructure	The formal systems and processes that reinforce the intentions of the organization's structure and strategies including the basic measurement, control, planning, information, human resource, operations, communication, and resource allocation systems.
People	The nature of the workforce, including work experience, skills, needs, preferences, maturity level, perceptions, orientations, and diversity, as well as the prevailing view of the role of the workforce in the organization.
Competencies	The core competencies of the organization as a whole. What an organization does *particularly* well.
Culture	The values and beliefs that are shared by most of the people in an organization and the style and behavior of its leaders. More a matter of what people and leaders do than what they say.

Without such a template and the language system it creates, an orderly orchestration of the elements of the organization toward the vision state can become hopelessly confused; there is little hope of preventing a plethora of well-intended but uncoordinated change initiatives or programs from overwhelming the total system and frustrating those who are trying to lead the transformation.

Moreover, because of the fundamental interdependence of the elements of organization, the absence of a well-understood, widely accepted organizing framework can result in major change initiatives canceling the effects of each other or even inadvertently pushing the organization in a direction different from the vector established by the vision.

Focusing on the Transformation Initiatives

The primary purpose of a total system analysis in the initial phase of corporate transformation is to identify the major "gaps" on each design element between the current and vision states, as illustrated in Figure 9.4. These gaps translate into creative tensions that help excite members of the organization to action, gauge the magnitude of transformation required, and reveal the direction or vector along which the vision journey must proceed.[10]

Gaps between current and vision states must first be prioritized according to the magnitude of change required to close them. Then the highest-priority gaps must be sorted into a few major clusters of related gaps. These clusters make up the *transformation initiatives* that receive primary focus during the journey to the vision state.

Transformation initiatives, or TIs, become the major areas of focus, the places where quantum change is needed in order to launch the transformation, complete a particular phase during the journey, and ultimately reach the vision state. In any given phase it is important to limit the number of TIs to between three and five to provide focus for the allocation of resources and enough simplicity in the midst of complexity to facilitate employee understanding, commitment, and concentration of effort. Such TIs serve as screening mechanisms for proposed investments in programs and projects to support the transformation effort. But it is important to note that the TIs and the programs and projects implemented to drive them are subject to modification or even replacement as their objectives are achieved or as new and different challenges emerge.

Bob Eaton, the current chairman and CEO at Chrysler Corporation who followed in the footsteps of Lee Iacocca, asserted at the onset of his assumption of command that he would not become the third "turnaround CEO" in a row at the company. Determined to make good on his vow, Eaton led the leadership of Chrysler through a vision-based transformation process, which

Figure 9.4. Total System Framework: Gap Analysis.

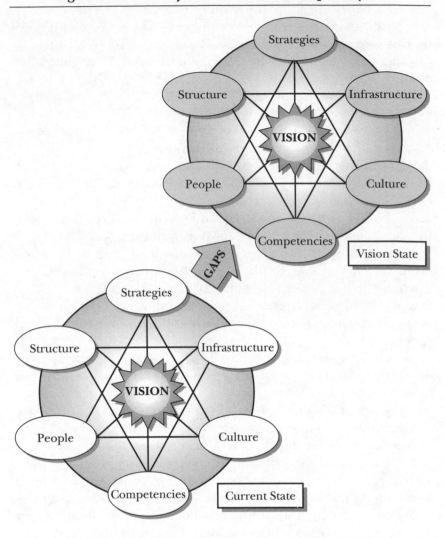

Source: Miles, 1997,[12] p. 39. Used by permission of Jossey-Bass Inc., Publishers.

among many things generated $10 billion in cash, believed to be more than enough to enable the company to weather the next worldwide recession in the automobile industry. The primary focus of Eaton's change process was on five major transformation initiatives: customer focus, inspired people, continuous improvement, financial success, and company reputation.[11] Jack Welch began his third phase in the transformation of General Electric by focusing in a similar way on six major TIs: new product introduction, quick market intelligence, supplier management, productivity, order to remittance, and globalization. Southern Company, the largest investor-owned electric utility in the United States, recently launched a fundamental transformation process across the fifty or so power generation plants in its portfolio by focusing on five TIs: empowered employees, adaptive culture, business focus, low-cost producer, and "fence management."[12] And Gordon Eubanks launched the "TakingCharge" transformational process at Symantec Corporation, a Silicon Valley software company whose growth trajectory had flattened, by focusing on just three transformation initiatives: Play to Win (focus on growth), Customer Excellence (focus on customers), and Winning Culture (focus on people). Each initiative had a couple of corporate-wide stretch goals, along with clear metrics, around which all Symantec businesses and employees could engage and align.

The specific content of these examples is important to the ultimate success of each company's change effort, but details are not so important here. What is critical is that one must *focus* resources and human energy for sustained periods of time in order to achieve quantum change without exposing the enterprise to unacceptable risk. The visioning process and the total system approach serve as reliable tools for crafting this focus. Another important characteristic of TIs may also be observed in the Chrysler, GE, Southern, and Symantec examples: each set of TIs includes business and cultural, hard and soft, externally focused and internally focused change initiatives. Finally, TIs and their underlying dimensions and programs tend to evolve to varying degrees as transformation unfolds. A financially oriented TI may emphasize asset management and gross profit when a company is attempting to restore its financial health. Later, when the financial crisis has passed, the company may shift to where its financial TI focuses on quantum revenue and market share growth. Indeed, a general test of whether the example companies will continue to be successful depends to a large degree on whether the objectives of their current TIs are realized *and* how well they identify and focus on subsequent TIs that better fit future phases of development.

Once the TIs have been identified they must be operationalized. For each TI there is a limited set of stretch goals with specific metrics that must be developed to cover the major gaps uncovered during the total system analysis. To close each gap or reach each stretch goal, the company must launch a limited set of programs or projects. Finally, each program or project should have broadly understood milestones to gauge progress and ensure accountability.

It is generally important for members of the senior executive team to be responsible for achieving quantum change in all TIs as part of the transformation process. In addition, it is often useful for senior executives to serve as champions or sponsors of a particular TI. In this capacity a senior executive is responsible for identifying internal and external best practices regarding their assigned TI and for disseminating this information on a timely and ongoing basis throughout the enterprise. Finally, responsibility for quantum change in all TIs must cascade down through the organization so that all levels may creatively align their efforts in response to the TIs. Indeed, it is customary to make plans and request resources with specific reference to one or more of the transformation initiatives.

Aligning the Organization and Culture

The vision-based total system analysis, which identifies the future and current states of the organization and prioritizes the gaps between them, yields a set of transformation initiatives that provide the specifications for the redesign of the organization. The alignment with the vision of this internal context, which consists of structure, infrastructure, culture, competencies, and people, powerfully shapes the patterns of behaviors, attitudes, and decision making and signals the magnitude and direction of the transformation. The more tightly these design elements are configured, the more powerful their combined influence will be on the people who have to fundamentally alter the way they think about and perform their work. Thus, the total system analysis performed to distill the core transformation initiatives also doubles as the template for the redesign of the enterprise to make it fit for the journey to the vision state.

But organizations do not safely move from their current state to the vision state in one giant leap. Often employee skills and organizational competencies must be built before significant contextual moves can be made. Because all the design elements must move in relative concert with one another, the organization often does not have adequate slack resources—money, management time and attention, surplus talent and underutilized skills—to achieve simultaneous quantum change on all dimensions. Moreover, some changes require that resource providers see the organization in a new light before they are willing to invest in the enterprise undergoing transformation. For example, it may be nearly impossible to bring in the needed management and functional talent or to engage in joint ventures with organizations that can provide needed resources and competencies before an organization undergoing revitalization can demonstrate in some tangible ways—through early wins or substantial reallocations of capital investments—its commitment to and progress toward the stated vision. Also, quantum changes are often impeded because the vision calls for a fundamental change in an enterprise's culture and core competencies, both of which require substantial time and intervention to achieve. A new structure may be announced and put in place in a matter of weeks, whereas a new culture that significantly departs from some deeply cherished, long-practiced values and assumptions may take years.

For all these reasons, the new internal context of the organization does not emerge in a single moment of cosmic creation. Instead, the leader must deliberately *orchestrate* all the elements of the total system to maintain a condition of dynamic alignment and to facilitate the processes of human development and organizational learning that allow forward movement without excessive risk exposure. The formal elements of strategy, structure, and infrastructure, and the informal elements of people, culture, and core competencies, must move in concert over time toward the vision state at a pace that accounts for the constraints of understanding, commitment, ability, resources, and credibility, as well as the inherent nature of each element of organization design.

Even though the period of transformation between current and vision states is characterized by a series of orchestrated moves from one transition state to another, the entire sequence of transition states should consistently signal the designated path toward vision state. Indeed, when one retrospectively views the progression through these transition states the feeling that one should get is that of finer and finer tuning of the whole organization. The tuning will be coarse at first, just enough to get a footing and general bearing, but later it will be finer high fidelity that is achieved with the vision state. The necessity of orchestrating change is one of the primary reasons why the leader must put in place a process architecture to support a corporate transformation.

Aligning Structure and Infrastructure. Structure and infrastructure are the design levers generally thrown first in aligning the internal context. Why begin redesign with these? Simply because they usually are the quickest to change. People, culture, and core competencies generally take more time to bring into alignment. Indeed, by resetting the more formal and tangible elements of organization design, leaders can provide early and relatively unambiguous signals about what kinds of people, culture, and competencies will be needed to make the journey to vision state while also serving as enablers of the development and alignment of these softer, more subjective elements.

Structural change is the primary mechanism for reallocating human and financial resources for better alignment. It also reallocates the basic patterns of authority, accountability, and decision making, and generally alters the balance of power among the major units of the organization. Thus, fundamental structural change almost always serves as a lead element in the redesign of the internal context of the organization as it comes into alignment with the new vision.

To provide greater urgency and clarity about needed changes in the softer elements, leaders must implement infrastructure to complement structure. Infrastructure refers to the formal systems and processes that reinforce the intentions of structure and strategies, including the basic measurement, control, planning, information, human resource, operations, communication, and resource allocation systems. These usually take somewhat longer to put in place than a new structure. Therefore, work on the redesign and implementation of the core elements of infrastructure first after agreement on the vision and transformation initiatives is reached. Otherwise the gross signals from the visioning and restructuring process will largely be ignored by employees in favor of sharper, more immediate signals that they receive by way of performance reviews and paychecks.

Reshaping the Culture. Changes in a company's vision and in the formal elements of its organizational context provide important signals and serve as reinforcers of what kind of processes and behaviors are needed to make the journey to the vision state. During less turbulent competitive times, the articulation of new strategies, structures, and infrastructure—the construction of a new internal context for decision making—was thought to be sufficient. If put in place and persistently applied it was believed that these formal elements of design would eventually induce changes in the slower-moving, more subjective design elements—that the right organizational context would cause culture, behavior, and process to "come around."

The problem is that this view presumed very little required change in people, culture, and competencies. But today's global competitive environment requires transformation, not incremental adjustment; a new formal context and incremental nudging and coaxing won't do the job. A more profound and direct intervention into the cultural elements of the organization is the order of the day. The values and beliefs shared by most employees, and the style and behavior of their leaders, must be critically examined for alignment with the new vision and strategies. Though they may have endured through good and bad times, old values and beliefs must be tested to see if they uniquely support the new vision. When they are found wanting, they must be changed. And when they are changed, mechanisms must be put in place to ensure that the new ways are practiced and that people have the awareness and abilities to make the changes without an extended getting-ready period of adjustment.

Ideally, any cultural change that supports a transformation attempt focuses on creating and sustaining three types of values and behaviors. Type 1 consists of everyday rules of the road: how people fairly, ethically, and constructively relate to one another in the workplace. Such *basic ground rules* are necessary for any organization to be successful in any circumstance. These values are of the long-held variety. They are deeply embedded in the culture and style of an organization and they may serve as anchors while everyone is attempting to navigate the stormy sea of transformation. Type II includes *strategically aligned values and behaviors,* those that uniquely align with the vision and primary initiatives of a particular period of transformation in the life of a company. For example, a value of individual autonomy and initiative at the business-unit level may be highly instrumental to achieving rapid business turnaround from the brink of financial disaster, but an emphasis on sharing and leveraging across business units and individual efforts may be more important during a transformation phase focusing on rapid growth in revenues or market share. There is evidence that basic ground rules and strategically aligned values and behaviors may be sufficient to achieve successful performance outcomes in a particular phase of corporate transformation that takes place over perhaps three to five years. But Type III, which contains core values and behaviors that promote *adaptiveness* to cope with changing competitive conditions, appears to be needed to cope with fundamental change over the long haul.[13]

In addition, although these types of values have been identified as necessary, it is important not to have more articulated values and related behaviors than absolutely necessary. Too many superfluous values can make Jack a dull boy. The objective is not to press everyone into a single, overdetermined mold. Rather than promote conformity with cultural change, executive leaders need to reinforce "creative individualism" by requiring subordinates to adhere only to pivotal values.[14]

Finally, the chosen values must be anchored to behaviors of people across all organizational units and levels if they are to be internalized and practiced. The adoption of these pivotal, required behaviors must be rigorously assessed early on, and the outcome of the assessment must be consequential for all members of the enterprise, starting at the top. This process of behaviorally anchoring the core values is an important part of the process of helping people understand, buy in to, and implement the vision at their own level in the organization. Failure to articulate the minimal elements of the needed culture, to translate those value elements into behavioral expectations, and to hold people accountable for modeling them will undermine the best-laid vision and internal organizational context.

Building Core Competencies. Building required core competencies is the final component in aligning the internal context of the organization to the new vision. Ideally, existing organization-wide competencies are identified as part of the development of strategic intent. But often transformation requires the development and refinement of new competencies as well. It would be foolish to assume that the process can be allowed to take its own course under the gross signaling and reinforcement provided by the formal elements of the organization's design. Instead, development and alignment of core competencies must be guided by direct intervention. En route to the vision state, some hard-earned core competencies will receive new investment and attention; others will have to be painfully abandoned to release resources. Some needed competencies will be developed, others will be imported; all will need to be leveraged throughout the enterprise.

A core competency is what an organization does *particularly* well. To qualify, a corporate resource must provide the company with access to a wide variety of markets and customers, be very difficult for competitors to imitate, and be leveragable across a variety of corporate units and product lines.[15] Without the requisite core competencies, an otherwise perfectly aligned and arranged organization will be incapable of completing the journey to the vision state.

Generally recognized core competencies of contemporary corporations include engines and drive trains at Honda, microprocessor technology at Intel, computer software expertise at Microsoft, general management bench strength at General Electric, and so on. These confer considerable competitive advantage because they tightly align with and provide broad support for the companies' vision and strategic intent. Conversely, like some traditional values, some core competencies limit a company's ability to pursue a new visionary course. Such was the case of Swiss watchmakers, who were so wedded to the mechanical technology of timekeeping that they missed the shift to digital electronics during the late 1970s and early 1980s.[16]

In summary, many, many changes must be made in the internal context of the organization in order to create sufficient alignment with the new critical path. Figure 9.5 reveals the changes that resulted in one of my transforming high-tech manufacturing clients just one year into its corporate transformation process. To keep up with this highly dynamic process while achieving higher and higher performance outcomes, leaders need a means of keeping track of and orchestrating all of the needed organizational changes. To accomplish this, a simple, efficient *process architecture* is needed.

Creating a Transformation Process Architecture

The total system approach to corporate transformation critically depends on the creation of a robust process of organizational learning and orchestration, without which the simultaneous implementation of change initiatives affecting all elements of the organization can expose the company to unnecessary risk and create debilitating uncertainty and frustration among the managers and employees. But if a total system launch is possible, the benefits are enormous. Perhaps the most important benefit is that it gives a leader the ability to intervene boldly across all elements of the organization simultaneously, rather than piecemeal or sequentially, greatly reducing the cycle time of quantum change.

Orchestrating transformation successfully requires that the leader put in place a process architecture consisting of a few mutually reinforcing mechanisms. Education, involvement, and communication mechanisms must be created or redirected to enable employees at all levels to acquire the understanding, ability, and motivation they need to modify their perceptions and behaviors. Coordination and feedback mechanisms must be installed to properly roll out and continue refinement of all the transformation initiatives. A way must also be provided to obtain needed expertise that does not reside in the organization, including ongoing process and just-in-time content consulting support. Finally, the responsibility for transformation leadership must be cascaded down to all levels to multiply its influence from above. These core components of the process architecture must be put in place at the earliest opportunity.

This process architecture draws from, but is in addition to, the normal infrastructure used to manage the ongoing business, such as the strategic planning process, the goal-setting and goal-alignment process, the new product planning review system, and

Figure 9.5. Total System Changes at End of First Year: High-Tech Company.

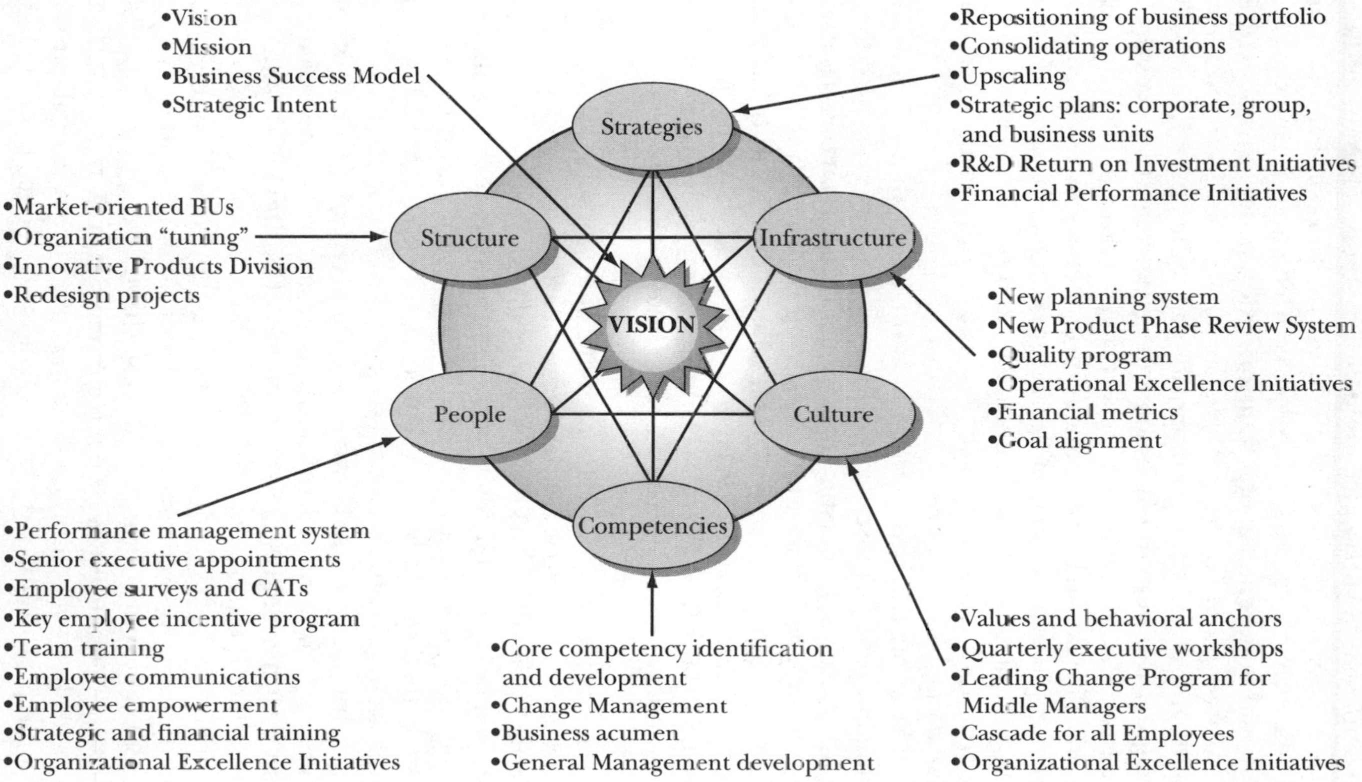

- Repositioning of business portfolio
- Consolidating operations
- Upscaling
- Strategic plans: corporate, group, and business units
- R&D Return on Investment Initiatives
- Financial Performance Initiatives

- New planning system
- New Product Phase Review System
- Quality program
- Operational Excellence Initiatives
- Financial metrics
- Goal alignment

- Values and behavioral anchors
- Quarterly executive workshops
- Leading Change Program for Middle Managers
- Cascade for all Employees
- Organizational Excellence Initiatives

- Vision
- Mission
- Business Success Model
- Strategic Intent

- Market-oriented BUs
- Organization "tuning"
- Innovative Products Division
- Redesign projects

- Core competency identification and development
- Change Management
- Business acumen
- General Management development

- Performance management system
- Senior executive appointments
- Employee surveys and CATs
- Key employee incentive program
- Team training
- Employee communications
- Employee empowerment
- Strategic and financial training
- Organizational Excellence Initiatives

Diagram labels: Strategies, Infrastructure, Culture, Competencies, People, Structure, VISION

the employee performance evaluation systems. Thus, in addition to strengthening the normal coordination and control functions, the leader must create slack resources dedicated to the development and maintenance of a transformation process architecture.

Educating and Involving People. Corporate transformation leads organizations and their members to places they have never been. A major investment in education and development is necessary to give people at all levels the perspectives and skills needed to make the transformation journey. Major investment is also needed to involve people in all aspects of decision making and action taking so they will truly understand, internalize, and become committed to the transformation and all the changes it implies for them and their work groups.

Education and involvement to launch and support the transformation process must begin at the top. A forum must be created for the executive leadership team to maintain an ongoing focus on the transformation and to achieve alignment with it. The team needs time together for working on the challenges of transformation, internalizing its requirements, comprehending its meaning, building skills to lead it, assessing progress, following through on commitments, and replanning to keep the process moving forward.

The single most powerful element of the process architecture for leaders at the top is a series of carefully designed and facilitated quarterly executive workshops devoted to the transformation, as illustrated in Figure 9.6. Such workshops need to be owned and led by the CEO with adequate consulting support, and they need to be scheduled regularly on the corporate calendar. Quarterly workshops lasting two to three days seem to best fit the rhythm of corporate transformation. Having these events in an informal off-site location not only minimizes interruptions, it removes the executives from their normal routines and symbols of position and status, enabling them to more easily shift into a corporate, as opposed to their normal business or functional, point of view. Attendees are usually executives representing all major functions and businesses, and it extends down through the top three layers.

Inviting multiple layers helps shorten the cycle of learning and open the lines of communication to those in charge of all parts of the enterprise. Managers with firsthand knowledge about the basic

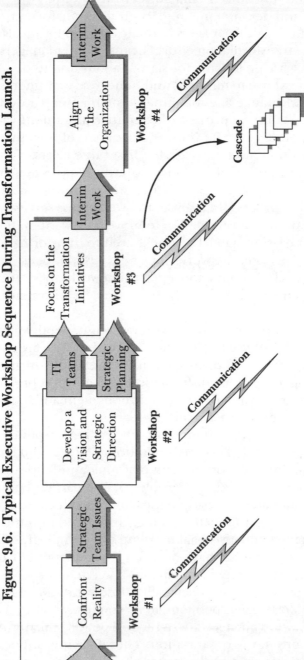

Figure 9.6. Typical Executive Workshop Sequence During Transformation Launch.

businesses and functions become directly involved in the process of dialogue and decision making about the transformation. Involvement of third-tier managers in the leadership forum also adds energy to the transformation effort because these managers often are the ones who are looking for signals about how to be successful over the next five to ten years and hence are very interested in the new performance agenda. Finally, such an expanded team helps speed the initial process of executive alignment with the transformation because it avoids the problem of selective filtering of information down through the first three layers.

The quarterly series of executive workshops serves as a primary vehicle for developing, orchestrating, and refining a corporate transformation process. In a sense, the workshops serve as tracks laid in front of the transformation to move it forward on the critical path to the vision state. The tracks are the transformation initiatives, and the executive workshops help sustain focus on them and expose leaders to new concepts, frameworks, best practices, and benchmark data to maintain the process of quantum improvement on them.

Participants bring to these workshops their in-depth knowledge of how their part of the organization works, but they are asked to adopt the perspective of the organization as a whole during all or most of the agenda. The transformation leader brings preliminary plans for change for initial testing and refinement and, ultimately, buy-in from the executive leadership team.

In the workshops, the framework for leading corporate transformation (Figure 9.1) becomes operational. The agenda of each workshop combines transformation planning and follow-through with just-in-time education and problem solving around obstacles. New transformation concepts and ideas are introduced, discussed, and vetted in this forum before being introduced into the mainstream of change initiatives that make up the overall effort. Other ideas and programs that have outlived their purpose or do not align with the transformation agenda are weeded out.

Transformation requires new skills, upsets traditional relationships and networks, alters positions, titles, compensation, and career opportunities, and changes the status and power of many individuals and groups in the organization. Therefore it is important to provide adequate time in the agenda of education and involvement activities for people to vent their frustrations and concerns as well as to explore the new vision in sufficient depth to be able to translate it into something relevant and positive for themselves and the group they represent. Thus, education cannot be of the intellectual variety only. It must allow for expression of human emotion and it must provide a neutral ground for experimentation with the new concepts and skills. To be successful, therefore, the executive workshops must join human and organization development. They must function as relatively safe places for executives to share their concerns and doubts, to let go of the past, and to acquire skills and practice new behaviors for which they must serve as role models when they return to their regular jobs.

Such workshops are where high-powered executives learn to engage in open dialogue and confront conflict in a constructive manner while seeking answers to tough challenges. To accomplish this the workshops heavily rely on debate in open forum together with multidisciplinary teamwork. Importantly, a lot of this dialogue takes place with all the major players "under the lights" with appropriate doses of process facilitation. I will always remember a comment made by an executive when he returned with his corporate team to the nine-month follow-up session to the Harvard managing change program. He said, "One of the advantages we had when we returned to our company to implement the change we planned was that the give and take discussion of the case method and the work with executive teams from other companies at Harvard had helped us become better listeners, more sensitive to the reactions of others to our plans. Therefore, when we returned to our company to implement the changes we had planned we were more ready to modify our ideas to accommodate the useful recommendations of others to obtain their commitment."

Executive education and involvement at the beginning and throughout a corporate transformation effort have a similar effect. It opens the minds of executives to new ideas and it sensitizes them in a very personal way to the intellectual and emotional hurdles that people down below will have to clear if the corporate transformation is to be successful. Thus, education and involvement of executives in a workshop process can be used by the leader to create a model of the kind of learning organization that the rest of the corporation must emulate if the transformation is to be successful.

It is important that these executive workshops not become islands unto themselves. Each should conclude with a commitment to action on issues and initiatives that need to be dealt with at the current phase of transformation. The CEO, as transformation leader, should personally close each workshop by reinforcing the basic learnings, summarizing commitments to action, and assigning accountabilities by charging executive teams to work on unresolved issues or launch new change initiatives for review at the next workshop. The leader should also open each workshop with a review of progress or closure on action items developed at the previous workshop. Thus, the series of workshops are linked by interim work by executive-led task forces.

It is essential that the rest of the organization be informed regularly about the progress of the executive workshops; otherwise informal grapevines and rumor mills will fill the gaps left by executives while on retreat. You cannot afford to wait to communicate until all of the pieces have come together. You have to help the organization develop its understanding of the process and its requirements as they become clearer to the executive leadership group during the corporate transformation journey.

Education and involvement opportunities created for the executive leadership level must be cascaded down through the organization as soon as the basic nature of the transformation takes shape. When education and involvement are aligned with the transformation agenda and implemented throughout the organization in a timely manner that is tailored to fit the audience at each level and in every part of the enterprise, it greatly leverages the influence of the CEO as transformation leader. It not only informs but actively engages participants in real transformation challenges about which they can do something and solicits feedback from them on how to improve the effort. This greatly amplifies communication and raises the likelihood that initiatives will be well received by those who have to implement them.

High-Engagement Employee Cascades. Education and involvement *cascades* are best received by employees at lower levels if line managers at each level have a major responsibility for their delivery to subordinates. Staff professionals and expert facilitators may need to play a major role in the design of these programs and may need to help with aspects of their delivery, but for the programs to have maximum credibility and impact, the line leaders should be in the driver's seat. This has the side benefit of speeding program roll-out, because there are never enough internal staff professionals to help without substantial protraction in the time it takes to get all employees involved. It also increases the depth of understanding of and the speed of commitment to transformation among managers, thereby helping with the challenge of executive alignment.

What should an education and involvement cascade contain to be effective? First, it should honor the past. No matter how difficult the situation, employees at all levels need to be recognized for the positive contributions they have made to the enterprise before they can let go of the old way of doing things and enlist in the new order. Moreover, the farther one goes down into the ranks, the more employees may be likely to blame the work of strategic decision makers rather than their own work for the dilemmas the company faces. Therefore, the process of buying in to the new vision and initiatives will generally be accelerated to the extent that education and involvement programs pay homage to past contributions of employees and make time for letting go.

The cascade should distill the general rationale and objectives of the transformation that has been formulated at the top and interpret it in a form relevant for each level and part of the organization. The cascade needs to expose employees to the business realities and introduce them to the vision, business success model, and transformation initiatives, as well as to the core supporting concepts, frameworks, and business basics. Employees must also be introduced to the general approach to transformation. Here, case examples of how other companies or parts of the focal company have used the approach are quite useful in helping employees understand what will be involved and how they will need to adjust. Instruction and discussion about the personal dynamics of change are also helpful, particularly in the first round of education and involvement cascades. All these inputs help create a common language and a shared set of meanings.

As Harvard researcher J. Richard Hackman recently concluded after more than two decades of research:

> [T]eam effectiveness is enhanced when managers are unapologetic and insistent about exercising authority about *direction*, the end states the team is to pursue. Authority about the *means* by which

those ends are accomplished, however, should rest squarely with the team itself.

Contrary to traditional wisdom about participative management, to authoritatively set a clear, engaging direction for a team is to empower, not de-power it. Having a clear direction helps align team efforts with objectives of the parent organization, provides members with a criterion to use in choosing among various means for pursuing those objectives, and fosters members' motivational engagement. When direction is absent or unclear, members wallow in uncertainty about what they should be doing and may even have difficulty generating the motivation to do much of anything.[17]

To be successful, therefore, education and involvement cascades must do more than distill, translate, and disseminate the work from senior executives to lower-level managers and employees. They must be action-learning vehicles. Participants must apply the new learnings to real issues and challenges facing their part of the organization before they leave the cascade program. They also must be required to deal with all the new information on both intellectual and emotional levels. Cascades must be explicitly designed to accomplish this. And participants must have structured time to translate the new corporate vision, success model, transformation initiatives, and core concepts into a relevant framework that they can take back to the job.

In addition, cascades must allow dialogue among participants—as peers representing different parts of the enterprise as well as with their leaders—in order to enrich their understanding and ascertain the commitment of those around and above them. Without affirmation, especially from their bosses, participants are not likely to become sufficiently enthusiastic when they return from the cascade program to their work units.

Cascades should also serve as important sources of feedback from specific subgroups about how the transformation is doing and where it needs refinement. Line managers should be the primary recipients of such feedback, but it should be captured in a systematic, organization-wide way to directly inform the primary architects of the process.

Finally, education and involvement cascades should conclude with a general call to action and specific accountabilities with planned follow-up for all participants, who should leave the cascade with a clear understanding of the role they are expected to play and what resources have been placed at their disposal in their area of responsibility. Ideally, they should depart with a new set of job-level performance objectives that have a clear line of sight to transformation initiatives and stretch goals being pursued by the enterprise as a whole, as shown in Figure 9.7.

Several rounds of cascades may be necessary to deliver a corporation to the vision state. Each new round helps move through the phases of transformation; each may require a reconfiguration of the core elements outlined in Figure 9.1.

Communication Campaigns. Transformation leaders who rely on standard forms of communication will have great difficulty launching and sustaining a transformation. The apparatus must be adapted, new elements added, and the whole process focused and intensified in support of the effort. The entire communication initiative must be focused on creating shared meaning and a common language so that everyone can begin understanding what the new vision is, why transformation as opposed to incremental or piece-part improvement is needed, and how employees need to adjust the roles they play to become an important part of it.

The communications campaign is the centerpiece in this part of the transformation process architecture. Although other components help reinforce it, a corporate-wide campaign is needed to launch the transformation, introduce new phases, share best practices and accelerate momentum.

The campaign consists of a series of timely releases that are pulsed throughout the organization so that everyone is constantly reminded of the central importance of the transformation, informed about its content, and alerted to leading practices that support it. Such information needs to be as consistent, simple, relevant, and timely as the transformation phase will allow, with the expectation that as learning occurs over successive phases the campaign will become more and more focused.

The amount of needed communication is easily underestimated. Core messages must be repeated over and over from multiple sources and through different communication vehicles. Any gaps or lapses in intensity will be filled with rumors; employees will revert to their old ways of doing things and the organization will risk

Figure 9.7. Cascading a Transformation.

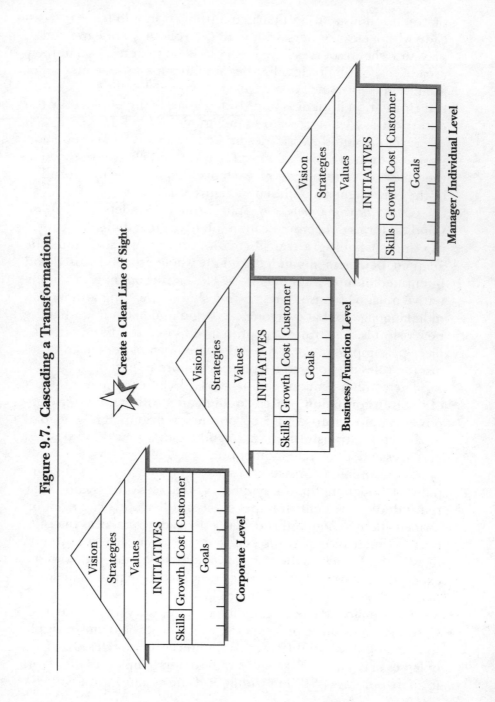

Create a Clear Line of Sight

Corporate Level

Vision
Strategies
Values

INITIATIVES

| Skills | Growth | Cost | Customer |

Goals

Business/Function Level

Vision
Strategies
Values

INITIATIVES

| Skills | Growth | Cost | Customer |

Goals

Manager/Individual Level

Vision
Strategies
Values

INITIATIVES

| Skills | Growth | Cost | Customer |

Goals

recapture by immediate issues and obstacles. In addition, the campaign needs to be complemented by more interactive mechanisms. Many other elements of the transformation process architecture—the education, involvement, coordination, and feedback mechanisms—help with this.

It also is essential that the commitment and alignment of the leadership to transformation be conveyed as part of the communication process. Opportunities to demonstrate such alignment must appear in as many communications as possible. Indeed, the most powerful source of meaning to employees is their immediate boss, if what he or she says squares with what is conveyed by other leaders and what is embedded in the overall communication campaign.

Finally, communication with external stakeholders may be as important as communication with employees. Some outside individuals and groups have the power to grant or withhold resources, loyalty, and goodwill that the company depends on; this necessitates a comprehensive external communication effort. And the design of that outreach effort should contain many of the features associated with a successful internal campaign.

Creating Coordination and Feedback Mechanisms. Because transformation requires quantum change in the total system, it cannot be accomplished by altering one element at a time. Coordination mechanisms, above and beyond the ones necessary to run the business, must be established to orchestrate simultaneous changes in all the pieces. An integrated approach is absolutely necessary.

The core integrative mechanism, of course, is the transformation leader. But in full-scale transformation a steering committee or support team is necessary to maintain vigilance over the coordination process. Often this team is composed of well-respected senior line and staff executives, as well as an ongoing process consultant whose expertise lies in the domain of corporate transformation. Sometimes the team is split in two: one group spends considerable time focusing on the design, assessment, and adaptation of the transformation process and is made up of staff professionals and consultants who are process specialists; the other meets less frequently and is made up of senior executives who have considerable business responsibilities in addition to those of orchestrating multiple change initiatives. It may also be useful to create an advisory team of key employees lower in the organization to serve as a sounding board for transformation ideas from above before they become full-blown initiatives.

Steering, support, and advisory groups tend to be quite active and visible during the launch phase of transformation, before the line function becomes fully aligned with the vision journey. After the first couple of years, however, the process architecture generally becomes more streamlined and less visible, and often advisory groups dissolve or become ad hoc as the line function takes more responsibility. Similarly, during the first year or so, the transformation leader tends to be the direct sponsor of the coordination apparatus. Later, such sponsorship may become more indirect as the support group begins to report to a second tier of senior executives to whom primary responsibility for the ongoing transformation is delegated.

Other important coordination mechanisms are cross-business and cross-functional councils and "communities of practice."[18] These may be organized around a major transformation initiative (such as quality), a core business process (manufacturing or value creation), or an important organizational level (middle management). They are useful, particularly early on, because they can help to interpret corporate-wide change initiatives for their level or area, weed out impractical ideas and replace them with better ones, and share leading practices affecting their part of the transformation agenda. As Rosabeth Kanter observed in *The Change Masters*, "Organizations that are change-oriented . . . will have a large number of integrative mechanisms encouraging fluidity of boundaries, the free flow of ideas, and the empowerment of people to act on new information."[19]

During transformation, an organization needs to shift to an intensive learning mode. That requires not only effective education and development processes, but also multiple feedback mechanisms beyond those needed day-to-day to operate the business. The leader must put listening posts at all levels in the organization and create scanning devices to learn how important external constituencies, such as customers and investment analysts, are responding to the changes.[20] Systematic feedback needs to be ongoing, timely, and reliable, and it needs to come from senior executives, middle managers, first-line supervisors, and employees, as well as customers and major stakeholders.

Feedback is especially useful during transformation because of the need to fill in the white spaces in the vision state and the pathway to reach it, both of which are so new and different for the organization that a tremendous amount of learning from changing has to take place en route. Feedback mechanisms are essential to reduce the time span of corporate transformation. Other things being equal, the shorter the cycle time of learning and mastery, the quicker the organization will be able to invent new futures or adapt to current challenges. The faster a transformation leader is able to put in place and nurture a robust set of high-fidelity feedback loops, the faster the learning and the shorter the duration of the transformation effort.

Many vehicles are available to obtain the quality and intensity of feedback leaders need to keep transformation on track. Most important is the extent to which leaders can personally involve themselves in interaction and dialogue with key internal and external constituencies to present their ideas, articulate the rationale for transformation, and solicit questions for clarification and suggestions for improvement. Nothing really substitutes for this; it is a direct connection through which both good and bad news is received unfiltered. But various interview and survey techniques are useful supplements. Benchmarking, the capture and sharing of best practices, intensive partnering with important customers, the use of focus groups, and continuing, open lines of information sharing may be other important feedback mechanisms. Also, the explicit creation of listening posts at various nodes in the organization can enhance the process of learning from changing. Many coordination vehicles mentioned earlier—steering committees, support teams, advisory groups, cross-business and cross-functional councils, and communities of practice—can also double as listening posts.

These feedback mechanisms seldom emerge on their own unless there is a crisis. Basically, organizations lack a nervous system, so transformation leaders have to create and nurture feedback loops if they want to be able to anticipate needed developments along a corporate transformation path rather than be overwhelmed by firefighting or missed opportunities along the way. Such leaders put in place a robust network of active feedback mechanisms early on and make sure that their channels stay wide open and unfiltered.

Filling Transformation Skill Gaps. Successful change means doing new and different things well; corporate transformation means doing lots of very new and different things very well. Not surprisingly, a transformation agenda often exceeds the current capabilities and skill sets in an organization by a wide margin. Thus there is a need for knowledge and expertise from outside the enterprise. Content consultants may help convey new concepts and frameworks. But it is important to recognize that an organization and its employees can only absorb and apply so many new ideas at a time before becoming overloaded. Thus content consultants tend to work best when they arrive just in time and leave as soon as they seed ideas. Otherwise the organization can become overrun by specialists, all trying to earnestly ply their expertise.

There is also a critical need for experts in the process of transformation. There are fewer of these, and they need to stay with the transformation during its first few phases until enough of their process skills are internalized by organization leaders and members so that the enterprise becomes change hardy—that is, of sufficient breadth and depth of skill to be able to continue to move the transformation process forward on its own.

In addition to the content and process expertise they bring to the organization undergoing change, external consultants can also be used by the leader to herald the transformation process and cause more intensity of focus on its core initiatives. Indeed, the arrival and in some cases continuation of external consultants can serve as a powerful symbol of a leader's commitment to transformation.

Are You Up to the Challenge?

This chapter lays out the required tasks of leaders of corporate transformation in a practice-based general framework. The four basic elements of the framework—generating energy for transformation, developing a vision of the future, aligning the internal organizational context, and creating a process architecture—provide not only a platform for launching a corporate transformation, but also for managing transitions from one phase of transformation to the next en route to the vision state. In so doing, the framework provides a field-tested guide to leaders for achieving quantum change without exposing their organization to excessive risk.

The essential elements of the transformation leadership challenge are summarized in the checklist that follows.

Checklist for Transformation Leaders

Have I created sufficient energy to launch and accelerate a fundamental transformation?

- ☐ Everyone has had an opportunity to confront reality in a meaningful way.
  - ☐ Everyone understands the industry trends, competitive dynamics, and customer challenges that we face.
  - ☐ Everyone understands the competitive benchmarks and actively shares best practices.
  - ☐ Everyone understands our internal strengths and weaknesses.
- ☐ Sufficient resources have been created to enable transformation to occur throughout the organization.
- ☐ Resources have been substantially reallocated to clearly signal the new direction.
- ☐ The bar of performance expectations has been sufficiently raised to encourage everyone to prepare stretch goals along the new critical path.
- ☐ Leaders at all levels in the organization are personally role modeling the new behaviors.

Have I focused the organization on a compelling vision corresponding to the business success model and the set of transformation initiatives?

- ☐ Everyone understands our new strategic intent, which is driven by customer needs.
- ☐ Everyone understands our new business success model.
- ☐ Everyone understands the gaps that separate the current state of the organization from the desired future state.
- ☐ Everyone has focused their attention and resources on a few major transformation initiatives.

Have I put in place an organization designed to uniquely support the transformation journey?

- ☐ The structure is uniquely aligned to reinforce the new vision and strategic direction.

☐ The infrastructure is uniquely aligned to reinforce the vision and strategic direction.

☐ The culture is adapted to uniquely support the new vision and strategic direction.

☐ The required core competencies of the organization are in place to support the journey to the vision state.

Have I put in place a process architecture that enables orchestration of all necessary changes?

☐ An ongoing and robust process of executive education and involvement is in place to develop and pursue the transformation agenda.

☐ High-engagement cascades to employees at all levels are generating broad-based understanding, commitment, and refinements regarding the transformation process.

☐ Sufficient coordination and feedback mechanisms have been put in place to guide the orchestration of all needed changes.

☐ A communication campaign is under way that constantly reinforces core transformation messages in a consistent, simple, and timely manner tailored to the needs of different constituencies.

☐ Adequate content and process expertise has been retained to complement the existing skill set of the organization.

Notes

1. Videotaped speech by Peter F. Drucker at the Organization of the Future conference, cosponsored by the Conference Board and the Drucker Foundation, New York, Feb. 19, 1998.

2. Speech by Gary Hamel at the Academy of Management annual meeting, Boston, Aug. 10, 1997.

3. I have referred to these resources that need to be set apart from the needs of the ongoing business operations to support the process of corporate transformation as "organizational slack." See Miles, R. H. *Macro Organizational Behavior.* Glenview, Ill.: Scott-Foresman, 1980 (esp. pp. 367–368); Miles, R. H. *Coffin Nails and Corporate Strategies.* Englewood Cliffs, N.J.: Prentice-Hall, 1982 (esp. pp. 248–254); Miles, R. H. *Managing the Corporate Social Environment: A Grounded Theory.* Englewood Cliffs, N.J.: Prentice-Hall, 1987 (esp. p. 288); and Miles, R. H., and Randolph, W. A. "Influence of Organizational Learning Styles on Early Development." In J. R. Kimberly, R. H. Miles, and As-

sociates, *The Organizational Life Cycle: Issues in the Creation, Transformation and Decline of Organizations.* San Francisco: Jossey-Bass, 1980, pp. 44–82. In the 1987 book I defined slack resources as "the resources possessed by an organization that are not consumed in the routine functioning of the business operations, and which may be called upon to cope with nonroutine issues. Such slack resources take many forms, including financial reserves, underutilized capacities and skills, employee commitment and loyalty, and goodwill among external constituencies" (p. 288).

4. Aguilar, F. J., Hamermesh, R. G., and Brainard, C. *General Electric, 1984.* Boston: Harvard Business School Press (9–385–315, Rev. Mar. 24, 1993), 1985.

5. I am indebted to John F. Welch, CEO of General Electric, for these insights about how to respond to different types of leadership effectiveness under conditions of corporate transformation.

6. Hamel, G., and Prahalad, C. K. *Competing for the Future.* Boston: Harvard Business School Press, 1994, pp. 19, 22.

7. For more complete treatments of the concepts of competitive advantage, strategic intent, and core competencies, refer to Porter, M. E. *Competitive Advantage: Creating and Sustaining Superior Performance.* New York: Free Press, 1985; Hamel, G., and Prahalad, C. K. "Strategic Intent." *Harvard Business Review,* May-June 1989; and Prahalad, C. K., and Hamel, G. "The Core Competence of the Corporation." *Harvard Business Review,* 1990, *68*(3), 72–78.

8. The importance of "fit" among the elements of organization in order to achieve effective business performance was originally established as part of the contingency theory of organization design developed by Paul Lawrence and Jay Lorsch. Refer to Lawrence, P. R., and Lorsch, J. W. *Organization and Environment.* Boston: Harvard Business School Press, 1967. The concept has been extended and refined by Ray Miles and Chuck Snow; see their book, *Fit, Failure and the Hall of Fame.* New York: Free Press, 1994.

9. I have used many total system templates in organization design and corporate transformation work: Beer, M. *Leading Change.* Boston: Harvard Business School Press (9–488–037), 1988, p. 3; McKinsey & Company, Inc. *Findings from the Excellent Companies: Three Yards and a Cloud of Dust.* McKinsey & Company, Inc.: 1980; and Pascale, R. T., and Athos, A. G. *The Art of Japanese Management.* New York: Simon & Schuster, 1981. Also refer to Waterman, R. H. Jr., Peters, T. J., and Phillips, J. R. "Structure Is Not Organization." *Business Horizons,* June 1980, pp. 14–26; Waterman, R. H. Jr. "The Seven Elements of Strategic Fit." *Journal of Business Strategy,* Winter 1982, *2*(1), 69–73; Galbraith,

J. R., and Nathanson, D. A. *Strategy Implementation: The Role of Structure and Process.* St. Paul, Minn.: West Publishing, 1978, p. 2.; and Nadler, D. A., and Tushman, M. L. "A Congruence Model for Diagnosing Organizational Behavior." In R. H. Miles (ed.), *Resourcebook in Macro Organizational Behavior.* Santa Monica, Calif.: Goodyear, 1980, pp. 30–49. See also another congruence model in Galbraith, J. R., and Kazanjian, R. K. *Strategy Implementation: Structure, Systems, and Process.* (2nd edition.) St. Paul, Minn.: West Publishing, 1986, p. 2.

10. The idea that performance gaps serve as major catalysts to organizational learning and change has been around for some time. See, as examples, Downs, A. *Inside Bureaucracy.* Boston: Little, Brown, 1967; and Hirshman, A. O., and Lindblom, C. E. "Economic Development, Research and Development, Policy Making: Some Converging Views." *Behavioral Science,* 1962, *8,* 211–222. For a more contemporary treatment of the creative tension caused by such gaps, see Senge, P. M. "The Leader's New Work: Building Learning Organizations." *Sloan Management Review,* Fall 1990, p. 9.

11. Best practices visit to Chrysler Corporation, Port Huron Conference Center, Port Huron, Mich., July 1994.

12. The launch of the transformation at the Southern Company is described in detail in Miles, R. H. *Leading Corporate Transformation: A Blueprint for Business Renewal.* San Francisco: Jossey-Bass, 1997, pp. 83–126.

13. A recent Harvard Business School study of the relationship between corporate culture and long-term performance reported that in cultures that contained adaptiveness values and behaviors, leadership encouraged initiating change in strategies and tactics whenever necessary to satisfy the legitimate interests of any major stakeholder—employees, customers, or stockholders. In contrast, the researchers found that in cultures containing few Type III values and behaviors, "the norm is that managers behave cautiously and politically to protect or advance themselves, their product, or their immediate work groups." Refer to Kotter, J. P., and Heskett, J. L. *Corporate Culture and Performance.* New York: Free Press, 1992.

14. Schein, E. "Organizational Socialization and the Profession of Management." *Industrial Management Review,* 1968, *9,* 1–15.

15. For more detail on core competencies refer to Prahalad, C. K., and Hamel, G. "The Core Competence of the Corporation." *Harvard Business Review,* 1990, *68*(3), 72–78.

16. Miles, R. H. "Findings and Implications of Organizational Life Cycle Research: A Commencement." In J. R. Kimberly, R. H. Miles, and Associates, *The Organizational Life Cycle: Issues in the Creation, Transformation, and Decline of Organizations.* San Francisco: Jossey-Bass, 1980, pp. 442–443.

17. Hackman, J. R. "Why Teams Don't Work." *Leader to Leader,* Winter 1998, pp. 24–38 (quote: p. 28).
18. Wegner, E. "Communities of Practice: Where Learning Happens." *Benchmark,* Fall 1991.
19. Kanter, R. M. *The Change Masters.* New York: Simon & Schuster, 1983, p. 32.
20. For extended discussions of the characteristics of learning organizations, refer to Argyris, C., and Schon, D. E. *Organizational Learning: A Theory of Action Perspective.* Reading, Mass.: Addison-Wesley, 1978; Bennis, W., and Nanus, B. *Leaders: Strategies for Taking Charge.* New York: HarperCollins, 1985, pp. 190–214; Senge, P. M. *The Fifth Discipline.* New York: Doubleday, 1990; and Beckhard, R., and Pritchard, W. *Changing the Essence.* San Francisco: Jossey-Bass, 1992, pp. 9–24.

Part Four

Beyond Leadership

Other Essential Elements
of Successful Change

Chapter Ten

Top Management Viewed from Below

A Learning Perspective on Transformation

Susan Albers Mohrman

During the past two decades, few corporations have been immune to the global economic forces that require large-scale change for survival. Deregulation, globalization, and technological advances that enable coordination of activities and real-time exchange of knowledge and information have altered the terrain on which organizations compete and add value to the markets and societies where they operate. The changes in organizational paradigms—in strategies, organizational designs, and relationships to market—have been profound.

The popular literature is replete with accounts of CEOs who have seized the moment, formulated a vision, and led their companies into new and uncharted waters. Case accounts abound that describe what CEOs do to lead these changes, including formulating the vision and underlying strategy to anticipate and respond to changes and trends in the environment and reshaping the organization to operate in new ways. But many take the perspective of the executive and are consequently somewhat "CEO-centric." One could walk away from many accounts feeling that if the CEO is prescient enough, charismatic enough, and, perhaps, smart enought to hire the reight consultants, a large and complex organization can be transformed.

Certainly the role of the executive is crucial in successful corporate-wide transformation. But accounts that focus primarily on the role of the executive in large-scale change mask a tremendous amount of activity in the guts of the organization that embeds new ways of operating and achieves success. This chapter examines the phenomenon of large-scale change from the perspective of organizational members and draws implications for change leadership.

The framework of this chapter is that large-scale change is a learning process in which units at all systems levels (business units, teams, individuals) learn to operate in new ways. New patterns and routines replace old ones; employees develop a new understanding of the organization and their relationship to it. Change occurs when the members of the organization collectively assume new ways of behaving and achieve new kinds of performance. Consequently, this chapter describes what leaders do that contributes to or prevents the organizational learning required to enact the new organizational model.

A key aspect of today's transitions is a new relationship between employees and employers. Downsizing and corporate restructuring have significantly disrupted the implicit or explicit loyalty between employee and employer that characterized many companies during the post-World War II era. As organizations transition to high-involvement management styles including flat and lean structures, broad distribution of responsibility for business success, pay at risk, and broader roles with more self-management, employees are finding themselves with greatly more complex, responsible, and demanding jobs, often with no change of status or salary. The traditional employment bargain has been disrupted. Thus, organizations are undergoing demanding transitions that require considerable organizational learning and that introduce considerable uncertainty into their relationship with their employees.

This chapter examines the role of top management during transition from the perspective of those within the organization. It is based on extensive qualitative data (more than a thousand interviews) in more than eighty business units within corporations undergoing large-scale change. Ten technology companies were part of a study from 1990–1993 of the transition to lateral team-based forms of organization in order to embed process management and market-orientation into their way of doing business.[1]

Eleven companies have more recently been part of a study of learning during transition. This study examined the internal learning dynamics that differentiated between business units that were able to put new ways of working into practice quickly and to experience performance improvement as a result and those that were having more difficulty with the transition.[2] In neither of these studies was the role of top management the prime focus; however, in both studies it was among the variables that were examined. These studies have provided a rich qualitative understanding of how executive leadership is seen from below during organizational transitions.

This chapter first provides a framework for conceptualizing large-scale transition as a learning process. It then examines the aspects of this learning process that are shaped and influenced by executive behavior.

Large-Scale Transformation as Learning

Established organizations manifest organizational learning that has occurred within a particular paradigm, or way of doing things, that sufficed in earlier environments. Organizations learned as they went through their growth cycles[3] and put in place new processes and structures to deal with increasing size and complexity. However, they often established a resilient mode of operating, an organizational "recipe,"[4] that fit with and was shaped by the environment in which they grew up. Subsequent learning was largely within that overarching recipe. Within a predominant model of hierarchical control and bureaucracy, organizations learned such things as how to design, produce, and distribute increasingly complex and diverse products, to employ sophisticated manufacturing control systems and knowledge bases, to utilize increasingly sophisticated information and control systems, and to put in place more sophisticated, hierarchically oriented performance management systems. All of this learning has been first-order change[5]—change that occurs within the overarching assumptions and governing principles of the hierarchical form.

Recently organizations have faced competitive environments that demand discontinuous performance: they call for qualitatively different levels and kinds of performances. Achieving this requires second-order learning—learning that entails the development of new organizational models and frameworks that challenge the assumptions of the hierarchical, bureaucratic form. Such transitions require employees to jump out of frame in their understanding of the organization and its environment, and in the way in which they carry out their jobs. The change may be from hierarchical governance to lateral governance and self-management, from technical to market orientation, from national or international to global— to name a few of the reorientations that have been occurring.

Many organizations today are undergoing strategically driven, large-scale change: lasting change in the character of the organization that significantly alters its performance.[6] Large-scale change tends to be organization-wide. It is pervasive in the sense that it involves almost all aspects of the organizational system, including strategy, structure, and processes. Finally, it is deep change, in that it challenges fundamental assumptions and values that previously underpinned the organization. In sum, large-scale change demands that the organization learn ways of operating that are based on different conceptualizations of the system, and new assumptions, values, and goals.

Learning Processes During Large-Scale Change

In the typical organization in the midst of such change, it seems to employees that everything is changing at once. Three aspects of the organizational architecture often are changing simultaneously.[2] First, advances in technical tools and knowledge and in telecommunications and computerized systems are combining with new ways of conceptualizing, organizing, and controlling technical and organizational processes to yield new technical architectures. New tools and methodologies to support cross-functional work such as optimization and trade-off tools, advanced simulation and modeling techniques, and integrated business systems and data bases make possible new ways of doing work.

The market architectures of organizations are also changing dramatically. Organizations are finding new ways to orient to and relate to customers, boundaries with customers and suppliers have become blurred, and a proliferation of organizational alliances has meant that competitors are also partners. Companies are changing from being international to being truly global. Organizations are distributing responsibility for market and financial success into small, dispersed, flexible units and moving it deeper into the organization.

Simultaneously the social architectures of most organizations are changing: new structures, work designs, processes, and systems are being put in place to underpin the web of relationships that are required within and between organizations, to take advantage of the capabilities of new communication systems, and to build the capacity for flexibility of action and business involvement throughout the organization. People find themselves in flat, lean organizations, working in teams and networks that may include customers and suppliers, delivering services from shared service structures, managing outsourcing relationships, and working in a variety of partnership structures.

Although the practitioner literature is filled with descriptions of these new approaches and often sings their praises, closer examination sometimes yields a less optimistic picture. For example, even consultants closely involved with process reengineering[7] report that these efforts lead to true improvement in organizational performance capabilities in just a small percent of companies.[8] Initial reported gains often are merely the result of downsizing in anticipation of expected operating efficiencies. Even the original proponents of the concept admit that the resilience of the entrenched organization was underestimated, and that the very executives who were propelling process engineering failed to become adequately educated about its essence and requirements for success.[9, 10] Even the initial advocates of process reengineering admit that they did not fully comprehend the depth of organizational change required to truly manage processes that span the empires of the segmented organization. One study of process reengineering in one company has found that the transition was most effective in units that experienced integrated change in their technical, market, and social architecture, rather than focusing primarily on one or two of these domains.[11]

There have been a number of diverse definitions of organizational learning. Some of these relate it to activities assumed to yield learning, such as TQM or training (for example, Ulrich, Glinow, and Jick[12]). Others reduce it to individual learning within an organization (such as Argyris and Schon[13]) or to generic competencies such as shared vision, team learning, and mental models (for example, Senge[14]). An alternative definition is in terms of outcomes—organizational learning can be conceptualized as the collective processes by which an organization is able to put in place new approaches that enable it to perform more effectively in its changing environment.[2] This definition explicitly defines learning in terms of what the organization is trying to accomplish strategically and operationally.

Clearly, effecting the simultaneous change in technical, market, and social architectures in order to perform more effectively entails considerable learning. The implementation of these new organizational forms entails the design of new structures, processes, and systems, which itself represents a formidable learning task for organizations that have spent years honing the structures, processes, and systems of the bureaucratic, functional form. For example, developing the ability to generate new products through cross-functional, global product development teams that include partnerships and alliances with other companies requires that cross-functional and cross-organizational structures be designed, as well as the systems and processes required to support and operate within them. In addition, new collective behavior patterns or programs[15] must be established if the new organizational design is to result in different kinds of performance. Not only must cross-functional and cross-organizational planning sessions be held, but the participants must develop ways to surface relevant information, integrate diverse information, create win-win solutions, and coordinate across functional "thought-worlds,"[16] national cultures, and distances. Underpinning the design of new organizational structures, systems, and processes and the enactment of new behavioral patterns are new cognitions—new and more systemic ways of understanding the organization, its purposes, the factors that impact performance, and the various knowledge sets that must be integrated.

Figure 10.1 arrays the various facets of the learning challenge embedded in large-scale change. Achieving the desired outcomes requires change in patterns of behavior—in organization-level phenomena. The learning process is necessarily a collective process as new shared cognitive frameworks emerge that form the basis for altered collective behavior patterns. The learning required to become global, for example, is not accomplished solely by creating a global vision, nor by exhorting businesses to become global. Rather, it happens because structures are set up for global design and production, processes are set up for worldwide participants to influence and shape goals and plans, reward systems recognize global growth, development systems build capability for effective global performance, and people collectively begin to behave in patterns that are globally oriented. Gradually a rich and deep shared understanding emerges of what it means to be a global company.

In our studies of organizational units involved in organizational transitions, we found it quite interesting that within the same organization (with the same top management) there are units that apply new approaches in an accelerated fashion while others struggle and continue to house old behavior patterns despite reconfiguration into new structures and the introduction of new formal processes and systems. Units that are "accelerated learners" are

Figure 10.1. Learning Domain of Organizational Transitions.

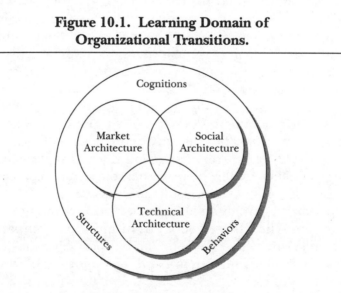

Source: Tensaki, R., Mohrman, S., and Mohrman, A. "Accelerated Learning During Organizational Transition." In S. Mohrman, J. R. Galbraith, and E. E. Lawler III and Associates, *Tomorrow's Organization: Crafting Organizations for a Dynamic World.* San Francisco: Jossey-Bass, 1997. Used by permission of Jossey-Bass, Inc., Publishers.

characterized by higher levels of collective learning processes that enable the members to develop a new shared understanding of their organizational system and how they operate.[2] There is considerably more dialogue about the changes, and more effort to learn from their own experiences with the changed approaches. They also engage in open system learning—by opening themselves up to information and feedback from outside the unit, and by building bridges to other units and organizations. These accelerated learning units develop a more systemic understanding of their organization that allows an integrated understanding of the technical, social, and market approaches.[11]

These collective learning processes enable the organizational unit to learn what kinds of organizational design features are effective for accomplishing the new operating capabilities that are the focus of the organizational transition, and to establish behavioral patterns to make them operate effectively. In essence, each organizational unit must self-design.[17, 18] There are no road maps for fundamental transitions. The high-level design features can be specified by executive leaders and their various change agents, but making them work and learning to work within them require considerable local learning as the unit tailors, fixes, and assimilates new approaches.[19] Take the example of organizations moving to cross-functional new product development teams in order to implement a strategy that calls for reduced development cycles and increased yield of new products to market. Some teams are able to learn quickly how to take advantage of this reconfiguration to achieve greater concurrence of operation and significant breakthrough thinking. Others recreate their old sequential, segmented way of doing business and historical status patterns. They essentially perform in a traditional functional manner despite being reconfigured. When these two kinds of units are compared, the former are characterized by considerable local sense-making, local design of practices and systems, and the importing of ideas from outside the group.

Because of the amount of learning required for transition, one way to conceptualize the role of top management is as the stimulator and orchestrator of a learning organization. Seen from this perspective, the challenge goes beyond charting a strategic and organizational course, taking tough action, and being the architect of the new organization. It requires that management establish a framework for organizational learning and lead the learning process.

The Changing Employment Relationship

When organizations undergo large-scale change, the relationship of employees to the company may change dramatically. This has been particularly true during the last decade when strategic restructuring has been accompanied by pervasive downsizing, flattening of hierarchical levels, outsourcing, and establishment of global operations. These changes in strategy and structure have often been accompanied by changes to human resource practices such as decreased loyalty to employees, altered career opportunities, and pay at risk. Such changes have violated the traditional psychological contract[20, 21] of employees—the individual beliefs about the employment relationship and terms of exchange between the individual and the employer. The psychological contract establishes an implicit balance in employees' minds between the level of effort and nature of the contribution the company expects from them and the outcomes they can expect in return. During the past decade, a change in the balance has been unilaterally imposed, with more being demanded of employees in return for a dramatically altered set of outcomes. Furthermore, the new contract has become increasingly transactional, placing a greater emphasis on formal provisions and being shorter in term than the traditional relationship-based contract that was less formal and longer in term.[21]

The changes have been particularly interesting because for the employees who remain part of the company after downsizing and restructuring, the changed organization has in many cases offered greatly increased outcomes in personal growth domains, such as the chance to learn new things, accomplish more, and make a difference. In fact, successful performance in the reconfigured organization practically demands that these occur. Simultaneously, hygiene-oriented outcomes such as security, the opportunity to make more money, and career advancement opportunities have decreased. Table 10.1 shows survey data from eleven diverse companies reporting employee perceptions of the impact that

Table 10.1. Positive Personal Impact on Organizational Transition.

The changes have allowed me . . .	11 Site Average	Sites										
		1	2	3	4	5	6	7	8	9	10	11
An Opportunity to Learn New Things	3.79	3.7	4.2	4.0	3.8	4.0	3.1	3.9	3.9	3.8	3.4	4.0
To Accomplish More than Before	3.40	3.3	3.8	3.5	3.3	3.7	2.7	3.9	3.2	3.4	3.0	3.5
To Have More Say in My Work	3.20	3.4	3.5	3.6	3.1	3.5	2.4	3.6	3.1	3.3	2.6	3.2
A Better Quality of Worklife	2.97	2.9	3.4	3.3	2.8	3.6	2.3	3.4	2.4	3.1	2.5	3.2
An Opportunity for Career Growth	2.90	2.7	2.7	2.6	3.1	3.5	2.8	3.0	2.8	2.9	2.2	3.6
Job Security	2.55	2.0	2.6	2.5	3.0	3.1	2.1	2.4	2.3	2.9	2.1	3.1
An Opportunity to Make More Money	2.49	2.3	3.0	2.2	2.4	3.1	2.1	2.2	2.4	2.8	2.0	3.1

Response code: 1 = Strongly Disagree, 2 = Disagree, 3 = Neither, 4 = Agree, 5 = Strongly Agree

Source: © 1996, Center for Effective Organizations, University of Southern California: "Learning During Transition Study" by R. Mohrman and R. Tensaki.

restructuring has had on their outcomes. It may not be stretching reality to say that we are in the midst of a very large social experiment—examining the impact of greatly decreasing the core bread-and-butter outcomes of employment while dramatically increasing the amount of growth and development that is both offered and required.

Most significantly, in most cases this change in the employment relationship has not been mutually crafted by the company and its employees; rather, the new psychological contract entails an adjustment by employees to new terms of employment created by unilateral employer action. Because of the increasingly short-term nature of the new relationship, the increasingly demanding expectations of employee performance in most organizations, and the dynamic nature of the organization and its strategies, the new relationship has carried with it a sense of threat. This threat can be expected to have an impact on the ability of the organization to learn as required for successful implementation of new organizational directions.

In our studies of learning during organizational transition, we found that, compared to members of struggling units, the members of accelerated-learning units were considerably more positive about the outcomes they were experiencing as a result of the organizational changes. They also felt that the changes were in their best interests and in the best interests of the company.[2] The degree of positive or negative effect with respect to the changing organization differed significantly between similar units within the same organization, indicating that interpretation of the changes is to a great extent socially constructed within the unit. It seems that the processes within each organizational unit affect even the perceptions of the employee outcomes that form a basis for the new psychological contract. Despite these differences in overall level of affect, it is fair to say that in the companies we studied, there was a prevailing sense that the shift has entailed an increase in growth outcomes and a decrease in hygiene outcomes.

The role of top management in leading large-scale change should be understood in the full context of the organizational dynamics that are set in motion during such change. Fundamental changes in organizational architectures require extensive organizational learning by a population of employees for whom the traditional psychological contract is being battered. In all the venues of the organization—business units, teams, and various kinds of work groups, collective processes are determining what is learned, how the new employment bargain is perceived, and what levels of performance will result. How top management leadership affects these collective processes is an important question.

Top Management Seen from Within

There have been a number of insightful treatments of the role of leaders and the nature of change leadership.[22-24] Indeed, a number of themes appear repeatedly: visioning, being the architect of the flexible organization, modeling ongoing learning, developing organizational capabilities, and inspiring and energizing. Numerous case studies demonstrate how these have been done by noteworthy leaders in highly visible corporations. This chapter does not purport to refute nor to recast this literature. Rather, it intends to complement it by providing the view from within. It reports themes from interviews and focus groups with people at all levels in organizations undergoing discontinuous change, and clusters them into three main categories that we have found to be critical to organizational learning: the learning system, shared meaning, and the psychological contract. First, it puts these findings into context by discussing the lenses through which many employees see top management.

Who Is Top Management and How Salient Are They in the Organization?

Most of the data in our studies of organizational transitions came from people within business units—divisions, product lines, regions, programs, and shared services. We interviewed top managers to get a sense of the strategy, vision, intended architectural changes, and change process being deployed. We took these features of the transition as givens, and set out to understand what is required to enable the organization to operate in these new ways. Our overall approach was to examine a variety of units and compare those that were making the changes effectively with those that weren't. The impact of top management was viewed from below—

not from the perspectives of top managers and their key change agents.

What was striking in our interviews was how infrequently top managers came up in response to open-ended questions such as, What are the facilitators of and barriers to putting these new organizational approaches into operation? or What role has management played in this transition? Questions about the nature of the transition indicated that people had registered a great deal of the message from top management: about the changing market environment, the strategy of the organization, the key focuses of the transition, and so forth. This was true in accelerated learning units and in the units that were struggling with the transition. However, there was a difference. In the accelerated units, the messages had been internalized and were being offered as one's own view: "We have to begin to reuse technology across our programs because otherwise we will be at risk in the changing market." In the units that were learning more slowly, the messages were often attributed to a generalized "they": "They want us to reuse technology to save money." In neither case was top management particularly salient in people's minds. This lack of reference to top management is not particularly surprising, given that these respondents are nestled within business units that are often several levels down; however, it does point out the importance of aligning the organization so that people get consistent messages from all levels. It also indicates that in units that are making the transition successfully, people have made the top management's message their own.

Another striking pattern is that interviewees often responded to inquiries about top management's role with comments about the behavior of their division or business unit management rather than with comments about the CEO and executives of the corporation. Some spoke of the expectations for performance, key initiatives, and sometimes the key elements of the vision that were coming from corporate management. But when asked about the dynamics of change, their focus was primarily on the change-related role that their local management was playing. In multidivisional companies, many have very little visibility beyond their divisional management. Beyond that there's often a fuzzy, almost depersonalized image—analogous to the rather vague referent when people talk about how "the company" does something. Indeed, in many cases responding to these questions in terms of local business unit management makes the most sense. Many aspects of the transition were often being crafted at the more local level; this was even the case when the corporation as a whole was in the midst of a strategic transition.[25] Even when top corporate management speaks directly to employees, the message is to some extent interpreted and heard through the voices of their more proximate managers. So one of the challenges to top management is how to get its message to echo with high resolution through the organization.

Although top managers tended not to be explicitly mentioned as barriers and facilitators, it is important to point out that many of the facilitators and barriers perceived by people are the result of executive focuses and action. They reflect the change activities and elements set in motion by or occurring in the name of top management: the new business strategy, new organizational architectures, and implementation processes. People experience top management in terms of the systems, structures, processes, and initiatives they put in place.

More particularly, employees experience top management in terms of the way these new systems, structures, and processes have an impact on them. However, personal impact is not a straightforward result of the content of the changes moderated solely by individual differences. Rather, it is a complex interactive phenomenon that both reflects and shapes the learning processes in the organization through which organizational members develop a new understanding of the changing architectures of the organization and their place in it. It also has a collective aspect, for the success of a unit in implementing new approaches relates to the nature of the shared meaning that is created among its members.[2] Within the same organization, similarly composed units doing similar work develop greatly divergent levels of perceived positive or negative personal impact from the change, diverse levels of shared understanding, and diverse learning processes. Furthermore, the perceived impact changes over time.

It appears that top management reaches the troops primarily through the voices of more proximate management, and that one of its main leverage points is through stirring up learning dynamics throughout the organization that lead to the behavioral, cognitive, and structural changes required to successfully enact new architectures. Simply charting the new architectures is not sufficient, for their successful enactment requires local learning and the development of new meaning. Top management does much that either fosters or impedes learning within the organization, the emergence of shared meaning, and the development of a new and positive psychological contract (see Figure 10.2). These focuses are discussed next, again from the perspective of members of the organization.

Leading the Learning System

It has been recognized by others that change leaders lead a learning system. For example, Bennis and Nanus[22] pointed out that true leaders are learners who model learning for the whole organization. Learning dynamics need to occur in all units. Management behavior can catalyze or stifle these dynamics in a number of ways.

Promoting Organization-Wide Open-Systems Learning

A key learning dynamic is open-systems learning through exposure to external information, feedback, and perspectives. In the transitioning organizations we have studied, it was apparent that leaders cannot learn for the organization. In several of the organizations that were moving to a team-based structure, for example, the general manager and several key staff members read voraciously, visited other companies, and attended a myriad of development activities. They had truly internalized a new mental model for how

Figure 10.2. Executive Focuses During Transition.

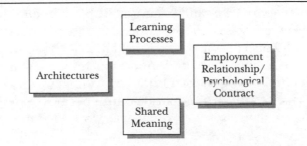

the organization might best work to quickly develop market-shaping products and maintain strategic leadership. Unfortunately, that learning did not extend down into the teams they were leading, where members were scrambling to figure out why they were suddenly in a radically reconfigured organization. The people who were actually going to develop these new products were aware that their managers were attending a lot of "off-sites" and undergoing some sort of transformation of thinking, but they themselves were still trying to figure out how to do business as usual within team structures that made it harder to do it.

That scenario can be contrasted with some other organizations and units where these kinds of learning events (visiting and benchmarking, attending conferences, and holding developmental off-site meetings) occurred throughout the organization, and where team members were able to more quickly develop new understanding. One top management role is to create the policies and frameworks that make such pervasive learning probable. For example, companies that had policies requiring a certain amount of development days per year, and that took a broad approach to what constitutes a development day (such as training, visiting, benchmarking, and the like) were more likely to have established an organization-wide dynamic of open-system learning.

Learning from Experience

The accelerated learning units not only imported learning, they also learned from their own experience more quickly and more intentionally than the struggling units. Even these local learning processes are to a great extent influenced by whether top management establishes a compelling message linking the new approaches to business performance and whether an atmosphere of trust is established such that risk taking will not be punished. Trying out new approaches and behaviors with the intention of learning from them implies the possibility of failure, a possibility that carries prohibitive personal career risk in many organizations. The alternative is a mechanical and superficial implementation of top-down dictated changes, with little learning about how to make them work effectively in the local setting because members continue to operate in ways they know have worked in the past.

The credibility of the message from top management and the way it is translated into the operating units of the organization are key. The messages encouraging experimentation and new approaches can get drowned out by anxiety about and intensity of the performance pressures being experienced by the organization and communicated by top management. Conveying a balanced set of expectations and a clear logic connecting the new architectures to business performance is critical to creating an atmosphere where people feel that they can be successful if they commit to trying new approaches and learning from their experiences. In one of the most accelerated organizational transitions we studied, top management repeatedly conveyed the kind of message paraphrased here:

> Our old way of doing work won't enable us to accomplish our goals in the new business environment. We have been technically preeminent and business naive and our performance has suffered as a consequence. We need to very quickly turn that around. We have to put in place new approaches that link every person in our organization more directly to our business purpose and our customers and give them the authority to do what's right for customer satisfaction and business success. This represents a major change from the past and we will experience a lot of bumps along the way. But we know we can achieve it because we have the most talented group of employees in the industry. We don't have all the answers. We're asking you to take the risk, extend yourselves, experience the bumps and learn from them, so that we can put in place a new way of operating that enables us to be a successful company into the future.

This was a message that gave a high-level case for action and statement of purpose and focus, gave permission to experiment, and at the same time built strong expectations of performance outcomes.

Systemic Understanding and Functioning

Even when management has thought through a systemic approach to change—one that examines market, technical, and social aspects of the organization and purports to establish an integrated change management approach—employees often experience the change process as a series of unrelated initiatives. The challenge is to create systemic understanding throughout the organization. In one insurance company that was undergoing major transformation to effect market flexibility and local business ownership by quite diverse geographical and cultural regions, units experienced very uneven success due in part to the different levels of understanding among the units of the systemic nature of the change. The units that successfully implemented the new model in an accelerated fashion understood how the structural changes that created intact local business units, technical changes that enabled quick flexible processing and responsiveness, and market changes to deliver enhanced analytical business support services to customers fit together to create a new business model. They focused on all three elements of the change. The struggling units tended to see the change in terms of one primary element—some focused on creating empowered teams to the exclusion of new relationships with the market; others focused on using the new technology to generate efficiencies but didn't work on new business and market relationships or on developing accountable teams. All units were exposed to a uniform set of change interventions from the corporation: the difference between the units was a function of local dynamics.[11]

Neatly articulated integrated change frameworks cannot be effectively conveyed by presentation or documentation. Over and over again, we heard people talk about the interactive process they went through to gain systemic understanding. Struggling teams would talk about how "management throws out all these words—like team, business accountability—and we don't know what that really means." In the transition to team-based organizations it is not uncommon to hear members of technology organizations say, "I don't know what's different. We've always been in teams," referring to the old organizational terminology that referred to anyone who got involved with a particular product as a team member. One fast-learning technical services team described the pains they took early on to talk about what it meant that they were now a "business unit" delivering a service to internal customers, and how they would have to change their technical processes and coordination processes to optimize the value they contributed to the business. This contrasted to similar units that were having difficulty grasping "what this transition is all about." The latter teams often said "this notion of teams as business units doesn't really fit us—we're a service unit"; and they proceeded to do work as usual, focusing on their own rather than their client's agenda.

Developing local systemic understanding is not accomplished through executive action and pronouncement. However, it can be helped along by executive focus. Exclusive focus on narrow business results, for instance, conveys a message that narrows the dialogue within units. Reiteration of the principles of the new architecture and review of progress in getting new social and technical systems in place extends focus. Reiteration of the logic of the new architectures is especially helpful. In one organization, for some units establishing integrated product development teams became its own focus: a better way of doing what we always did but faster. In other units in that organization, the teams were understood as a means of developing a new relationship with the customer, dealing with the lifelong cost issues of product ownership, and using cross-discipline exchange to generate innovative approaches. The differences in understanding reflected differences in unit management emphases: in the latter, accelerated units, local management kept repeating, in every possible forum, the multifaceted business rationale for establishing integrated product teams. Quickly the teams internalized that rationale.

Leading the Development of Shared Meaning

The transformed organization is one that has developed new capabilities; it is also one that has developed a new meaning system. The preexisting shared understandings, including explicit and implicit values, norms, and routines, have been altered, enhanced, or replaced. A myriad of new understandings may have needed to be put in place: about the need to address the customer's business needs in conjunction with one's own technical and business considerations in making ongoing trade-offs and decisions; about what it means and requires to be global rather than international; about factors that yield performance in the changing environment and the need for a balanced performance that yields both current and future outcomes; and about new ways of leading and controlling organizational performance. In one insurance company, for example, the members of the new decentralized cross-functional business teams had to learn to understand what constitutes good and bad business, as they were now being asked to operate like a business and focus on return on equity rather than purely on revenue. In the past, central actuarial groups had been the watchdogs for bad business; now, team members were governing their own behavior in this regard. These are broad systemic understandings that require cognitive shifts as well as new behavioral patterns. Each has layers of implications for the organizational architecture and its programs. Earlier, we talked about the need for the executive to act in a way that catalyzes local learning. To establish a new shared meaning requires attention to new programs that will embed these new understandings in the way the organization operates and create a coherent and flexible whole.

Shared Meaning Around Principles, Processes, and Language

Creating shared meaning requires more than being an architect of the new system. As we mentioned earlier, learning how to make new architectures work requires a great deal of local learning. The new systems should be crafted in such a way that local interpretation, assimilation, and accommodation are possible—indeed, required. For it is through these local processes that shared meaning develops and is made concrete in new ways of doing work. On the other hand, commonalities across the organization enable effective and efficient commerce across units and leverage and flexibility in the application of resources. Top management, it appears, walks a tightrope between setting in motion forces that require unneeded uniformity and discourage local learning and optimization, and setting in place change forces that yield unwieldy diversity of practice. The people in our studies reacted negatively to both over- and underprescription. The reaction to overprescription came because it attenuates local learning, designing, and ownership; the reaction to underprescription occurred because people feel at risk of doing the wrong thing, or of charting an idiosyncratic course that results in isolation from the larger corporate context—as, for instance, for career purposes.

The shared meaning that people sought is in such areas as general operating principles and values and how the various parts of the organization relate to one another. Ultimately these have to be made concrete in common practices and clear designs. The question is how common do approaches need to be and how dynamic will they need to be?

One way that management can achieve a new shared meaning that is not experienced as constraining is to embed new meanings in high-level processes within which each unit goes through its own local interactions to establish internal shared meaning, and that can yield different designs and approaches in various units. In one organization moving to self-contained integrated product development units, for example, a common nine-phase life cycle phase model was introduced with three formal checkpoints that were required of all units and served as the basis for relating the unit to the larger organizational context. By providing a reconfigurable software package to the units, each was encouraged to tailor the phase model to fit its situation, including adding and removing steps and focuses. In several other companies business models were introduced whereby each business unit was required to do a value chain business assessment, determine key drivers, and formulate goals and objectives accordingly. Certain corporate drivers were prescribed, but units with different market or product constraints could generate unique configurations of drivers and goals. Each division and business unit in the company went through a similar process, yielding diverse, locally sensitive plans. Shared meaning developed around the importance and process of focusing on key business levers in order to have an impact on short- and long-term results.

The key implication for top management is that shared meaning is a combination of prescription and local self-direction. Change interventions do not create a neat, uniform ripple through the organization; rather they catalyze diverse activity in diverse units that enables high-level meaning systems to be made concrete in local practice. Members of the units that went through the business model planning processes just described singled them out as perhaps the key contributor to learning: "We floundered about for a year, and when we went through that business planning process we kept trying to figure out what it had to do with our work [exploring for oil in the Gulf of Mexico]. Why didn't management just tell us our metrics? Then all of a sudden it clicked. We had a collective 'aha' and figured out what it meant that we are a business team. We don't think the same way anymore."

Consistency of Messages

The development of shared meaning is also enabled by the consistency of messages in the system, a point that is certainly not new in the change literature. Aspects of this issue relate in part to the infrastructure and architecture of the organization: Do the reward systems acknowledge the new performances and capabilities? Are the corporate support groups redesigned to fit with the new organizational logic? Is the organization measuring and focusing on the outcomes it says are important? These are all systems that our respondents pointed to either as inhibitors or enablers of learning, depending on whether they were aligned with the new logic or not. In one organization, for example, a number of respondents made a similar point: although the company was pursuing a new low cost strategy, there was not a single system that gave good cost feedback. Instead, feedback focused entirely on schedule. Thus, constructing the various organizational systems is one of the major ways management sends a consistent message and establishes common meaning.

Consistency in what top managers say and do is also important for building shared meaning. Discrepancies in the messages that come from different members of the executive staff, for example, work against the development of shared understanding, especially in cross-functional units. When an espoused direction is perceived to be held by only one or two of the top managers (even if one is the CEO), people give little credence to the transformation because they are continually receiving conflicting information, often from the people at the top of their own reporting chain. Conversely, commonality in message, focus, and behavior across the management team can temporarily offset incompatibilities that result while the organization is trying to bring its systems into alignment. In one defense firm, for example, one program manager received a very consistent message from his group-level managers:

> Our president, controller, manufacturing vice president, and chief technology officer are making a concerted effort to help us achieve commercial operating capability. We applied for special [Perry initiative] status with our government customer that allows us to deviate from traditional approaches by common agreement. My program team feels perfectly comfortable and in fact we feel a compelling need to depart from company practice in almost all re-

spects and do everything possible to achieve the operating efficiencies of a commercial firm. For example, we've gerry-rigged some systems and gotten the military to agree to some new ways of reporting things.

This contrasts with a program manager in another group in the same company, who felt there was a great deal of dissension in his group-level staff about the desirability of achieving commercial operating approaches:

Our president says we need to go in that direction, but our CFO is saying to us, "just make sure you don't change the way you report data" and our quality officer is saying that it doesn't matter what the president says, he knows his neck is on the line to make sure we don't deviate one iota from mil-spec processes. So we're pretty much doing business as usual with some lip service to benchmarking commercial practices.

Both of these groups were hearing the same messages from the corporation's CEO about a strong strategic commitment to commercial practice.

Inconsistency of message can also be a problem when multiple messages are coming from the same source. In one organization that was transitioning to product line business teams, the engineering vice president was a major proponent of the changes, championing training, the introduction of new processes, new measurement systems, and rotational career paths. However, his explicit message to the organization about rewards was that "when it comes to rewards we won't go by this team stuff; we all know that people contribute at different levels and that some disciplines contribute more than others. You'll have to make it visible to me that your contribution is greater than that of your peers in order to get a good raise and promotions around here." That simple message was reported by people to be far more powerful in determining how they thought about their work than the structures and processes that were put in place to support integrated teamwork.

Continuity

It is also not a new theme in the change literature that continuity permits learning and gives the opportunity for a new shared meaning to develop in the organization. "The thing that has helped the most is that our president has stayed the course despite everyone's bellyaching and the initial pain we felt. We've actually had a chance to learn how to make this work." In some organizations, continuity was mentioned over and over by interviewees as the single biggest facilitator of learning. This pattern of response was particularly likely to be present when the transition was a reconfiguration to a new architecture that embedded a new systemic model of organizing rather than being a sequential series of programmatic initiatives. When there is a "switch-over" of organizational model, subsequent changes can be introduced that are portrayed and understood as the supporting features for the new model. Programmatic initiatives, though, are often experienced as the "change de jour." Interestingly, initiative-driven transformation is often described by top management and its advisors in a systemic manner—there's a master plan guiding the unfolding of various interventions—but it is almost impossible for recipients to experience it in a systemic way because they are not set up to operate with the full new logic. This is illustrated by a commonly expressed theme: "There are so many initiatives that we just pick and choose which ones are worth the energy and which ones aren't"—apparently failing to see systemic fit and mutual reinforcement between them.

Another deterrent to continuity is change of top management and subsequent changes in message and architecture that undo the organizational learning that has occurred. New managers often haven't been present to learn with the system and may not have an understanding of the logic. Changes to divisional or group-level management, for example, often occur in the middle of a multi-year transition in that business unit, in a corporate environment that has insufficient shared understanding to ensure continuity across managers. In our small sample of companies, two transitions that were achieving marked organizational performance improvement were interrupted midstream because of the promotion of the general manager and his replacement by managers unfamiliar with the new operating logic that had been established. Although an argument can be made that infusing new top management promotes learning because there is a continual infusion of new perspectives and leadership, new managers also tend to want to put their stamp on the organization, and in the process often undo a lot of learning and can actually move the organization backward in terms of its performance capabilities. New organizational forms tend to be fragile during the learning process; their full benefit often cannot be experienced until iterations of learning bring the whole system into alignment. A succession of managers often means that there is never enough stability to put a robust system in place and that the organization is destined to interventions that pick low-hanging fruit.

Perhaps the most troublesome form of lack of continuity pertains to behavior during adversity. Most top managers lead a transition in order to reap performance benefits, and may make promises to keep stock analysts and stockholders happy and to accrue large executive performance bonuses. This raises a dilemma for leading change that implies fundamental shifts of capability. In a number of our companies a fundamental lack of continuity resulted because every time there was a performance crunch the messages of capability development, risk taking, and transition were abandoned and the organization went through a "budgeting process" that included downsizing as the primary "performance enhancing" focus. Without exception, the companies in our studies had gone through some downsizing and were in the process of rebuilding. For those that kept ratcheting back into a downsizing mode, however, keeping continuity in an organizational transformation was extremely difficult. In part this is because of the key role that the psychological contract plays in learning during transition. This is discussed next.

Leading the Development of New Psychological Contracts

New organizational models are changing the relationship of employees to their organizations in some fundamental ways. The traditional benefits that employees have come to expect from loyalty and hard work—security, growth of compensation, chances to advance—have been eroded at the same time that job demands and responsibility have increased. People have the opportunity to do more (perhaps to do more with less—often in a downsized environment), to learn more (in order to adapt to broader responsibilities), and to make a difference (within empowered settings characterized by much less management presence and attention). Each of these opportunities can have a positive or negative meaning attached to it. Many companies that we studied have acknowledged the changes; they have openly admitted that they can't be loyal to employees and that they don't therefore expect loyalty from them. Preparing people for employability has become some companies' way of understanding their new obligations to employees. On a much more fundamental level, however, no one really has a good idea of what the new contract is and how it will have an impact on performance. Until recently, many organizations have been in a buyer's market with respect to talent, and employees have accepted the changed contract because they had few alternatives. The tides have turned and companies are now experiencing the other side of the cycle as their experienced employees are able to go across the street and get a raise and a promotion. This is the true test of the suitability of the emergent employment contract.

As mentioned, employee views of the personal impact of the transition relate to the acceleration or retardation of learning (see Figure 10.3). That views of personal impact differ across similarly composed units undergoing the same transition indicates that more is involved than individual differences in the value attached to the growth-oriented outcomes such as responsibility and learning. The large differences across units in the level of positive or negative effect of unit members seem to indicate that collective sense making is at work. The members of some units are apparently able to create a new, more balanced sense of the changing relationship whereas members of other units continue to see it as imposed and negative. For example, in one design program that was having great success operating as a minibusiness, members extensively described the benefits of being in their new environment: "Other companies are going in this direction too and having been in a cross-functional product team and being able to move laterally through different functions will be a real plus in the job market"; "We now have a choice of career directions since we don't have to worry about staying narrowly focused in order to move up a hierarchy"; "Since the company isn't loyal to us, we can pay more attention to our own development needs and not feel guilty when we put in fewer hours in order to attend a class"; "Closer connection to the needs of the factory and to manufacturability poses a more challenging and interesting design task"; and so forth. In another design program in the same company, members explained that they didn't feel there were any career tracks left in the company; that they were being treated like commodities that can be purchased, used, and discarded; that these new ways of doing design for manufacturing were eroding their ability to focus on their technical task and do good technical work; and that their jobs were so demanding that they no longer had a life and lived in fear of being laid off if they slacked off.

An area where members of accelerated and struggling units alike reported a great imbalance in the new employment relationship is rewards. A common complaint was that management was moving a great deal of responsibility and accountability downward without giving employees commensurate compensation. Factory employees, R&D scientists, and middle-level managers alike could recite their CEO's performance bonus, and pointed out that it was made possible by them coming in for forty-three weekends out of fifty-two, skipping vacations, covering the night shift during a particularly busy period, or quitting their evening class halfway through the semester because they couldn't get away from work for a seven o'clock class. Although many of the companies we studied had introduced some form of incentive bonus, people were often quite cynical about its size in relationship to the contribution

Figure 10.3. Psychological Contract: A Key Element of Cognition in Organizations.

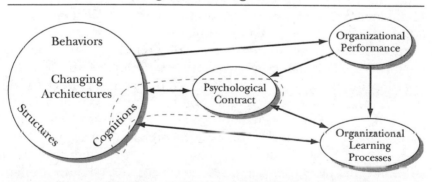

A psychological contract consists of individual beliefs, shaped by the organization, regarding terms of the exchange agreement between individuals and their organization.[20, 21]

they felt they were making, and about the various gates to payout that ensured that there would be no bonus if overall company targets were not made so that executives received theirs. Even some fairly upbeat employees in the most accelerated units felt that one way their top managers were ensuring their own bonuses was by suppressing the benefits their employees received.

The psychological contract relates to the speed of learning during transition and to the ability of the organization to put in place new architectures that underlie new capabilities and have a positive impact on performance. The establishment of a new contract should be a major executive focus; in most of the companies in our studies, this potentially enormously impactful CEO role in managing change was not occurring. The formidable task facing management is to define a new relationship that establishes for employees a true stake in the organization's performance, one that makes sense for individuals and companies that exist in a dynamic environment in which organizations require much higher levels of contribution from employees but cannot in return guarantee a stable relationship. This is an arena where executive action or inaction can be a negative force in transition—one that has until recently been masked by the overall trauma of the restructuring that has occurred in the economy.

Conclusion

This chapter looks upward from the perspective of the organizational member at the impact of top management's leadership of large-scale change. Such change involves alteration of the architectures of the organization to achieve different levels and types of performance in a changing environment. It entails considerable organizational learning: new cognition, behavioral patterns and structures, and systems need to be crafted. Interviews with participants show that top management behavior is to most people not a particularly salient factor in enabling the organization to learn new approaches; however, many of the factors they mention are strongly influenced by top management behavior. Organizational units successfully implementing new approaches have gone through local learning processes so that they see themselves as the energy behind the change and have internalized a local understanding of the new approaches. Struggling units tend to place blame on an amorphous "company," to feel a negative impact, and to be passive about the changes. They have not established the learning processes to develop new meanings and new behaviors.

The implications for the top management role are profound. These managers must not only be the architects of the change, they must also create conditions that energize learning throughout the organization. They must attend to the impact they have on the learning dynamics of the organization, on the creation of a new shared meaning in the organization, and on the shifting psychological contract.

Notes

1. Mohrman, S. A., Cohen, S. G., and Mohrman, A. M. JR. *Designing Team-Based Organizations: New Forms for Knowledge Work.* San Francisco: Jossey-Bass, 1995.
2. Tenkasi, R., Mohrman, S. A., and Mohrman, A. M. JR. "Accelerated Learning During Transition." In S. A. Mohrman, J. R. Galbraith, E. E. Lawler III, and associates. *Tomorrow's Organization: Crafting Organizations for a Dynamic World.* San Francisco: Jossey-Bass, 1998.
3. Greiner, L. E. "Evolution and Revolution as Organizations Grow." *Harvard Business Review,* 1972, *50*(4), 37–46.
4. Starbuck, W. H. "Organizations and Their Environments." In M. D. Dunnette (ed.), *Handbook of Industrial and Organizational Psychology.* Chicago: McNally, 1976, pp. 1,069–1,123.
5. Bateson, G. *Steps to an Ecology of Mind.* New York: Ballantine, 1972.
6. Ledford, G. E. JR., Mohrman, S. A., Mohrman, A. M. JR., and Lawler, E. E. III. "The Phenomenon of Large-Scale Organizational Change." In A. M. Mohrman JR., S. A. Mohrman,, G. E. Ledford JR., E. E. Lawler III, and Associates, *Large-Scale Organizational Change.* San Francisco: Jossey-Bass, 1989.
7. Hammer, M., and Champy, J. *Reengineering the Corporation: A Manifesto for Business Revolution.* New York: HarperCollins, 1993.
8. Bashein, B., Markus, M. L., and Riley, P. "Preconditions for BPR Success." *Information Systems Management,* 1994, *11*(2), 7–13.
9. Hammer, M. "You Get What You Deserve." *CFO: The Magazine for Senior Financial Executives,* 1996, *12*(9), 9.
10. Hammer, M., and Champy, J. "Who Will Reengineer?" *Executive Excellence,* 1995, *12*(2), 13–14.
11. Mohrman, S. A., Tenkasi, R. V., and Mohrman, A. M. JR. "An Organizational Learning Framework for Understanding Business Process

Redesign: A Case Study from the Financial Services Industry." *Journal of Applied Behavioral Science,* forthcoming.

12. Ulrich, D., Von Glinow, M. A., and Jick, T. "High Impact Learning: Building and Diffusing Learning Capability." *Organizational Dynamics,* 1993, *22*(1), 52–79.

13. Argyris, C., and Schon, D. A. *Organizational Learning: A Theory of Action Perspective.* Reading, Mass.: Addison-Wesley, 1978.

14. Senge, P. M. *The Fifth Discipline: The Art and Practice of the Learning Organization.* New York: Doubleday/Currency, 1990.

15. March, J. G., and Simon, H. A. *Organizations.* New York: Wiley, 1958.

16. Dougherty, D. "Interpretive Barriers to Successful Product Innovation in Large Firms." *Organization Science,* 1992, *3*(2), 179–202.

17. Weick, K. E. "Organizational Redesign as Improvisation." In G. P. Huber and W. H. Glick (eds.), *Organizational Change and Redesign: Ideas and Insights for Improving Performance.* New York: Oxford University Press, 1993, pp. 346–382.

18. Mohrman, S. A., and Cummings, T. G. *Self-Designing Organizations: Learning How to Create High Performance.* Reading, Mass.: Addison-Wesley, 1989.

19. Orlikowski, W. J. "Improvising Organizational Transformation Over Time: A Situated Change Perspective." *Information Systems Research,* 1996, *7*(1), 63–92.

20. Barnard, C. *The Functions of the Executive.* Cambridge, Mass.: Harvard University Press, 1938.

21. Rousseau, D. M. *Psychological Contracts in Organizations: Understanding Written and Unwritten Agreements.* Thousand Oaks, Calif.: Sage, 1995.

22. Bennis, W. G., and Nanus, B. *Leaders: Strategies for Taking Charge.* New York: HarperCollins, 1985.

23. Tichy, N. M., and Devanna, M. *The Transformational Leader.* New York: Wiley, 1986.

24. Wheatley, M. J. *Leadership and the New Science: Learning About Organization from an Orderly Universe.* San Francisco: Berrett-Koehler, 1992.

25. Beer, M., Eisenstat, R. A., and Spector, B. *The Critical Path to Corporate Renewal.* Cambridge, Mass.: Harvard Business School Press, 1990.

Chapter Eleven

The Role and Limits of Change Leadership

Thomas G. Cummings

The subject of leadership and organization change is embedded deeply in the lexicon and discourse of business executives, management consultants, and organizational scholars. Business periodicals, the trade press, and academic publications are brimming with information and knowledge about leading organization change. Widespread attention to leading change is largely a reflection of the times. Fueled by unprecedented changes in technologies, markets, and economies, organizations are experiencing rapidly changing environments and enormous competitive pressures. Responses to these challenges are resulting in a virtual revolution in new organizational forms and systems. Organizations are increasingly seeking to transform themselves to become more adaptable and competitive, with leaner, more flexible structures, more empowered and committed employees, and more performance-driven human resource practices.[1]

As organizations strive to implement these innovations, they discover that change is incredibly arduous, requiring a great deal of expertise, resources, and luck. The sheer difficulty of transforming organizations is evident in their enormous inertial qualities as well as the scope and magnitude of the required changes. Organization transformation typically involves radical changes in strategy and structure, in work practices and methods, and in members' perceptions, norms, and work behaviors. As many observers have pointed out, because transformational change involves the total organization including strategic relationships with the competitive environment, top leaders or CEOs need to lead the change process and are essential to its success.[2-4]

The key role that top leaders play in transformational change is reflected in how the topic is currently written and talked about. Descriptions of transformational change tend to be leader-centric. The change process is typically depicted from the perspective of senior executives; the lessons to be learned are often exemplified by the behaviors of successful CEOs, such as Iacocca at Chrysler, Welsh at General Electric, and Carlzon at SAS. Accounts of transformational change tend to portray leaders in almost mythical terms—as charismatic, visionary, heroic. Their roles in the change process tend to be similarly described: envisioning, empowering, energizing.

It is easy, therefore, to assume that top leaders make a significant difference in change outcomes. Indeed, belief in the power of change leaders is widespread, often taken for granted, and rarely questioned, particularly by practitioners and popular writers. But this contrasts sharply with persistent debates among academics. Strategic choice theorists argue that top leaders really matter;[5] external control proponents contend that they do not.[6] Attempts to reconcile these views suggest a contingency perspective, specifying situations where top leaders can and cannot be expected to have powerful effects.

In the spirit of contingency thinking, this chapter seeks to present a balanced view of the role of top leaders in transformational change. It first explains how assumptions about change leadership develop and are reinforced. This shows the need to question current assumptions and to develop better-balanced contingency views. The chapter then identifies, in a preliminary manner, change situations where top leaders are likely to have their greatest effects and those where they are not. Finally, the chapter speculates on whether powerful substitutes for change leadership exist in organizations and their environments, thus raising the possibility that top leaders may be unnecessary or redundant in certain change contexts.

Assumptions About Change Leaders

So far, there has been little debate or question in the organization transformation literature about the effects of change leaders. Based largely on anecdotal evidence from practitioners and consultants, it is commonly assumed that top leaders make a difference in how well organizations transform themselves. This belief underlies current prescriptions about transforming organizations; it persists despite almost no scientific data to either confirm or refute it.

To understand why leader-centric assumptions about transformational change are so prevalent, it is useful to examine how they develop and are reinforced. Insight into the genesis of such beliefs raises issues about their validity and provides a starting point for developing a more open and balanced view of change leaders.

Current assumptions about change leaders derive primarily from two related sources: the sense making that people do to explain and account for organizational activities and outcomes, and the reports of experts who become, often unintentionally, the servants of top leaders.

Sense Making

Assumptions that top leaders make a difference in transformational change can be understood as part of a larger sense-making process that occurs among observers and members of organizations.[7] This process involves the social construction of organizational realities. People develop theories or explanations to account for their organizational experiences, and these implicit theories enable them to make sense of organizational phenomena; they provide useful information about how to behave in organizations.

Leadership plays a significant role in the way people interpret and give meaning to organizational events.[8] Powerful organizational effects, both positive and negative, tend to be attributed to top leaders, who are often seen in highly romanticized, heroic ways. This perception is particularly prevalent when it is difficult to understand the complex causes underlying important organizational events, such as significant changes in performance. In these important and highly ambiguous situations, people's causal attributions depend heavily on their own interests, preferences, and biases. This results in sense making that favors leadership.

> The romanticized conception of leadership results from a biased preference to understand important but causally indeterminate and ambiguous organizational events and occurrences in terms of

leadership. Accordingly, in the absence of direct, unambiguous information that would allow one rationally to infer the locus of causality, the romanticized conception of leadership permits us to be more comfortable in associating leaders—by ascribing to them control and responsibility—with events and outcomes to which they can be plausibly linked.[8]

Research supporting this romance of leadership perspective shows that it is most likely to prevail in ambiguous situations involving extraordinary events with extreme outcomes.[9] This explains why CEOs are often extolled when organizational performance is spectacular and vilified when it is dismal. This research also provides insight into why accounts of transformational change are so leader-centric. Transformation is a radical event involving significant changes in most features of the organization. It is a highly uncertain process generally undertaken to achieve exceptional results. These are precisely the conditions likely to give rise to romanticized attributions about the effects of top leadership. When faced with the ambiguity and importance of transformational change, observers and participants are likely to look to highly visible executives for an explanation. Because it is reasonable to assume that top leaders are in control of and responsible for the transformation, it is relatively easy to attribute the changes and their outcomes to them.

Romanticized attributions about leadership effects are likely to extend to the perceived qualities of change leaders themselves. Research suggests a relationship between implicit theories that romanticize leadership and the tendency to perceive transformational or charismatic qualities in top leaders.[10] This helps explain the current fascination with transformational leaders in the organization change literature and the charismatic and visionary qualities typically ascribed to them. It suggests that those qualities exist, in part, in the minds of observers and followers, and are tied closely to their implicit theories about leadership effects on transformational change. Moreover, people can develop perceptions about the qualities of change leaders without having direct contact with them. Attributions of charisma to change leaders, for example, can result from social contagion processes occurring among followers in organizations.[9] These powerful social processes, such as modeling, communication, persuasion, and social conformity, take place laterally among members. They are part of the shared sense making that occurs continually in organizations. Social contagion can contribute to the spread of charismatic leadership attributions throughout the organization; it can reinforce romanticized conceptions of change leaders, regardless of their actual characteristics.

Servants of Power

A key source of sense making about change leadership is the experts who write and professionally converse about the topic. These scholars, journalists, and practitioners typically have direct experience with change leaders, either as consultants to them or chroniclers of their efforts. They typically disseminate their expert knowledge widely in such popular forums as trade books, newspapers, magazines, and professional speeches. Their accounts of change leadership contribute significantly to romanticized conceptions of it. There is a strong inclination among experts to attribute transformational effects to top leaders; they often describe them as having charismatic or heroic qualities.

The propensity of experts to romanticize change leaders derives, in part, from the nature of their relationship with them. Many experts are employed by change leaders as consultants; others rely on leaders' goodwill to gain access to study them. These special relationships enable experts to gain the kind of detailed information needed to advise top leaders and to report about their change leadership. Unfortunately, the dependency inherent in these relationships can lead to biased accounts of change leaders. Experts who depend on top leaders for employment or privileged access can become, often unwittingly, "servants of power."[11] They can promote the interests of top leaders at the expense of critical judgment and reporting. Because top leaders want to appear powerful and effective, they are likely to reward experts who provide favorable accounts of them. The dynamics of this mutually reinforcing cycle are evident and can result in systematic positive bias in reporting about change leaders.

As servants of power, experts' economic interests can color their perceptions of change leaders. This can result in favorable biases toward change leaders, thus increasing the chance that positive qualities and effects will be attributed to them. Moreover, because experts tend to be opinion leaders, their accounts of change leaders can strongly influence current sense making about change leadership. Indeed, a growing and lucrative industry has developed around disseminating expertise in organization change and leadership. Consultants have learned that a top-selling book, a *Harvard Business Review* article, or a reference in *Fortune, Business Week,* or *Forbes* can propel them into the higher echelons of corporate money making. This is especially the case if the names of senior executives and their organizations are linked to consulting success. Scholars have followed suit. Under the academic banner, an abundance of books, articles, and speeches extolling the transformational effects and qualities of top leaders have appeared in the past decade with little if any criticism of them and no rigorous assessment of their claims. Some senior executives have gotten into the act themselves, writing highly favorable memoirs about their experiences leading and changing organizations.

Taken together, the dynamics of organizational sense making and expert accounts of top leadership help explain why leader-centric assumptions about organization change are so prevalent. They show how romanticized notions of change leadership are likely to develop in situations involving organization transformation. They describe how favorable biases toward change leaders and their effects can emerge when experts become servants of power. These explanations question the validity of current attributions about change leadership that tend to be overly positive and taken for granted. They challenge assumptions that change leaders are as effective or heroic as commonly portrayed, or that they make as much difference to change as is generally presumed.

Where Change Leadership Matters

At this nascent stage of knowledge about change leadership, it is prudent to question positive attributions about change leaders and their effects, particularly when those assumptions have been so one-sided and uncontested. This can lead to a more balanced view of change leaders. It can spur contingency thinking that attempts to determine where change leadership is likely to matter and where it is not.

Research on chief executive discretion provides a useful starting point for identifying situations where change leadership is likely to matter.[12, 13] This stream of inquiry seeks to determine those factors that contribute to management discretion, defined as the "latitude of action" available to top leaders. High-discretion or wide-latitude contexts afford leaders considerable room for choice and action. Such situations provide executives with relative freedom to change the organization, if they perceive that it is appropriate and if they have the inclination, skills, and power to do so. Thus, change leaders are likely to have their greatest effect in situations affording them wide latitude of action.

Researchers have identified several factors that can contribute to executive discretion. These fall into three general categories having to do with the task environment, the organization, and the leader. Those factors that have particular significance for the latitude of action of change leaders are described next.

Task Environment

Task environments vary in the amount of discretion they afford senior executives. Environments where means-ends linkages are poorly understood or where competitive conditions are shifting rapidly are particularly conducive to change leadership. These external factors tend to lessen the inertial tendencies found in most organizations and can provide change leaders with considerable leeway to make strategic changes.

Uncertainty about means-ends connections is typically found in industries where products are differentiable, where industry standards are weak, where market growth is rapid, or where demand is unstable.[12] These situations provide change leaders with ample opportunities for transforming the organization. For example, in industries that produce differentiable products or where industry standards are weak, executives generally have wide latitude for product innovation. They can make significant changes in how the organization markets, manufactures, and distributes products or services. Similarly, industries where growth is high or demand is unstable are likely to require considerable innovation and entrepreneurial action for success. These situations provide change leaders with opportunities to transform the status quo.

Rapidly shifting competitive environments are generally found in industries with short product cycles or rapid technological change. Such high-velocity situations demand almost constant innovation and change to compete successfully.[14] They provide change leaders with considerable freedom to introduce new products and technologies. Moreover, dynamic environments typically require quick market moves and countermoves among competitors.[15] This places a premium on organization flexibility and response rate, thus allowing senior executives to make necessary changes almost continuously.

Organization

Researchers have identified several factors internal to the organization that can affect management discretion. Those with special relevance to change leadership have to do with the inertial qualities of the organization, the composition of its top leadership team, and the features of its board of directors.

Organizational factors that contribute to rigidity include age, size, availability of resources, capital intensity, and strong culture.[12] Generally, the weaker these inertial forces within an organization, the more opportunities for change. For example, younger and smaller organizations are likely to have less bureaucratic momentum and investment in the status quo than larger, more established firms, thus providing change leaders with greater freedom to innovate and change. Abundant resources can provide the slack needed for organizational innovation. When capital intensity is low, monetary commitments to courses of action and production processes are likely to be sufficiently low to permit significant organization change. Organizations with weak cultures are unlikely to have strong investments in norms and values that can be difficult if not impossible to change. Of course, if organizational norms and values promote innovation and change, a strong culture can facilitate transformation.

Change leadership typically occurs in the context of a top management team that is responsible for making strategic choices and implementing them. The demography of that team can affect opportunities for organization transformation. It can determine whether top leaders are likely to embrace the status quo or to seek change. Generally, top teams having the following demographic features are most conducive to organization change: younger, more educated members with relative short organization tenure, high team tenure, and heterogeneity in educational backgrounds.[16, 17] Members of top teams having these characteristics tend to be receptive to change and willing to take risks inherent in transforming the organization. They are likely to engage in creative decision making using a diversity of information and perspectives.

Organizations typically have a board of directors that monitors and controls executive behavior on behalf of owners. The relative power of the board over senior executives can affect the amount of discretion they have to change the organization. Generally, top leaders are likely to have the most freedom when the board is not cohesive, board members are demographically similar to the leader, and the percentage of insider board members is high.[18] In these situations, top leaders have considerable autonomy to change the organization without having to worry about excessive oversight and control from the board. They can transform the organization according to their own interests and values.

Leader

The last set of factors that can affect executive discretion has to do with characteristics of top leaders themselves. Senior executives differ on a number of personal features that can influence their freedom to transform organizations. Generally, leaders having high levels of professional aspiration, tolerance of ambiguity, cognitive complexity, or internal locus of control are willing to change organizations.[12] They believe that they can affect change and seek opportunities to enact their convictions. They can deal with the complexity and uncertainty inherent in organizational transformation, and thus can function effectively in such situations.

Top leaders can differ in their level of commitment to organization change. Moderate levels of commitment provide the most freedom for change. If commitment to change is too low, executives are unlikely to have sufficient motivation to depart from the status quo. If commitment is too high, their personal investment in a particular course of action is likely to be so extreme that alternative opportunities for change are ignored. Such myopia can severely limit executives' flexibility and discretion to innovate.

To transform organizations successfully, change leaders need considerable power and political insight. They must be able to overcome entrenched interests and to gain the commitment of stakeholders with different values. Thus, top leaders with a broad power base and strong political skills are likely to have more freedom to change organizations than their less powerful counterparts.[12, 19] They can consider and undertake a diversity of change options with relatively limited risk of resistance. They can use their power and expertise to persuade others of the need to change and of the appropriate direction to take.

As summarized in Table 11.1, these three sets of factors—task environment, organization, and leader—identify the kinds of situations where change leadership is likely to matter least and most. They provide a preliminary list of contingencies for understanding change leader effects. Empirical studies are needed, however, to assess whether these contingencies actually moderate the relationship between change leadership and its effects. Further research could also examine the relative importance of the different factors in constraining or enhancing change leader effects. This could lead to a more parsimonious theory of where change leadership matters.

At present, the factors identified in Table 11.1 are probably best used to stake out the ends of the continuum of where change leadership is least and most likely to matter. At the low end, change leaders are unlikely to have much effect, either positive or negative, in industries operating in relatively certain task environments that are changing slowly, such as chemicals, mining, and industrial equipment. Here, top leaders would be highly constrained in changing the organization, particularly if it was large and well established with a strong culture, a top management team composed of seasoned veterans, and a strong board of directors. Change would be even more limited if senior executives lacked the commitment and personality for innovation as well as the power and political skills necessary to achieve it.

Conversely, change leaders can be expected to matter most in industries operating in uncertain task environments that are changing rapidly, such as electronics, entertainment, and telecommunications. Here, top leaders would have relative freedom to innovate and to transform the organization to keep pace with external demands. Discretion to change would be especially high if the

Table 11.1. Where Change Leadership Matters Least and Most.

	Matters Least	*Matters Most*
Task Environment		
Means-End Linkages	Certain	Uncertain
• Product Differentiability	• Low	• High
• Industry Standards	• Strong	• Weak
• Market Growth	• Slow	• Fast
• Demand Instability	• Low	• High
Rate of Change	Slow	Rapid
• Product Cycle	• Long	• Short
• Technological Change	• Low	• High
Organization		
Inertial Factors	Strong	Weak
• Age	• Old	• Young
• Size	• Large	• Small
• Resource Availability	• Low	• High
• Capital Intensity	• High	• Low
• Culture	• Strong	• Weak
Top Team Composition	Closed	Open
• Member Age	• Old	• Young
• Education Level	• Low	• High
• Team Tenure	• Short	• Long
• Organization Tenure	• Long	• Short
• Heterogeneity of Education	• Low	• High
Board of Directors	Strong	Weak
• Cohesion	• High	• Low
• Demographic Similarity of Leader	• Low	• High
• Percentage of Insiders	• Low	• High
Leader		
Personal Features	Maintainer	Innovator
• Professional Aspiration	• Low	• High
• Tolerance for Ambiguity	• Low	• High
• Cognitive Complexity	• Low	• High
• Locus of Control	• External	• Internal
• Commitment to Change	• Low/High	• Moderate
• Organization Tenure	• Long	• Short
Power	Weak	Strong
• Power Base	• Narrow	• Broad
• Political Skills	• Low	• High

organization was relatively small and new with a developing culture, a top management team composed of young, highly educated executives, and a weak board of directors. Change would be even more favorable if top leaders were highly innovative and committed to change, and had the power and political skills needed to enact it.

Substitutes for Change Leadership

So far, this chapter has addressed assumptions about change leader effects and situations where they are least and most likely to occur. A key premise underlying this discussion is that change leadership is a function carried out by the top leader or CEO. The relevant literature portrays top leaders as essential to strategic change; it offers a plethora of advice about what roles they should play to transform organizations successfully.[2, 4] In keeping with the speculative nature of this chapter, this last section addresses whether CEOs need to perform these leadership functions or whether there might be substitutes for their change leadership in the situation itself.[20] As the term implies, substitutes would act as surrogates for CEO change leadership; they would perform the top leader functions needed for strategic change. Identification of substitutes for CEO change leadership could expand the range of options available to organizations seeking to transform themselves. It could provide promising alternatives for organizations that do not have the executive talent to lead organization change.

The literature suggests special functions that top leaders need to perform for strategic change to be successful. These leadership functions typically derive from the behavioral characteristics of charismatic or mythic leaders who have unique abilities to change people and organizations. Such leaders exhibit three broad kinds of behaviors that together comprise change leadership functions: envisioning, energizing, and enabling.[4, 21]

Envisioning involves describing the future of the organization in a way that is clear and compelling to organizational members. This vision focuses member behavior in a valued direction. It provides a challenging objective toward which members can become excited and committed.

The energizing function entails motivating members to change. It involves showing personal excitement for the vision and confidence that it can be implemented successfully.

Enabling has to do with helping members perform the tasks and make the behavioral changes necessary to enact the vision. This leadership function provides resources and assistance for change. It includes showing emotional support and empathy for the problems that members invariably encounter in trying to change themselves and the organization.

Substitutes for Envisioning

Substitutes for CEO envisioning include factors in the change situation that can provide members with a clear and compelling vision for the organization's future. At least three surrogates for top leader envisioning seem applicable: organization role models, behaviorally integrated top management teams, and management consultants.

Organizations often adopt new structures and administrative innovations through imitating other organizations. Such mimetic behavior can contribute to organizational efficiency and legitimacy, particularly when organizations are embedded in interorganizational networks that include highly visible role models.[22] Organization role models tend to be successful early adopters of innovations. As their innovative achievements become more visible and socially accepted, there is strong normative pressure for other organizations to copy them.

Imitating organization role models can serve as a substitute for CEO envisioning. It can provide organizations with a clear and challenging vision for the future. Information about the innovative practices of organization role models is readily available and can provide a template for organization change. For example, detailed descriptions of organization innovations appear in the popular media; consulting firms and industry groups have developed benchmarks or best practices that provide clear objectives for organization change. A cottage industry has even formed around visiting innovative organizations. For a fee, organizations can visit successful innovators to learn firsthand what they are doing. All of these sources of information about organization innovations can serve as a substitute for CEO envisioning.

Behaviorally integrated top management teams can also substitute for CEO envisioning. Generally, top management teams are responsible for formulating and implementing adaptive responses to the competitive environment. Such tasks require a good deal of information exchange, collaborative behavior, and joint decision making among team members. Behaviorally integrated teams are effective at engaging in such mutual and collective interaction.[17] They are proficient at sharing perceptions about environmental change, and designing and implementing organization-wide responses to it. Such teams should be capable of creating a clear and compelling vision for the organization without heavy reliance on CEO direction and influence. Members should be able to share diverse perceptions about the organization and its future, openly confront differences, and arrive at sufficient consensus to move forward in a clear and committed direction. Conversely, top management teams with low behavioral integration would have difficulty performing this envisioning function. They would tend to be fraught with political infighting, limited information exchange, and individualized decision making. Such teams are likely to be overly reliant on the CEO to initiate and manage strategic change.

Organizations often use management consultants, either internal or external to the firm, to help transform themselves. Consultants can act as a surrogate for top leader envisioning as well as energizing and enabling, and thus their applicability to all three functions will be discussed here rather than separately later. Management consultants generally bring a wealth of competence and experience to organization clients. They have knowledge about how to change organizations, and information about competitive environments and how other organizations are adapting to them. Consultants can provide a vision of how the organization should structure itself to compete successfully in the future. They can furnish benchmarks of innovative practices toward which organizations can direct their change efforts. Similarly, management consultants can help to motivate change. They can provide insightful analyses showing the demands of the competitive situation and the organization's need to change to meet them. This can promote readiness for change; it can energize members to move toward the vision. Management consultants can also provide enabling activities for helping organizations implement changes. They can provide a strategy for change and an assessment of how the organization is progressing. Consultants can emotionally support members; they can assure them that what they are experiencing is normal and that they are on the right path toward their vision.

Substitutes for Energizing

Substitutes for top-leader energizing include elements in the change situation that can motivate members to change. At least two factors appear likely to perform this function: highly visible enemies or competitors and environmental jolts.

Organizations are highly inertial and are unlikely to change unless there is a deep-felt need to do so. Highly visible enemies or competitors can provide that motivation. They can present a challenge to members' organizational identities and interests. This can spur members to seek better, more effective ways of competing. Highly visible adversaries can serve as a rallying point for strategic change. They can focus members' energies on transforming the status quo so the organization can outperform its key opponents. Microsoft and Coca-Cola, for example, help to perform this energizing function for Netscape and Pepsico, respectively. These highly visible competitors can substitute for CEOs performing this energizing function.

Environmental jolts can also motivate members to change the organization.[23] Such shocks can result from abrupt shifts in technologies, resources, regulations, markets, and a host of similar competitive conditions. They can signal to organizations the need to change themselves. Environmental jolts are most likely to result in adaptive responses when they increase organizations' resource contingencies and operational autonomy.[24] Under these conditions, organizations are likely to perceive the need for change and have the opportunity to enact it. This can energize members to transform the organization, although the success of those efforts will depend on their abilities and skills to design and implement the required changes.

Substitutes for Enabling

Substitutes for CEO enabling have to do with factors in the change situation that help members implement organization changes. These can include resources, assistance, and emotional support for change activities. At least three surrogates for top leader enabling seem likely to perform this leadership function: organization learning processes, reward systems, and widespread leadership talent.

To implement change successfully, organizations need to engage in considerable action learning.[25] Members generally have to learn new behaviors and ways of working; they have to learn how to implement new structures and processes. Such learning is an integral part of organization change and comprises a feedback-adjustment process where members learn from their implementation actions what is working and what is not, and make modifications if necessary. Organization learning processes can serve as a substitute for CEO enabling. They can provide the infrastructure needed to learn how to implement innovations; they can facilitate the widespread shared learning that is required to transform organizations. Organization learning processes enable members to discover implementation errors, to invent and implement improvements, and to share their knowledge throughout the organization.[26] They help to ensure that learning is continuous and embedded in the organization rather than periodic and concentrated at the top of the firm.

People generally perform those behaviors for which they are rewarded, and consequently the organization's reward system can be a powerful enabler of change.[27] It can substitute for top-leader enabling by reinforcing new behaviors and practices needed to transform the organization. Such reinforcement can derive from making extrinsic rewards, such as pay, promotion, and recognition, contingent on enacting the changes. It can originate from the intrinsic satisfaction of performing challenging tasks and learning new competencies.

Organization transformation is a systemwide process involving most parts and layers of the organization. The breadth and magnitude of such change require considerable assistance and emotional support throughout the organization. Widespread leadership talent can substitute for CEO enabling by providing that help and facilitation. Competent leaders at different levels of the organization can help members learn new behaviors. They can empathize personally with members and engage directly with them in the action learning needed for change.[28] Widespread leadership talent can provide a support network for change leaders themselves. It can provide leaders with collegial support for managing the stresses typically experienced in leading change.

The proposed substitutes for CEO change leadership are summarized in Table 11.2. They include factors in the change situation

**Table 11.2. Substitutes for CEO
Change Leadership Functions.**

	Change Leadership Functions		
Substitutes	Envisioning	Energizing	Enabling
Organization Role Models	x		
Behaviorally Integrated Top Management Team	x		
Management Consultant	x	x	x
Highly Visible Enemies or Competitors		x	
Environmental Jolts		x	
Organization Learning Processes			x
Reward Systems			x
Widespread Leadership Talent			x

that can perform the top leader functions needed for transformational change: envisioning, energizing, and enabling. It is important to emphasize that the substitutes do not replace top leaders, nor do they perform all of the innumerable tasks needed to manage and change organizations. For example, senior leaders still need to make key decisions about what role models to follow, what consultants to hire, how to respond to environmental jolts, and the like. They need to implement appropriate responses, reward practices, and learning processes. Thus, the substitutes are probably best viewed as surrogates for the more mythical or heroic aspects of the change leadership role. They can complement senior leadership that is basically competent and effective, yet may be deficient in the envisioning, energizing, and enabling needed for strategic change.

At this preliminary stage of knowledge, the substitutes notion is highly speculative and needs considerable conceptual and empirical refinement. Research is needed to assess whether the top leader functions of envisioning, energizing, and enabling are essential for strategic change, and, if so, whether the proposed surrogates can perform them effectively. Further research might discover additional change leadership functions; it might find that the proposed substitutes are differentially effective; other factors might be identified as substitutes for the top leader functions.

Conclusion

The current literature and discourse about organization change is heavily weighted toward top leaders or CEOs and the essential role they play in transforming organizations. This chapter seeks to provide a more balanced perspective. It calls to question leader-centric assumptions about organization change. It shows how organizational sense-making processes and experts' roles as servants of power can lead to systematic positive biases about the change effects of top leaders and their charismatic qualities. To offset this biased and often unquestioned view of change leadership, a contingency framework is presented suggesting where change leaders are likely to matter least and most. In a more speculative mode, substitutes for CEO change leadership are explored, thus raising the possibility that in certain situations top leaders may be unnecessary or redundant for strategic change.

This chapter is purposefully skeptical about the role of top leaders in organization change. Such questioning is intended to elucidate often taken-for-granted assumptions about change leaders, and to bring balance to what so far has been a one-sided view on the topic. Hopefully the points raised will promote more open debate and systematic research about leading organization change.

Notes

1. Lawler, E., Mohrman, S., and Ledford, G. *Creating High Performance Organizations: Practices and Results of Employee Involvement and Total Quality Management in Fortune 1000 Companies.* San Francisco: Jossey-Bass, 1995.
2. Tichy, N., and Devanna, M. *The Transformation Leader.* New York: Wiley, 1986.
3. Greiner, L., and Bhambri, A. "New CEO Intervention and Dynamics of Deliberate Strategic Change." *Strategic Management Journal,* 1989, *10,* 67–86.

4. Nadler, D., with Nadler, M. *Champions of Change.* San Francisco: Jossey-Bass, 1997.
5. Child, J. "Organization Structure, Environment and Performance: The Role of Strategic Choice." *Sociology,* 1972, *6,* 2–21.
6. Salancik, G., and Pfeffer, J. "Constraints on Administrator Discretion: The Limited Influence of Mayors on City Budgets." *Urban Affairs Quarterly,* 1977, *12,* 475–498.
7. Weick, K. *Sensemaking in Organizations.* Thousand Oaks, Calif.: Sage, 1995.
8. Meindl, J. R., Ehrlich, S., and Dukerich, J. "The Romance of Leadership." *Administrative Science Quarterly,* 1985, *30,* 78–102.
9. Meindl, J. R. "On Leadership: An Alternative to the Conventional Wisdom." In B. Staw and L. Cummings (eds.), *Research in Organizational Behavior.* (Vol. 12.) Greenwich, Conn.: JAI Press, 1990.
10. Meindl, J. R. *On the Romanticized Perception of Charisma.* Unpublished paper, School of Management, University of New York at Buffalo, 1988.
11. Baritz, L. *The Servants of Power: A History of the Use of Social Science in American Industry.* Westport, Conn.: Greenwood, 1960.
12. Hambrick, D., and Finkelstein, S. "Managerial Discretion: A Bridge Between Polar Views of Organizational Outcomes." In B. Staw and L. Cummings (eds.), *Research in Organizational Behavior.* (Vol. 9.) Greenwich, Conn.: JAI Press, 1987.
13. Finkelstein, S., and Hambrick, D. *Strategic Leadership: Top Executives and Their Effects on Organizations.* Minneapolis: West Publishing, 1996.
14. Brown, S., and Eisenhardt, K. "The Art of Continuous Change: Linking Complexity Theory and Time-Paced Evolution in Relentlessly Shifting Organizations." *Administrative Science Quarterly,* 1997, *42,* 1–34.
15. D'Aveni, R. *Hypercompetitive Rivalries: Competing in Highly Dynamic Environments.* New York: Free Press, 1995.
16. Wiersema, M., and Bantel, K. "Top Management Team Demography and Corporate Strategic Change." *Academy of Management Journal,* 1992, *35,* 91–121.
17. Hambrick, D. "Top Management Groups: A Conceptual Integration and Reconsideration of the 'Team' Label." In B. Staw and L. Cummings (eds.), *Research in Organizational Behavior.* (Vol. 16.) Greenwich, Conn.: JAI Press, 1994.
18. Westphal, J., and Zajac, E. "Who Shall Govern? CEO/Board Power, Demographic Similarity, and New Director Selection." *Administrative Science Quarterly,* 1995, *40,* 60–83.
19. Greiner, L., and Schein, V. *Power and Organization Development.* Reading, Mass.: Addison-Wesley, 1988.

20. Kerr, S., and Jermier, J. "Substitutes for Leadership: Their Meaning and Measurement." *Organizational Behavior and Human Performance,* 1978, *22,* 375–403.
21. Nadler, D., and Tushman, M. "Leadership for Organizational Change." In A. Mohrman and others, *Large-Scale Organizational Change.* San Francisco: Jossey-Bass, 1989.
22. Westphal, J., Gulati, R., and Shortell, S. "Customization or Conformity: An Institutional and Network Perspective on the Content and Consequences of TQM Adoption." *Administrative Science Quarterly,* 1997, *42,* 366–394.
23. Meyer, A. "Adapting to Environmental Jolts." *Administrative Science Quarterly,* 1982, *27,* 515–537.
24. Allmendinger, J., and Hackman, J. R. "Organizing in Changing Environments: The Case of East German Symphony Orchestras." *Administrative Science Quarterly,* 1996, *41,* 337–369.
25. Mohrman, S., and Cummings, T. *Self-Designing Organizations: Learning How to Create High Performance.* Reading, Mass.: Addison-Wesley, 1989.
26. Snyder, W., and Cummings, T. "Organization Learning Disorders: Conceptual Model and Intervention Hypotheses." *Human Relations,* 1998, *51,* 873–895.
27. Lawler, E. *Strategic Pay: Aligning Organizational Strategies and Pay Systems.* San Francisco: Jossey-Bass, 1990.
28. Tichy, N., with Cohen, E. *The Leadership Engine: How Winning Companies Build Leaders at Every Level.* New York: HarperBusiness, 1997.

Chapter Twelve

Leadership and Collaboration

Raymond E. Miles
Grant Miles

The leader's task is to articulate and legitimize an organizational vision and the means of achieving it. The emerging twenty-first century organizational vision focuses on continuous innovation as the engine of corporate wealth and emphasizes collaborative behavior within and across firms as the means of creating and utilizing the knowledge essential to innovation. The leader's role is to facilitate that collaboration, and both theory and practice suggest it will be enormously difficult.

Historically, this new leadership challenge is the fourth in a related series that has emerged over the last forty or so years. In each instance, as we will illustrate, the new vision of the successful organization gained easy acceptance. The means of achieving each new vision, however, have run up against a persistent set of acceptance barriers.

For example, the leadership challenge of the 1950s and early 1960s was to reduce bureaucratic constraints and increase productivity, an easily articulated vision. However, the prescribed means for achieving this vision was participative management, and leaders found it difficult to convince themselves and other stakeholders that participative approaches could tap underutilized member capabilities in order to achieve productivity gains.

Moreover, subsequent means toward more demanding leadership visions—for example, the calls for job enrichment in the seventies and for individual and team empowerment in the eighties—have posed equal if not greater challenges.

Against this backdrop, analysis suggests that the emerging leadership vision faces an almost insurmountable set of barriers because the means by which twenty-first century organizations will succeed requires a fundamental shift not only in the practices and beliefs of those involved but also threatens the basic philosophical underpinnings of modern business practice.

In the following pages we briefly review prior leadership challenges and legitimacy hurdles. We then explore the new organizational vision that we believe is emerging for twenty-first century firms, particularly those in knowledge industries. Finally, we examine the legitimacy barrier twenty-first century leaders must overcome and how this might be achieved.

Changing Conceptualizations of the Leadership Challenge

In this brief review, we examine the perceived leadership challenges in three post–World War II periods: first, (very roughly) the fifties through the mid-sixties; second, the late sixties through the seventies; and third, the early eighties into the early nineties (see Figure 12.1). Our discussion of the legitimacy issues leaders have faced in each period will help frame the twenty-first century challenge.

The Fifties and Early Sixties

This period was one of relatively predictable economic growth. The underlying dynamics of some industries (automobiles, for example) were shifting, but the pace of change across the economy, particularly across the leading firms in most industries, seemed well within manageable limits.

In such a climate, strategic change was not a pressing issue for most firms. Indeed, the term was seldom if ever used. Instead, maintaining or increasing productivity improvements seemed the logical path to long-term revenue and profit growth—the firm did not need to do different things, it simply needed to do what it was

**Figure 12.1. Evolution of Economic Demands
and Leadership Challenges.**

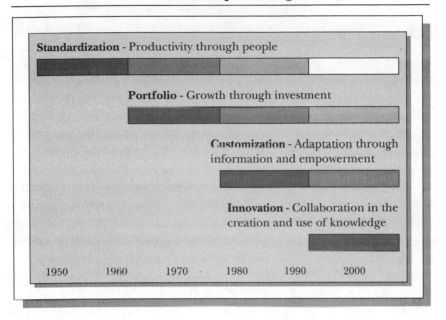

doing better. Leadership was thus perceived primarily as an operational lever, the mechanism by which human effort and capability were aligned and maintained on organizational objectives.

This view of leadership was of course not new—morale had been viewed as the key to wartime productivity and writers from the twenties to the early fifties (Mayo, Barnard, Drucker, and others) linked leader behavior and worker cooperativeness.

What did emerge as a major difference later in this period was a growing view that much more than simply worker loyalty was involved in long-term organizational success. Leadership began to be perceived as either a barrier to or a means of tapping the underutilized capabilities of organization members at all levels. Scholars argued that leaders' negative assumptions about people[1] and their focus on procedures rather than performance[2,3] stifled member creativity and constrained their opportunity to exercise acquired skills, judgment, and initiative in the pursuit of organizational needs. The new vision was apparent not only in the literature but in the titles of corporate officers. Early in the period, directors of human relations designed supervisory training courses to improve worker morale. Late in the period, vice presidents of human resources stressed "theory Y" approaches to joint goal setting and improved job design as means of increasing the utilization of members' full capabilities.[4, 5]

Finally, by the end of the period, the leader's responsibility for facilitating the growth of peer cooperation and leadership within his or her work group and even across units within the organization was beginning to be emphasized.[6-8] Correspondingly, leadership training began to be broadened from an emphasis on leader style and behavior to a focus on team building and development.

As suggested earlier, the challenge of creating more flexible and more productive organizations by reducing bureaucratic constraints required little legitimization. Organization stakeholders had experienced enough constraints during World War II and the recovery period and the growth of large-scale private organizations had created a ready list of grievances and prescriptions for change. Moreover, earlier forms of subordinate involvement in organizational issues (such as suggestion systems) had provided little real challenge to managerial authority or responsibility—management retained the right to decide which if any suggestions might be accepted. Similarly, early approaches to job redesign (job enlargement, for example) broadened the scope of subordinate duties, but again the new duties did not intrude on management's authority or challenge existing control procedures.

The approaches advocated in the sixties, however, focused less on morale and more on performance. Members' ideas and their ability to exercise responsible self-direction and control were essential to long-term organizational success. In the new message, participation was not aimed simply at providing "feelings" of involvement, it was aimed at focusing worker ideas directly on improved systems and procedures. New job design was not about relieving boredom, but about "enriching" positions with new responsibilities for quantity and quality control.

The problem with this message, of course, was that it challenged virtually every principle of management previously in vogue. Joint goal setting, increased member self-direction, job redesign—all appeared to put stockholder's property at risk by reducing managerial authority and control (though its advocates argued that the new approaches increased the total organization effort at control). Because of this, the effort to operationally legitimize worker involvement as a key means of adding economic value faced major hurdles in the sixties and has yet to achieve universal acceptance.

The Late Sixties and Seventies: A Strategic Diversion

By the late sixties, and in accelerating fashion during the seventies and into the early eighties, a schism developed between the perceptions of the leadership challenge at the operational level and at the strategic level. At the office and shop level, team building became a continuing process in progressive firms and expanded to full-blown "organizational development"—integrated, system-wide efforts to build intra- and interdepartmental competencies—in some firms.[9, 10]

At the corporate level, however, senior executives were increasingly attracted by growth opportunities associated with wide-ranging diversification through acquisition and merger. Indeed, outward-looking "strategic planning" began to be perceived as the proper focus for top managers, and strategic planning departments staffed by market and financial analysts began to grow in size and importance. The success of early movers such as Geneen at ITT[11] added energy to the movement and gave new meaning to the concept of "portfolio" strategies, diversifying risk across industries and regions and creating cash flow synergy to finance additional growth. Moreover, where dramatically underpriced assets could be found, acquisitions could be quickly assimilated (and even paid for) by selling off underperforming resources and refocusing the more efficient remaining lines.

Not surprisingly, the legitimacy of the movement toward portfolio strategies and the delivery of stockholder returns from financial maneuvering rather than from productivity gains was seldom challenged in the seventies and early eighties. For one thing, the U.S. position as the global standard of productivity had not yet been broadly challenged and U.S. firms were clear leaders in most industries. Perhaps more importantly, the approach of using money to make money fit neatly in the mind-set of both managers and shareholders. The huge gains in corporate assets achieved by strategic acquisitions and mergers, whether truly profitable or not, provided whatever empirical support was needed.

Against this backdrop, the underlying linkage between firm success and the broad-scale leadership and organizational development efforts already under way in many firms was being eroded. That is, the contribution of team-based improvements in productivity and earnings was perceived to be relatively small and long term in comparison to the gains thought to be possible by the strategic reshuffling of assets.

Thus, in the minds of many key executives (even those in progressive firms), team building and organizational development efforts were once again mechanisms primarily useful for maintaining morale and cooperation rather than as major instruments for the improvement of corporate performance. In fact, for many, these leadership efforts at the operational level were acceptable as the cost of doing what was popular and expected—what the firm "ought" to do—rather than a key means to profitability. Thus the continuing quest for the utilization of untapped member capabilities and broadened self-direction expanded slowly, if at all, and was supplanted in many organizations by other "oughts," such as the push for advancement and opportunity for women and minorities.

The Eighties and Early Nineties

The combined forces of accelerating technological change, rapidly expanding global trade, and the deregulation of transportation, communications, and banking during the eighties and early nineties exposed the shaky underpinnings of many corporate business structures. In their rush to accumulate assets and build business portfolios, many firms had reduced the attention paid to long-term competitive improvements and returns on investments. Foreign and domestic firms with better cost structures and more agile mechanisms for product and service adaptation and improvement began to take away market share from the more cumbersome and cost-laden industry leaders.

In the early part of this period, the strategic leadership challenge was stark: firms had to reduce costs and speed responsive-

ness if they were to survive. At first gradually, and then with growing speed, firms began selling off underutilized assets, outsourcing
lower-value-adding activities to up- and downstream partners for
whom they were more profitable, and reducing layers of hierarchy
no longer needed to manage coordination mechanisms across the
shrinking array of corporate assets.

In the less effectively managed firms, these cost-cutting efforts
became a continuing process—an end in and of itself—and leadership struggled to maintain some level of morale and loyalty despite job insecurity and increasing work loads. In these firms,
empowerment meant simply being freed to do one's own work and
that of several others who had been downsized. That is, in many
firms, systems redesign did not keep pace with layoffs, so that procedures that had depended on, say, twenty people to operate were
now being serviced, without change, by half as many.

In the more effectively managed firms, however, sheer cost cutting soon gave way to an articulated strategy for focusing firm attention on high-value-adding assets and processes. In these firms,
the linkage between operational leadership and strategic objectives, lost in the previous period, began to reemerge. The key was
to empower a smaller, leaner, and more flexible workforce capable of achieving higher customer responsiveness, improved quality levels, and overall cost effectiveness.

As a broader segment of firms rationalized their new focused
strategies and their downsized, "networked" structures, the leadership challenge at both the strategic and operating levels began
to move even more tightly into alignment. The route to improved
customer effectiveness—to efficient "customization"—clearly required the rapid assembly of resources among firms along the
value chain so that product or service designs that fit customer
needs could be produced quickly and cheaply. And, if these rapid
"hook-ups" were to be made across organizations, firms needed to
create mechanisms—usually self-managing teams—to carry them
out. Finally, as progressive firms moved into the nineties, it became
commonplace to rapidly assemble interfirm teams to work through
the challenges of producing products or services across several
firms linked along the value chain, creating simplified contracts
reflecting agreed-upon returns on actual costs for new or modified
designs.

Thus, in the hypercompetitive world of the late eighties and early nineties, with economic success clearly hinging on efficient customization, the message of the sixties finally began to achieve legitimacy. In a growing number of firms, empowerment—the reliance on member competencies for self-direction and a growing acceptance of their ability to play reasoned roles in entrepreneurial decisions—was now not only an acceptable but a necessary managerial goal.

The Future Challenge

The nineties have brought the beginnings of a new leadership challenge: the need to develop the capacity for continuous innovation. This challenge is being felt first and most directly in leading-edge firms in knowledge industries such as computer software and biotechnology. It is also being felt by design firms at the front end of network value chains in other industries.

The new challenge represents a significant transition. It not only presents managers with a new goal, but also with a new key asset, knowledge (see Figure 12.1). That is, the key to organizational success throughout the fifties, sixties, and into the seventies was to produce standardized output more efficiently utilizing ever-improved capital equipment and growing operational and investment know-how. A major shift occurred in the late seventies and eighties, when the new goal became efficient customization and information became the key asset—with adequate information, customer needs and organizational resources within and across firms could be efficiently matched. Now, in the nineties, the new goal is efficient innovation—continual, low-cost development of new products and services—and the key asset is knowledge. The explosion of knowledge around the globe offers a ready source of new product and service ideas to those firms with the competence to utilize them.[12]

To achieve this goal, firms must learn how to create, transform, transfer, and utilize knowledge inside and outside the firm. For example, in biotechnology, useful knowledge is spread across hundreds of "cells" of scientists around the world, connected by a self-organized network of information flows. Revelations often occur around the exchange of data sets, where unarticulated and perhaps unrecognized knowledge is turned into explicit understandings of possible compound or technique development and utilization.

Thus, the process of discovery outside of biotech firms is essentially self-managed, though it may be facilitated by funding and tapped into by affiliation. Inside biotech firms, although the discovery process appears more orderly, it is also self-managed to a large extent by the scientists involved. The more successful firms recognize this and search for mechanisms to facilitate effective self-management.

Similarly, in computer software and its myriad related industry segments (the notions of hardware and software are of course converging), similar innovation processes are visible. New products are created continuously inside and outside of existing firms in both a self-organized and firm-organized manner. Indeed, with the high proportion of contract designers operating in the industry, inside and outside are also losing their meaning.

To a lesser extent, the processes employed in design firms look very much like those in biotechnology and software, though they are usually initiated by a specific request rather than occurring continuously. As well, in organizations as diverse as banks, utilities, clinics, and equipment manufacturers, there is growing recognition that only a fraction of the knowledge available in the firm is being widely and productively utilized. What is more, there is now the recognition that those who do learn to capture and manage knowledge will clearly have a competitive advantage.

Legitimacy Issues

As was the case in the eighties with the goal of efficient customization, the new challenge of efficient, continuous innovation is recognized at both the strategic and operational levels. Further, this challenge is being articulated with growing skill and understanding by both scholars and executives. As has been true in previous periods, the legitimacy of the vision is not generally at issue.

Such is not the case, however, with the means necessary to achieve this vision. Although there is a growing awareness that major changes must occur in the way that organizations are designed and managed if the new vision is to be achieved, the mechanisms being suggested for accomplishing this are again clashing with traditional beliefs, this time at their most basic levels.

In the shortest form, the process of discovery generally revolves around sharing—knowledge creation is the outcome of collaboration. Collaboration occurs as scientists share data sets and discuss methods, as designers brainstorm new outcomes and approaches, as cross-functional and cross-firm teams share insights and ideas, and as companies seek partners with complementary knowledge, skills, and processes.

But although collaborative behavior, particularly the creation and sharing of knowledge, occurs all around us, it is not viewed as a legitimate process in the business world. On the surface, collaboration is questioned because, like delegation and participation before it, the process appears to conflict with hierarchical authority and control. Within the firm, collaborative processes frequently occur across lines and ranks and may not hold to any set boundaries. Across organizations, collaboration may be recognized as having many potential benefits, but here again neither the process nor its returns are fully controllable by any of the partners. Beneath the surface, collaborative processes, even those that are successful, create unease because they seem to be at odds with basic concepts of business behavior.

Philosophical Underpinnings

At this deeper level, as the late Aaron Wildavski noted, collaboration is a process without a philosophical base in most western societies. In these societies, basic life philosophies tend to cluster around two polar positions, libertarian or collectivist. Libertarian views, as we know, emphasize the virtues and importance of individual freedom—the freedom to choose one's occupation and lifestyle—and individual responsibility—the requirement to meet one's own needs without the demand for social support. This philosophical position is expressed in neoclassical economics, which argues that aggregate social welfare will be maximized if individuals are allowed to pursue the maximization of their own utility functions through free-market interactions.

In this view, organizations are launched by entrepreneurs, utilizing capital acquired through savings, and all factors of production enjoy returns equivalent to their contributions to added value. Hierarchical organizations are shaped and directed by owners or their representatives, exercising the rights accruing to the protection of their property at risk. Critics of the libertarian philosophy, though, point out that although the unbridled pursuit of individual goals may stimulate aggregated output, unequal distributions of returns and unequal access to societal resources will develop as the result of initial differences in resources and capabilities. They argue further that these inequalities will be perpetuated and expanded over time.

Collectivist views, however, endorse the concerns expressed by the critics of libertarianism and argue, as we know, that distributions of societal goods and services should reflect effort and need rather than initial resources or capabilities. Social ownership and control of capital is advocated as essential if all members are to be protected from exploitation and assured appropriate returns and equal access to societal resources. Social control of capital is exercised through state-run hierarchical organizations utilizing a flow of resources guided through centralized planning.

Critics of the collectivist view, however, point out that subordinating individuals to the requirements of central plans diminishes creativity. Moreover, they contend, effort and initiative are lowered by restricting rewards for individual accomplishment.

Compromise Views

In most modern societies, neither the pure libertarian nor pure collectivist views are widely endorsed. Society members may agree with certain of the principles of libertarian or collectivist philosophies, but most also acknowledge the costs of each and thus the need for economic and governance systems based on compromises between the two philosophical streams.

Thus, most governance systems reflect a compromised philosophy and most modern economies are mixed. Governmental agencies provide common (infrastructure) goods, such as roads and education, and regulate the negative social outcomes of private action (externalities), such as pollution, while private capital and markets are allowed to allocate the broader flow of goods and services. In the main, individual returns are determined by the market system, supplemented by social welfare programs designed to provide temporary services for those in need.

Within this middle ground, the appropriate balance between institutions and systems reflecting libertarian and collectivist views and concerns is the everyday grist for local and national political mills. Social welfare systems are periodically "reformed" to provide both improved services to the truly needy and to institute higher standards of individual responsibility. Similarly, mechanisms providing for public services and those preventing private abuse are regulated, deregulated, and reregulated to reflect both empirical evidence and new political balances between libertarian and collectivist views.

Thus, in this arena between the two main philosophical streams, the stability and legitimacy of most institutions in most modern societies are at some risk. They rest on a compromised philosophy that makes no claim to welfare maximization but only to the minimization of the costs associated with the two dominant philosophies.

Compromise Theories of Organization

As noted, both libertarian and collectivist views are typically translated into some form of centrally planned hierarchical organizations, pursuing either owner-directed or socially directed plans and objectives. Neither philosophy suggests the development of leadership approaches or organizational forms utilizing collaborative self-governance.

Indeed, the organizational perspective most closely linked with neoclassical economics and libertarian views, agency theory,[13] focuses on misdirected or opportunistic agent behaviors that may thwart the objectives of principals (owners). The theory promotes the search for incentives that meet both agent utilities and owner objectives. It recognizes the necessity of allowing some agent discretion, but is concerned that the outcome of that discretion will be adverse. Thus, although effective positive reward systems are crucial to collaboration, agency theory has to date focused primarily on the control of opportunism and the negatives that it might bring.

One theoretical perspective, transaction cost economics,[14] does offer some guidance in the middle ground that is economic reality between the two philosophical standards. Transaction cost theorists recognize that pure markets seldom, if ever, exist. As such, they seek to explain the shape and behavior of organizations as the product of efforts to economize on the costs associated with market failures.

That is, libertarian-supported neoclassical economic concepts of markets and firms ignore the imperfections created by transactions that are not guided by large, impersonal markets. When information is unevenly held and only one or a few buyers or sellers is present, the efficiencies expected from rational economic choices may not prevail and managers will seek relief through organization. Transaction cost theorists explain, for example, that vertically integrated firms may evolve because managers seek to protect themselves from possible exploitation by suppliers with unique and critical competencies.

Thus, what is in the organization are those resources and capabilities that can be coordinated and allocated at lower (transaction) costs through hierarchical control than through less-than-perfect market mechanisms. Conversely, those resources and capabilities that are competitively arrayed are left outside the organization and allocated by cost-minimizing market forces.

From this perspective, however, transaction cost concepts, like the compromise philosophies supporting hybrid political and economic institutions, are essentially themselves compromises—mechanisms for economizing on the costs associated with imperfect institutions. The theory argues for the benefits of the best available solution, but offers no positive support for leadership nor organizational complexity and the resulting dependence on collaborative self-governance. Management practices and organizational mechanisms are, instead, seen as necessities forced by the absence of a preferred solution.

A Trend Toward More Supportive Views

Neither agency theory or transaction cost economics provide any real support for collaboration, but several more recent developments from economists and organization theorists would appear to provide the beginnings of a foundation on which a philosophy supportive of collaborative self-governance might be based. The resource-based perspective on organizational economics, for example, focuses management attention on the development and utilization of key resources as the primary tool for economic success.[15, 16] Where industrial organization economics focused managerial attention on industry attractiveness and the achievement of market control as the source of profits, the resource-based view urges attention be paid to firm resources which can be managed to create a strong competitive position—for example, the creation of scale-efficient processes, brand recognition, superior sales and distribution methods, and the like. Thus, whereas strategic approaches based on traditional industrial organization economics focused on creating "monopoly" rents (profits) by erecting barriers to competition, the resource-based approach focuses on achieving profits by building a resource capability (including human resources) superior to that of competitors.[17]

A related approach, evolutionary economics,[18] ties organizational achievement to the creation and implementation of superior know-how. Technical proficiency is acquired over time as firms move along a production learning curve. This know-how is accumulated in routines and procedures that can be honed and passed along to new members. Thus, the established firm with experience-based routines expects to outperform a new firm with untested procedures. There are, of course, various forms of know-how that can be accumulated and "routinized," including those guiding resource allocation approaches, adaptation approaches, and the like. Clearly, firms with superior routines and superior resources anticipate a strong competitive position. (Note that know-how can be considered a resource and thus the resource and evolutionary perspectives flow together in an essentially complementary manner.)

Most recently, Teece, Pisano, and Shuen[19] have reemphasized and expanded a key dimension of the resource-evolution perspective by focusing on the creation of "dynamic capability"—the organizational capacity to adapt its resources and know-how to changing market demands. This capability involves not only the organizational coordination and reallocation of existing resources but strategic investments to create new resources and new, more effective organizational coordination and allocative abilities.

The resource-based, evolutionary, and dynamic capability views all acknowledge a common debt to Edith Penrose, whose 1959 book *The Theory of the Growth of the Firm*[20] tied organizational achievement and firm growth to the expansion of managerial capability. In Penrose's view, the growth of managerial capability through learning induced firm growth—firms grew to absorb excess managerial capacity and then paused as new know-how accumulated. The newer theories expand managerial know-how to include the know-how of all of its members accumulated in all of its routines—its production, coordinating, allocation, and investment capacity. The recognition of this total package clearly raises utilization questions beyond the simple concept of firm growth.

Implications for Organizational Design

As Penrose suggested in the preface to the third (1995) edition of her classic work, in a world of rapidly changing markets, resources, and competencies, the constraint shaping firms may not be know-how availability but the ability of the firm to find a structure that can utilize its accumulating capability. Indeed, Penrose noted that the rapid growth of alliances and networks in the eighties and early nineties is pushed along by firm efforts to find ways to unlock and utilize underemployed resources and abilities.

Unfortunately, leaders attempting to create and operate the newer organizational forms still run into theoretical and ideological constraints that may interfere with the success of their ventures. Alliances and networks are expected to increase the value of resources by combining the efforts, knowledge, and capabilities of two or more firms, but much of the literature related to them focuses on issues such as how to avoid opportunism, how to capture knowledge and skills from partners without giving any away, the dangers of "spillovers" of know-how, and the like. These concerns are clearly more in line with a philosophy focused on cost minimization and individual firm profit gains than they are on collaboration as the means of maximizing interfirm resource and capability utilization. Surrounded by these views, it is not surprising that many collaborative ventures either fail or achieve only a fraction of their potential resource utilization gains.[21]

In sum, the resource based, evolutionary, and dynamic capabilities approaches would appear to provide support for collaborative behaviors to increase intra- and interfirm resource and capability utilization, but the legitimization process is incomplete because these concepts still rest on a foundation of neoclassical concepts of the firm.

The Advent of Collaboration

Although the theoretical underpinnings of collaboration remain incomplete, the notion of collaboration is slowly gaining ground both in practice and in theory. In these final pages, we attempt to highlight both the current efforts under way and the direction of future work that will allow collaboration to become fully legitimate, both as a leadership vision and an operational reality.

The New Firm in Practice

Despite the philosophical barriers, within- and between-firm experiments in collaboration are expanding, driven in large measure by the recognition that knowledge is increasing far faster than the capability of firms to utilize it. We have described some of these experiments in detail elsewhere, and a brief explanation is warranted here.

Collaboration between firms (for example, software designers and PC producers) is being expedited by creative contracting. Licensing and cross-licensing agreements are increasingly written to create "litigation-free" zones that unlock resource utilization. As Gilbert and Shapiro point out, cross-licensing of intellectual property for technologies that are complements or are in a blocking relationship can "help solve the complementarity monopolist problem identified long ago by Cournot, and they can avoid costly infringement disputes." Further, they note, in addition to promoting the dissemination of technology, royalty-free cross-licensing can serve "as a means to short-cut the complexities of valuing each item of intellectual property."[22]

On more mundane levels, "Seven Eleven Japan has fostered multi-organizational knowledge-creating systems to develop new products through strategic alliances with manufacturers who possess complementary knowledge," according to Nonaka, Umemoto, and Saski.[23] These consortia include such diverse interests as box-lunch and delicatessen makers who cooperate in procurement, quality control, and new product development, and the developers of cooked noodles—more than twenty companies in all, including flour mills, soup makers, and Seven Eleven itself.

In a similar vein across progressive U.S. networks, data that once was guarded as the potential basis for leverage in bargaining is now often freely shared among up- and downstream partners to allow more effective resource utilization and greater efficiency and profits throughout the network. Moreover, among analysts of alliances and networks there is increasing focus on the positive social effects that may result from technical spillovers—the unplanned sharing of know-how across firms.[24] Finally, there is a growing recognition that demonstrating trustworthiness as a network partner (through data sharing and other techniques) may create a competitive advantage.[25]

Within firms, as suggested earlier by our biotech example, the trend is toward encouraging more and more members to exercise self-direction and to engage in collaborative entrepreneurship—pooling know-how to create new products and services. We have described the design of many of these organizations as "cellular"—clusters of teams (or even small firms) that interact to produce larger organisms of shared resources and know-how as tasks demand. In the most advanced cellular firms, individuals and teams interact in accordance with protocols they have helped shape. These protocols are designed to facilitate everyone's access to the full know-how of the organization and to facilitate the creation of new know-how through shared experience and the communication of explicit knowledge. With all members sharing access to full firm know-how, each member or team is expected to exercise entrepreneurial responsibility in finding ways to exploit that know-how in the design of new products and services.

For example, TCG, an organization engaged in the design of computer graphic solutions such as portable and hand-held data terminals and loggers and bar coding systems, is in fact a collection of thirteen small firms (cells). Each firm, like a cell in a larger organism, has its own purpose and ability to function independently, but it also shares common features and purposes with all of its sister firms.

In each design venture, the TCG firm leading the venture creates an external network with a principle customer and a joint venture partner (Hitachi, for example, which provides venture capital in the hope of gaining broader manufacturing rights). Equally important, the TCG lead firm also creates an internal network, linking at least two other TCG firms into the design team. TCG protocols treat the internal linkage as mandatory. That is, the hook-ups should occur even if the lead firm feels capable of handling the project alone. The reason, as suggested earlier, is that design know-how is at least partially acquired through doing, and thus knowledge sharing cannot be complete without collaboration.

On a larger scale, the Acer Group, a multinational designer, manufacturer, and assembler of personal computers, is also cellular. The firm is on its way to the creation of a federation of twenty-one independent national firms (Acer U.S., Acer Mexico, and others), designed to be held together only by the value of the synergies achieved through resource and know-how exchange. Although each firm is designed to be either a client (such as a parts and components purchaser) or server (market data, design concepts, parts and components producer) to every other firm in the group, the firms are rapidly moving toward complete financial (stock listing) and operational independence.

As such independence is achieved, the economic and governance limits of the cellular structure will be tested. Refinements will likely have to be made and additional barriers overcome as TCG, Acer, and others continue to utilize and struggle with the form.[26] Across these emerging alliance, network, and firm designs, however, key features can be identified: a focus on creative collaboration guided by voluntarily adopted protocols rather than by authority hierarchies; the widespread responsibility for entrepreneurship—finding the innovation that allows the utilization of untapped resources and know-how; and an enlightened perspective on ownership rights and the distribution of rents (profits) flowing from collaboration.

In the fast-paced world of the innovation era—with the prime asset, knowledge, widely diffused within and across firms and constantly multiplying—self-organizing, collaborative behavior increasingly offers the best mechanism for economic achievement. Cross-firm alliances and networks and groupings of autonomous units within firms allow the continuous flexibility that mirrors expanding opportunities and accommodates continuous innovation. Diffusing entrepreneurial responsibility to partner firms and spreading the responsibility across internal units promotes a higher level of utilization than might occur within a more specialized, hierarchical structure. Finally, and importantly, flexible perspectives on ownership and rent sharing remove barriers to rapid resource utilization. Increasingly, firms are agreeing on resource and know-how sharing first and then worrying about the particulars of rent sharing. Similarly, most cellular organizations appear to be moving toward broad member ownership, recognition that knowledge is widely generated and owned and that only a portion of total intellectual property is capturable by the firm or attributable to traditional investment processes.[27]

The New Firm in Theory

Both the "within" and "between" characteristics of the new firm are driven by an underlying economic perspective that recognizes the uniqueness of knowledge as the foundation for economic value. Knowledge obviously is difficult to contain, account for, and own through traditional economic mechanisms. Moreover, technical knowledge, at least, is highly time-bound; more firms are beginning to understand that they must either use it or lose it.

Continuing experimentation within alliances, networks, and cellular structures will most likely push a restatement of neoclassical economic perspectives on the firm. Our view, and that of at least some economists,[28] is that such a restatement will rest on a resource-capabilities base and acknowledge the reality of expanding rather than diminishing returns from resource and capabilities utilization, within broad limits. We further expect that the new economics will focus on the positive externalities of collaboration and point to a welfare model that emphasizes resource utilization rather than rent seeking as its driving force.

Such a theory is beyond this discussion, but it would follow current trends in theory building and will, we believe, be pushed toward development by recognized practice. Providing a theory of the firm that accommodates the richness of knowledge as both a resource and a capability for resource utilization would be a major step toward legitimizing leaders' efforts to pursue creative utilization strategies.

From Economics to Broader Ideological Issues

To fully justify collaborative behavior, within the firm and in society at large, requires more than simply adapting the theory of the firm to recognize the economic benefits of collaboration—modern economic theory is only one expression of society's core ideology. Beyond but related to economic theory, concepts of governance, property rights, and individual freedoms and responsibilities are all part of modern, mainstream values and perspectives. The legitimacy issues posed by a leadership challenge to facilitate intra- and interfirm collaboration as the means of more fully utilizing the knowledge and know-how available to the firm confront these values and perspectives at many points and levels.

Indeed, the core notion of collaboration, that one may simultaneously be concerned with the utilization of one's own capabilities and rewards and those of others, remains deeply at odds with core governance and ownership beliefs. Earlier leadership challenges confronted elements of economic and social ideology, including belief about the separation of thinking and doing and the necessity of unitary control and responsibility. They did not, however, suggest that organizations, and perhaps societies, can be structured around the voluntary assumption of responsibility for the equitable distribution of the fruits of joint resource utilization.

But just as we expect continued experimentation with collaborative intra- and interfirm behaviors to induce a more flexible and persuasive economic theory of the firm, we also expect social experimentation and the growing recognition of global interdependencies to push societies toward a more enlightened ideology of individual and collective rights and responsibilities. It seems likely that it will flow more from the recognition of the requirements and benefits of interpersonal and international collaboration than from the current focus on individual and national achievements and returns.[29]

Closing Comment

This chapter deals very briefly with issues of very broad social importance and we acknowledge its shortcomings. The older of us closed another work in the seventies with the comment that theory building in turbulent times is akin to painting a mural on the side of a charging elephant: it is difficult to be complete or tidy, but one must move quickly if a mark is to be made at all. Now that we recognize the enormity of the leadership legitimacy challenge posed by the age of knowledge and innovation, we might broaden the metaphor to incorporate a cyber mammoth and a new set of collaborative commandments within the mural.

Notes

1. McGregor, D. *The Human Side of Enterprise.* New York: McGraw-Hill, 1960.
2. Argyris, C. *Integrating the Individual and the Organization.* New York: Wiley, 1964.
3. Bennis, W. *Changing Organizations.* New York: McGraw-Hill, 1966.
4. Miles, R. "Human Relations or Human Resources." *Harvard Business Review,* 1965, *43*(4), 148–163.
5. Miles, R. "The Affluent Organization." *Harvard Business Review,* 1966, *44*(3), 106–114.
6. Likert, R. *New Patterns of Management.* New York: McGraw-Hill, 1961.
7. Likert, R. *The Human Organization.* New York: McGraw-Hill, 1967.
8. Lawrence, P., and Lorsch, J. *Organization and Environment.* Homewood, Ill.: Irwin, 1969.
9. Schein, E. *Process Consultation: Lessons for Managers and Consultants.* (Vol. 2). Reading, Mass: Addison-Wesley, 1987.
10. Blake, R., and Mouton, J. *Building a Dynamic Corporation Through Grid Organization Development.* Reading, Mass.: Addison-Wesley, 1969.
11. Araskog, R. *The ITT Wars.* New York: Henry Holt, 1989.
12. Miles, R., Snow, C., Mathews, J., Miles, G., and Coleman, H. Jr. "Organizing in the Knowledge Age: Anticipating the Cellular Form." *Academy of Management Executive,* 1997, *11*(4), 7–20.
13. Jensen, M., and Meckling, W. "Theory of the Firm: Managerial Behavior, Agency Costs and Ownership Structure." *Journal of Financial Economics,* 1976, *3*(2), 305–360.
14. Williamson, O. *Markets and Hierarchies: Analysis and Antitrust Implications.* New York: Free Press, 1975.
15. Wernerfelt, B. "A Resource-Based View of the Firm." *Strategic Management Journal,* 1984, *5*(2), 171–180.
16. Grant, R. "The Resource-Based Theory of Competitive Advantage." *California Management Review,* 1991, *33*(3), 114–135.
17. Miles, G. "In Search of Ethical Profits: Insights From Strategic Management." *Journal of Business Ethics,* 1993, *12*, 219–225.

18. Nelson, R., and Winter, S. *An Evolutionary Theory of Economic Change.* Cambridge, Mass.: Harvard University Press, 1982.
19. Teece, D., Pisano, G., and Shuen, A. "Dynamic Capabilities and Strategic Management." *Strategic Management Journal,* 1997, *18*(3), 509–533.
20. Penrose, E. *The Theory of the Growth of the Firm.* (3rd ed.). Oxford, England: Basil Blackwell, 1995 (originally published 1959).
21. Miles, G., and Preece, S. "Strategic Alliances and Strategy Formulation: Challenging the Dominant Logic of a Firm." Paper presented at the Strategic Management Society 15th Annual International Conference, Mexico City, Mexico, 1995; see also Miles, R., Miles, G., and Snow, C. "Good for Practice: An Integrated Theory of the Value of Alternative Organizational Forms." In H. Thomas and D. O'Neil (eds.), *Strategic Flexibility: Managing in a Turbulent Environment.* New York: Wiley, 1998.
22. Gilbert, R., and Shapiro, C. "Antitrust Issues in the Licensing of Intellectual Property: The Nine No-No's Meet the Nineties." Brookings Papers on Economic Activity, September 1997.
23. Nonaka, I., Umemoto, K., and Sasaki, T. "Building Business Process Innovations: Three Tales of Knowledge-Creating Companies." Working paper, 1997.
24. Garud, R., and Kumaraswamy, A. "Changing Competitive Dynamics in Network Industries: An Exploration of Sun Microsystems' Open Systems Strategy." *Strategic Management Journal,* 1993, *14*(5), 351–370.
25. Barney, J., and Hanson, M. "Trustworthiness as a Source of Competitive Advantage." *Strategic Management Journal,* 1994, *15* (Special Issue), 175–190.
26. A variety of other organizations are currently utilizing at least some aspects of the cellular concept. Kyocera has used the idea to align cells focused on manufacturing with its respective suppliers and customers. Oticon followed many cellular principles in dramatically reengineering its entire company, removing as many bureaucratic barriers as possible so that firm members could focus on self-organizing efforts directed at the development of new business products. See Miles, Snow, Mathews, Miles, and Coleman (note 12) for a fuller discussion of these and other firms, and the issues that they have, and will have, to address.
27. Given the emphasis on knowledge rather than tangible assets, an argument can be made that it may be more efficient for labor to hire capital rather than the more traditional approach of capital hiring labor to work under its direction. See Hansmann, H. *The Ownership of Enterprise.* Cambridge, Mass.: The Belknap Press of Harvard University Press, 1996, for a discussion of the economics of ownership.

28. There is growing recognition that, unlike tangible assets and resources that have a finite limit and thus drive an economic theory built around scarce resources, ideas and knowledge are nearly infinite and can be used to find ways to both create more and to get more out of what is already there. As such, economists such as Paul Romer are now exploring the implications of models that accept growth rather than scarcity as a central feature.

29. Theorists and practitioners, particularly in Europe, are currently pushing concern for the inclusion and evaluation of "social capital"—the investment in human capabilities and human institutions that promote creative collaboration. An important aspect of this work is finding ways to treat expenditures on the development of social capital as an asset (a development investment with likely future payoffs) rather than as a cost.

Chapter Thirteen

Take-Away Lessons
What We Know and Where We Need to Go

Jay A. Conger
Gretchen M. Spreitzer
Edward E. Lawler III

The authors of this volume have introduced a variety of themes about leading change. We see several areas of thematic consensus among them, and some divergent perspectives as well. In this closing chapter, we summarize what we have learned about leadership and highlight areas that remain unresolved. We end with a discussion of the key leadership issues that we foresee for tomorrow's organizations.

Leadership Makes a Difference

We introduced this volume by asserting that in today's environment of growing complexity and increasing competition, perhaps only one thing is certain: the importance of the leader's role in guiding change. The authors support this assertion. In chapter after chapter they mention how critical the CEO is in leading change. Nadler describes how Henry Schacht provided a guiding hand to the nascent Lucent as it was spun off from AT&T. Bartlett and Ghoshal recount how Jack Welch led General Electric through radical transformation without the luxury of an obvious crisis. Quinn and Snyder describe how David Whitwam engineered a change process to transform Whirlpool into a global organization. Heifetz and Laurie describe the role of Sir Colin Marshall in trying to make British Airways become the "World's Favourite Airline."

In each of these cases the leader made a striking difference. Their visions were instrumental in transforming their organizations into today's success stories and in creating competitive advantage for their future. They have taken on legendary status in their company and arguably in their industry as well. They are the stuff of Harvard Business School cases and textbooks on leadership. They epitomize the heroic leader so popular in Western culture.

Several authors in this volume (such as Beer, Cummings, and Mohrman) assert that heroic leadership is not necessary for leading change, but they do agree that leadership can make a difference through the creation of structures and processes that align the organization to a common direction. Thus, one message comes across loud and clear within this volume: leadership matters.

How Does Leadership Make a Difference?

The authors go beyond convincing evidence that leadership matters: they weave a story about how and why it matters. They provide an understanding of some key behaviors that senior executives use in leading change, including direction setting and strategy development, creating a felt need for change, and communication.

Direction Setting and Strategy Development

Perhaps the first thing a leader must do is determine the organization's appropriate vision and underlying strategy. Without a compelling vision, the leader's efforts are likely to flounder. Hambrick and Stucker found that establishing and communicating a clear vision was particularly critical in spinoffs, where leaders must create a new identity separate from the parent company. Kotter emphasizes that a key reason why change efforts fail is the lack of a compelling vision. Plans, directives, and programs are not a vision: vision goes beyond profit or market-share objectives. Unless the organization has a clear direction for change, it becomes impossible to align its constituencies.

Heifetz and Laurie describe the difficulty of recognizing the need for radical—"adaptive"—change. It is easier to take an incremental approach that builds on the status quo, much harder to build a vision that takes the organization in a radically new direction. Miles and Miles suggest that radically new visions are necessary as society moves from hierarchical, bureaucratic systems to more knowledge-based systems. Often this envisioning process requires that the leader spend a great deal of time talking to people both inside and outside the organization, collecting data, and gathering as much information as possible about the appropriate direction for the future.

The chapters do indicate that leaders can take different approaches to direction setting. Some develop a strategy almost single-handedly with little input from lower levels. Bartlett and Ghoshal describe how Jack Welch envisioned an organization made up of divisions that ranked first or second in their respective industries. Other leaders, especially those who are relatively new or where a vision is not immediately evident, seek more input. Quinn and Snyder describe how David Whitwam developed his vision for Whirlpool only after a rather lengthy process where he sought the input of key internal constituencies that had different perspectives on the future of the firm and the needs of customers. Heifetz and Laurie suggest that the creation of a real vision for change demands the involvement and responsibility of managers and workers from all parts of the organization, and that deep change requires everyone to address problems and opportunities, not just an omnipotent senior manager. Although they differ on how vision or direction should be developed, the authors agree on the compelling need for it.

Creating a Felt Need for Change

Once a compelling vision has been formulated, the leader has to help followers understand the necessity of change. This is essential because it creates the motivation for employees to embrace change. Yet Kotter estimates that more than 50 percent of companies fail to establish a sufficient sense of urgency. Creating a felt need for change means communicating to employees the business case and competitive realities and then identifying major opportunities for change.

In some situations, the need for change is obvious. As Lucent Technologies was spun off from AT&T, Henry Schacht had little trouble convincing employees that Lucent needed to operate differently than when it was under the strong arm of its parent AT&T (see Chapter One). In other situations the need for change is less obvious. Neither GE nor Whirlpool were in crisis, but the CEOs realized that to sustain competitive advantage they would have to make radical changes. Jack Welch created a felt need for change when he downsized large numbers of employees to bring costs down, focused on key business areas, and demanded that each business be first or second in its market (see Chapter Two). David Whitwam created felt need for change by bringing in three critical industry analysts to provide a painfully honest assessment of Whirlpool's image in the financial community (see Chapter Seven). Clearly, a key role of the leader is to create a sense of dissatisfaction with the current state of organization to stimulate a felt need for change.

Communicating the Vision

For the vision to become reality, it must be communicated to key organizational constituencies. Most leadership theories recognize that top-down communication of the vision is needed to align employees to it. As Miles and Miles assert, the new vision and the means of creating it must be articulated and legitimized so as to make it meaningful. Hambrick and Stucker emphasize this when they argue that senior managers of successful spinoffs communicate a new identity for the spinoff and symbolically distance it from the parent company. Communication can come through a variety of intracompany communication networks ranging from video conferences to company newsletters to town-hall meetings. It can and in most cases must come in the form of role modeling: executives who "walk the talk" of their new vision. Typically, employees believe in a vision only when they see senior management actively living it.

Several chapters also suggest the importance of bottom-up communication—from the lower levels of the organization to the leader about their readiness for change. Beer argues for creating an organizational conversation or dialogue between the leadership team and lower level employees connected to the strategic task of the organization. The aim is to provide valid data about how well the strategy, organization design, organizational capabilities, and leader behavior fit with the vision of the new organization and each other. This dialogue is needed to help the leader tap the ingenuity of lower-level employees in determining the most appropriate way to implement the change.

The Environment is Crucial

There is clear agreement in this volume that the key stimulus for change in contemporary business organizations is the environment. Demands for change and transformation are at an all-time high due to intense global competition, deregulation, rapid technological change, and international capital markets. Moreover, organizations that span nations and that experience rapid growth through acquisitions and mergers (or rapid changes in status and visibility after spinoffs) are part of a more complex world that creates dramatic need for change. This challenges the way organizations coordinate activities and exchange knowledge and information,[1] and it alters the bases of competition and changes the way they add value to the market.[2]

Most successful change efforts begin when some senior manager or group of managers takes a hard look at a company's competitive situation, market position, and financial performance. Then they assess what the ramifications of the environment are for the organization's performance. Identified areas of misfit or opportunity become the focus of the change efforts. Of course, as Cummings suggests, environments vary in the amount of discretion that they afford leaders. Times of poorly understood means-ends linkages or rapidly shifting competitive conditions are environments that allow significant leadership discretion.

Systemic Change is Necessary

Heroic or charismatic leaders are emphasized in much of the literature on leadership, but the authors of this volume argue that more is needed to make change a reality. Although charisma and a radiant personality can help, effective leadership requires much more. For change to be embraced and sustained, systemic change in the structures and processes of the organization is required. Cummings argues that a key role for the leader is as a designer of new structures, processes, and rewards to support and encourage change. Hambrick and Stucker emphasize "high-powered incentives" such as employee stock ownership to create ownership opportunities for the senior executives of spinoffs; otherwise they will have little reason to take risks. Nadler describes how the leadership team at Lucent Technologies created a new reward system that built understanding and ownership of the vision, strategy, and principles of the new organization. Senior managers at Lucent also worked to create a more participative culture that embraced the ideas and energies of all employees.

Mohrman argues that a key role for the leader is creator of social, market, and technical architectures to support the new vision. Robert Miles calls this a transformation process architecture. The leader must stimulate and orchestrate new structures and processes for this purpose. Otherwise, given that most existing systems promote stability and inertia, the current processes and structures are likely to create major obstacles to change. For example, hierarchical companies usually find it difficult if not impossible to stimulate employee involvement. If the reward system emphasizes today's financial performance, employees have little reason to take risks and learn new skills and competencies. If its culture and structure has a strong domestic orientation, an organization cannot operate as a global entity. Thus, a key role for the leader is as creator of social, market, and technological architectures that foster a new shared meaning of the organization and how it should operate. There needs to be clear logic connecting the new systems and processes to the vision and ultimately to business performance.

Because of the complex and changing business environment, Mohrman argues that a key role for today's leader is as developer of a new psychological contract to facilitate the commitment and loyalty of employees to the change vision. Downsizing and corporate restructuring have ended the expectations about loyalty and lifetime employment characteristic of employment relationships in the post–World War II era, so leaders must find other mechanisms for engaging the commitment of employees. Mohrman as well as Bartlett and Ghoshal suggest that employability is one alternative to lifetime employment. Their logic is that employees should be offered opportunities for frequent training and development to keep them on the cutting edge with regard to their skills and competencies, thereby positioning them to find a new job with little difficulty. Other elements of a new psychological contract might include designing work to be interesting and challenging to appeal to employees' intrinsic motivation, and creating a reward system that gives employees a stronger sense of ownership of the organization.

Leaders Can Be Developed

A key theme in this volume is that the requisite skills for leading change can and must be developed. Quinn and Snyder explain that the leader must change first before he or she can reasonably expect others to do so, and that means behaving in ways consistent with the values embedded in the vision of change. Beer describes a learning process for leaders called Organizational Fitness Profiling. Through this participatory process, leaders learn about their own skill deficiencies as well as the fitness of the organization for embracing and implementing change. The leader learns from those at lower levels of the organization about the skills and competencies needed by the leader and by the organization for the change to become reality. Mohrman likewise argues that the leader can learn from lower-level employees about his or her role in the change process.

Outsiders Can Help

Finally, the authors emphasize the key roles for several types of outsiders in leading change. Sometimes radical change requires bringing in a new leader from outside to lead it. New leaders can bring a fresh perspective without the usual baggage carried by insiders and important skills that the current senior team lacks. For example, Henry Schacht, the retired CEO of Cummins Engine and an AT&T director, was appointed CEO of Lucent Technologies. The task of starting up a new $25 billion enterprise, including managing the separation from AT&T, doing the IPO, and building a new culture would have been difficult for a brand new CEO to accomplish. Schacht's experience on the AT&T board and at Cummins and his propensity to act as a teacher and coach were critical in developing Lucent's culture and organization and Richard McGinn's capability to take over the reins as CEO.

Consultants can provide needed resources for facilitating change, as we learned in Chapter Nine. Many companies do not have these resources in-house, so they must bring in outsiders who do. In addition to doing training and giving change advice, consultants may assist with data gathering to get a read on employees' readiness for change. Beer's Organizational Fitness Profiling calls for a consultant to help the firm assess the competencies needed for managing in its changing environment. In this way, the consultant facilitates a learning process that eases the change process.

Consultants may also help stimulate and facilitate change. Quinn and Snyder described Quinn's role as a consultant in the transformation of Whirlpool. Quinn challenged the CEO to change himself before he could expect others in the organization to heed the change message. Once the CEO changed himself, Quinn went to work with him and his team to blueprint a process for guiding the rest of the organization through the change process. Thus, in today's fast changing business environment, outsiders, whether they be new senior managers or consultants, can bring important information, resources, and skills to the change process.

Unresolved Issues

We have explored many facets of leadership and organizational change, but there remain a number of unresolved questions and issues. Four of the most significant and fundamental are the relative importance of leadership in successful change efforts, the impact of change driven by chief executive officers versus leaders at other levels in an organization, managerial versus leadership roles in change, and differing change strategies and their differing leadership requirements.

How Important Is Leadership to Successful Change?

Most chapters argue that leaders play an essential role, not only as catalysts for change but as designers and implementers of change strategies. Several chapters, however, question whether leaders— even top leaders—consistently define or are even necessary in defining successful change. Cummings, for one, describes possible substitutes. Highly effective top management teams or consultants may provide vision that is normally associated with a senior leader. Changes in reward systems, and performance measures that reinforce new behaviors and practices, may also assist change.

It is difficult to resolve polar positions concerning the value and necessity of leadership in change efforts. Our ability to decide whether leaders actually contribute to organizational change is clouded by the multiplicity of events and our romantic notions. We need to see our leaders as responsible for performance outcomes, and that biases our assessment of them. Much of this has to do with our psychological makeup and the limits on our capacity to process information. Generally speaking, we strive to make sense of the complex causes that shape important events by simplifying root factors and attributing them to the people involved. We particularly direct our attention to those who hold formal leadership positions.

Our romance with leadership is particularly pronounced during periods of significant organizational change when causal forces are more complicated and the outcomes more extreme. As Cummings points out, this explains why so many CEOs become heroic figures when turnarounds succeed or villains when they fail. Further reinforcing these notions are the experts, consultants, and journalists who write about senior leaders; the often symbiotic relationship between the former and the latter frequently leads to positive "spin" on the importance of leadership.

Change experts are often retained in advisory positions by the very leaders that they write about. Not surprisingly, they want to show the effectiveness of their advice and the wisdom of their clients in hiring them, but this can lead to distorted reporting. Wishing to gain access to such leaders and to publish their findings, writers and academics may find themselves compromised by producing enhanced accounts of leaders and the importance of leadership. For that matter, leaders who want to be perceived as powerful and wise may grant access and rewards to experts who produce positive accounts. Little wonder, then, that romantic notions about heroic leaders are frequently reinforced, and that it remains difficult to know the actual extent to which leaders make a difference.

CEO-Driven Change Versus Champions from Other Levels

Is change best accomplished from the CEO's office, or can others drive it equally well? If lower-level leaders can drive it, must there

be a critical mass of them or can solitary champions create sufficient momentum to bring about large-scale change?

A number of researchers argue convincingly that major change
requires, at minimum, very active support from the CEO and other
senior executives,[3-6] because only these leaders have the power and
influence to drive change across all functions of a company and to
dramatically alter reward and performance measurement systems.

But it is increasingly clear that transformation occurs in large
part because of leaders at all levels.[7, 8] For example, we know that
lower-level champions can promote new strategies and foster
change events that gain momentum throughout the entire company. Burgelman,[9, 10] for one, has shown how some individuals or
small groups have engaged their organizations in activities outside
the current scope of the company's competencies. A critical mass
of such activities can lead to new strategies that ultimately transform the company. Burgelman's research shows that although
autonomous initiatives may have their origins at any level of management, they are most common among managers who are directly in contact with new technological developments and market
changes, and who have some budgetary discretion. Interestingly,
in large organizations these individuals are less likely to be found at
the highest levels, mainly because executives are often at a distance
from new technology and new markets. Furthermore, executive
worldviews are often formed around the earlier strategies of the
firm, making senior managers less likely to even perceive early
shifts in technology and markets.

Thus, although senior leaders can and should play a pivotal role
in organizational change, they are clearly not always the primary
drivers of transformation. But it is not so clear whether junior leaders alone can reorient organizations without at least political and
resource support from the very top.

The Role of Leadership Versus Management in Successful Change

Over the past decade and a half, academics and others have interpreted leading and managing as separate activities. Before that,
however, the distinction was rarely drawn; it was assumed that anyone in management was essentially in a leadership role. But by the
mid-1980s a growing consensus emerged that leadership had to be

distinguished from managership.[7, 11-13] As a result, today we think of management as involving the administrative and operational demands of an organization—for example, the procurement and deployment of resources to maintain day-to-day operations, or the use of human resources to accomplish objectives. Management relies to a large extent on formal systems of rewards and performance measures to achieve its aims. Leadership, however, involves longer-term and more adaptive challenges. The essential characteristics of leadership include the ability to challenge the status quo, engage in creative visioning for the future of the organization, and bring about appropriate changes in followers' values, attitudes, and behaviors through inspiration and empowerment.

Since the 1980s, it has been widely assumed that the inability of many North American corporations to rapidly adapt to intense competition could be traced to their having too much management and too little leadership.[7, 11] This led to an interest in charismatic and visionary leaders,[14-16] but the role and importance of management in organizational change has been neglected.

One of the more thoughtful treatments of leadership and change is by Nadler and Tushman,[12] who argue that charisma or visionary leadership is insufficient in itself to effect large-scale change. On the positive side, they note that the charismatic senior leader does serve several important functions: psychological focal point and source of vision for the energies and aspirations of employees, role model for desired behaviors, and source of support and confidence building. But these are not enough. A set of more instrumental activities is needed to effect change, including structuring, controlling, and rewarding behaviors.

According to Nadler and Tushman, structuring involves the setting of operational goals, establishing standards, defining responsibilities and roles, and building effective management teams that possess the competence to implement desired change. Controlling focuses on the creation of formal systems to measure and monitor behavior and results. Rewarding focuses on the administration of rewards and punishments contingent on whether behavior is consistent with change requirements.

The dilemma for many charismatic leaders is that they often are motivated by the need for positive feedback from employees. As a result, say the authors, it is difficult for them to successfully do what is needed to achieve control. In other words, rarely can they incorporate the behavioral demands of the more instrumental side. As a result, they need to be complemented or paired with individuals who possess strong managerial and operational skills. In our quest to understand leadership's role in organizational change, we may well have overlooked certain essential managerial competencies that are as crucial as the leadership competencies we have been describing.

Approaches to Change and Their Differing Leadership Requirements

We can divide change efforts into roughly two classes, revolutionary and evolutionary. In revolutionary or "big bang" change efforts, time frames are short and the aim is to radically remake the organization virtually overnight. Evolutionary efforts are less hurried and changes are paced; time is taken to build effective coalitions and to gradually reshape the tasks, behaviors, and architecture of the organization. The issue here is whether these two approaches demand different leadership styles. Little research has been conducted in this area, but we can speculate.

With some exceptions, say Nadler and Tushman, revolutionary changes are made under conditions of crisis. In addition, they almost always involve changes in the core values of the organization and important shifts in power. As a result, they are characterized by significant resistance and political behavior. To be successful therefore usually involves changes in senior leadership and, frequently, a new leader or leaders coming from outside. As such, we might speculate that leaders under revolutionary conditions need an outsider's viewpoint on the organization and its central shortcomings. They must feel little or no obligation to the status quo.

These leaders must necessarily be bold in their actions and remarkably accurate in their assessments. They must be able to quickly formulate a clear and well-communicated vision that builds confidence and diminishes anxiety under conditions of extreme uncertainty. Moreover, they must be adept at rapidly assessing talent throughout critical levels in the organization and must promote talented individuals into positions of great responsibility. They have to be fearless in their willingness to confront and overturn the existing power structure. It is very likely that such individuals are rare.

Incremental and evolutionary change presumably demands a leadership style that is cooperative and highly effective at coalition building. Leaders under such conditions often have the luxury of managing change through existing management structures and processes using special transition structures.[17] They are also in a position to use pilots and prototypes to test new ideas and initiatives before revamping entire areas. In general, it is likely that evolutionary leadership can be more varied and less heroic than its revolutionary counterpart. But again, our knowledge in this area is still extremely limited.

On to the Future

The last decade of the twentieth century was a golden era for leaders and the study of leadership. The bookshelves of corporations and bookstores were filled with new books on leadership. Heroic leaders such as the ones discussed in this book gained increased prominence and became folk heroes. They were repeatedly featured in articles, not just the *Wall Street Journal, Business Week,* and *Fortune,* but in local newspapers, *Time, Newsweek,* and a host of other magazines. The compensation levels of executives, particularly in the United States, reached truly unprecedented levels. The salaries of top CEOs rose more than 10 percent annually; the highest-paid received ten, fifteen, twenty, even a hundred million dollars a year.

But is the bubble about to burst? Will the focus on leaders and leadership continue to be as strong in the early years of the twenty-first century? We predict that it will; a number of forces conspire to keep it that way. The same forces will, however, most likely change some of the issues addressed in the research and thinking about leadership. A look at some of the major trends that we predict will affect the study and practice of leadership in the next decade follows.

New Forms of Organization

New forms are constantly being invented, test driven, and, in some cases, institutionalized as standard operating procedure. We are clearly in an era where businesses see organization as an increasingly important source of potential competitive advantage. This has led to a much greater focus on organization design and to a series of innovations focused on new designs.[18] It seems unlikely, however, that these will lead to a singular new approach to organizing that will replace the traditional functionally organized multibusiness corporation. Rather it most likely will result in a wide variety of different types of organizational form.

Organizations are not likely to be consistently either smaller or larger, virtual or networked. Rather, different types likely will proliferate. All probably will share a few common characteristics, most notably an abandonment of traditional hierarchical, functional structures in favor of structures that are flatter, designed on a global basis, and adaptable to deal with a continuously changing environment.

What about leaders and leadership in these new organizational forms? We believe that leaders are likely to be looked upon as substitutes for hierarchy, centralized control, and bureaucracy. Here the contrasts between leaders and managers come very much front and center. Traditional organizations need many managers and very few leaders. The new forms need few managers if any, but many leaders; otherwise they will be rudderless and unable to engage in coordinated activities. In the absence of traditional structure, something is needed to direct, motivate, and coordinate behavior. Leadership is a logical candidate.

Leading Continuous Change

The rapidly changing business environment has one clear implication for the role of leaders, and most of the chapters in this volume identify it: leading continuous change. Decades ago, leaders worked in steady-state environments that allowed them to carefully build relationships and performance strategies. Today the challenge is to constantly adapt to rapidly changing competitive environments. Product life cycles that were five or more years long are now ten to eighteen months long, and customer preferences change faster. The result is that leaders must learn to juggle current performance with change management.

We believe one key is to sort out what is relatively permanent and what is subject to continuous change in the work environment and in the relationship between individuals and their organizations.

Leaders are important here, as they help define these relationships and provide vision and direction for the organization. Further, they can play a role in helping design new organization structures and in convincing individuals to accept them. Major change is a leap that must be based on faith, but faith in what? In most cases the only answer is an effective leader. There are few if any obvious substitutes.

Shared Leadership

Several chapters in this volume argue that an important change in the leadership world is the movement from a few heroic leaders to a shared leadership model. At this point, the details of how a shared leadership organization can be developed and supported are not well developed. Nevertheless, the argument that they will develop and be effective is convincing.

In many respects, the case for shared leadership returns to the argument that in the absence of bureaucracy and hierarchy, leadership is needed to provide direction and coordinate behavior. It is virtually impossible for senior management to provide that direction throughout an entire large organization. The only alternative is to develop leaders throughout the organization who can translate, implement, and further develop the vision and direction for all employees. In this sense, more and more individuals will need to become not simply good followers of the top leadership, but leaders in their own right—redefining and adapting the messages from senior management so that they can inspire the people they work with to perform effectively.

Leadership in Virtual Organizations

Virtual organizations are likely to become more popular. Exactly what constitutes a virtual organization depends on who you ask, but in general their members are only loosely or temporarily connected; they typically are not all employed by a single corporate entity and do not have a long-term relationship with any entity. The lack of common employment and adherence to a particular hierarchical direction creates even greater need for effective leadership. In the virtual organization, leadership may be the only mechanism that can unite the organization and create coordinated behavior.

In some cases, organizations may be so virtual that individuals do not actually have face-to-face contact—they may simply be connected on the internet or through some other electronic means. This raises a number of tremendous leadership challenges. It makes it more important, but in many respects more difficult. Indeed, very little is known about how leaders can influence and lead in situations where they have neither face-to-face interactions with nor formal authority over those they are supposed to be leading.

One prediction is that a different set of leadership behaviors and skills will be required to be effective in a virtual organization. For example, leader effectiveness may depend much more on the ability to communicate through the vehicles of e-mail and video conferencing. The demand for very clear and concise guidelines for action and direction are likely to become greater. As a result, leaders must be very adept at articulating their visions, plans of action, and values. The demand for coordinating actions becomes greater without daily face-to-face contact.

Leading Teams

A tremendous body of evidence says that teams are already very much a part of the typical corporation today.[19] That said, it is also important to note that there are many different kinds of teams, and they may require different types of leadership. The kind of teams in present corporations range from temporary problem-solving teams to high-pressure cross-functional new product development teams that face tough challenges and are vital to the firm's ongoing viability. The leadership behavior that is effective in one type of team may not work as well in another, and an individual effective in leading one type of team may be less effective with another.

Having different types of teams in one organization creates the possibility that an individual will lead some teams but simply be a member of others—perhaps going between the two roles regularly, maybe even hourly. This has interesting implications about needed skills. A person may well need the ability to lead several different kinds of teams and to be a member and contributor to several other kinds.

One type of team warrants special mention here: leadership teams. Nadler's chapter on Lucent describes one and provides interesting insights into certain of the conditions necessary for this type of team to be effective. A good guess is that an increasing number of large corporations will be led by leadership teams. This raises a number of issues, not the least of which is the fundamental issue of how individuals will respond to being led by a team instead of an individual. Also, how will teams of leaders divide up the leadership activities? Will they simply duplicate each other, or compensate for one another and create synergies that make the team greater than the sum of its parts?

One safe prediction is that some individuals will find it difficult to adjust to being on a team of leaders, as well as to being led by a team. Particularly in Western societies, the idea of team leadership is not well developed and may be difficult for many individuals to adapt to.

Despite the problems of developing leadership teams, some clear pressures are likely to result in a growing reliance on them. Among these are the tremendous difficulty of leading a global organization and the inability of most individuals to fill all of its leadership needs. At the most basic level, few individuals have the time to provide continuous leadership to a twenty-four-hour global firm. Even if they did, even fewer could grasp the complexities of different cultures and business situations and provide effective leadership in situations where multiple products and services are being sold in a hundred or more countries.

Much of the early attention to leadership teams has been focused at the very top of organizations, where the time and knowledge demands are the greatest. It is quite possible that leadership teams will increasingly be used throughout organizations. Some work already suggests that entire organizations can be built on the basis of teams, and that teams can produce better cross-functional decision making and performance on an organization-wide basis.[20] In some respects, having team leadership at multiple levels in an organization may help lower-level teams be more effective. It can, for example, provide an integrated view of what lower-level teams need to do to be successful. It can create managers who understand the dynamics of teams and the challenges that teams reporting to them face because the managers themselves are on teams.

Leadership in Global Organizations

Global organizations aren't just bigger in most cases, they are typically much more complex than those that operate in a single or small number of countries. They face many different local conditions that challenge acceptance of their products and services. From a leadership point of view, it not only raises the hurdle in terms of the technical and cultural knowledge that a leader requires in order to be successful—it raises fascinating questions about how leadership behaviors will be perceived in different countries and cultures.

Leadership behavior that is quite effective in the United States may be quite ineffective in an Asian country. Leaders are faced, therefore, with the challenge of either finding behaviors that are universally effective, or somehow modifying their behavior so that it is appropriate to the local culture. This is not easy—indeed, it is one of the forces that pushes some organizations toward leadership teams, as this is a way to create not only an understanding of different cultures but leadership behaviors that are appropriate for each culture.

One likely consequence of globalization and the leadership requirements it creates is an increased demand for leaders who can lead across cultures. At a very senior level, this may mean developing more executives who are citizens more of their corporation than of a particular country. If demand grows as expected, it is safe to predict a severe shortage of individuals with global leadership skills. It is unclear where the leaders will come from. Given what is known about the importance of experience in leadership development, there is at least one obvious point to make here:[21] they are likely to be individuals who have lived in a variety of countries and had leadership positions in several of them.

Knowledge-Based Organizations

The growing consensus is that increasingly, organizations, particularly in the developed world, must be excellent at knowledge creation and management. This has led to an increased interest in intellectual capital, competency assessment, and the development of organizational capabilities; a focus on protecting intellectual property; and a host of other initiatives concerned with the knowledge assets of a company. At this point, it is not clear how all this will affect the way organizations operate and the role of leaders. It seems certain, however, that it will make a significant difference. At the very least, the human assets of an organization are likely to become more important, and the ability of leaders to attract and retain them will become a more critical determinant of organizational success.

But the attraction and retention of human assets is not sufficient for organizational effectiveness. Effective organizations need to grow not just individuals but their own intellectual capital and property and their ability to deploy them effectively. In many cases effective deployment means focusing individuals with those assets on the strategic mission and agenda of the business. This presents an enormous challenge to leaders, one made significantly greater because traditional management approaches tend not to be effective in responding rapidly to knowledge-based problems. One thing seems certain: the movement toward knowledge-based organizations is likely to shift needed executive behaviors even further away from those of managers and toward those of leaders.

The typical managerial tools and behaviors associated with the traditional organizing were not designed to facilitate building intellectual capital and dealing with knowledge workers. In many cases, knowledge workers understand their work better than their bosses. This is exactly the reverse of the assumption of traditional management thinking, which is that managers can control and direct subordinates because they have not only authority but they understand and know best how to do the work.

But when the manager cannot do the work better than the subordinate (or cannot do it at all), the managerial role must change. So what does leadership mean in this situation? Does it mean providing a mission or vision for the project? Defining roles and agendas and facilitating communication? Facilitating the group getting resources and interfacing effectively with customers and suppliers? The answer is most likely yes, yes, and yes.

In one sense, the manager in knowledge work situations needs to be much less a supervisor and much more a facilitator. But the manager may also need to help leadership emerge among the individuals who have the intellectual knowledge and the technical expertise to do the work. In this sense, the leader may need to be an expert at developing shared leadership behaviors.

Leaders of the future must not be threatened by emergent leaders nor have the need to be in control. They must encourage emergent leadership and accept that even though they have authority it is sometimes irrelevant to getting the work done. They need to let the person who understands the work and the work process lead even as they support that person. As the next project appears, the leader may need to change roles and again engage in more managerial behaviors, such as defining projects, setting targets and goals, and the like.

Sources of Power

The theory and research on leadership has for many decades discussed how leaders capture the power to influence others and get things done. The source of power is obvious when leaders are in a highly authoritarian organization and in control of rewards and punishments. Then they can influence others by wielding the resources they control and distribute.

To say the least, traditional authority is not what it used to be. Leaders are less and less able to rely on command and control. Most trends about how organizations operate and what they must do to be successful undermine traditional authority as an effective way to influence behavior. This is particularly true of knowledge-based organizations, where individuals often have highly portable skills and will move if they are controlled and managed with traditional rewards and punishment. In addition, the rise of cross-functional teams means that more and more team members are peers rather than bosses and subordinates. Technology is also undermining the traditional sources of power. For example, the virtual organization is often impossible to run from the top down; it must operate through individuals and small organizations that reach mutually agreeable working relationships by negotiation, not by fiat.

Furthermore, there has been an overall political shift in the world toward democratic governance. This is part of a long-term, worldwide social evolution away from traditional autocracy. The same appears to be going on in organizations, so that more and more leaders govern because they are endorsed by the individuals that they lead. This suggests that leaders increasingly need to be effective in creating a willingness to be governed. Inevitably, this brings the discussion of leadership and power back to persuasion, vision, charisma, and the ability of leaders to organize and articulate goals and agendas for others. These appear likely to become the coins of the realm with respect to obtaining power and leading change. This fits with the idea of intellectual capital being key to an organization's success, and the importance of knowledge workers and knowledge development. It also returns us to the interesting issue as to whether leaders have to be knowledge experts and technical experts. On the one hand, as we noted earlier, it will be increasingly difficult for leaders to know and keep up with all the details given the rapid pace of change in knowledge. On the other hand, leaders will need a firm grasp of the big picture and general directions facing technical knowledge in their fields. They must be able to articulate these convincingly in order to both lead and retain their credibility.

Does the growth of knowledge organizations and democracy mean that leaders will cease to be able to effectively use traditional rewards and authority as a source of power? We don't think so. These are clearly important tools that leaders are still likely to be able to use to influence organizations and lead change. Indeed, particularly when it comes to leading change, being able to offer financial rewards and career opportunities may be quite powerful. The challenge leaders face is integrating them with a sense of mission, direction, and vision. Without the latter, extrinsic rewards and formal authority are useless. But without the former, leaders may fail to be able to enroll a significant part of the workforce in a vision and direction for the company. Leading the new work organizations means effectively combining and in some cases replacing the traditional sources of leader power with new ones that reflect the changing nature of the workplace and the workforce.

Notes

1. Lawler, E. E. III. *From the Ground Up*. San Francisco: Jossey-Bass, 1996.
2. Mohrman, S. A., Galbraith, J., and Lawler, E. E. III. *Tomorrow's Organization*. San Francisco: Jossey-Bass, 1998.
3. Beer, M. *Organization Change and Development: A Systems View*. Santa Monica: Goodyear, 1980.
4. Gouillart, F. J., and Kelly, J. N. *Transforming the Organization*. New York: McGraw-Hill, 1985.

5. Kearns, D. T., and Nadler, D. A. *Prophets in the Dark*. New York: Harper-Collins, 1992.
6. Nadler, D. A. *Champions of Change*. San Francisco: Jossey-Bass, 1997.
7. Kotter, J. P. *The Leadership Factor*. New York: Free Press, 1988.
8. Tichy, N. M. *The Leadership Engine*. New York: Harper Business, 1997.
9. Burgelman, R. A. "Strategy Making as a Social Learning Process: The Case of Internal Corporate Venturing." *Interfaces*, 1988, *18*(3), 74–85.
10. Burgelman, R. A. "Intraorganizational Ecology of Strategy Making and Organizational Adaptation: Theory and Field Research." *Organizational Science*, 1991, *2*(3), 239–262.
11. Bennis, W., and Nanus, B. *Leaders: Strategies for Taking Charge*. New York: HarperCollins, 1985.
12. Nadler, D. A., and Tushman, M. L. "Beyond the Charismatic Leader: Leadership and Organizational Change." *California Management Review*, Winter 1990, pp. 77–97.
13. Zaleznik, A. "The Leadership Gap." *Academy of Management Executive*, 1990, *4*, 7–22.
14. Bass, B. M. *Leadership and Performance Beyond Expectations*. New York: Free Press, 1985.
15. Conger, J. A. *The Charismatic Leader*. San Francisco: Jossey-Bass, 1989.
16. Shamir, B., House, R. J., and Arthur, M. "The Motivational Effects of Charismatic Leadership Theory: A Self-Concept Based Theory." *Organizational Science*, 1993, *4*(4), 577–594.
17. Beckhard, R., and Harris, R. *Organizational Transitions*. Reading, Mass.: Addison-Wesley, 1977.
18. Lawler, E. E. III. *From the Ground Up*. San Francisco: Jossey-Bass, 1996.
19. See, for example, Lawler, E. E. III, Mohrman, S. A., and Ledford, G. E. Jr. *Creating High-Performance Organizations: Practices and Results of Employee Involvement and TQM in Fortune 1000 Companies*. San Francisco: Jossey-Bass, 1995.
20. Mohrman, S. A., Cohen, S. G., and Mohrman, A. M., Jr. *Designing Team-Based Organizations*. San Francisco: Jossey-Bass, 1996.
21. McCall, M. W. *High Flyers*. Boston: Harvard Business School Press, 1998.

Index

Brainard, C., 265
Bristol-Myers Squibb, 87
British Airways (BA), 64, 71, 72, 73,
  83, 84, 87, 202, 345
Brown, M., 163, 166, 177, 193
Brown, S. L., 159, 319
Burgelman, R. A., 353, 365
Burt, H. E., 160
Bush, G., 71
Business Week, 306, 356

C

Cagney, J., 159
Campbell, J., 166, 193
Carlzon, J., 73–74, 78–82, 130, 302
Champy, J., 86, 299
Change, critical elements of: and
  CEO role in teaching and coaching, 17–18; developing strategy
  for, 11–13; diagnosing need for
  change, 9–11; and managing executive succession, 20; and
  processes to broaden participation, 14–17; and value of symbolic acts, 18–19; vision for,
  13–14
Change leadership: assumptions
  about, 302–306; and organizations, 308–309; and power, 305–
  306; role and limits of, 301–318;
  and sense making, 303–305; substitutes for, 312–318; and task environment, 307–308; from theory
  to practice in, 22–25
Change Masters, The (Kanter), 260
Change, phased sequence of: description of, 27–32; and rationalization phase, 32-38; and
  regeneration phase, 45–50; and
  revitalization phase, 38–45
Charan, R., 52
Child, J., 319
Chin, 163, 164–165, 193
Chrysler, 71, 130, 228, 239, 241,
  302

Citibank, 134
Coca-Cola, 103, 315
Cohen, A., 160, 299
Cohen, E., 320
Cohen, S. G., 365
Coleman, H., Jr., 341, 342
Collaboration: advent of, 336–340;
  and broader ideological issues,
  340; and changing conceptualizations of leadership challenge,
  322–330; and compromise views,
  331–333; and leadership, 321–
  341; and organizational design,
  335; philosophic underpinnings
  of, 330–336; and trend toward
  more supportive views, 333–335
Complex Adaptive Systems (Complexity): and harnessing setbacks,
  215–216; and intricate understanding of business, 213–214;
  and inventive accountability, 216;
  and relentless discomfort with
  status quo, 217–218; sustaining
  gains from, 212–218; and uncom-
  promising straight talk, 214–215;
  and understanding the *quid pro
  quo*, 216–217. *See also* Leadership,
  Complexity view of
Complexity. *See* Complex Adaptive
  Systems (Complexity)
Conger, J. A., 344, 365
Continuous change, 357
Continuous self-renewal, 45–50. *See
  also* Self-Renewal
Corning, 28, 45, 133, 134
CPC International, 110
Crotonville, New York, 35, 42, 43
Culture: alignment of organization
  with, 242–248; and alignment of
  structure and infrastructure,
  244–245; and building core com-
  petencies, 247–248; reshaping of,
  245–246;
Culture change: and culture audit,
  180; and high-performance cul-
  ture workshops, 182; and senior